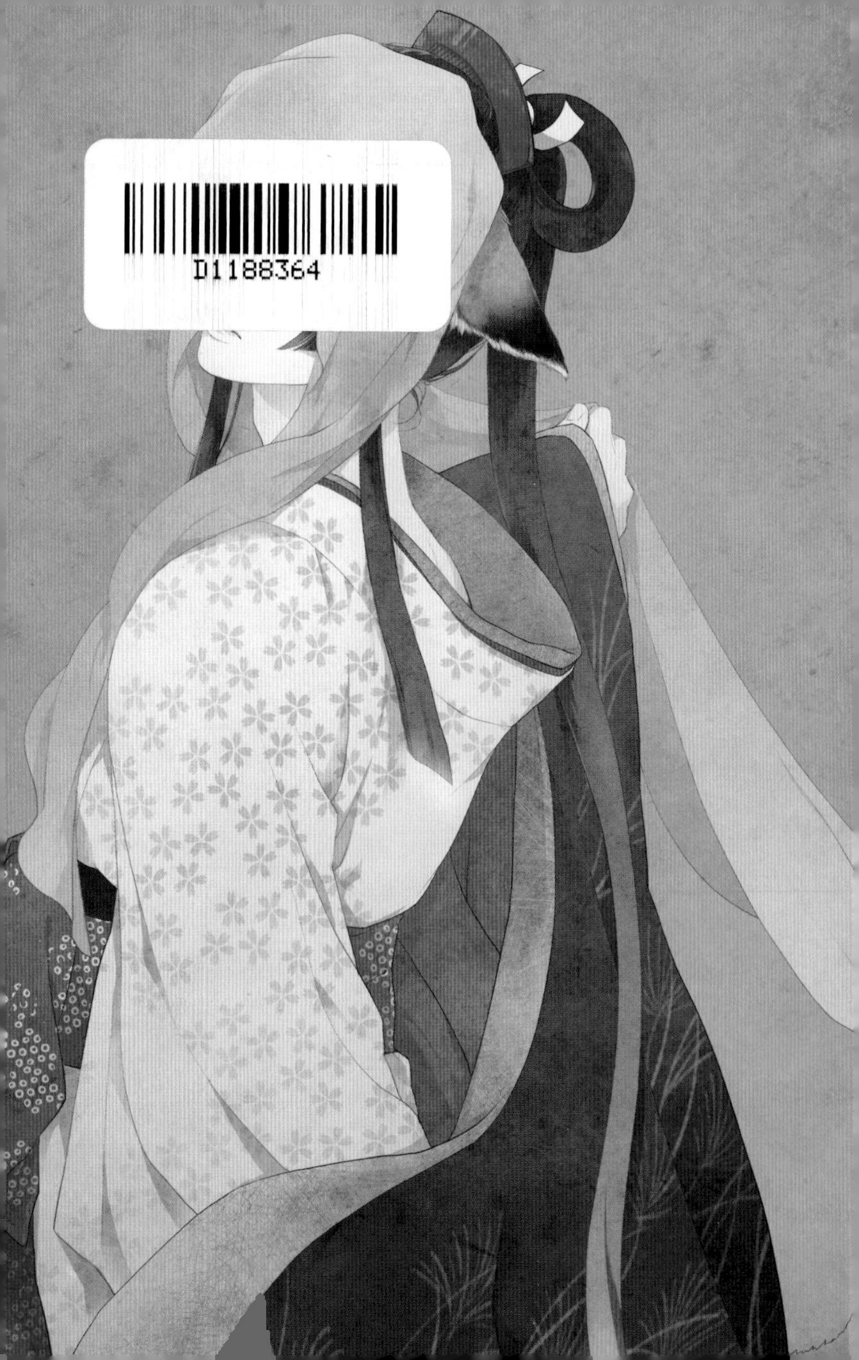

A Strange & Mystifying Story

Story and Art by **Tsuta Suzuki**

volume **7**

CONTENTS

SUBLIME

SuBLime Manga Edition

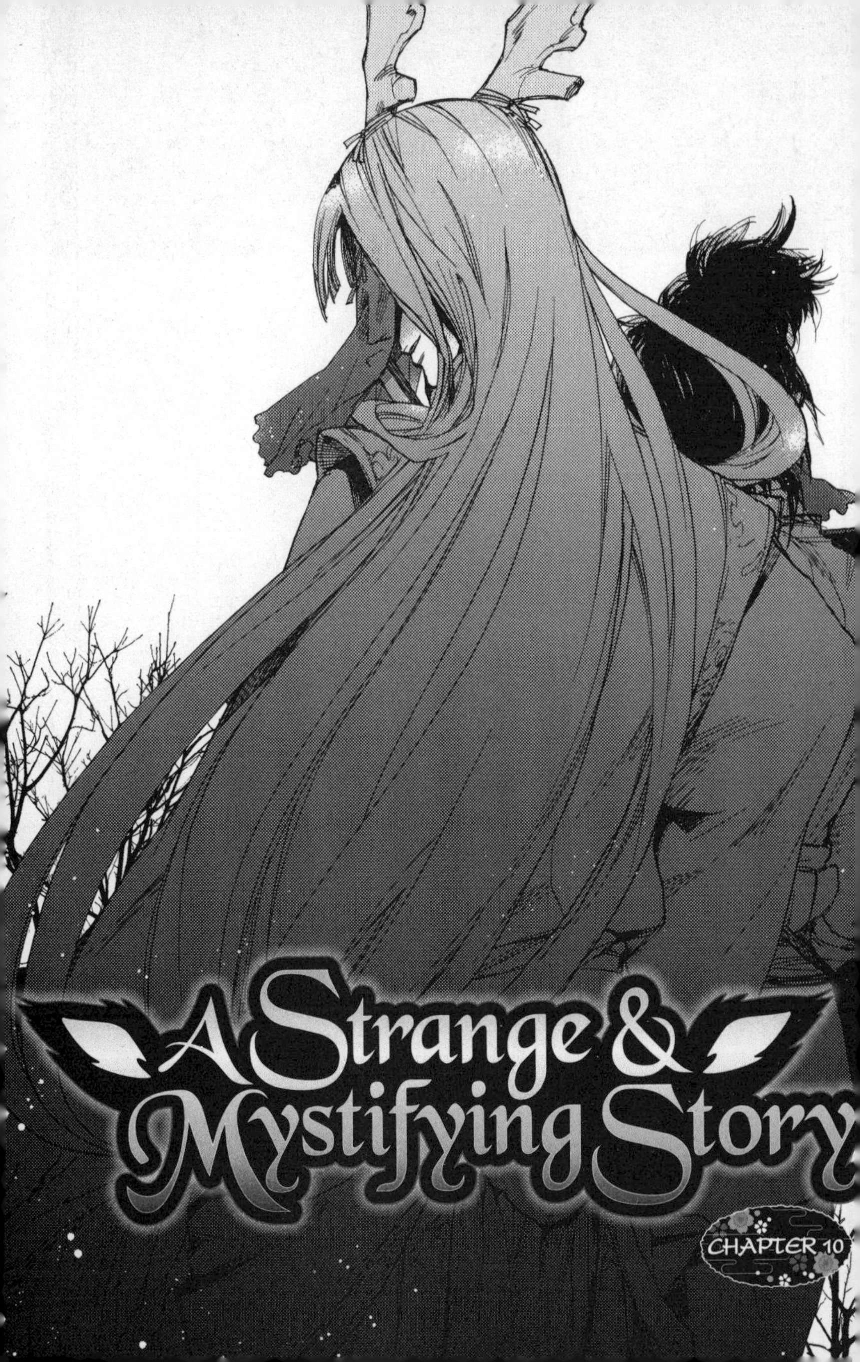
A Strange & Mystifying Story
CHAPTER 10

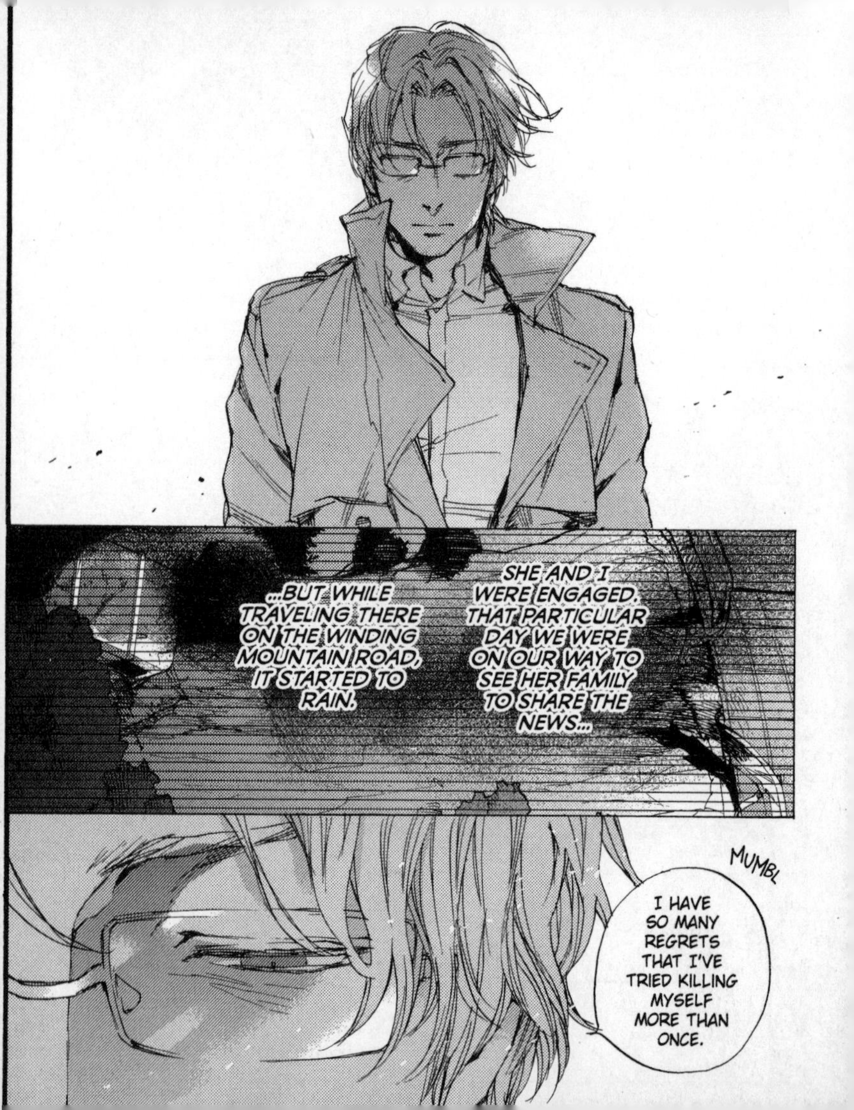
SHE AND I WERE ENGAGED. THAT PARTICULAR DAY WE WERE ON OUR WAY TO SEE HER FAMILY TO SHARE THE NEWS...
...BUT WHILE TRAVELING THERE ON THE WINDING MOUNTAIN ROAD, IT STARTED TO RAIN.
MUMBL
I HAVE SO MANY REGRETS THAT I'VE TRIED KILLING MYSELF MORE THAN ONCE.

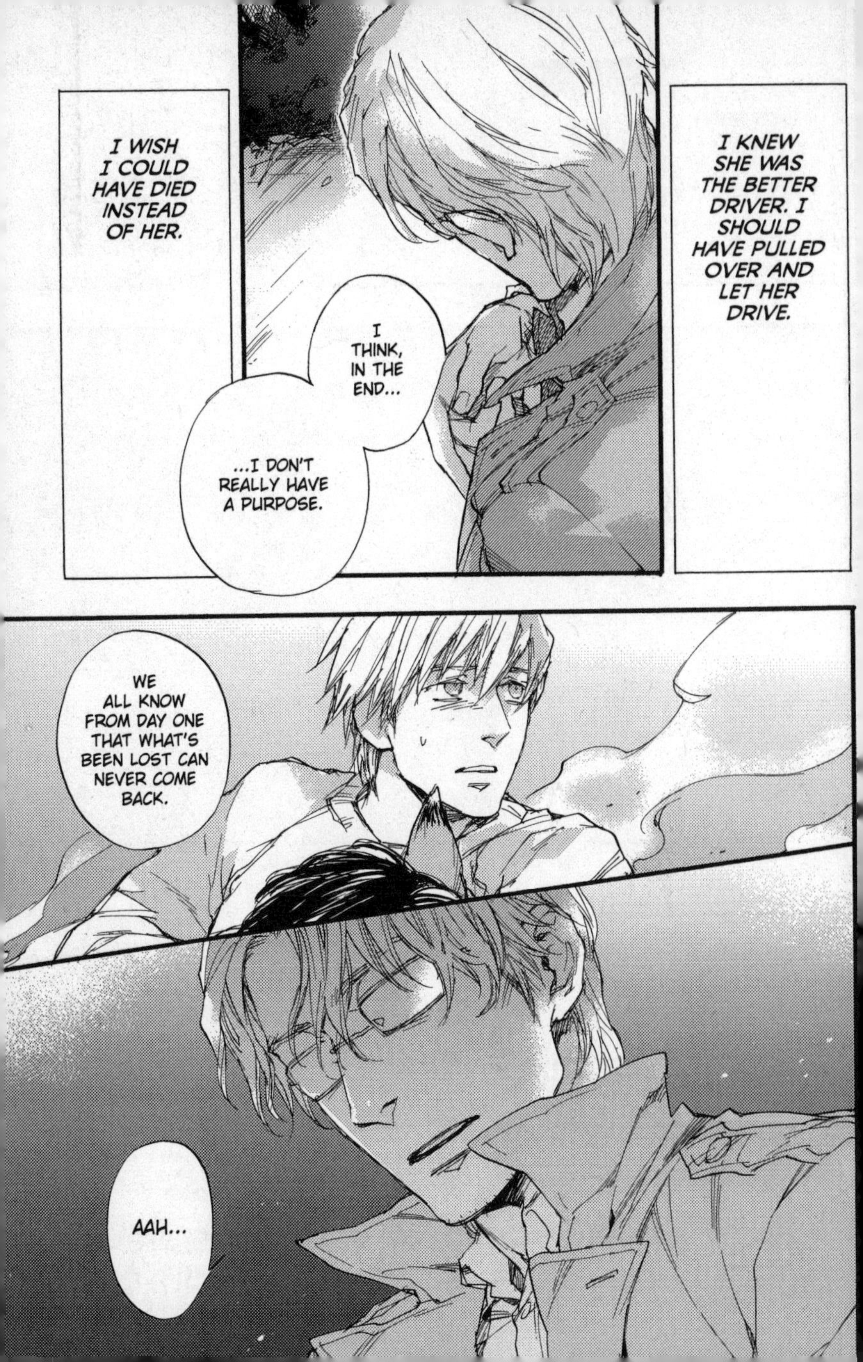
I KNEW SHE WAS THE BETTER DRIVER. I SHOULD HAVE PULLED OVER AND LET HER DRIVE.
I THINK, IN THE END...
...I DON'T REALLY HAVE A PURPOSE.
I WISH I COULD HAVE DIED INSTEAD OF HER.
WE ALL KNOW FROM DAY ONE THAT WHAT'S BEEN LOST CAN NEVER COME BACK.
AAH...

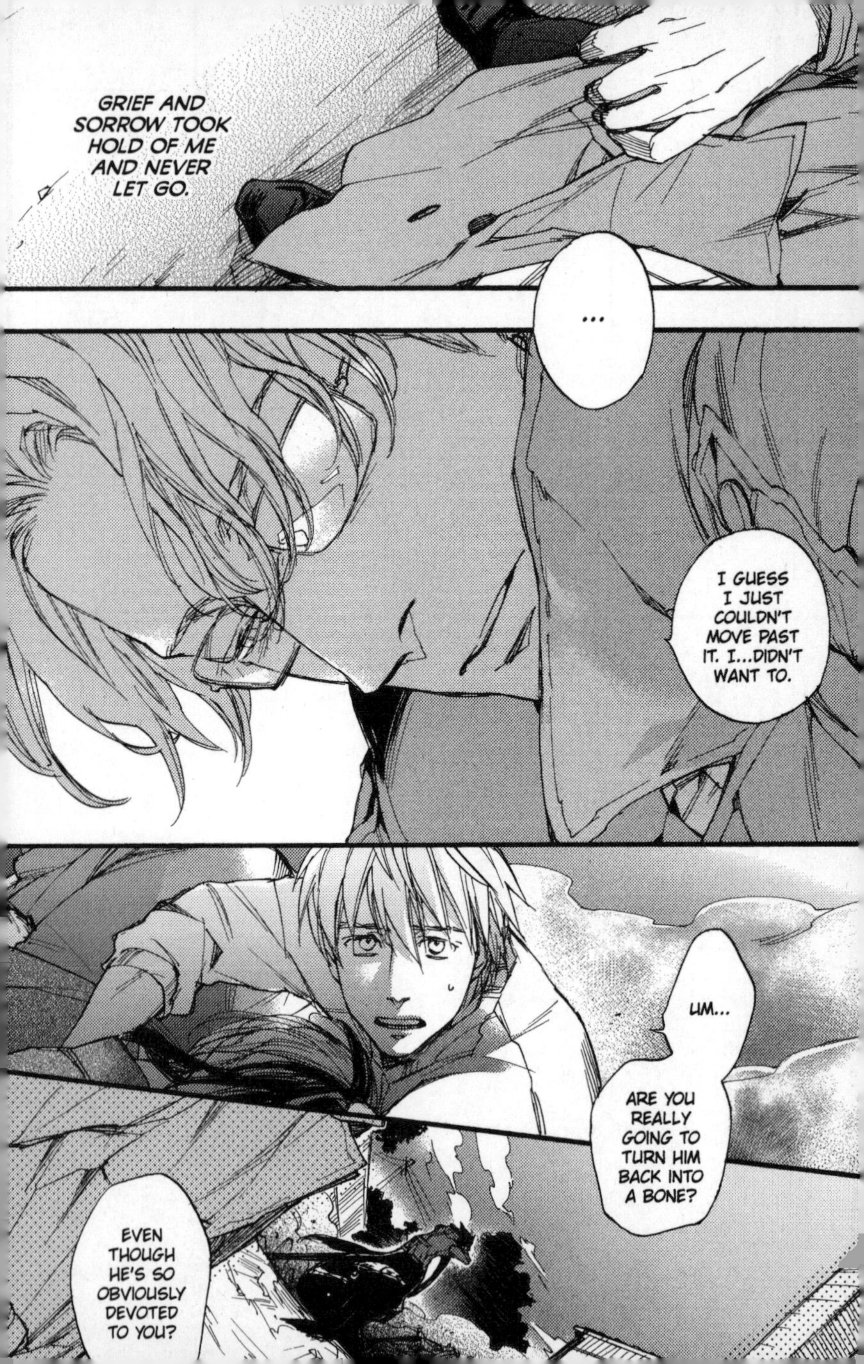
GRIEF AND SORROW TOOK HOLD OF ME AND NEVER LET GO.
...
I GUESS I JUST COULDN'T MOVE PAST IT. I...DIDN'T WANT TO.
UM...
ARE YOU REALLY GOING TO TURN HIM BACK INTO A BONE?
EVEN THOUGH HE'S SO OBVIOUSLY DEVOTED TO YOU?

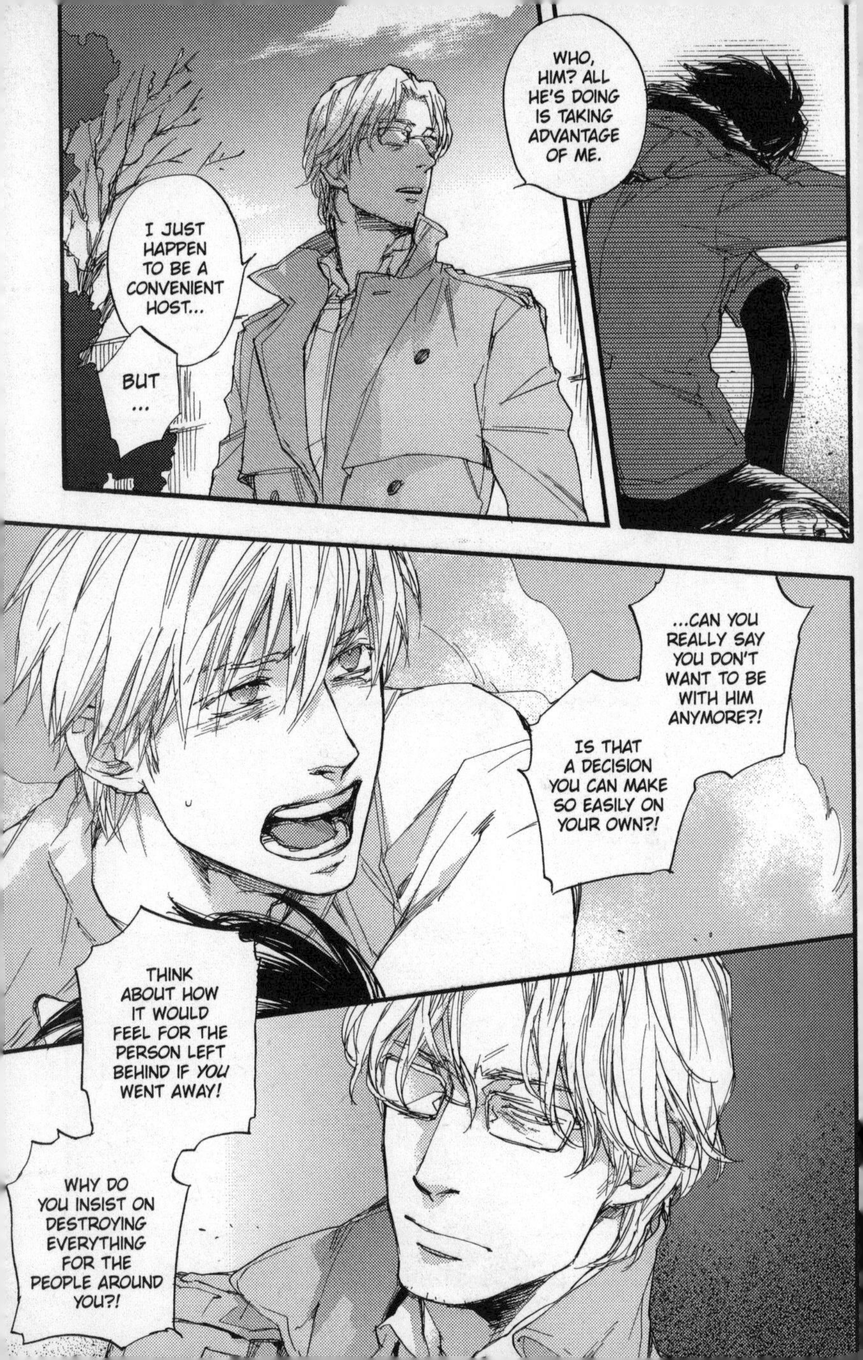
WHO, HIM? ALL HE'S DOING IS TAKING ADVANTAGE OF ME.
I JUST HAPPEN TO BE A CONVENIENT HOST...
BUT ...
...CAN YOU REALLY SAY YOU DON'T WANT TO BE WITH HIM ANYMORE?!
IS THAT A DECISION YOU CAN MAKE SO EASILY ON YOUR OWN?!
THINK ABOUT HOW IT WOULD FEEL FOR THE PERSON LEFT BEHIND IF *YOU* WENT AWAY!
WHY DO YOU INSIST ON DESTROYING EVERYTHING FOR THE PEOPLE AROUND YOU?!

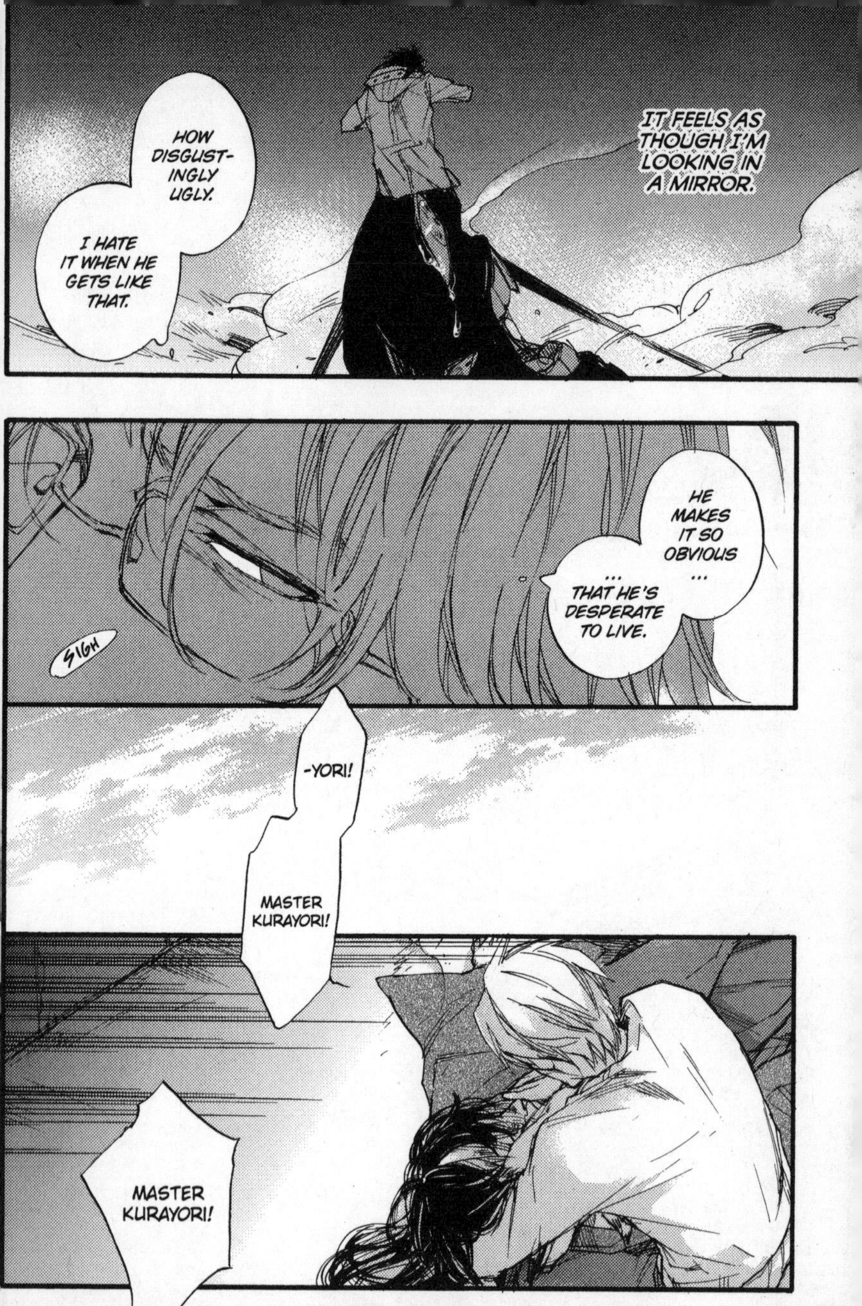
IT FEELS AS THOUGH I'M LOOKING IN A MIRROR.
HOW DISGUST-INGLY UGLY.
I HATE IT WHEN HE GETS LIKE THAT.
HE MAKES IT SO OBVIOUS ...
... THAT HE'S DESPERATE TO LIVE.
SIGH
-YORI!
MASTER KURAYORI!
MASTER KURAYORI!

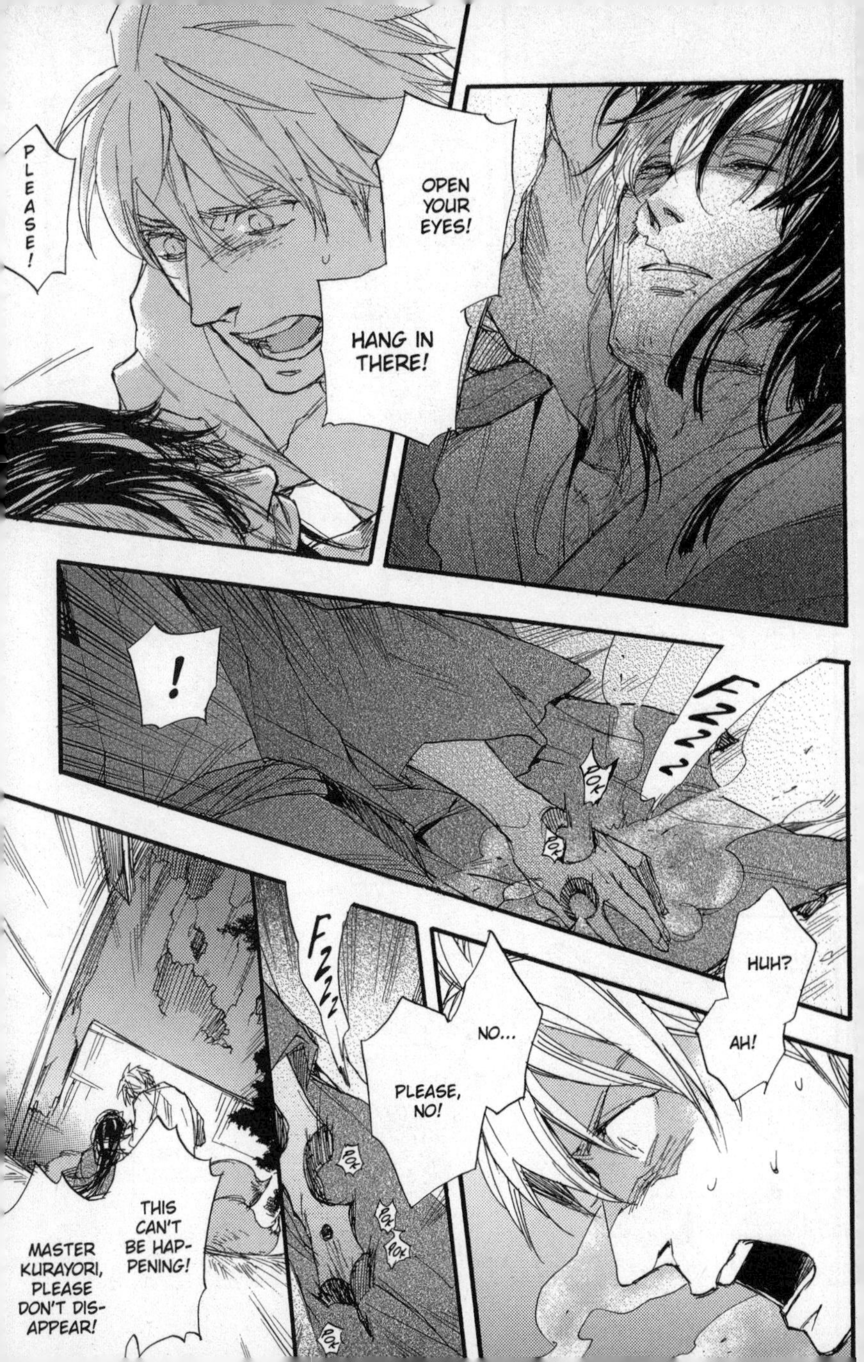
OPEN YOUR EYES!
HANG IN THERE!
PLEASE!
!
FZZZ
POK
POK
HUH?
AH!
NO...
PLEASE, NO!
FZZZ
POK
POK
POK
POK
THIS CAN'T BE HAP-PENING!
MASTER KURAYORI, PLEASE DON'T DIS-APPEAR!

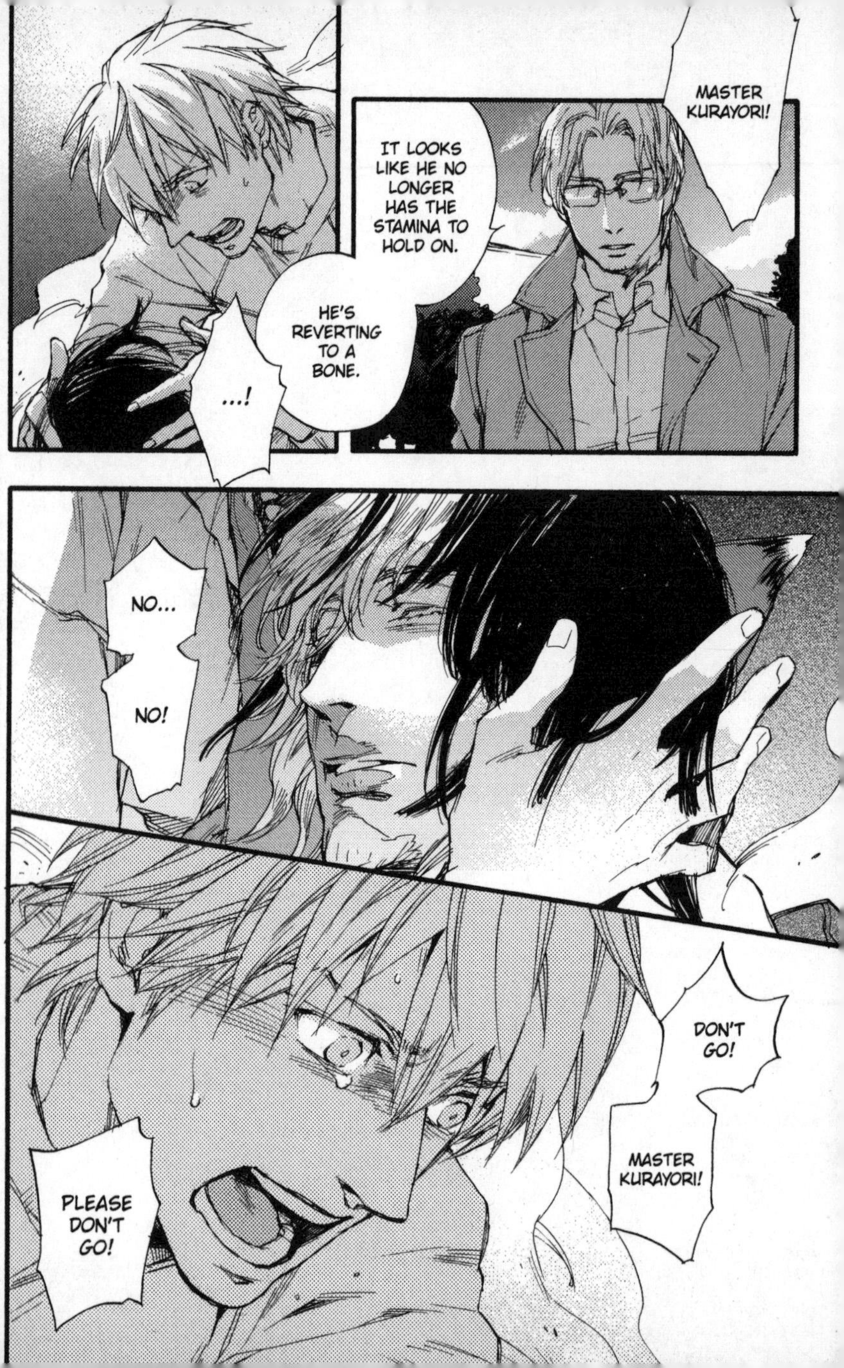
MASTER KURAYORI!
IT LOOKS LIKE HE NO LONGER HAS THE STAMINA TO HOLD ON.
HE'S REVERTING TO A BONE.
...!
NO...
NO!
DON'T GO!
MASTER KURAYORI!
PLEASE DON'T GO!

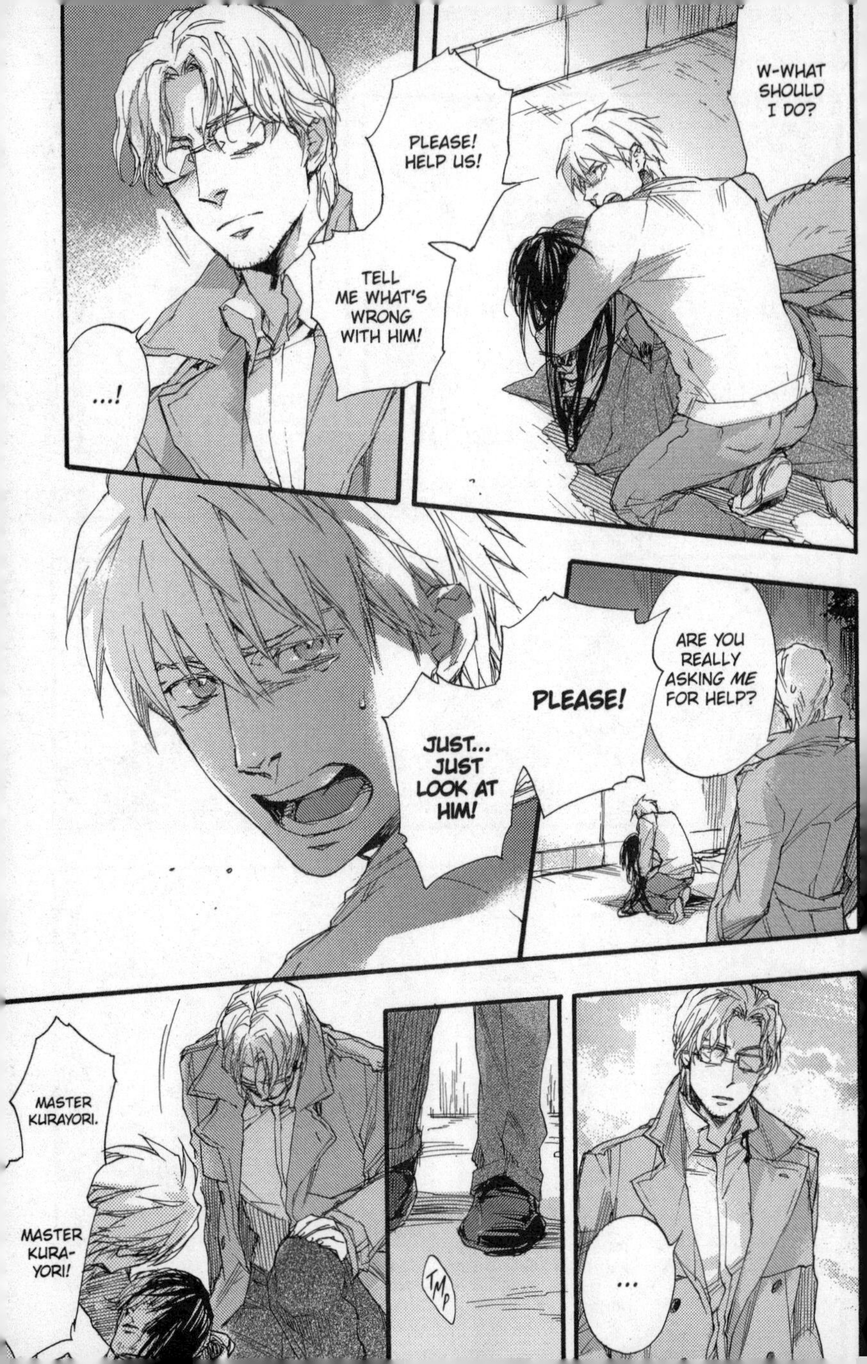
W-WHAT SHOULD I DO?
PLEASE! HELP US!
TELL ME WHAT'S WRONG WITH HIM!
...!
ARE YOU REALLY ASKING ME FOR HELP?
PLEASE!
JUST... JUST LOOK AT HIM!
...
TMP
MASTER KURAYORI.
MASTER KURA-YORI!

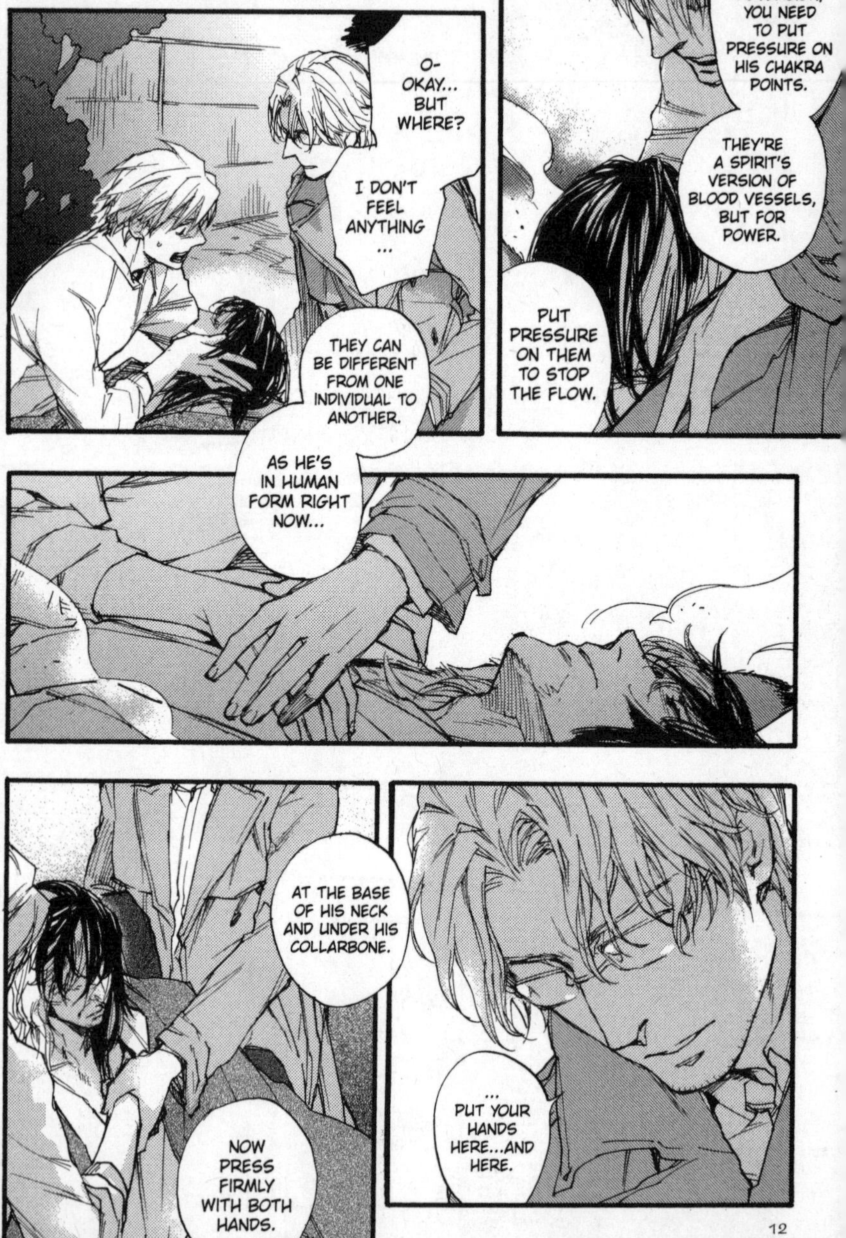
TO STOP THE REVERSION, YOU NEED TO PUT PRESSURE ON HIS CHAKRA POINTS.
THEY'RE A SPIRIT'S VERSION OF BLOOD VESSELS, BUT FOR POWER.
PUT PRESSURE ON THEM TO STOP THE FLOW.
O-OKAY... BUT WHERE?
I DON'T FEEL ANYTHING ...
THEY CAN BE DIFFERENT FROM ONE INDIVIDUAL TO ANOTHER.
AS HE'S IN HUMAN FORM RIGHT NOW...
...
AT THE BASE OF HIS NECK AND UNDER HIS COLLARBONE.
... PUT YOUR HANDS HERE...AND HERE.
NOW PRESS FIRMLY WITH BOTH HANDS.

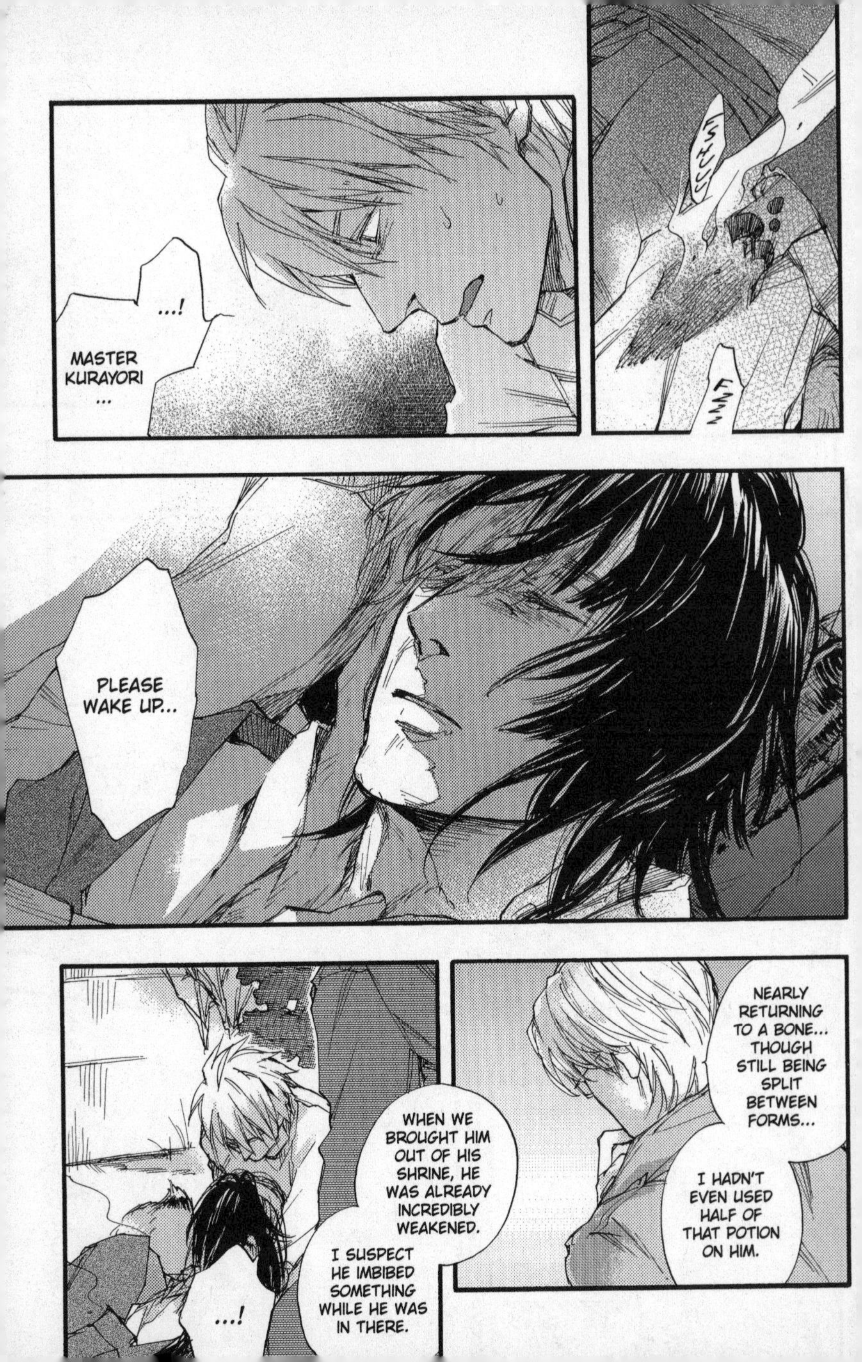
FSHUU
FZZZ
...!
MASTER KURAYORI...
PLEASE WAKE UP...
NEARLY RETURNING TO A BONE... THOUGH STILL BEING SPLIT BETWEEN FORMS...
I HADN'T EVEN USED HALF OF THAT POTION ON HIM.
WHEN WE BROUGHT HIM OUT OF HIS SHRINE, HE WAS ALREADY INCREDIBLY WEAKENED.
I SUSPECT HE IMBIBED SOMETHING WHILE HE WAS IN THERE.
...!

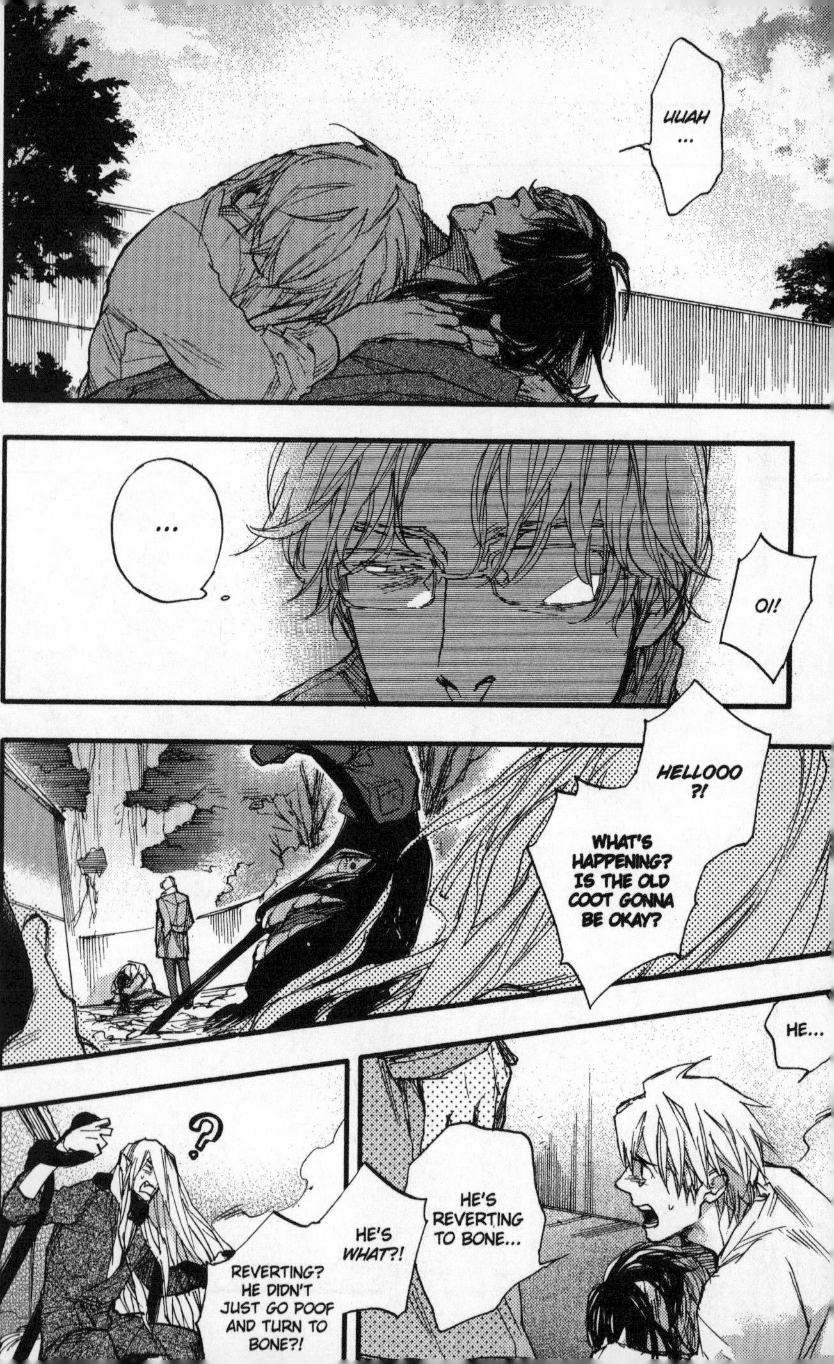
UUAH ...
OI!
...
HELLOOO ?!
WHAT'S HAPPENING? IS THE OLD COOT GONNA BE OKAY?
HE...
HE'S REVERTING TO BONE...
HE'S WHAT?!
?
REVERTING? HE DIDN'T JUST GO POOF AND TURN TO BONE?!

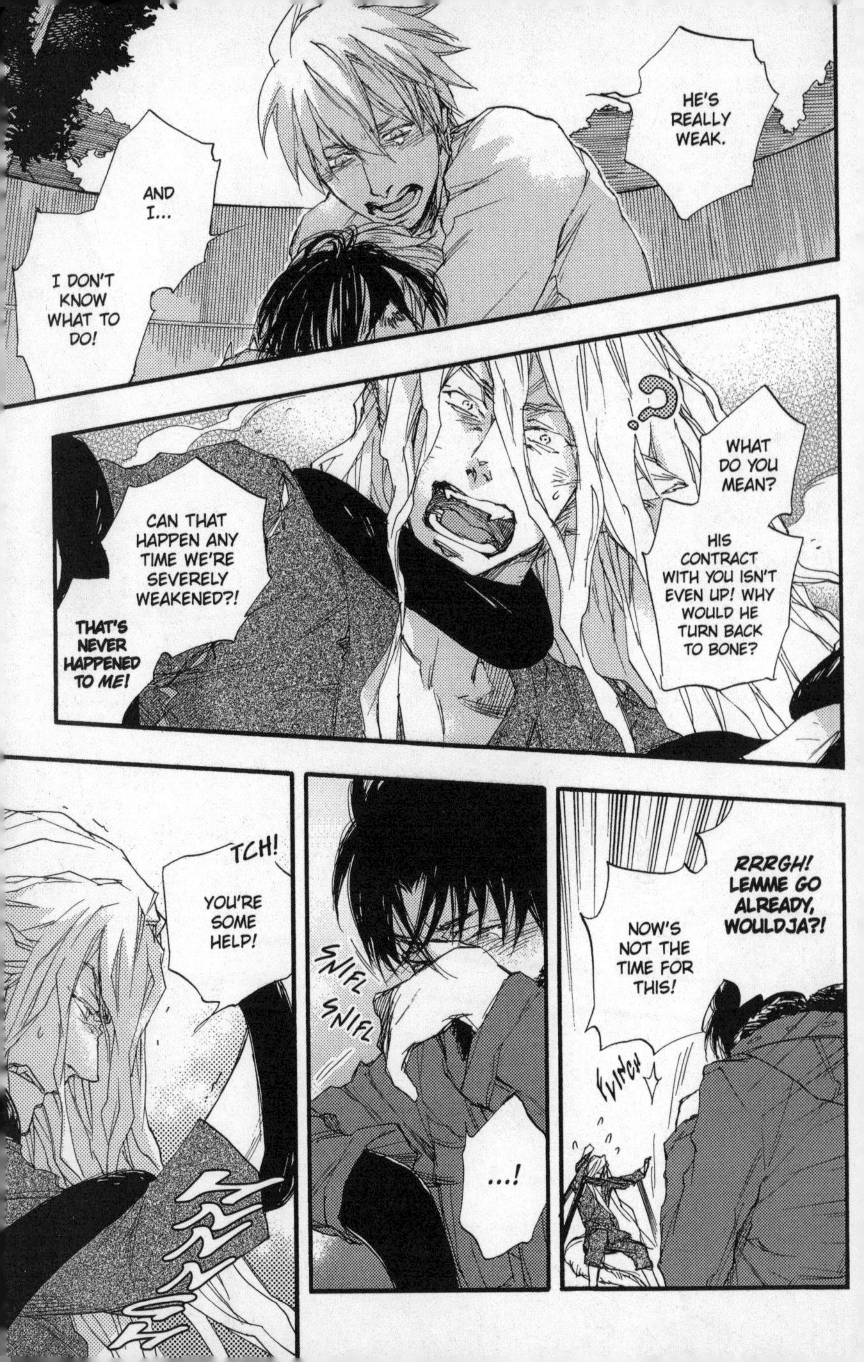
HE'S REALLY WEAK.
AND I...
I DON'T KNOW WHAT TO DO!
?
WHAT DO YOU MEAN?
HIS CONTRACT WITH YOU ISN'T EVEN UP! WHY WOULD HE TURN BACK TO BONE?
CAN THAT HAPPEN ANY TIME WE'RE SEVERELY WEAKENED?!
THAT'S NEVER HAPPENED TO ME!
RRRGH! LEMME GO ALREADY, WOULDJA?!
NOW'S NOT THE TIME FOR THIS!
SNIFL
SNIFL
...!
TCH!
YOU'RE SOME HELP!

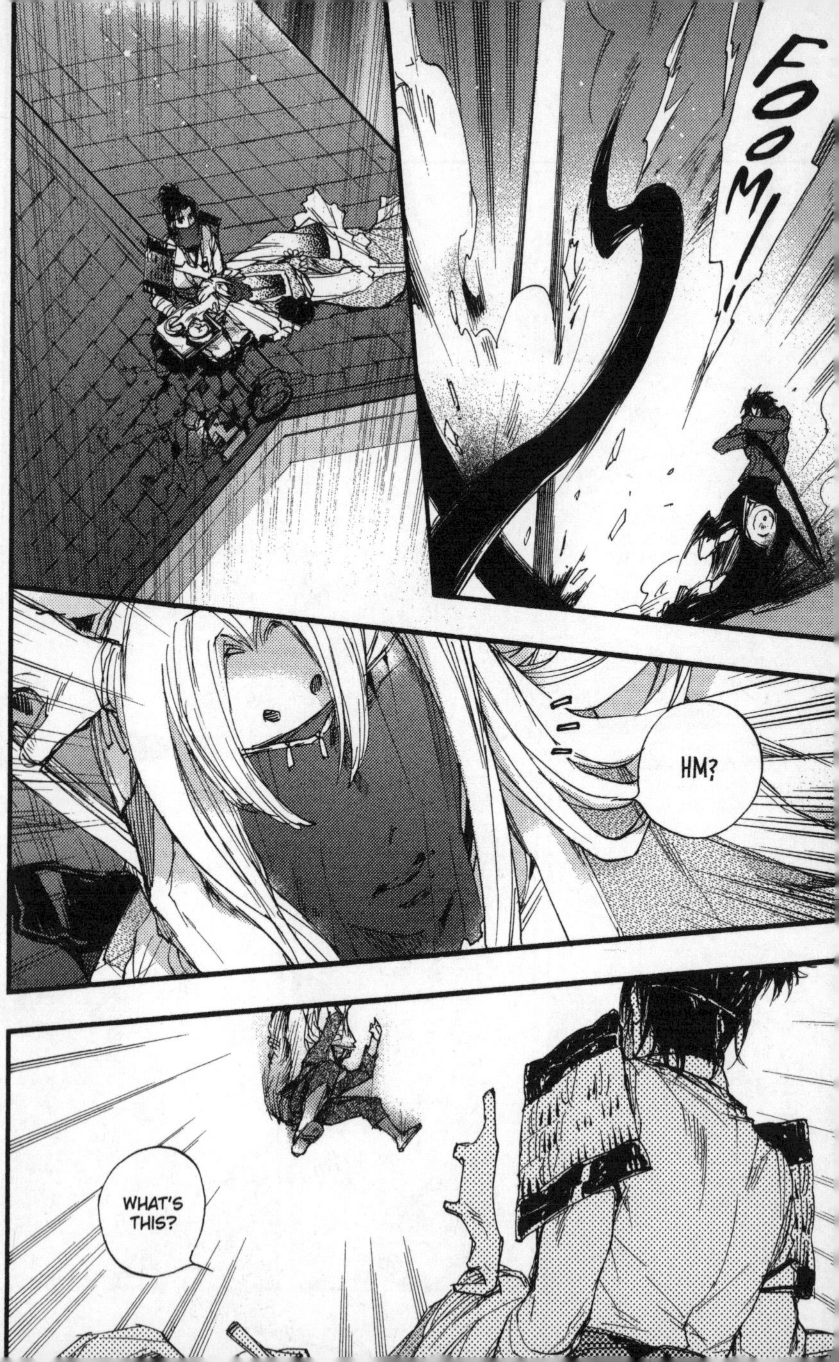
FOOOM!!
HM?
WHAT'S THIS?

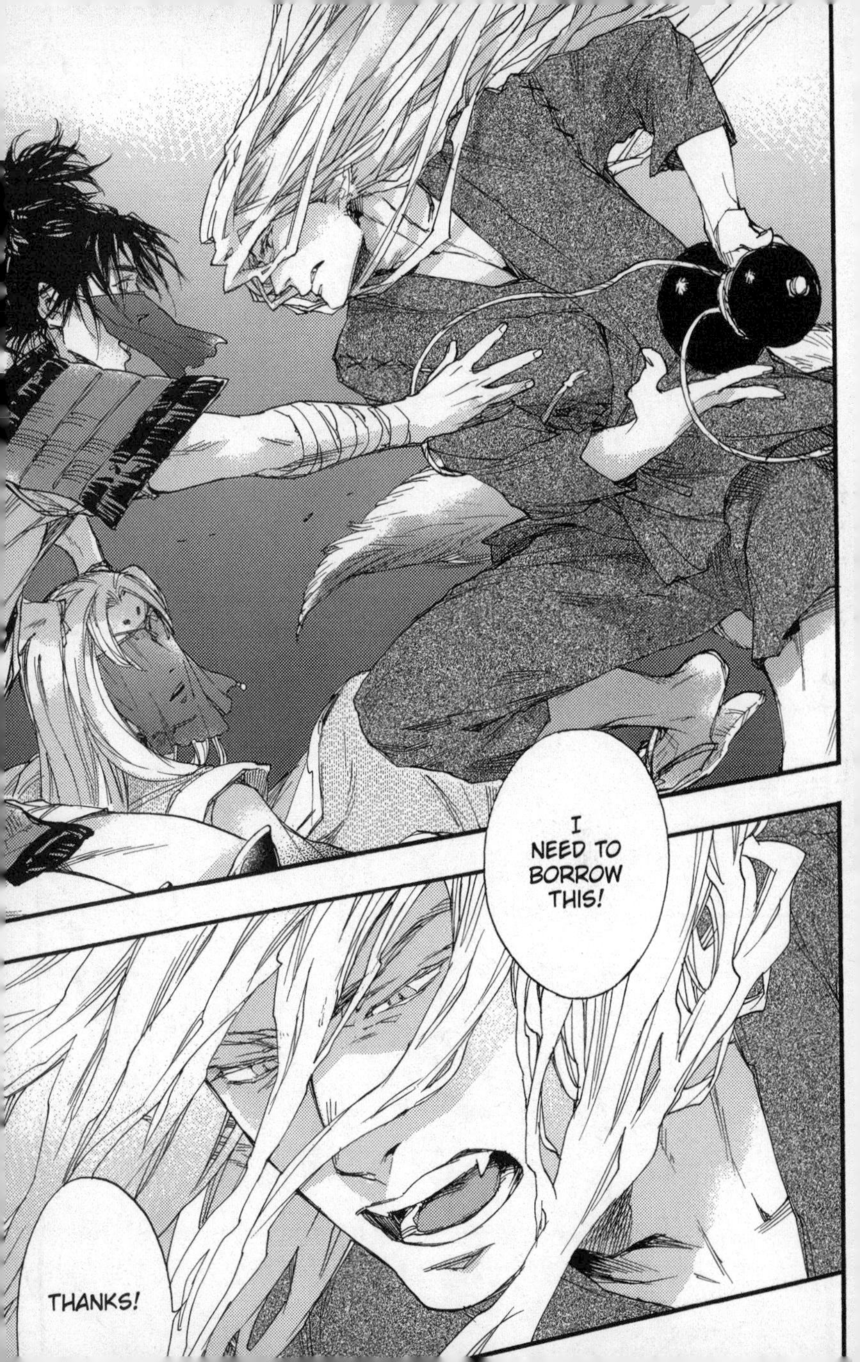
I NEED TO BORROW THIS!
THANKS!

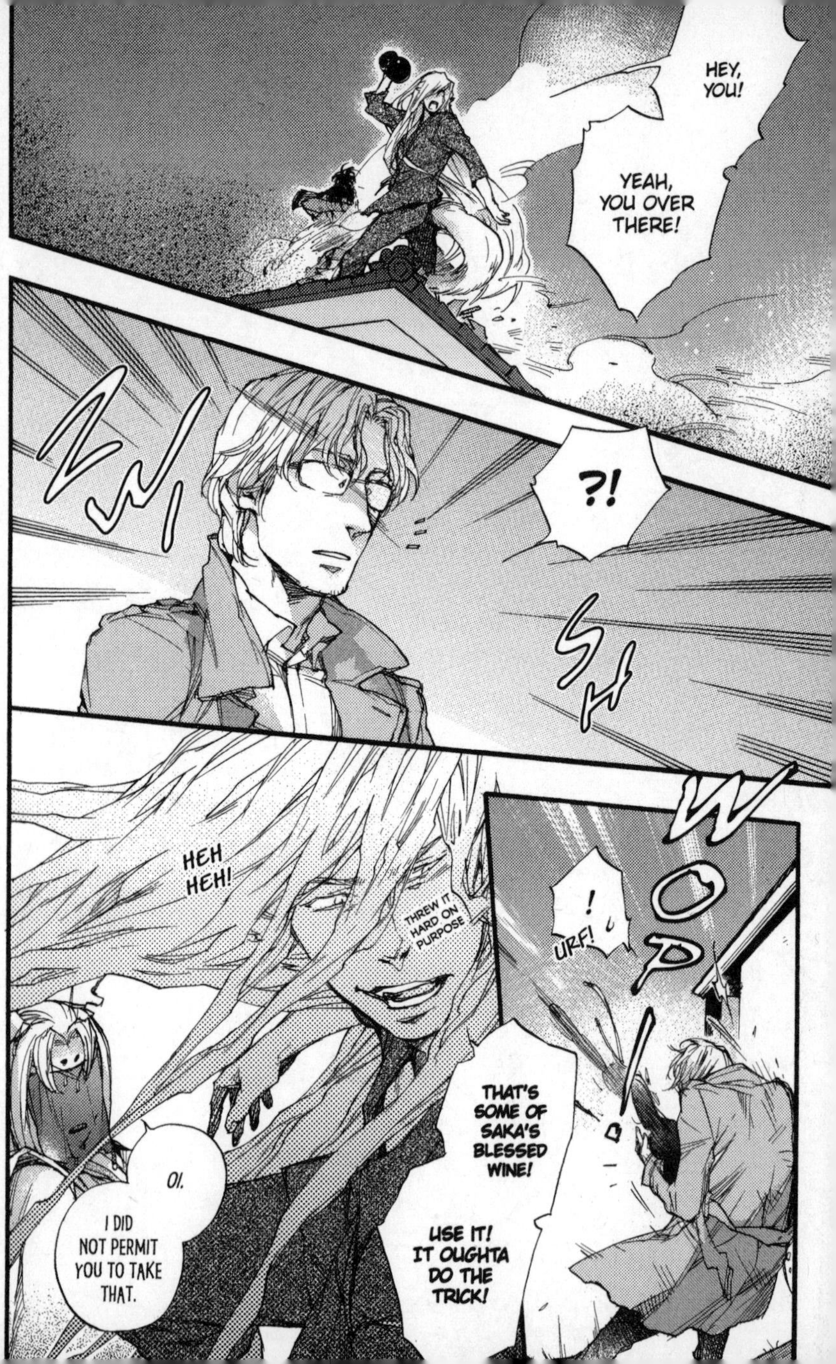
HEY, YOU!
YEAH, YOU OVER THERE!
?!
SH
WOP!
!
URF!
THAT'S SOME OF SAKA'S BLESSED WINE!
USE IT! IT OUGHTA DO THE TRICK!
HEH HEH!
THREW IT HARD ON PURPOSE
OI.
I DID NOT PERMIT YOU TO TAKE THAT.

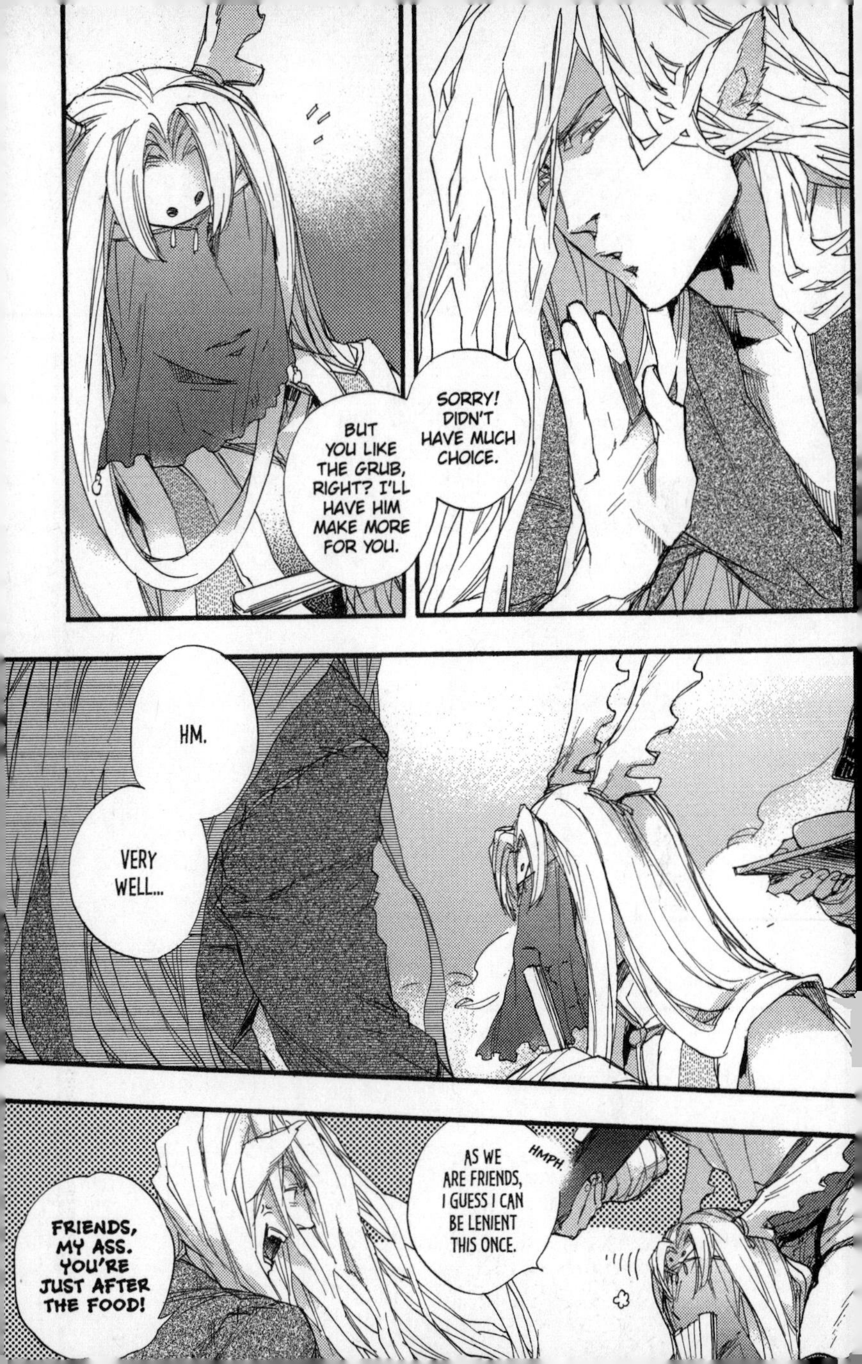
SORRY! DIDN'T HAVE MUCH CHOICE.
BUT YOU LIKE THE GRUB, RIGHT? I'LL HAVE HIM MAKE MORE FOR YOU.
HM.
VERY WELL...
HMPH.
AS WE ARE FRIENDS, I GUESS I CAN BE LENIENT THIS ONCE.
FRIENDS, MY ASS. YOU'RE JUST AFTER THE FOOD!

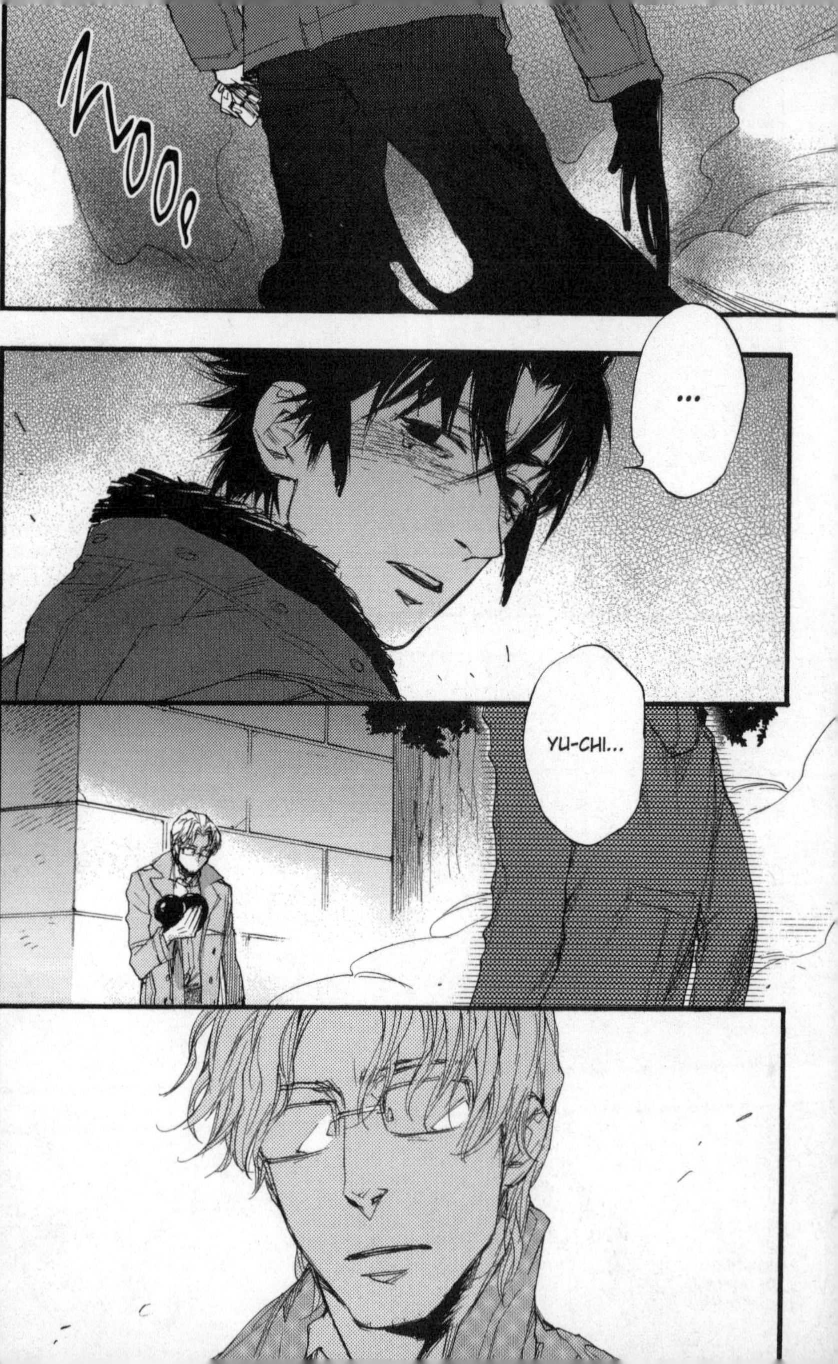
...
YU-CHI...

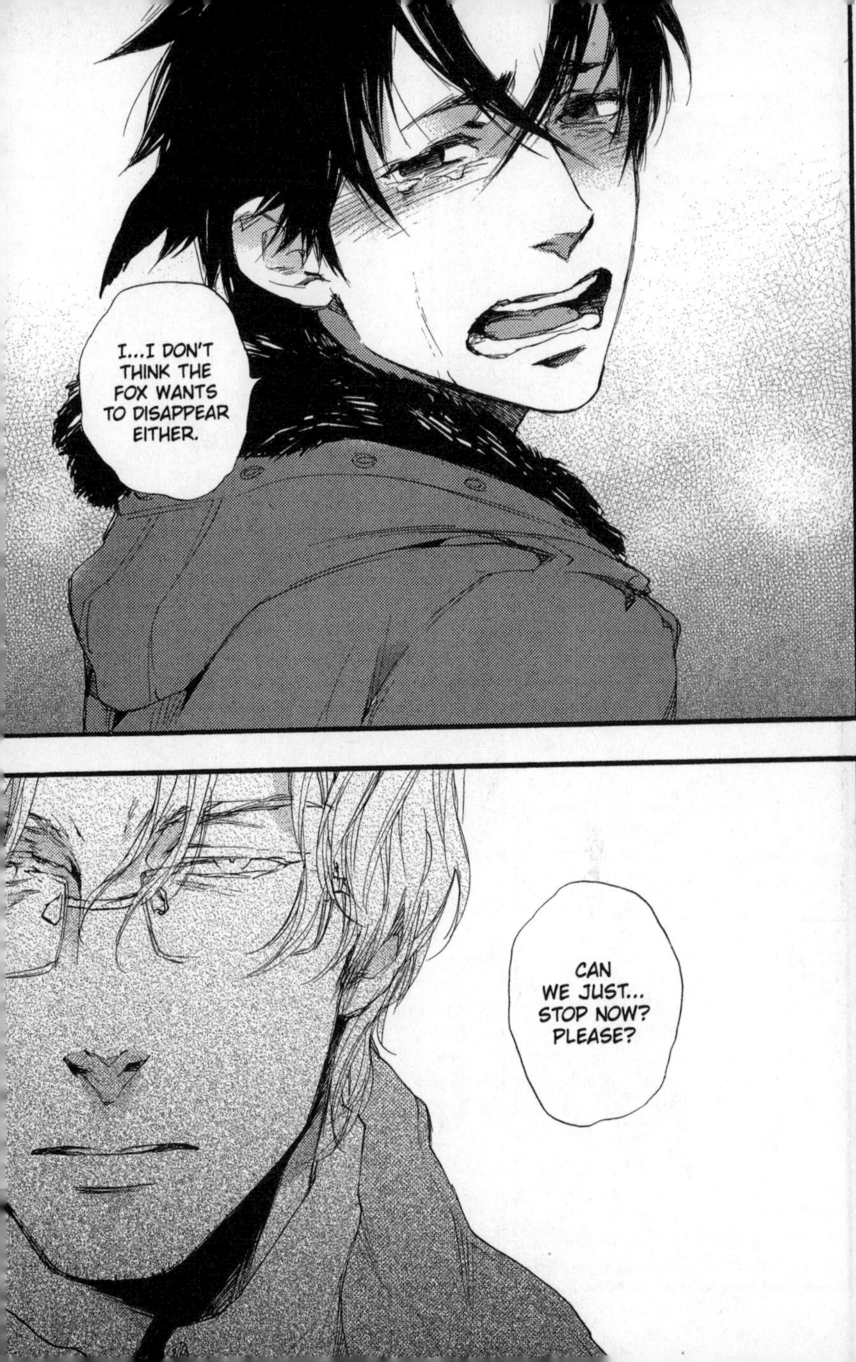
I...I DON'T THINK THE FOX WANTS TO DISAPPEAR EITHER.
CAN WE JUST... STOP NOW? PLEASE?

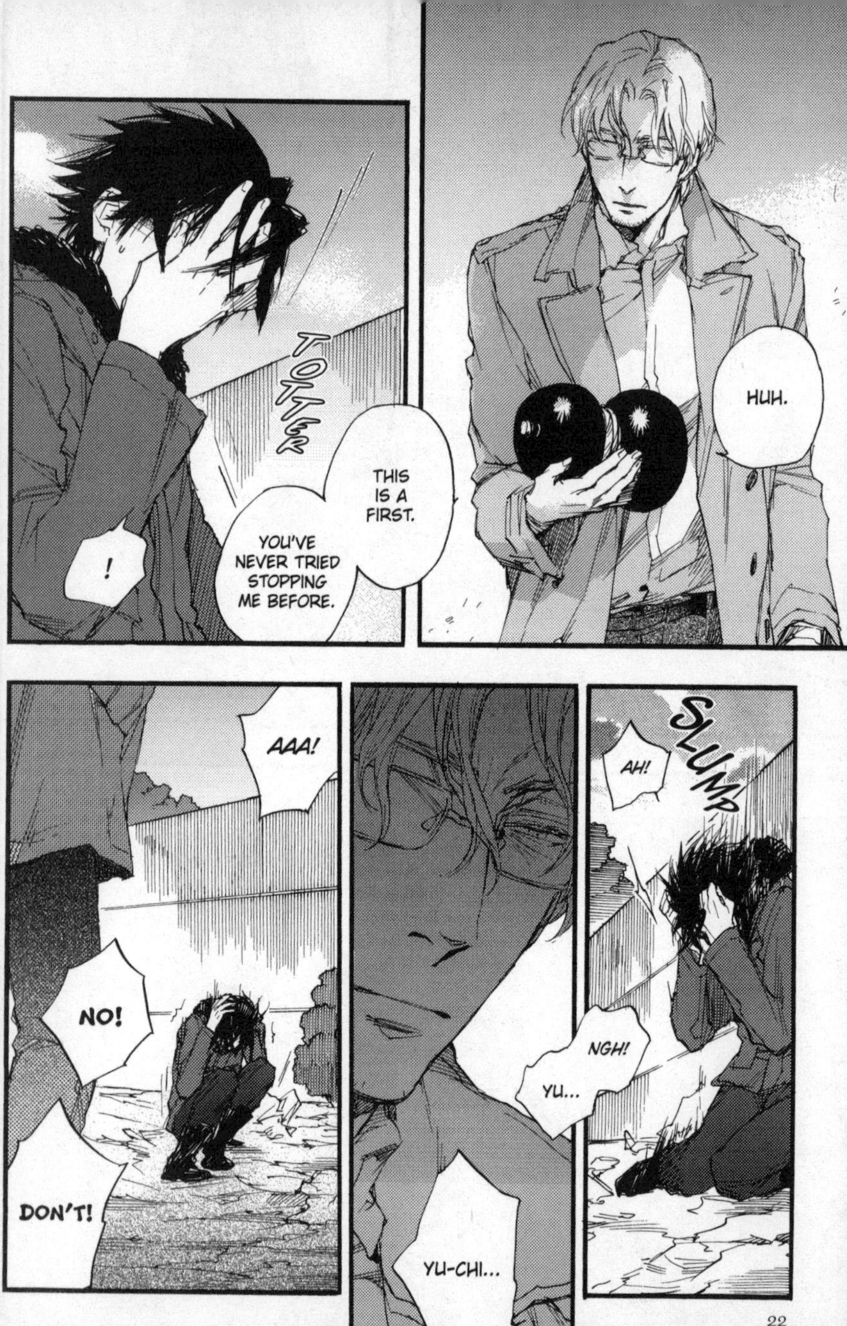
HUH.
THIS IS A FIRST.
YOU'VE NEVER TRIED STOPPING ME BEFORE.
TOTTER
!
SLUMP
AH!
NGH!
YU...
YU-CHI...
AAA!
NO!
DON'T!

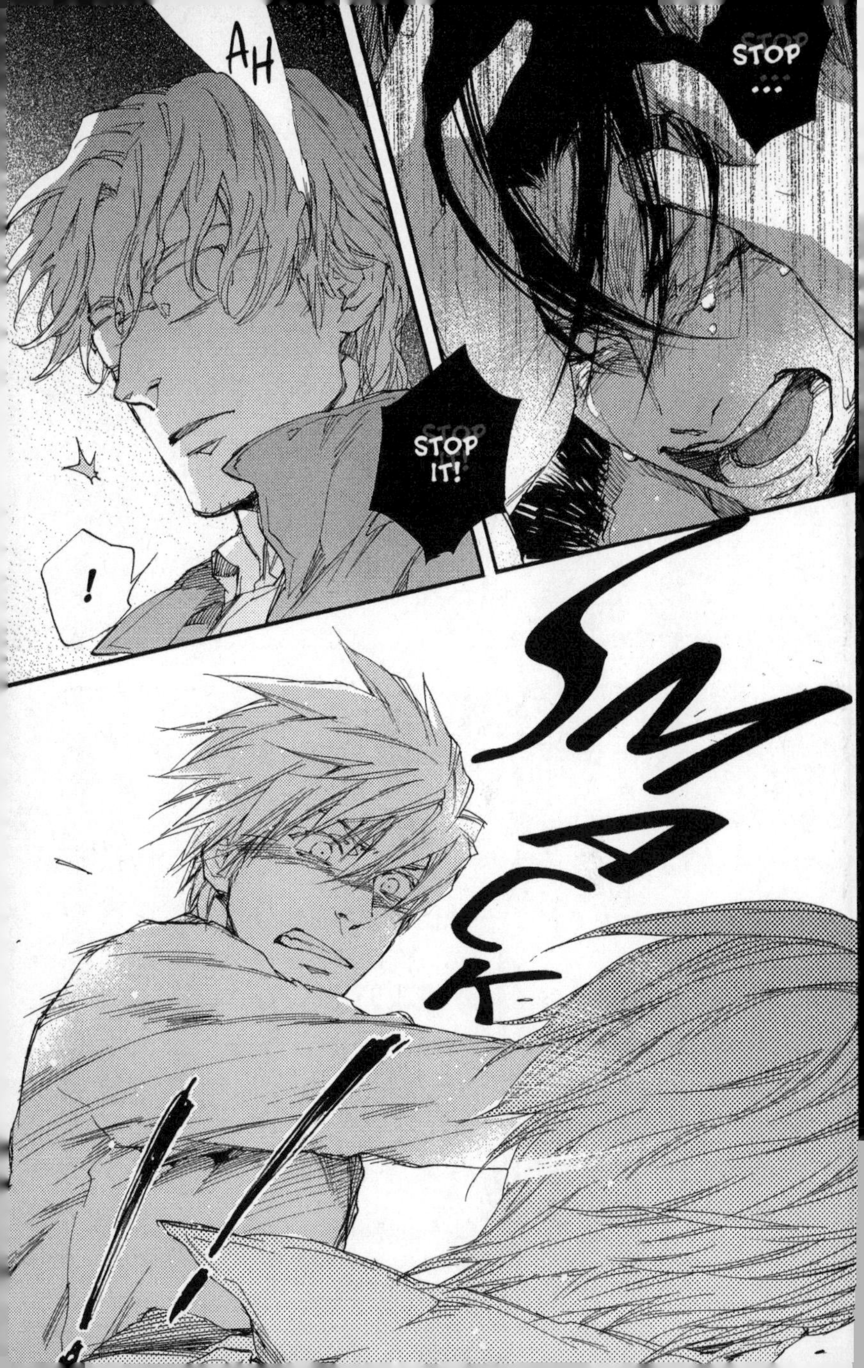
STOP...
STOP IT!
AH
!
SMACK

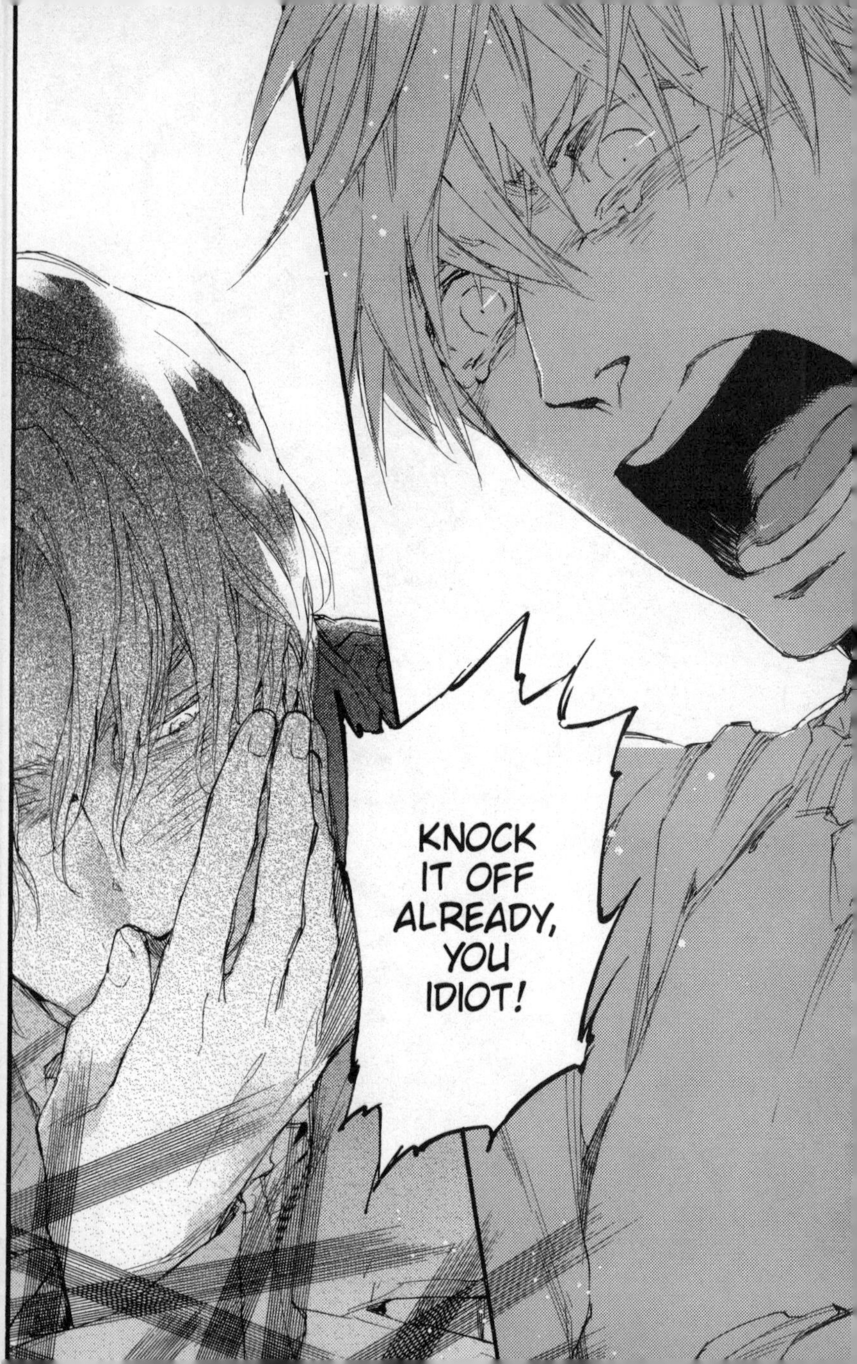
KNOCK IT OFF ALREADY, YOU IDIOT!

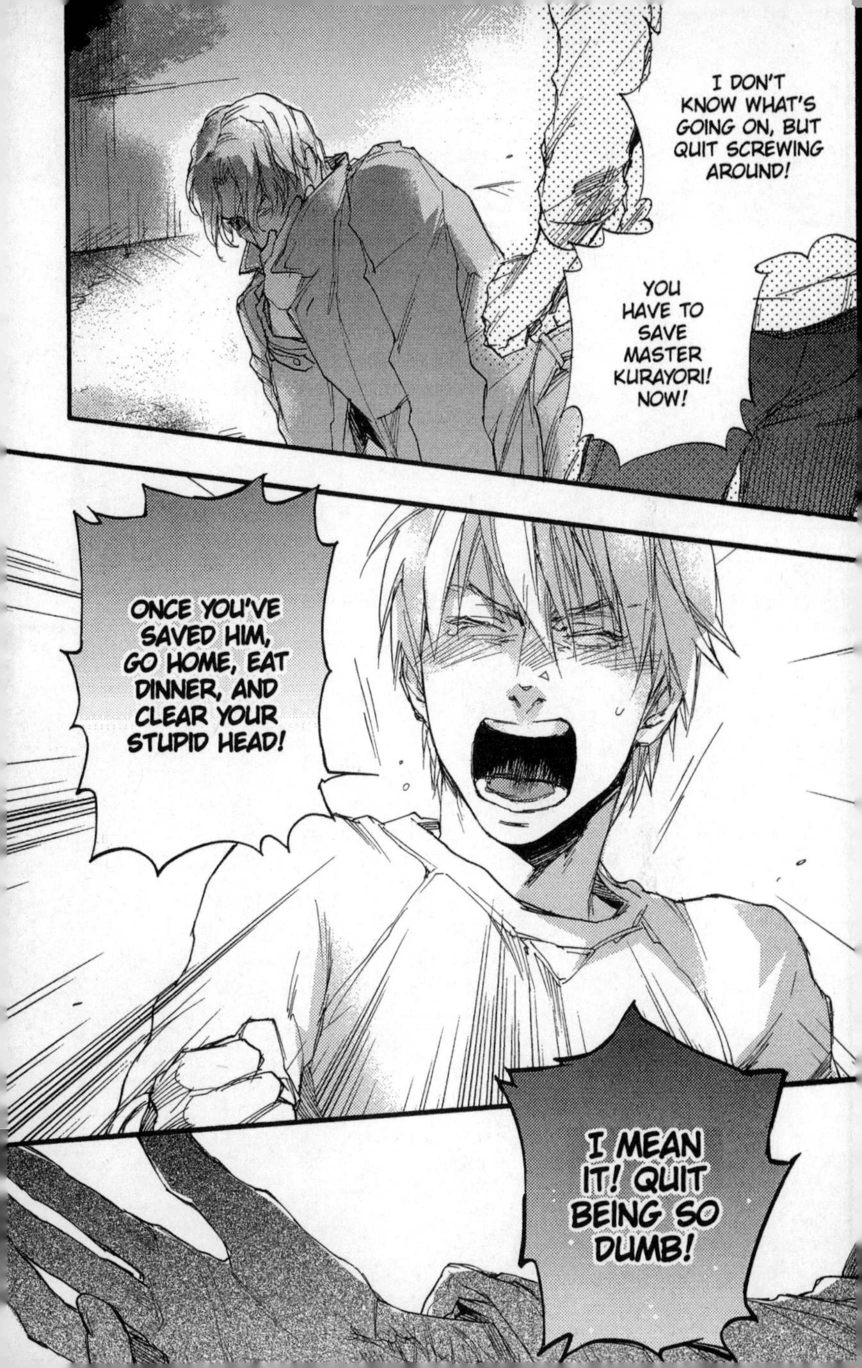
I DON'T KNOW WHAT'S GOING ON, BUT QUIT SCREWING AROUND!
YOU HAVE TO SAVE MASTER KURAYORI! NOW!
ONCE YOU'VE SAVED HIM, GO HOME, EAT DINNER, AND CLEAR YOUR STUPID HEAD!
I MEAN IT! QUIT BEING SO DUMB!

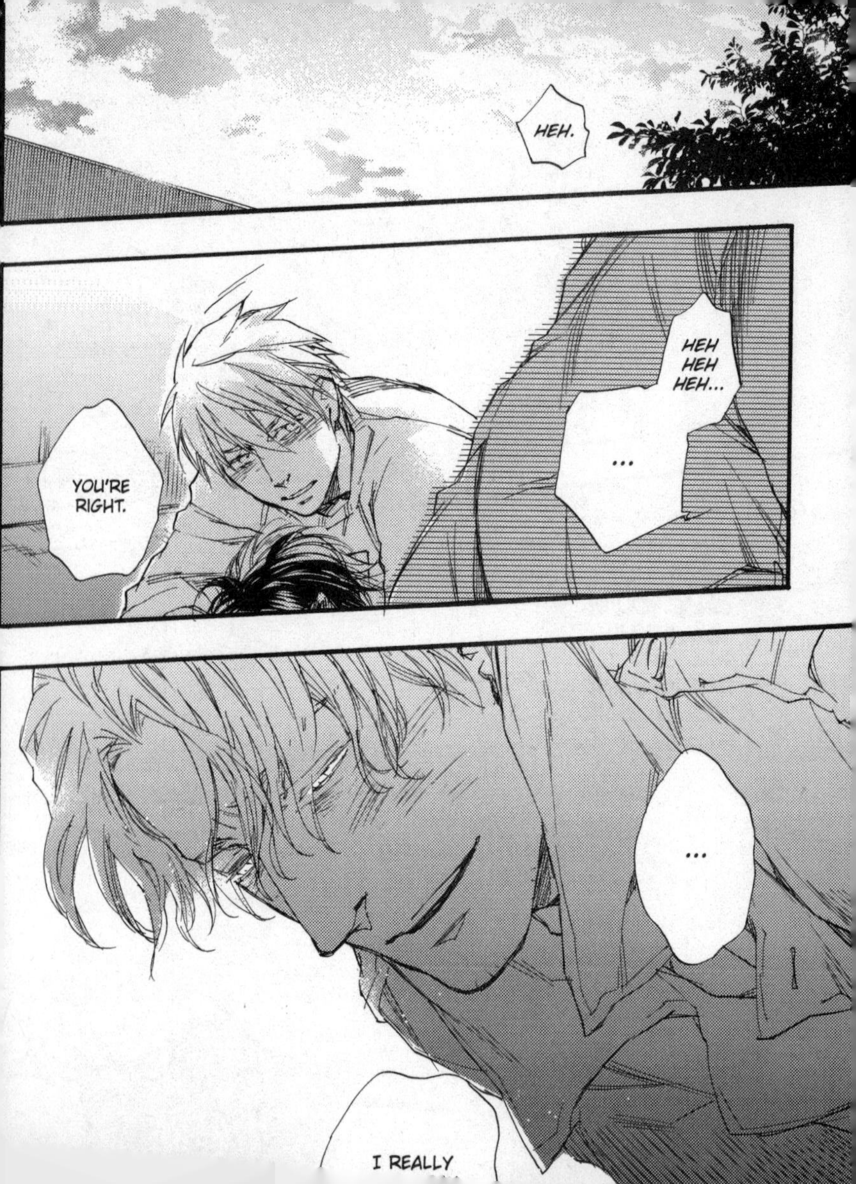
HEH.
HEH HEH HEH...
...
YOU'RE RIGHT.
...
I REALLY

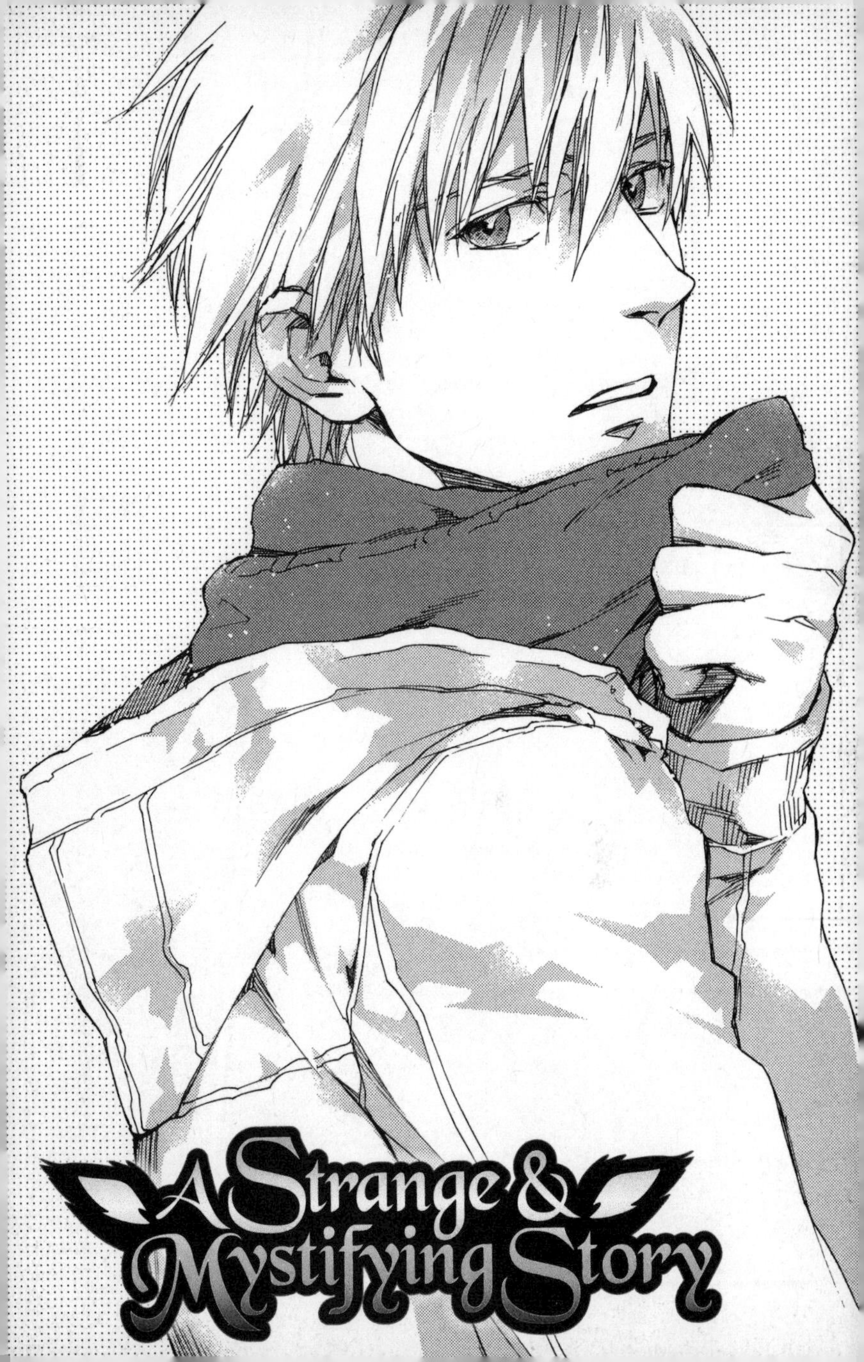
A Strange & Mystifying Story

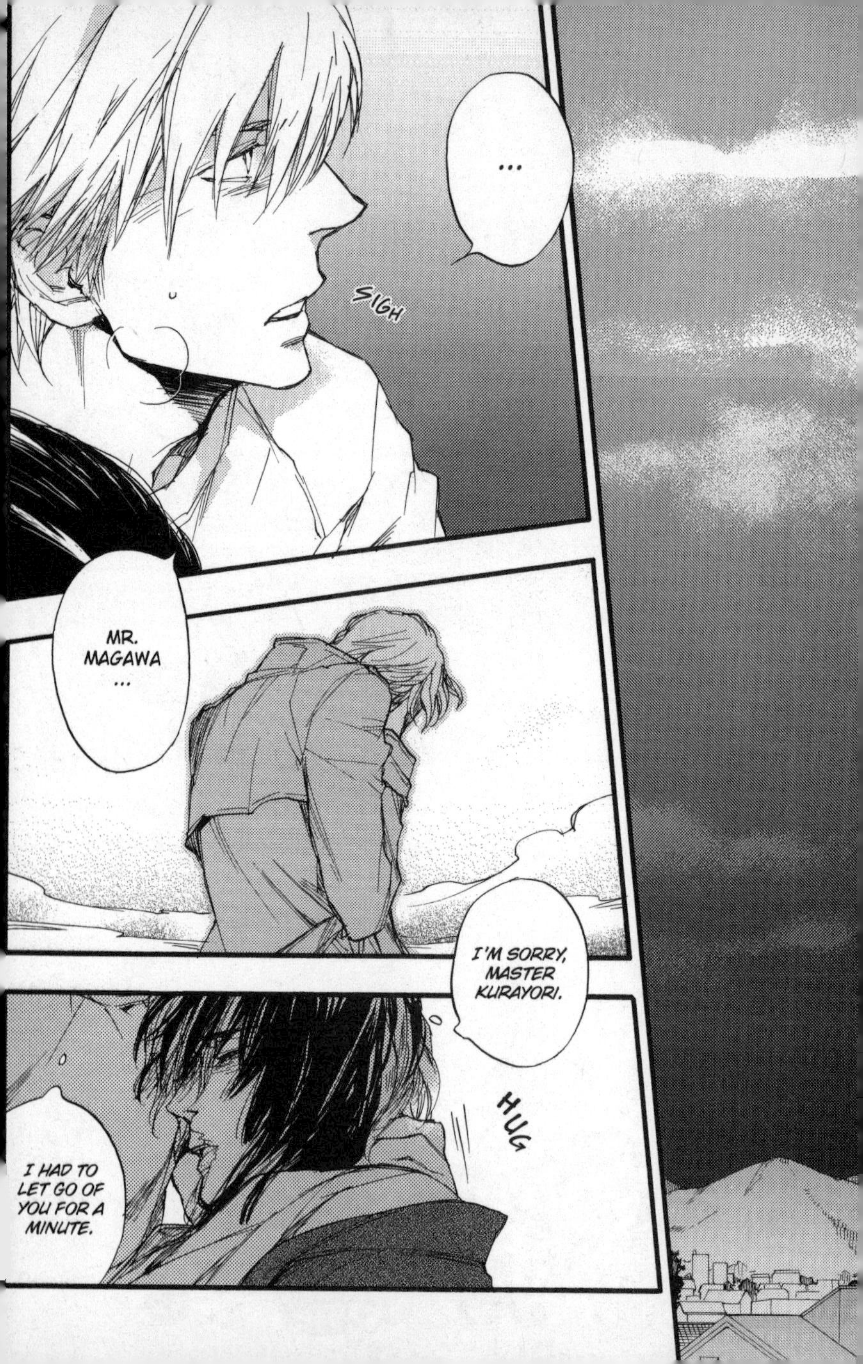
...
SIGH
MR. MAGAWA ...
I'M SORRY, MASTER KURAYORI.
HUG
I HAD TO LET GO OF YOU FOR A MINUTE.

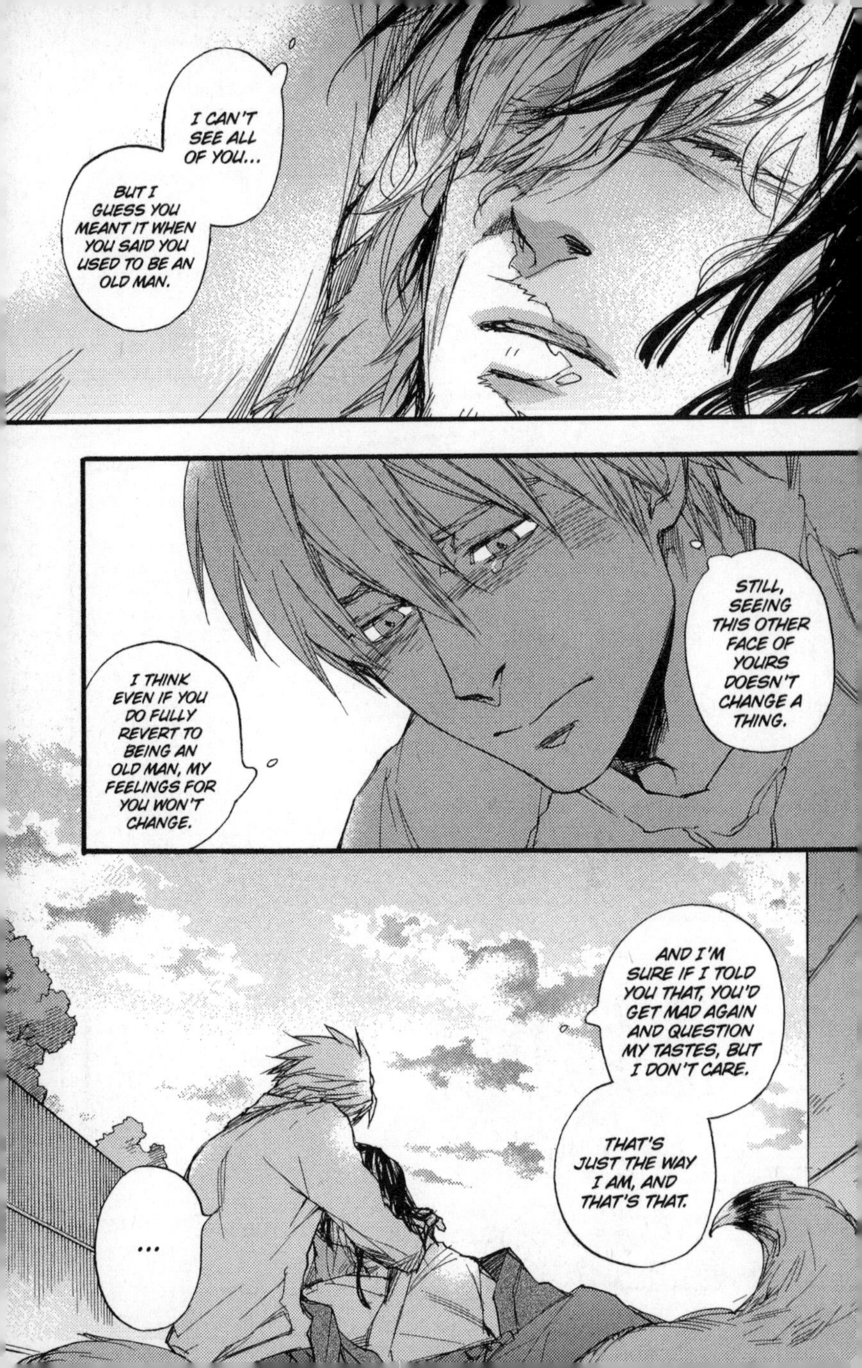
I CAN'T SEE ALL OF YOU...
BUT I GUESS YOU MEANT IT WHEN YOU SAID YOU USED TO BE AN OLD MAN.
STILL, SEEING THIS OTHER FACE OF YOURS DOESN'T CHANGE A THING.
I THINK EVEN IF YOU DO FULLY REVERT TO BEING AN OLD MAN, MY FEELINGS FOR YOU WON'T CHANGE.
AND I'M SURE IF I TOLD YOU THAT, YOU'D GET MAD AGAIN AND QUESTION MY TASTES, BUT I DON'T CARE.
THAT'S JUST THE WAY I AM, AND THAT'S THAT.
...

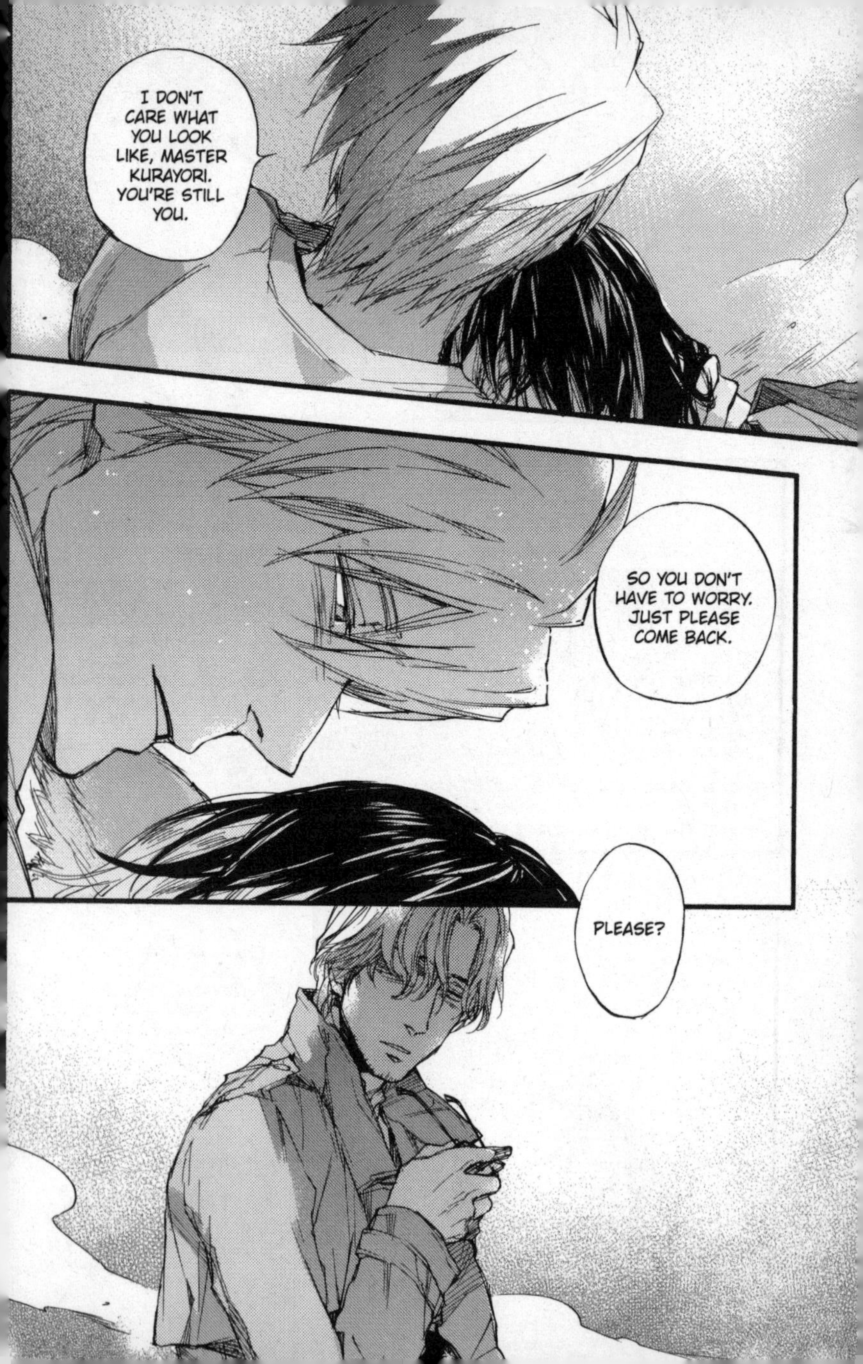
I DON'T CARE WHAT YOU LOOK LIKE, MASTER KURAYORI. YOU'RE STILL YOU.
SO YOU DON'T HAVE TO WORRY. JUST PLEASE COME BACK.
PLEASE?

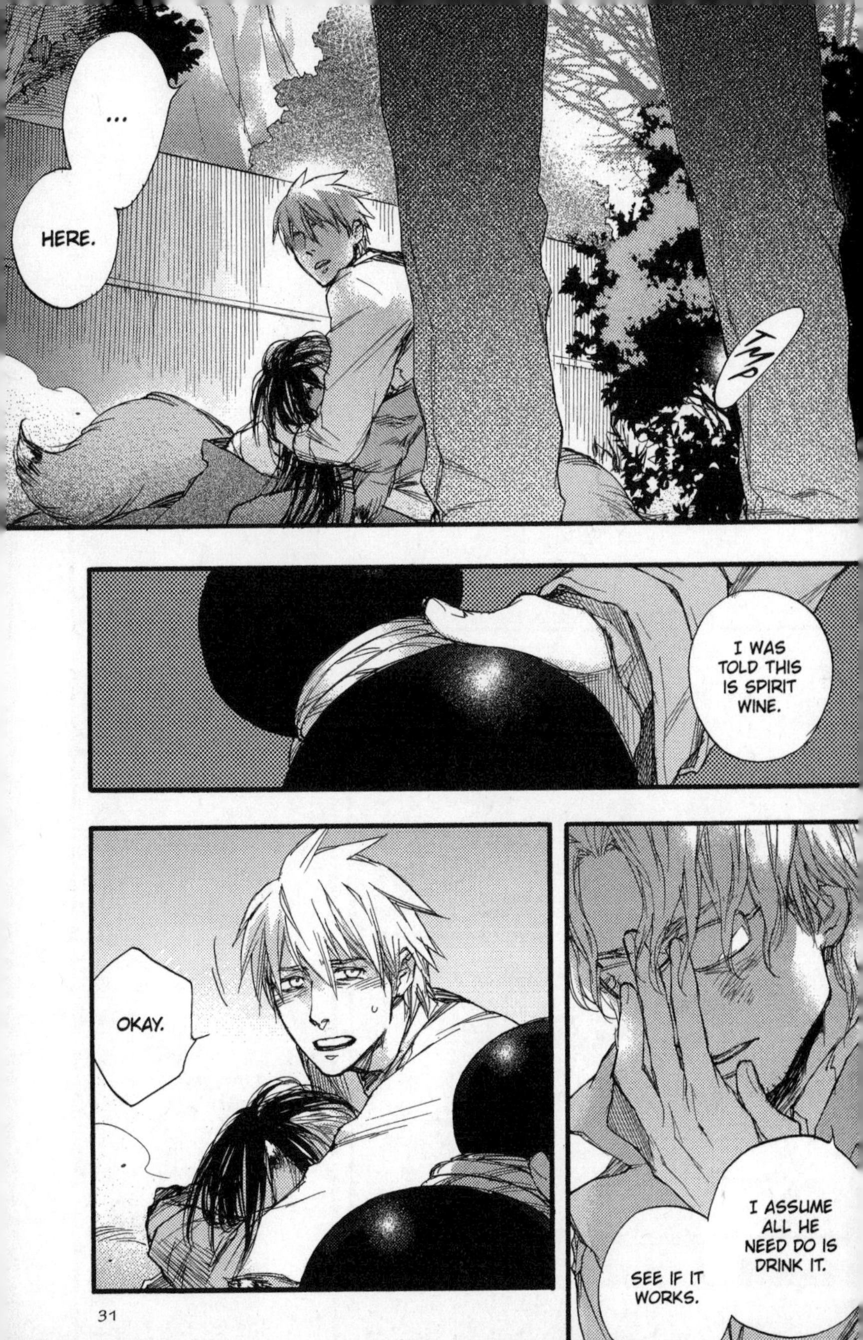
TMP
...
HERE.
I WAS TOLD THIS IS SPIRIT WINE.
I ASSUME ALL HE NEED DO IS DRINK IT.
SEE IF IT WORKS.
OKAY.

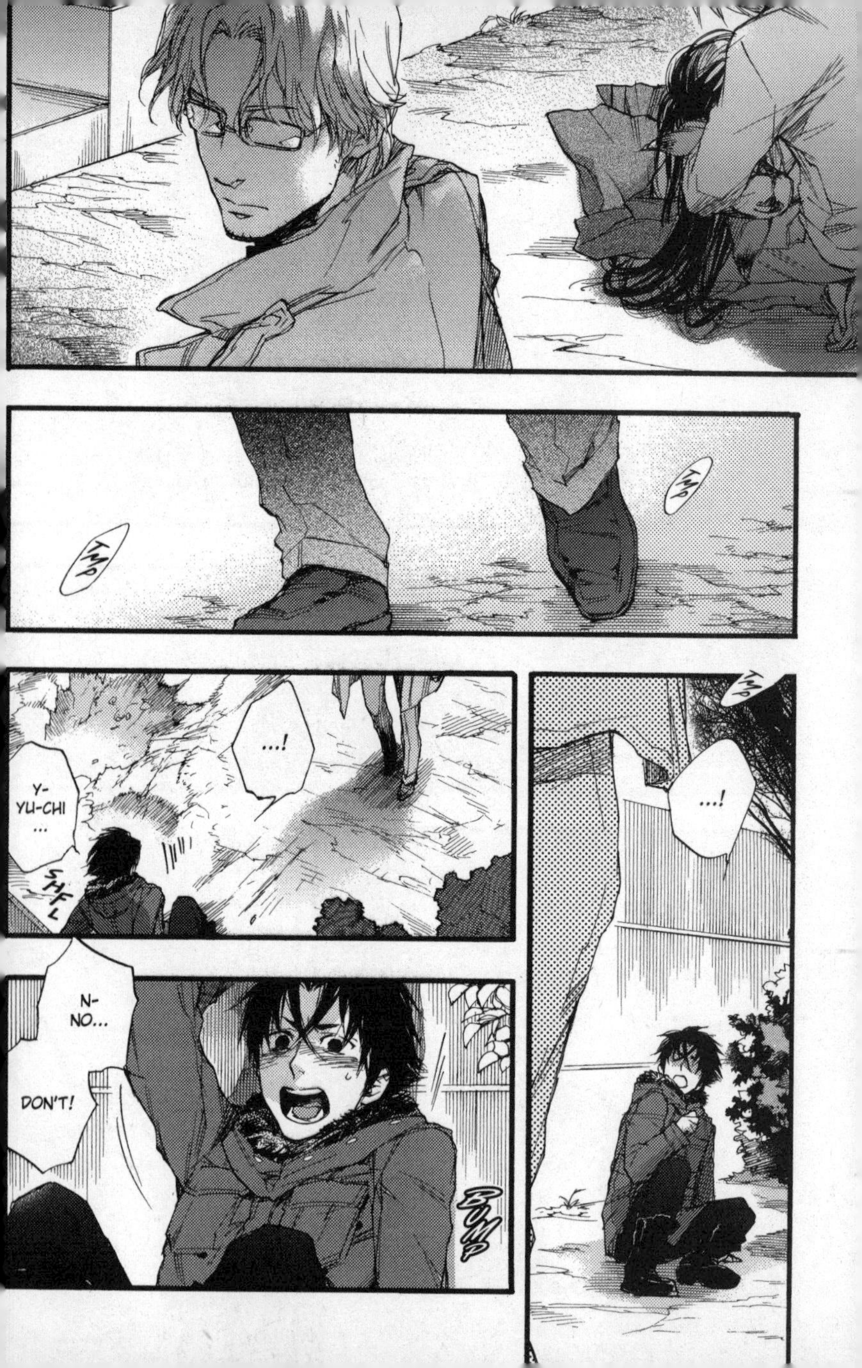
TMP
TMP
TMP
...!
...!
Y-YU-CHI ...
SHFL
N-NO...
DON'T!
BUMP

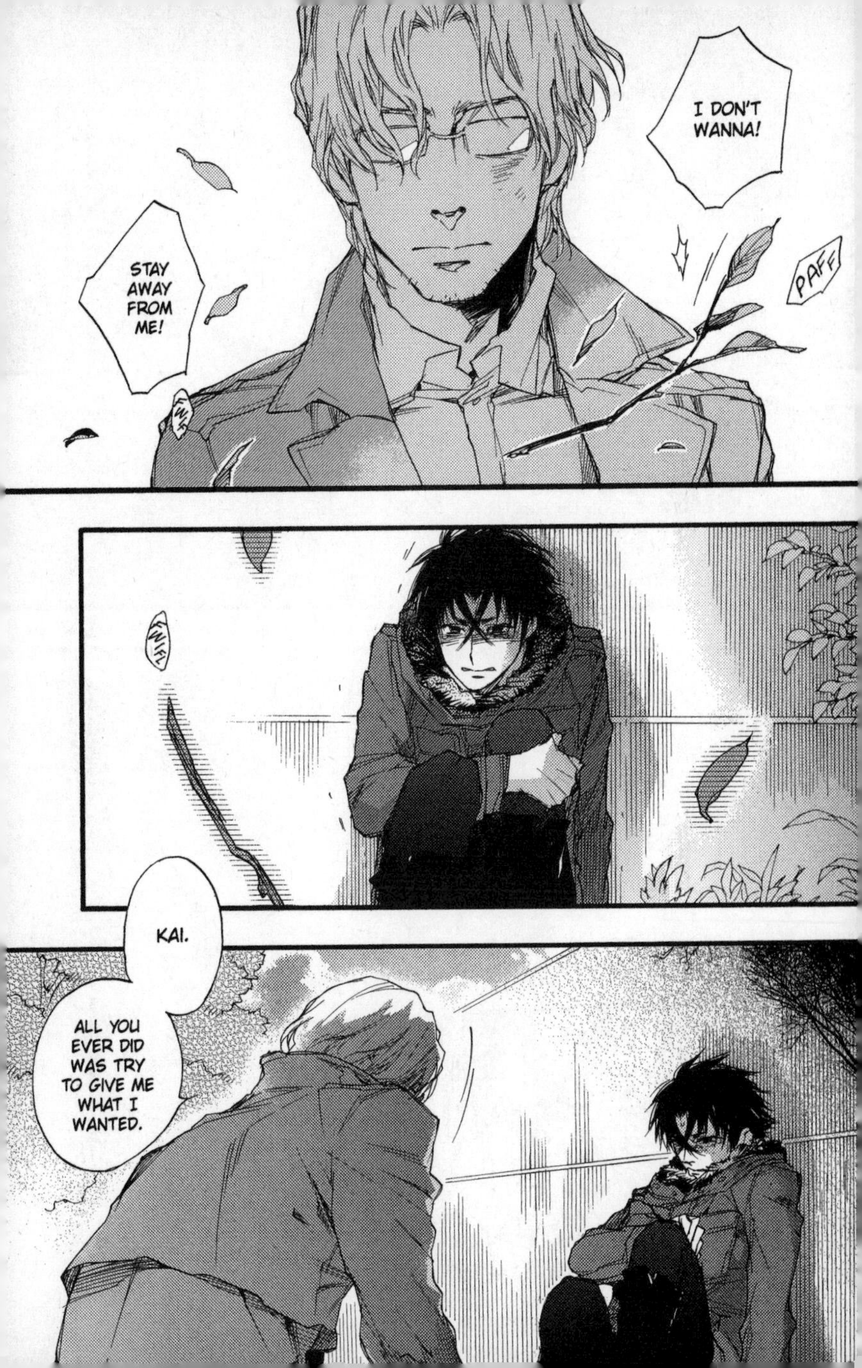
I DON'T WANNA!
PAFF
STAY AWAY FROM ME!
KAI.
ALL YOU EVER DID WAS TRY TO GIVE ME WHAT I WANTED.

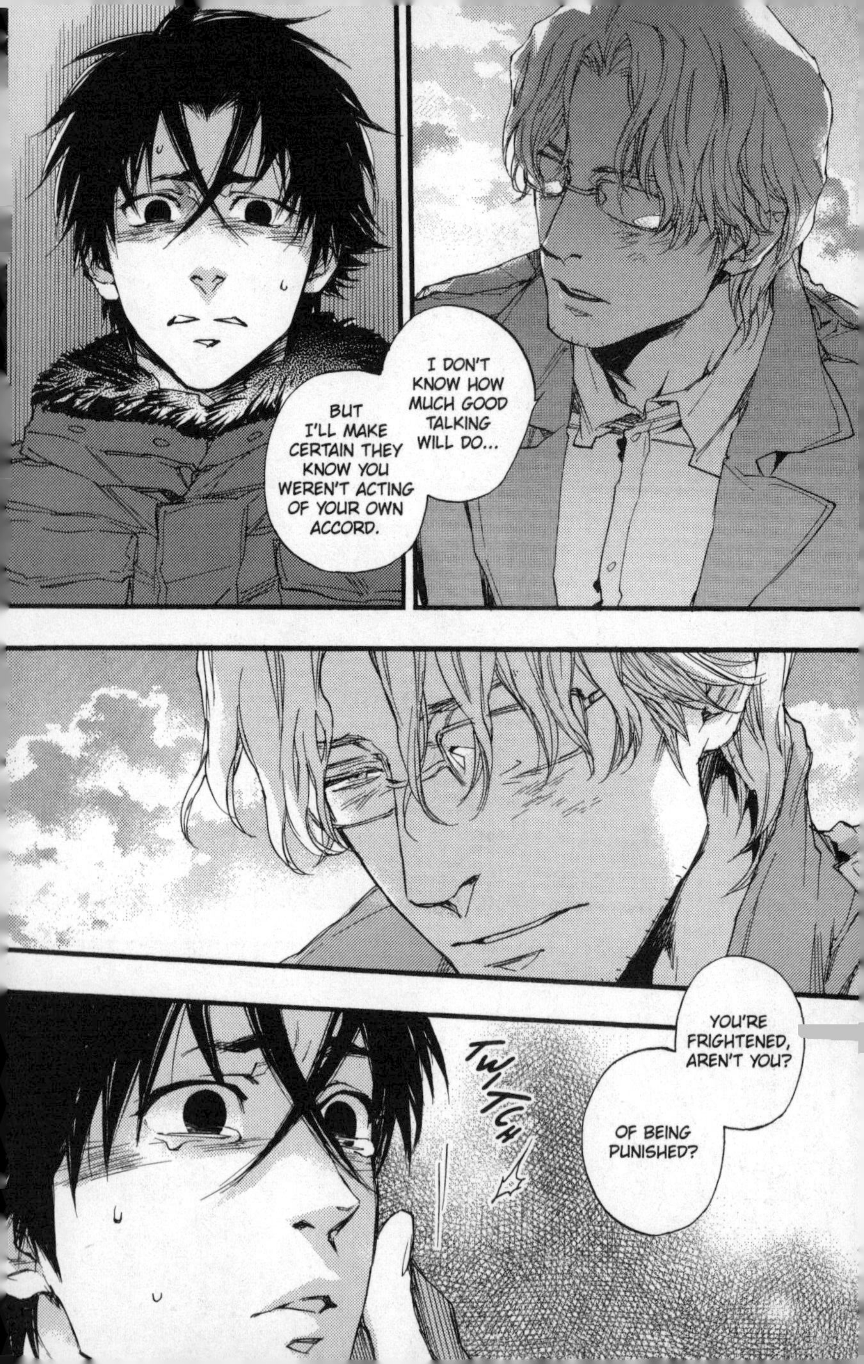
I DON'T KNOW HOW MUCH GOOD TALKING WILL DO...
BUT I'LL MAKE CERTAIN THEY KNOW YOU WEREN'T ACTING OF YOUR OWN ACCORD.
YOU'RE FRIGHTENED, AREN'T YOU?
TWITCH
OF BEING PUNISHED?

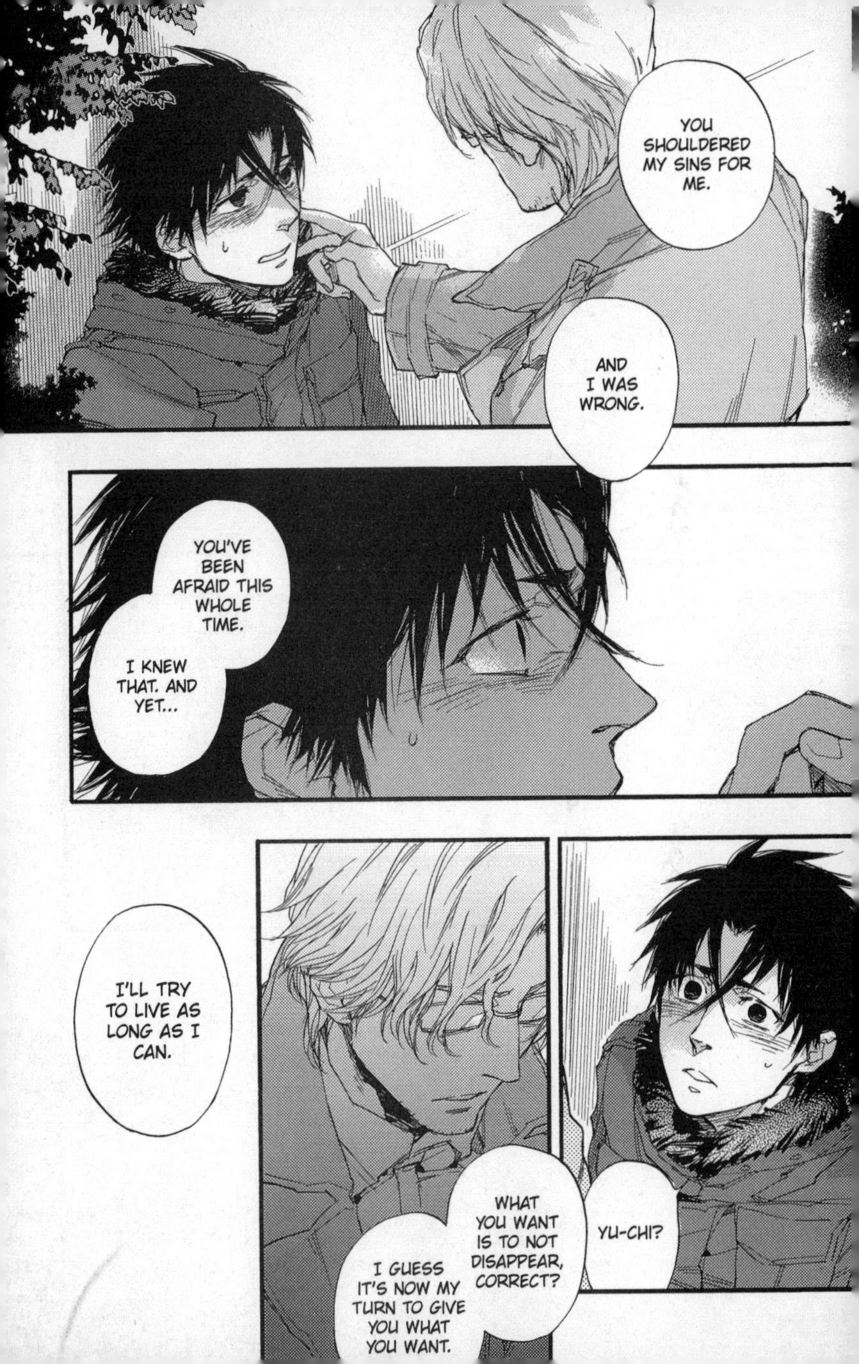
YOU SHOULDERED MY SINS FOR ME.
AND I WAS WRONG.
YOU'VE BEEN AFRAID THIS WHOLE TIME.
I KNEW THAT. AND YET...
YU-CHI?
WHAT YOU WANT IS TO NOT DISAPPEAR, CORRECT?
I GUESS IT'S NOW MY TURN TO GIVE YOU WHAT YOU WANT.
I'LL TRY TO LIVE AS LONG AS I CAN.

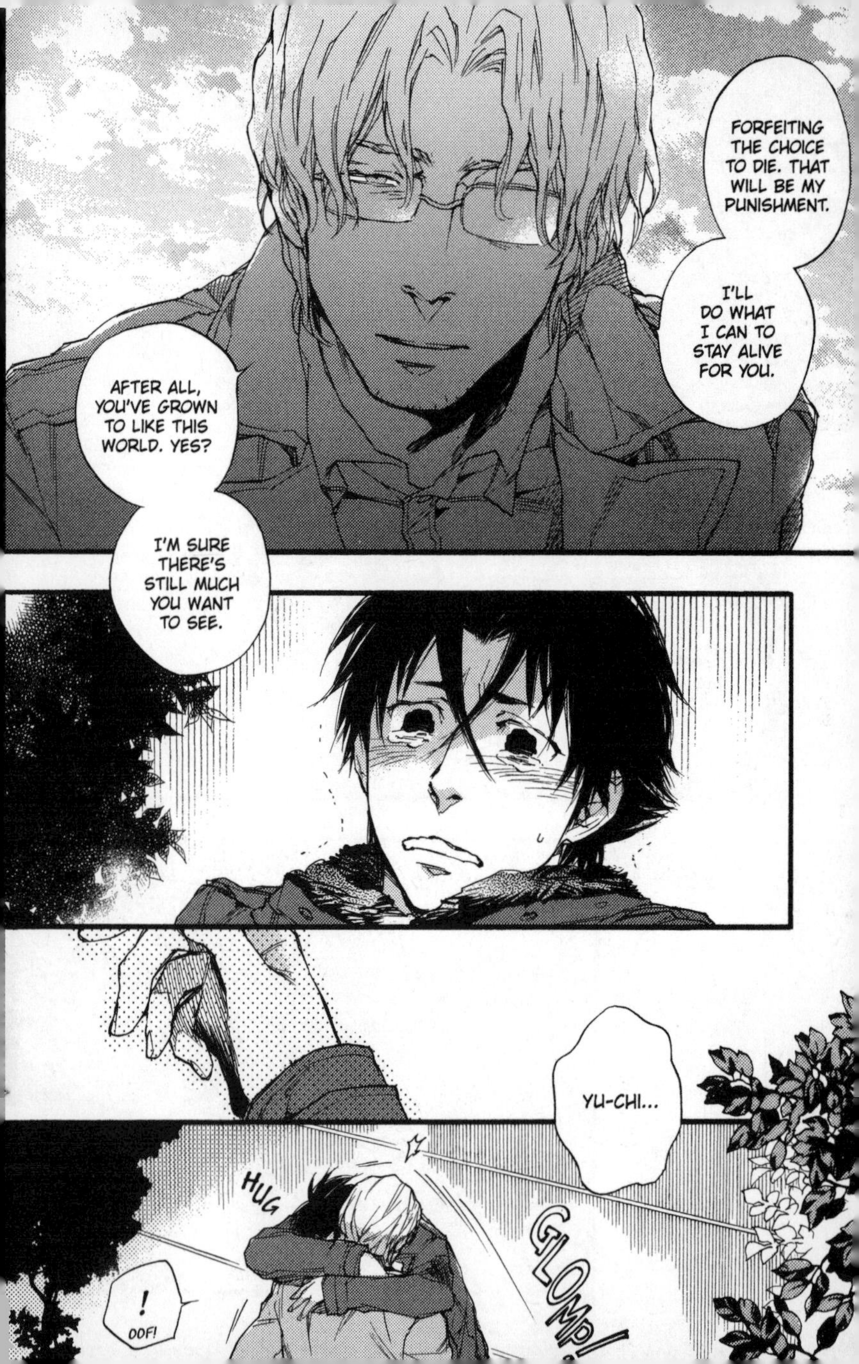
FORFEITING THE CHOICE TO DIE. THAT WILL BE MY PUNISHMENT.
I'LL DO WHAT I CAN TO STAY ALIVE FOR YOU.
AFTER ALL, YOU'VE GROWN TO LIKE THIS WORLD. YES?
I'M SURE THERE'S STILL MUCH YOU WANT TO SEE.
YU-CHI...
GLOMP!
HUG
!
OOF!

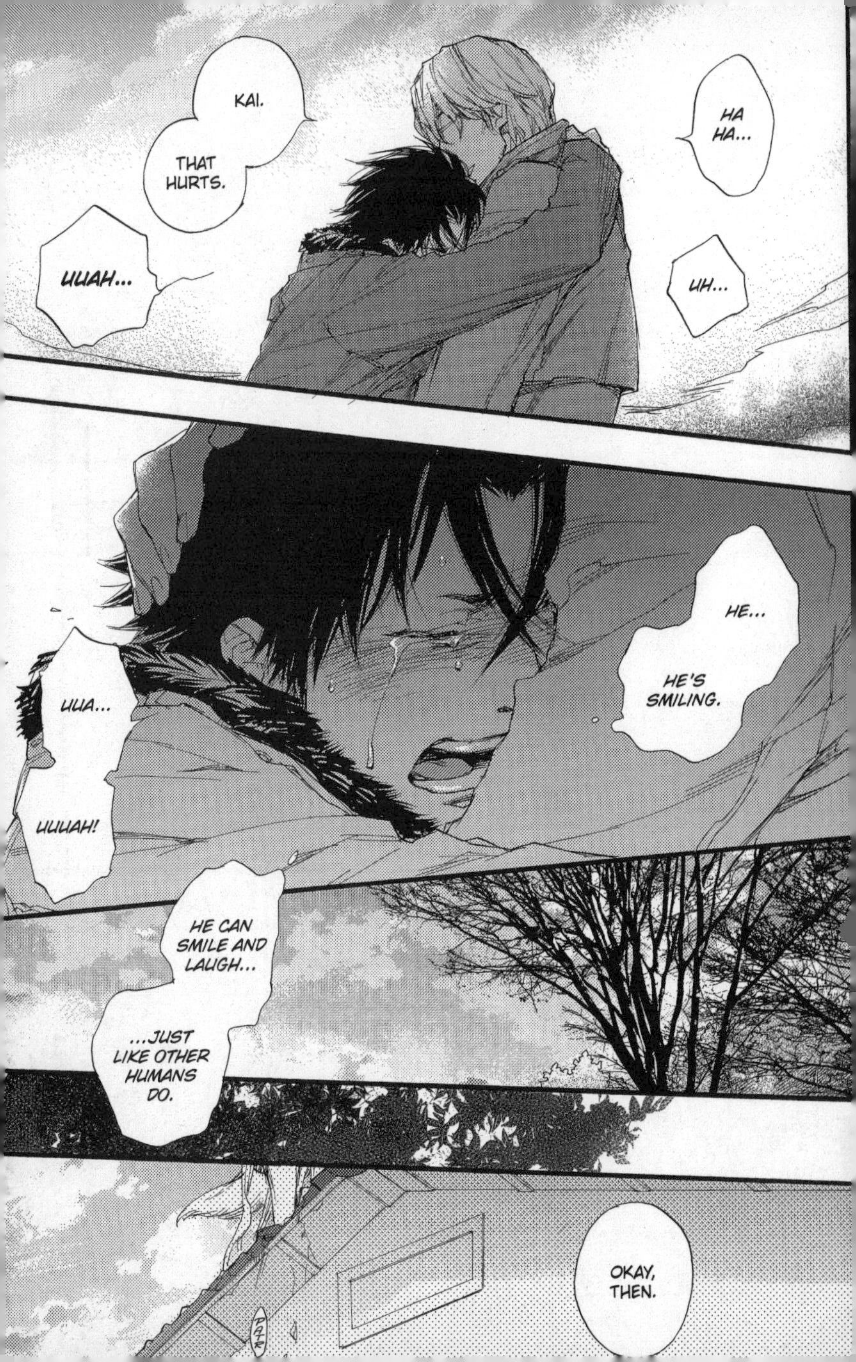
HA HA...
KAI.
THAT HURTS.
UH...
UUAH...
HE...
HE'S SMILING.
UUA...
UUUAH!
HE CAN SMILE AND LAUGH...
...JUST LIKE OTHER HUMANS DO.
OKAY, THEN.

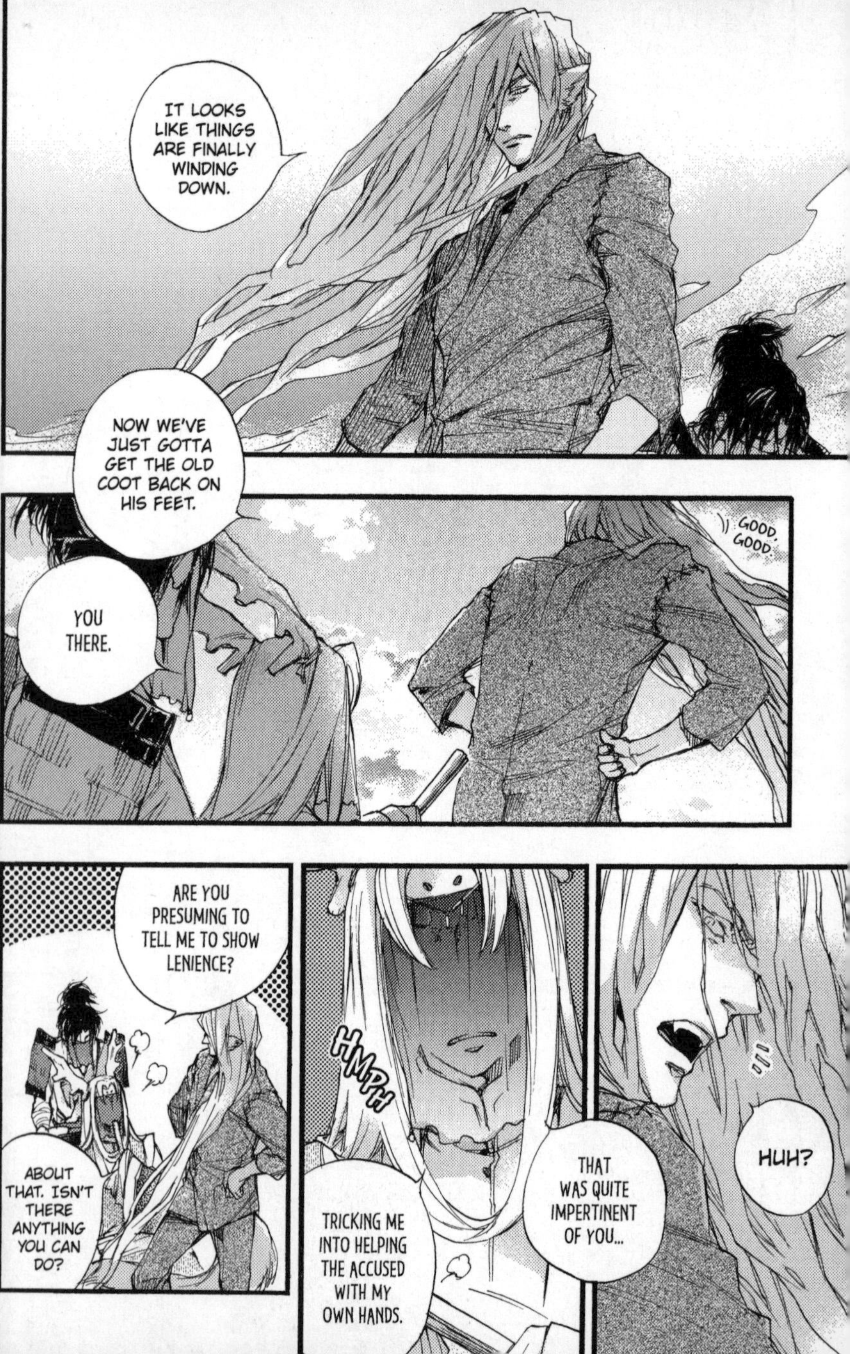
IT LOOKS LIKE THINGS ARE FINALLY WINDING DOWN.
NOW WE'VE JUST GOTTA GET THE OLD COOT BACK ON HIS FEET.
GOOD, GOOD.
YOU THERE.
HUH?
HMPH
THAT WAS QUITE IMPERTINENT OF YOU...
TRICKING ME INTO HELPING THE ACCUSED WITH MY OWN HANDS.
ARE YOU PRESUMING TO TELL ME TO SHOW LENIENCE?
ABOUT THAT. ISN'T THERE ANYTHING YOU CAN DO?

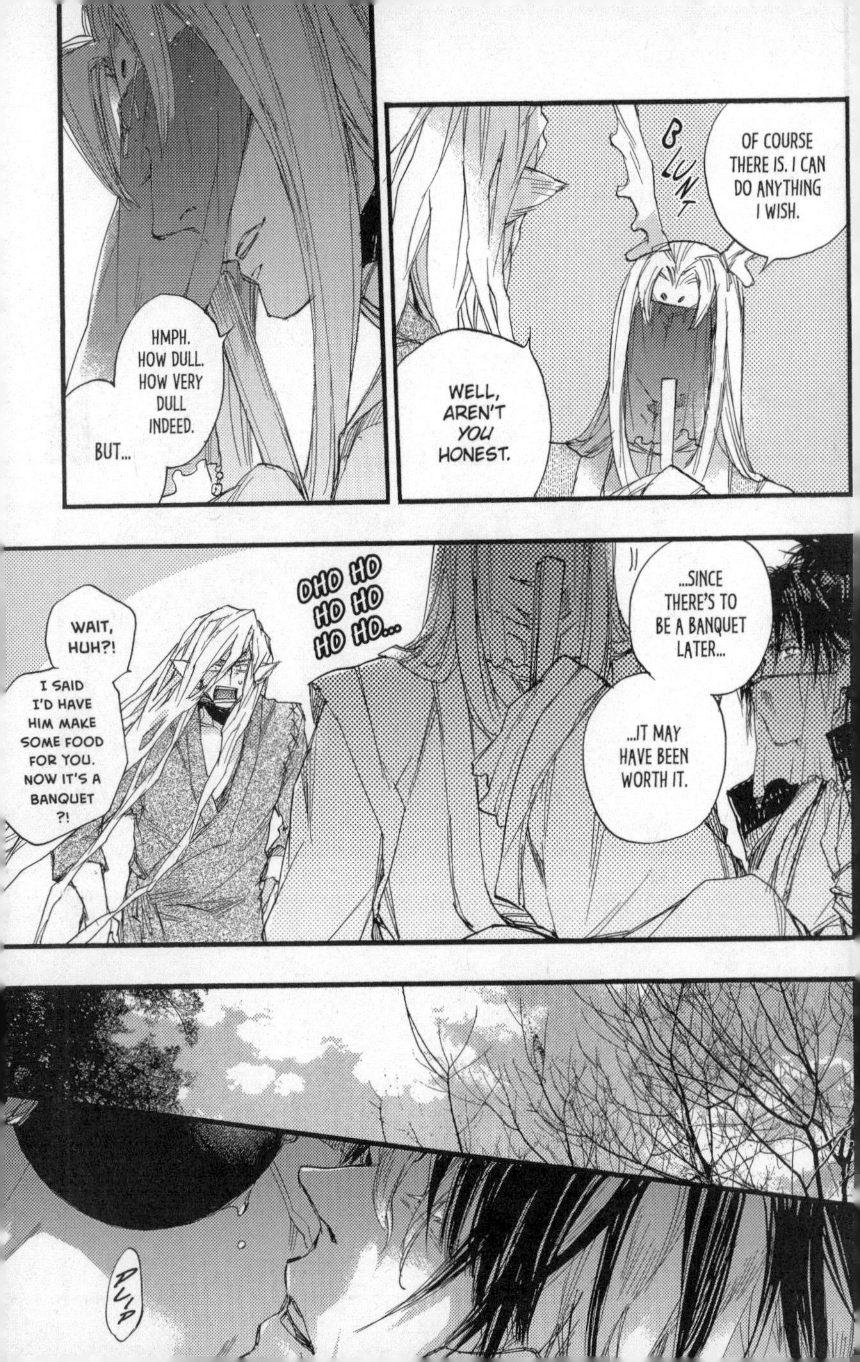
OF COURSE THERE IS. I CAN DO ANYTHING I WISH.
BLUNT
WELL, AREN'T YOU HONEST.
HMPH. HOW DULL. HOW VERY DULL INDEED.
BUT...
...SINCE THERE'S TO BE A BANQUET LATER...
...IT MAY HAVE BEEN WORTH IT.
OHO HO HO HO HO HO...
WAIT, HUH?!
I SAID I'D HAVE HIM MAKE SOME FOOD FOR YOU. NOW IT'S A BANQUET ?!

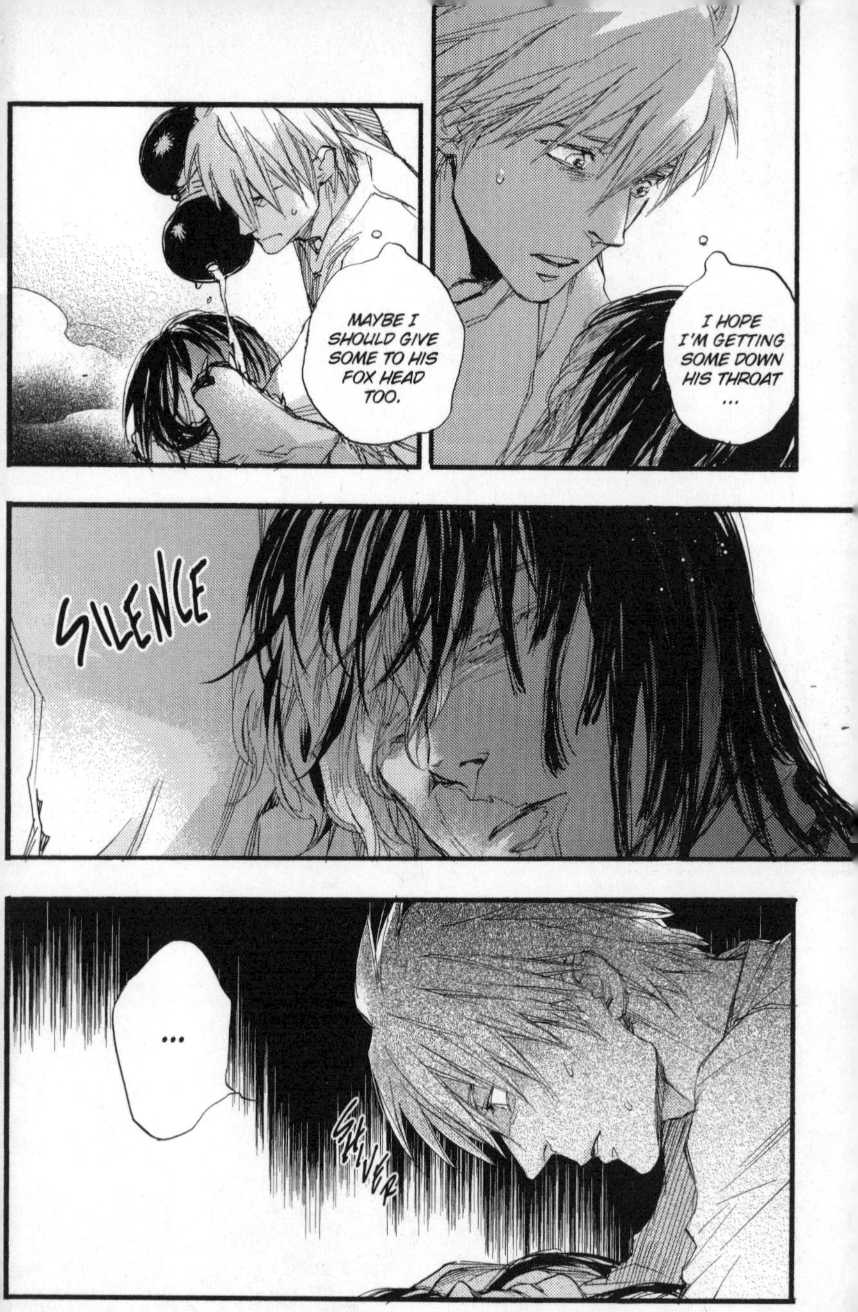

I HOPE I'M GETTING SOME DOWN HIS THROAT ...
MAYBE I SHOULD GIVE SOME TO HIS FOX HEAD TOO.
SILENCE
...
SHIVER

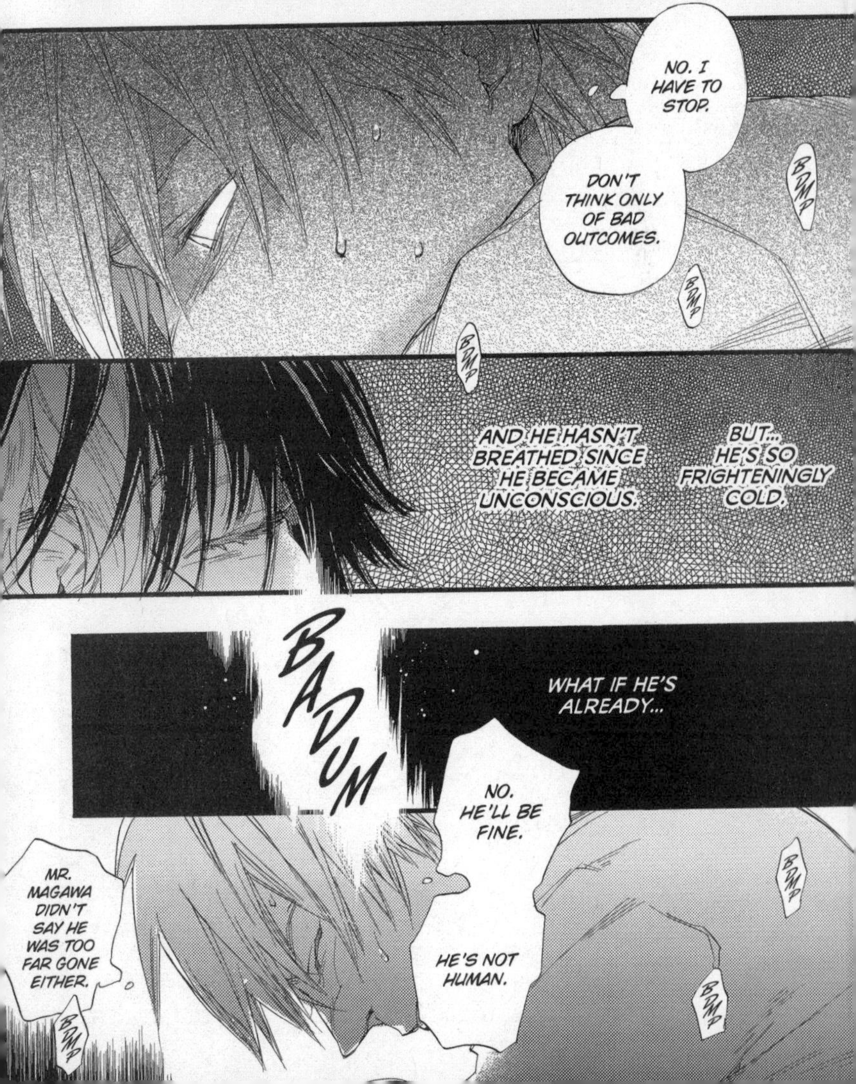
NO. I HAVE TO STOP.
DON'T THINK ONLY OF BAD OUTCOMES.
BDMP
BDMP
BDMP
BUT... HE'S SO FRIGHTENINGLY COLD.
AND HE HASN'T BREATHED SINCE HE BECAME UNCONSCIOUS.
WHAT IF HE'S ALREADY...
BADUM
NO. HE'LL BE FINE.
BDMP
HE'S NOT HUMAN.
BDMP
MR. MAGAWA DIDN'T SAY HE WAS TOO FAR GONE EITHER.
BDMP

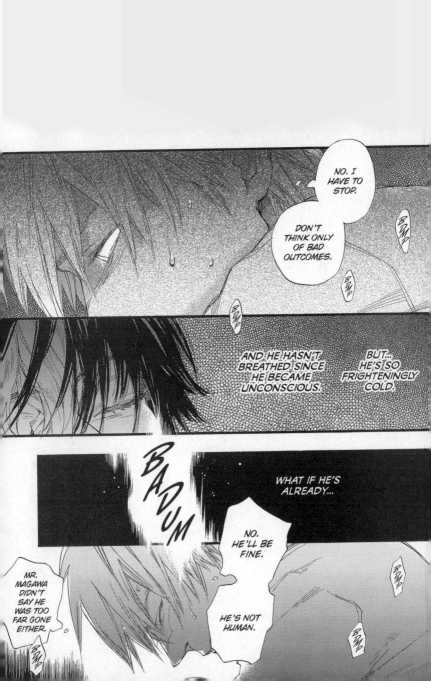

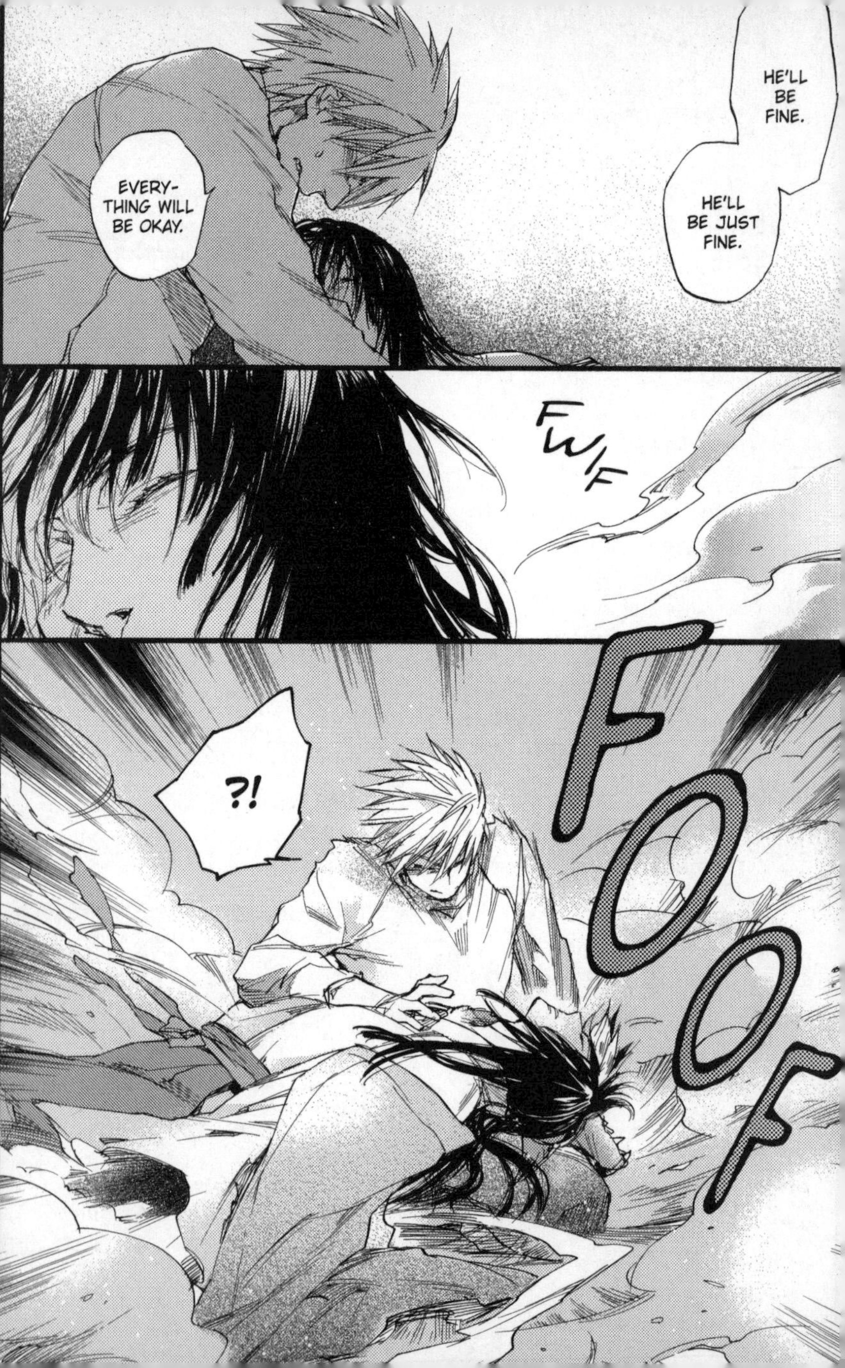
HE'LL BE FINE.
HE'LL BE JUST FINE.
EVERY-THING WILL BE OKAY.
FWIF
FOOF
?!

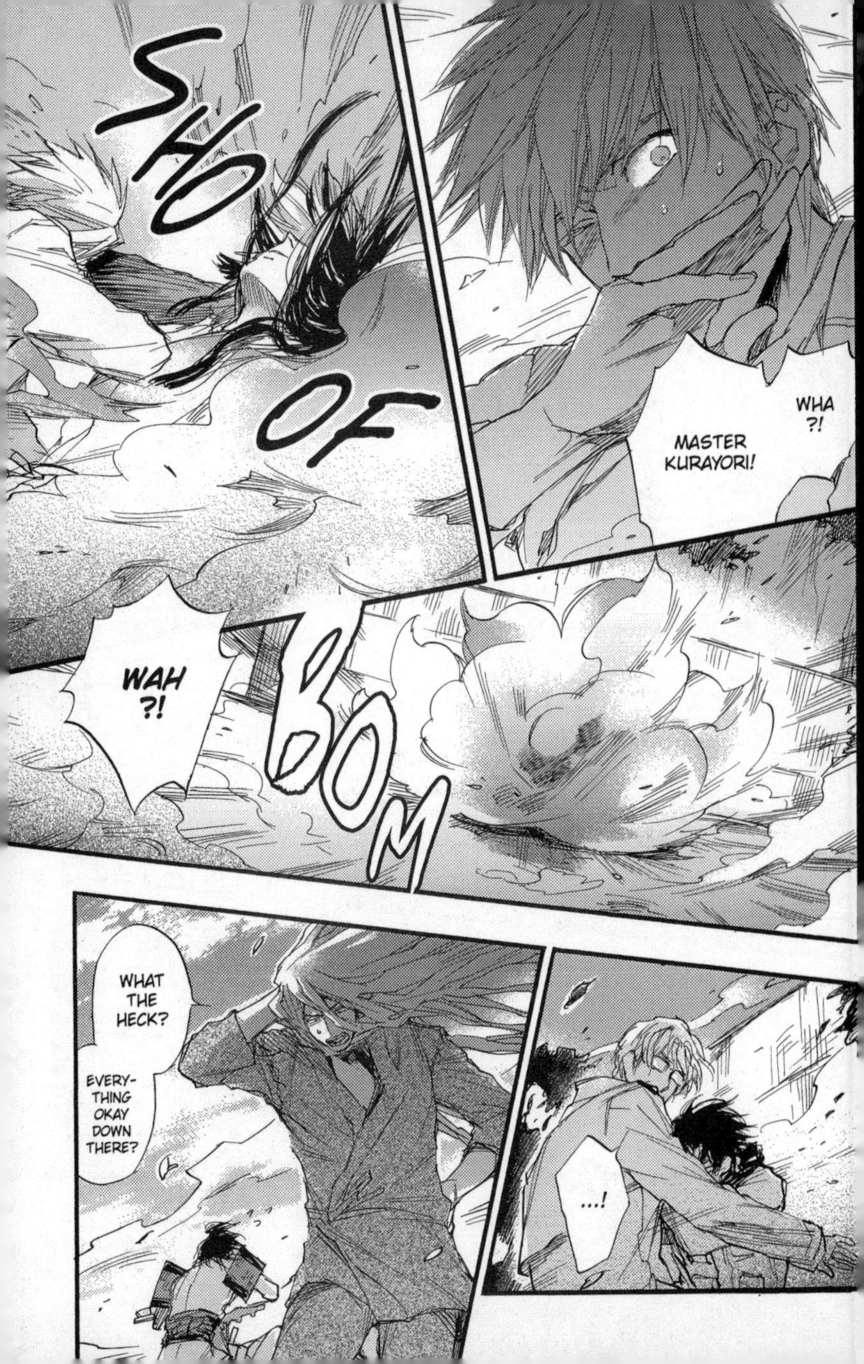
WHA ?!
MASTER KURAYORI!
SHOOF
BOOM
WAH ?!
...!
WHAT THE HECK?
EVERY-THING OKAY DOWN THERE?

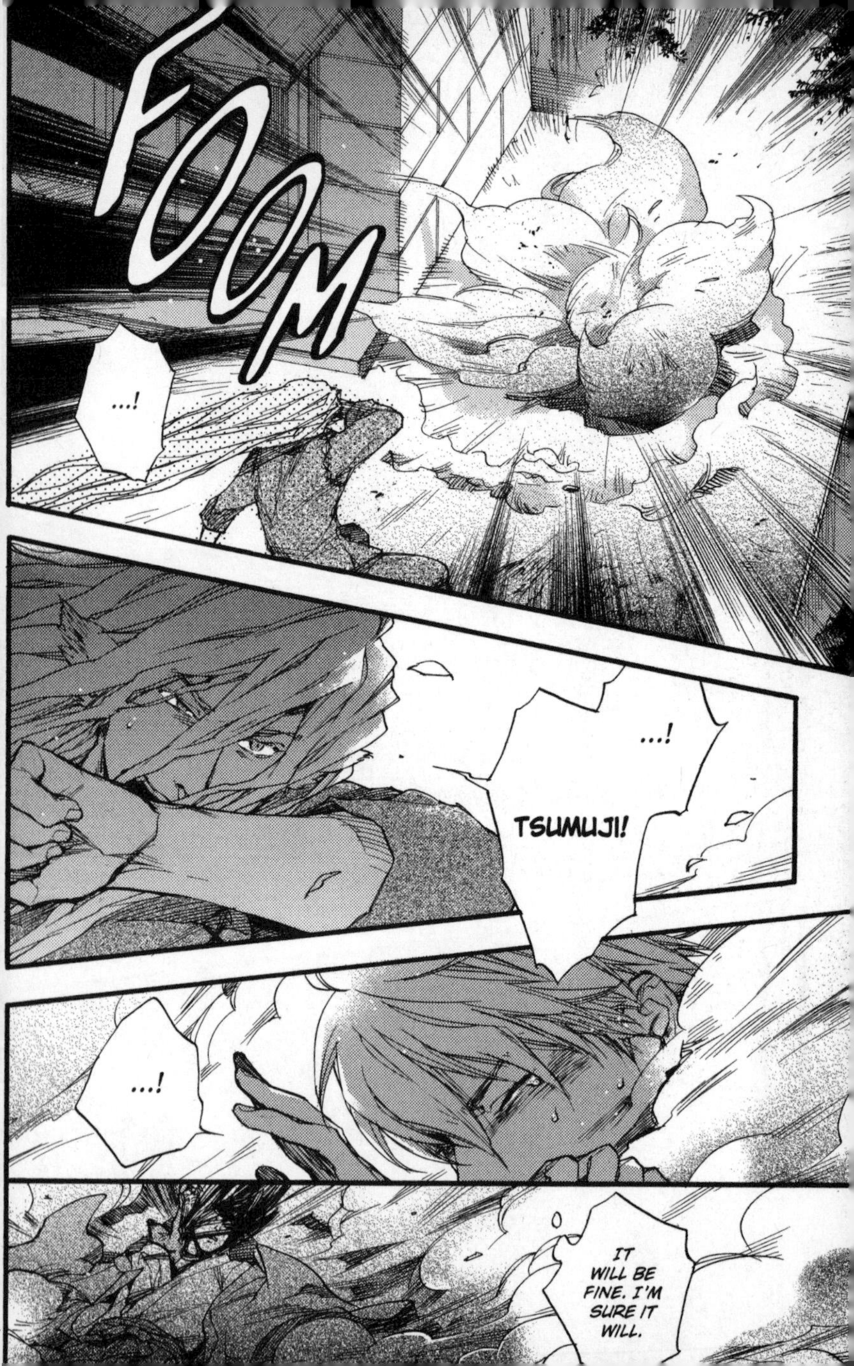
FOOM
...!
...!
TSUMUJI!
...!
IT WILL BE FINE. I'M SURE IT WILL.

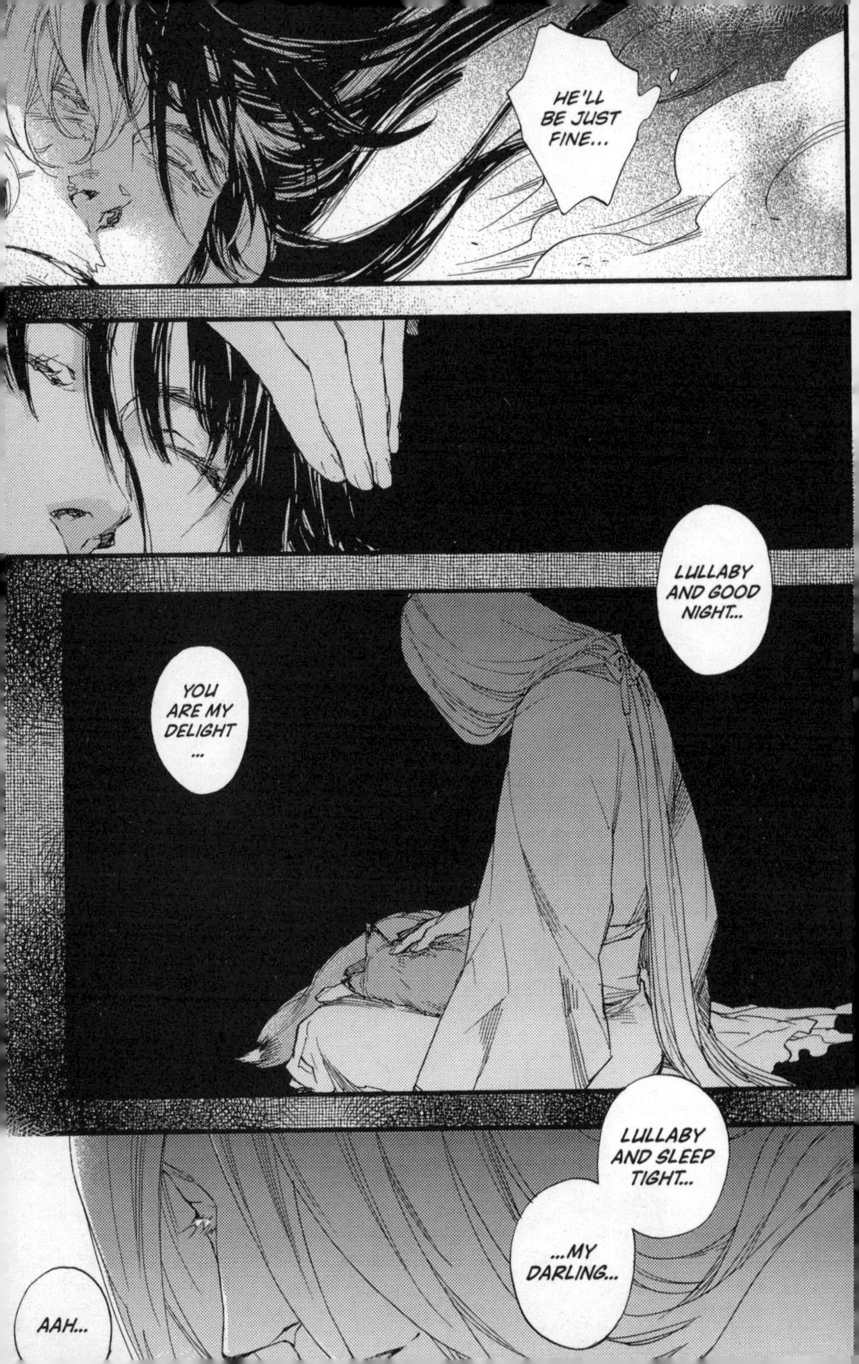
HE'LL BE JUST FINE...
LULLABY AND GOOD NIGHT...
YOU ARE MY DELIGHT ...
LULLABY AND SLEEP TIGHT...
...MY DARLING...
AAH...

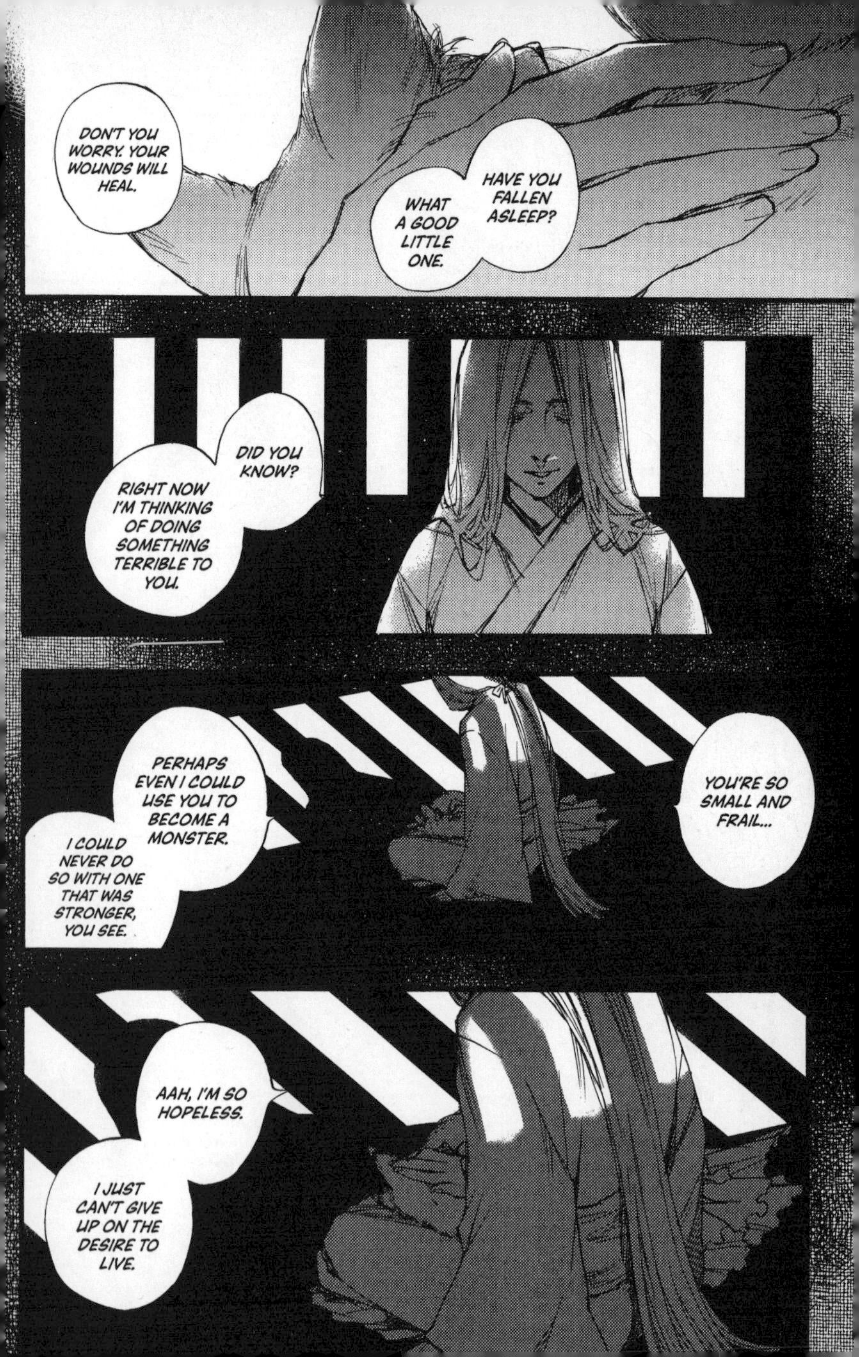
HAVE YOU FALLEN ASLEEP?
WHAT A GOOD LITTLE ONE.
DON'T YOU WORRY. YOUR WOUNDS WILL HEAL.
DID YOU KNOW?
RIGHT NOW I'M THINKING OF DOING SOMETHING TERRIBLE TO YOU.
YOU'RE SO SMALL AND FRAIL...
PERHAPS EVEN I COULD USE YOU TO BECOME A MONSTER.
I COULD NEVER DO SO WITH ONE THAT WAS STRONGER, YOU SEE.
AAH, I'M SO HOPELESS.
I JUST CAN'T GIVE UP ON THE DESIRE TO LIVE.

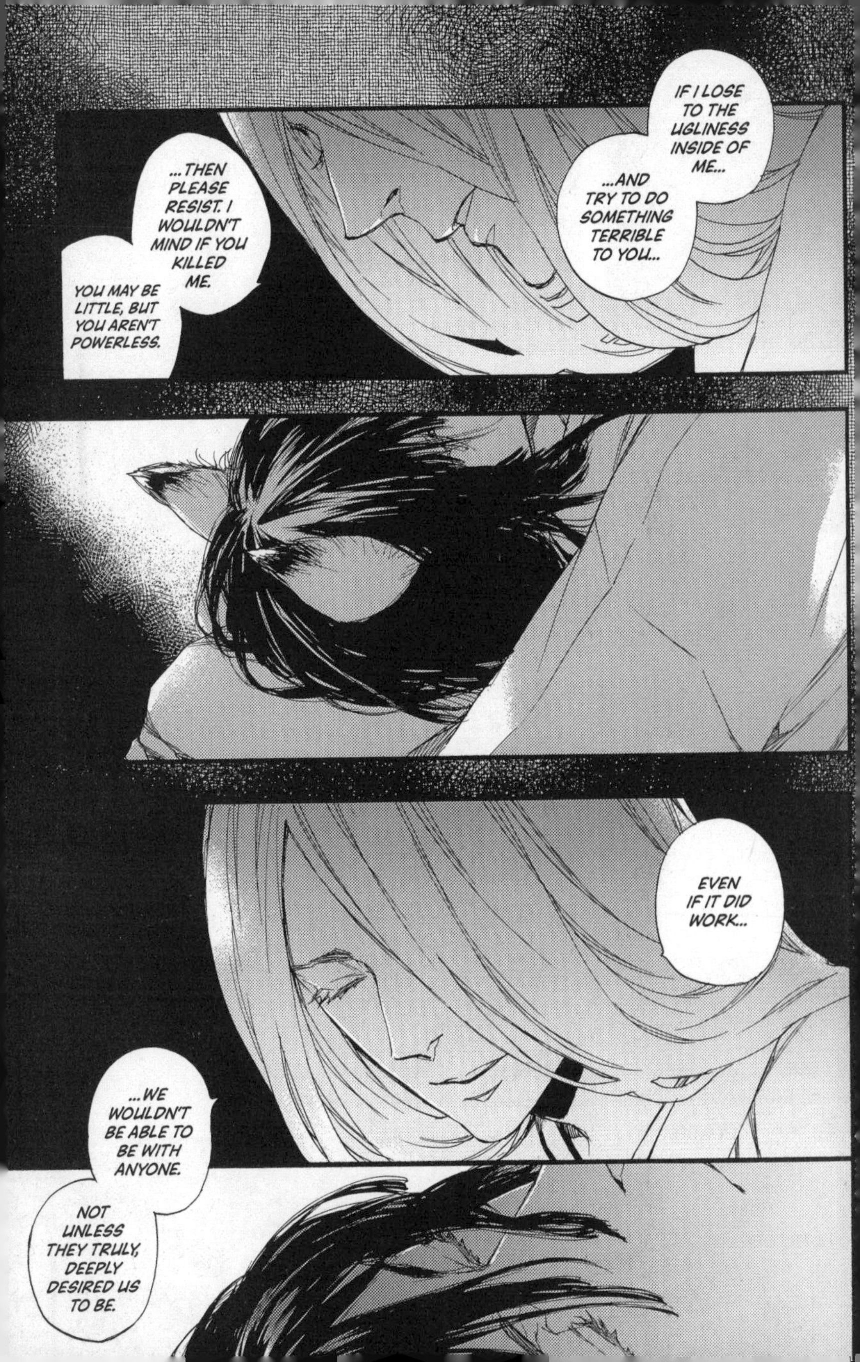
IF I LOSE TO THE UGLINESS INSIDE OF ME...
...AND TRY TO DO SOMETHING TERRIBLE TO YOU...
...THEN PLEASE RESIST. I WOULDN'T MIND IF YOU KILLED ME.
YOU MAY BE LITTLE, BUT YOU AREN'T POWERLESS.
EVEN IF IT DID WORK...
...WE WOULDN'T BE ABLE TO BE WITH ANYONE.
NOT UNLESS THEY TRULY, DEEPLY DESIRED US TO BE.

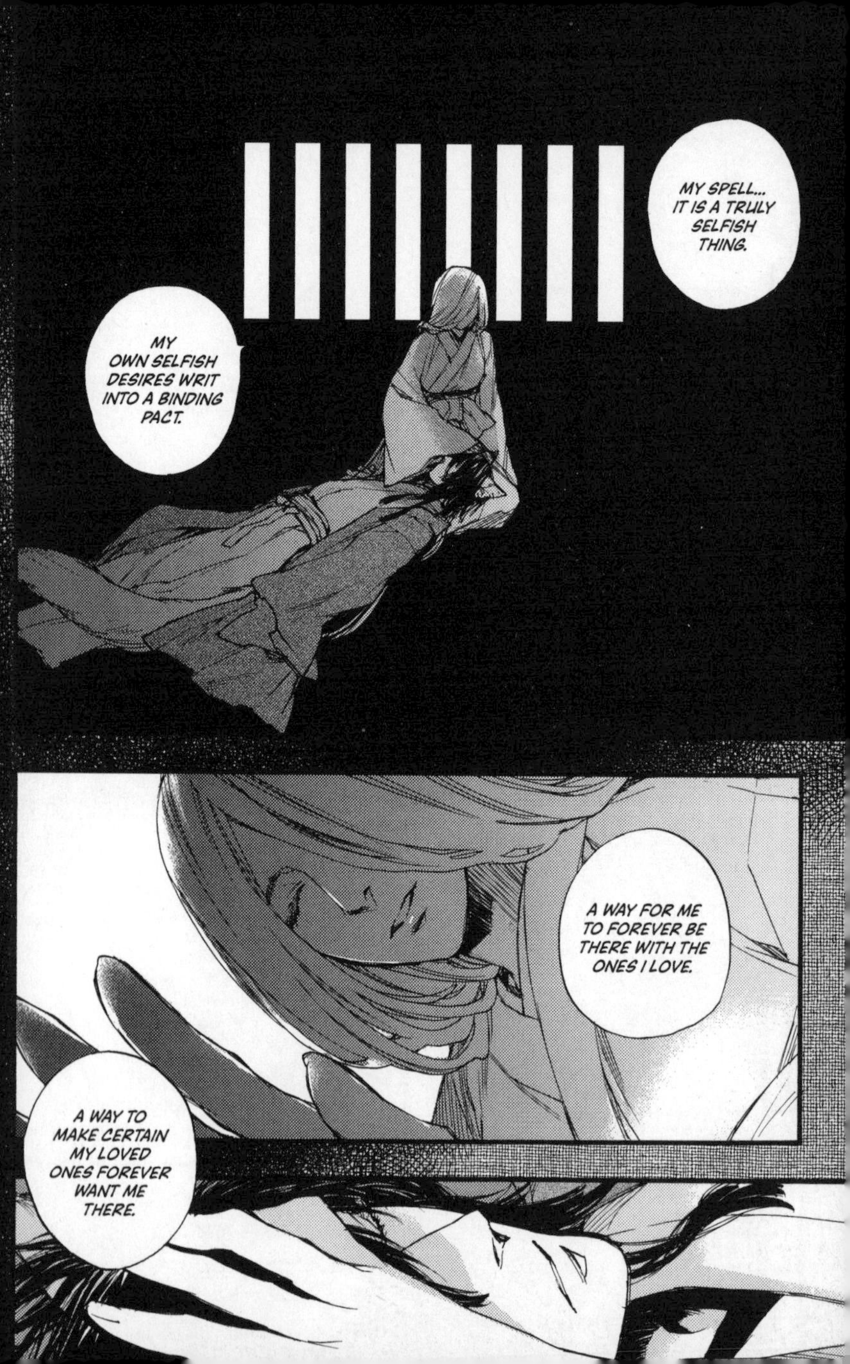
MY SPELL... IT IS A TRULY SELFISH THING.
MY OWN SELFISH DESIRES WRIT INTO A BINDING PACT.
A WAY FOR ME TO FOREVER BE THERE WITH THE ONES I LOVE.
A WAY TO MAKE CERTAIN MY LOVED ONES FOREVER WANT ME THERE.

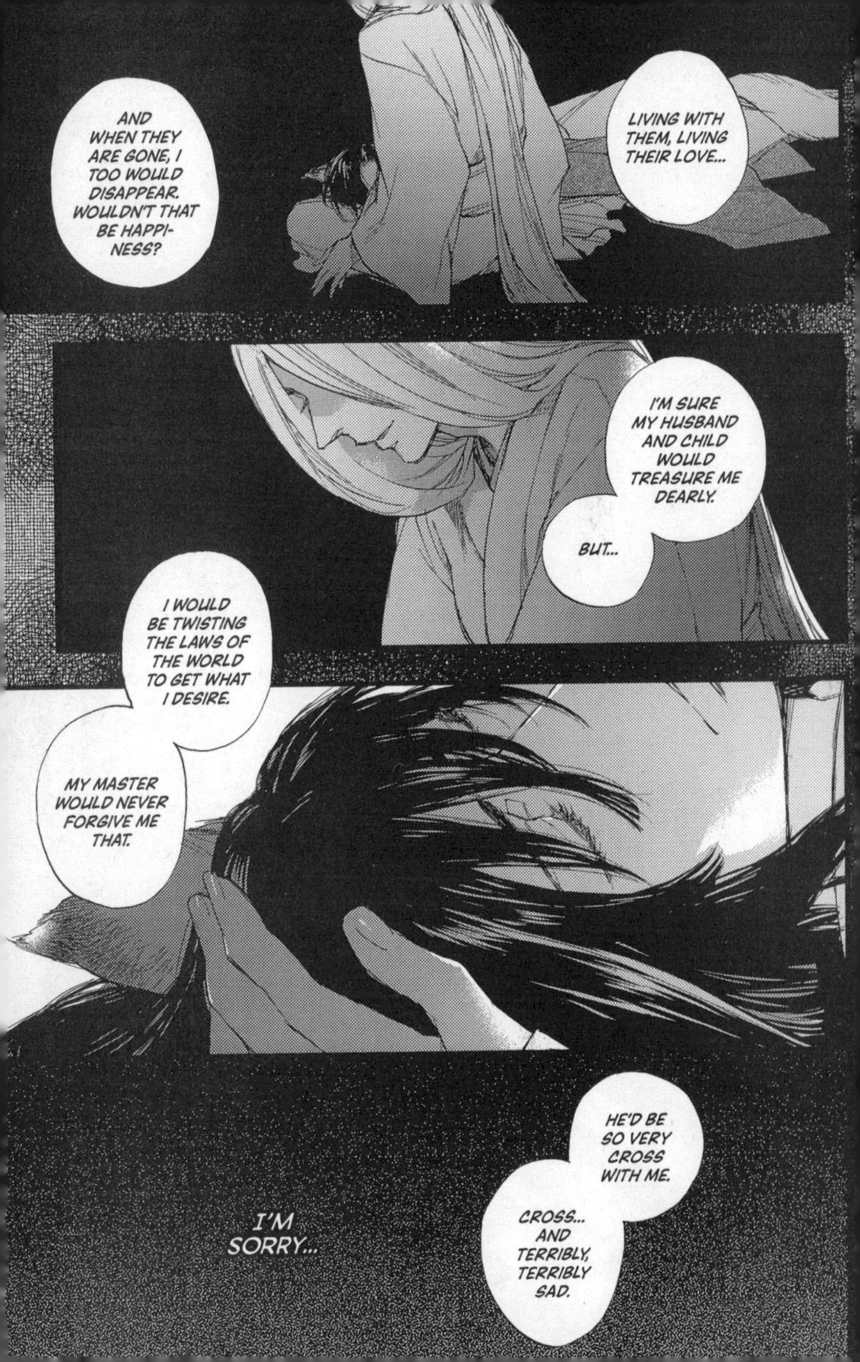
LIVING WITH THEM, LIVING THEIR LOVE...
AND WHEN THEY ARE GONE, I TOO WOULD DISAPPEAR. WOULDN'T THAT BE HAPPI-NESS?
I'M SURE MY HUSBAND AND CHILD WOULD TREASURE ME DEARLY.
BUT...
I WOULD BE TWISTING THE LAWS OF THE WORLD TO GET WHAT I DESIRE.
MY MASTER WOULD NEVER FORGIVE ME THAT.
HE'D BE SO VERY CROSS WITH ME.
CROSS... AND TERRIBLY, TERRIBLY SAD.
I'M SORRY...

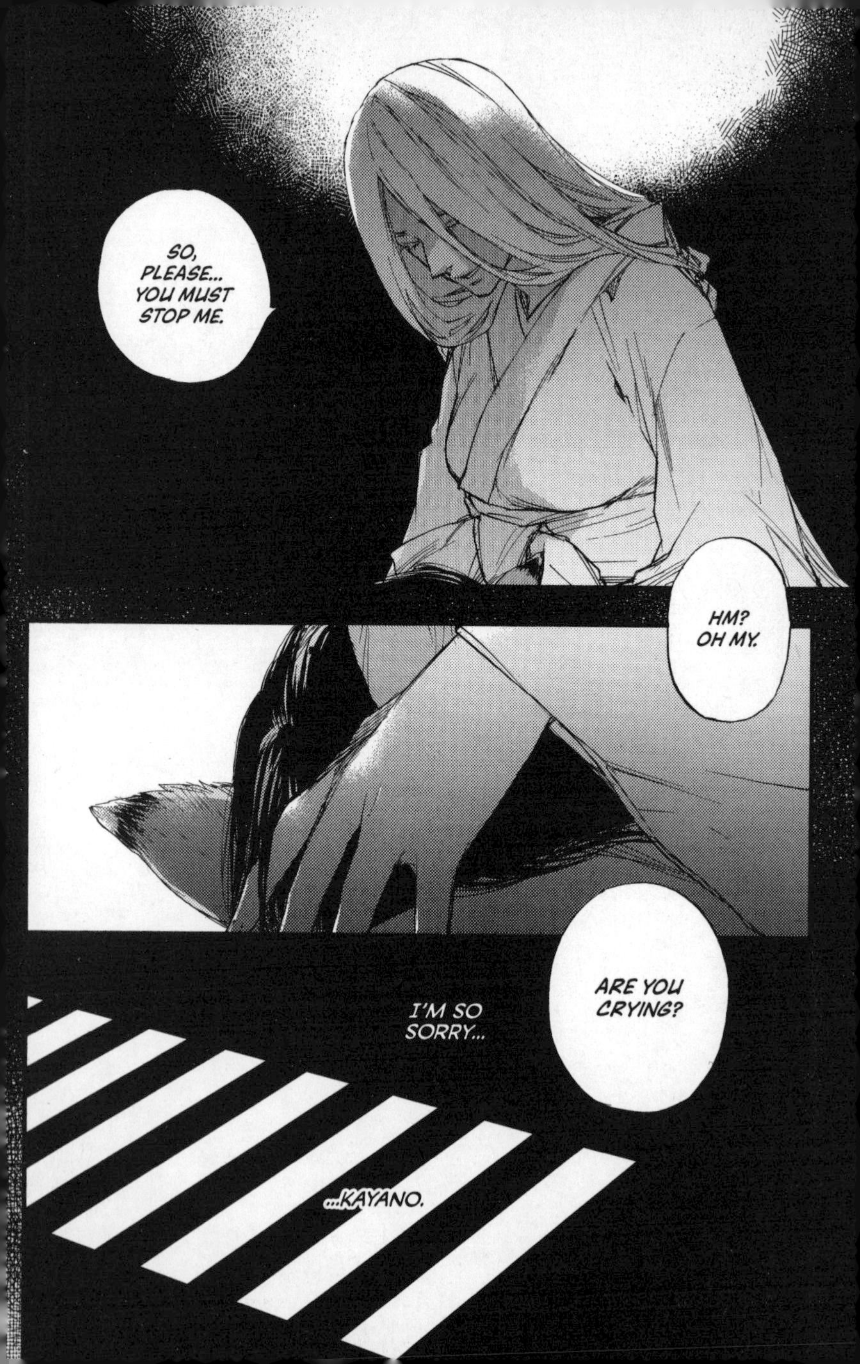
SO, PLEASE... YOU MUST STOP ME.
HM? OH MY.
ARE YOU CRYING?
I'M SO SORRY...
...KAYANO.

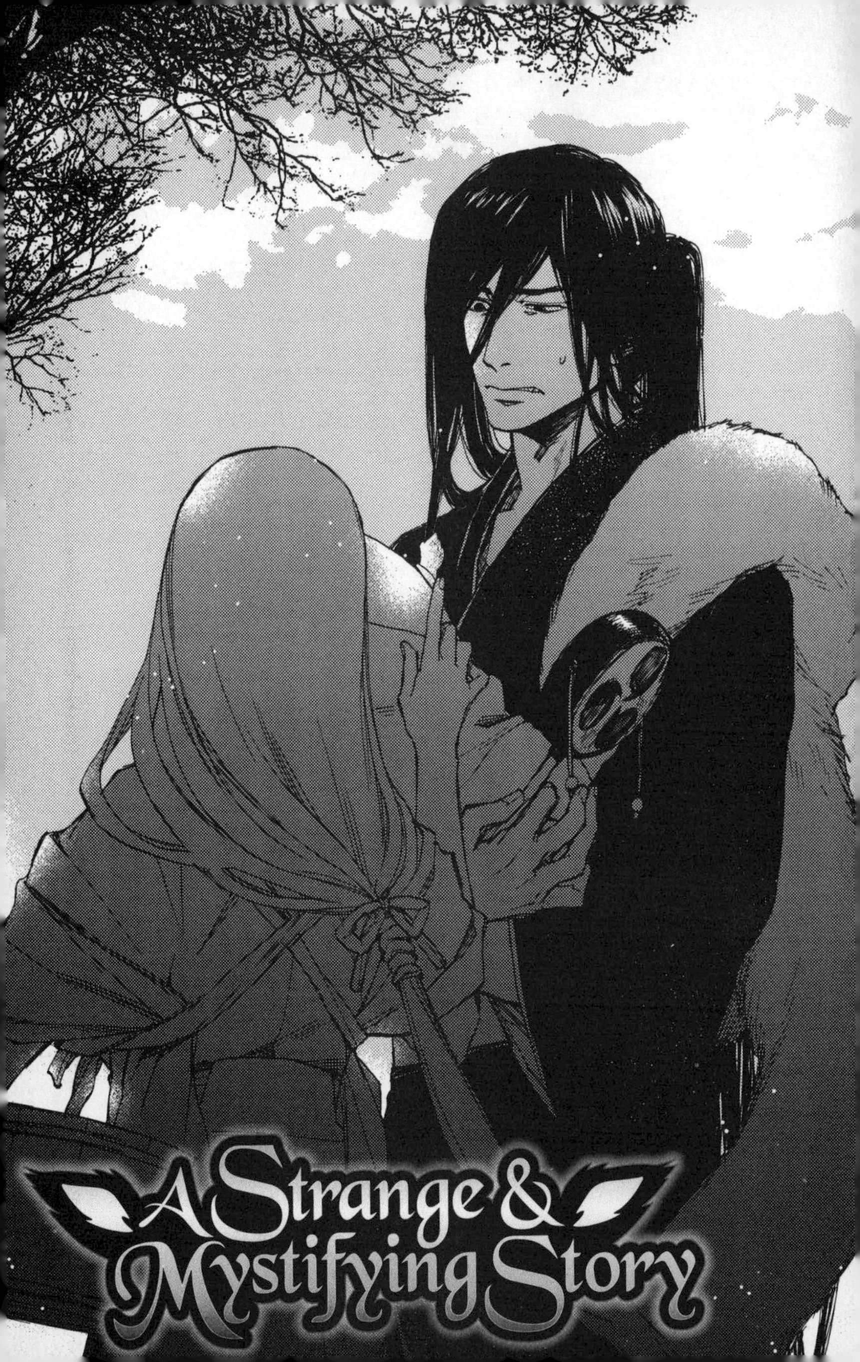
A Strange &
Mystifying Story

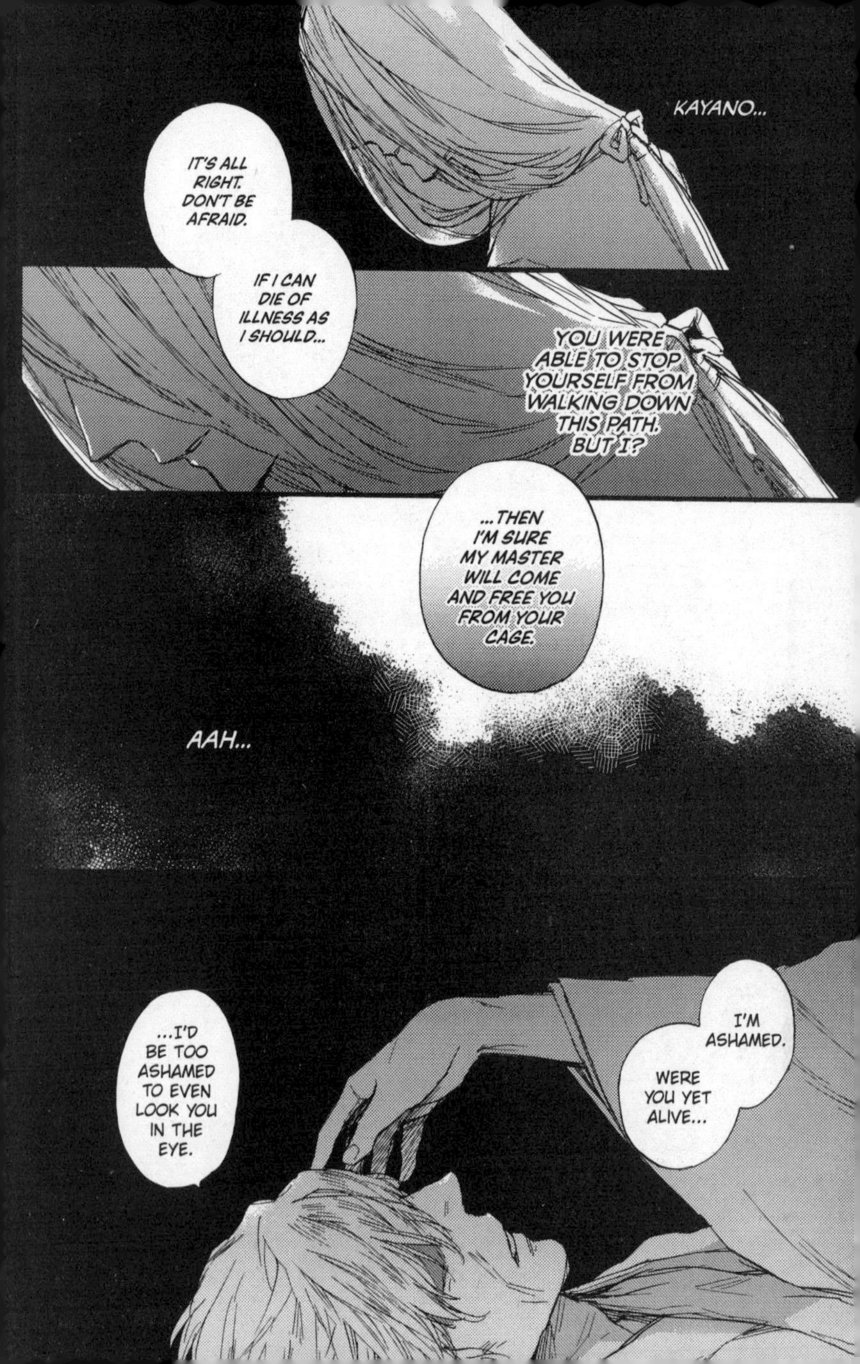
KAYANO...
IT'S ALL RIGHT. DON'T BE AFRAID.
YOU WERE ABLE TO STOP YOURSELF FROM WALKING DOWN THIS PATH. BUT I?
IF I CAN DIE OF ILLNESS AS I SHOULD...
...THEN I'M SURE MY MASTER WILL COME AND FREE YOU FROM YOUR CAGE.
AAH...
I'M ASHAMED.
WERE YOU YET ALIVE...
...I'D BE TOO ASHAMED TO EVEN LOOK YOU IN THE EYE.

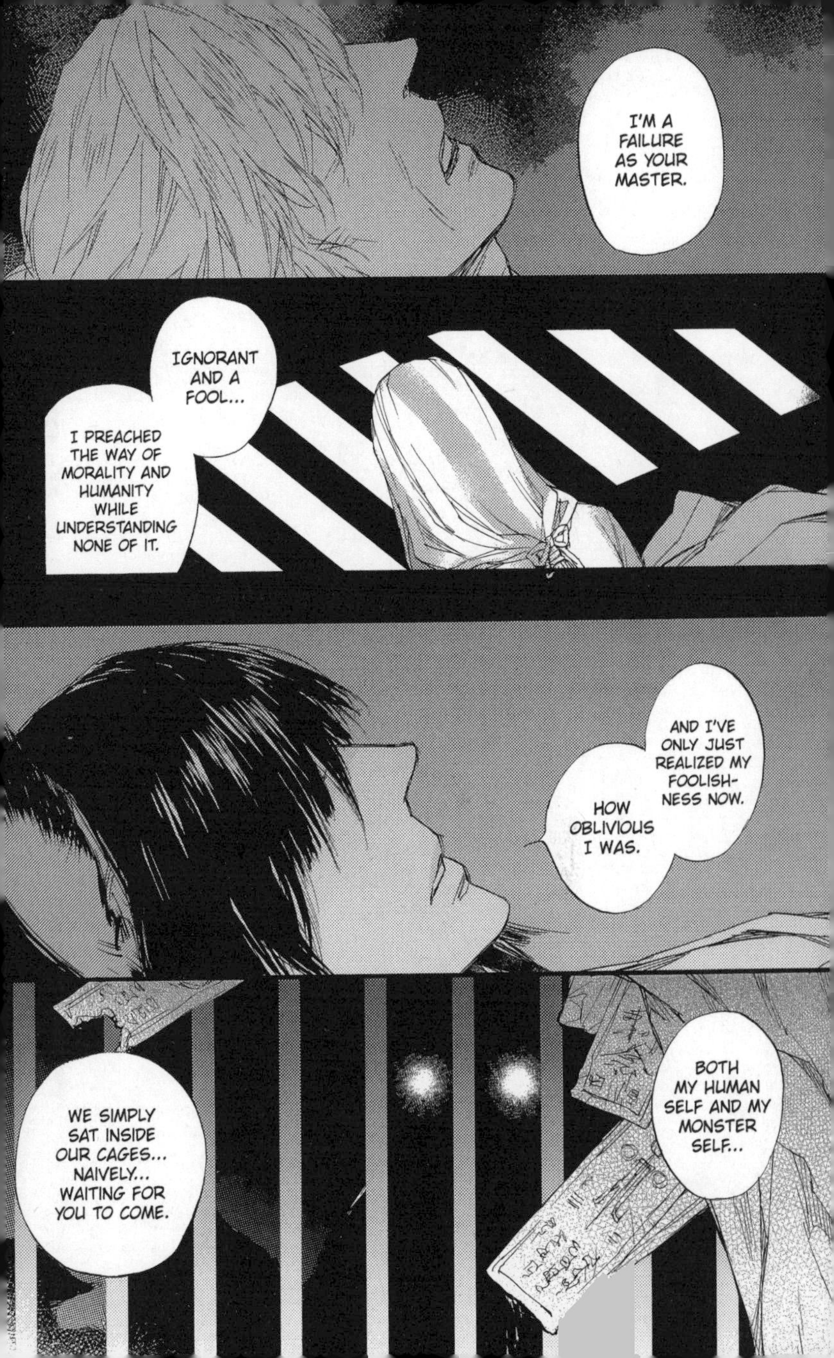
I'M A FAILURE AS YOUR MASTER.
IGNORANT AND A FOOL...
I PREACHED THE WAY OF MORALITY AND HUMANITY WHILE UNDERSTANDING NONE OF IT.
AND I'VE ONLY JUST REALIZED MY FOOLISHNESS NOW.
HOW OBLIVIOUS I WAS.
BOTH MY HUMAN SELF AND MY MONSTER SELF...
WE SIMPLY SAT INSIDE OUR CAGES... NAIVELY... WAITING FOR YOU TO COME.

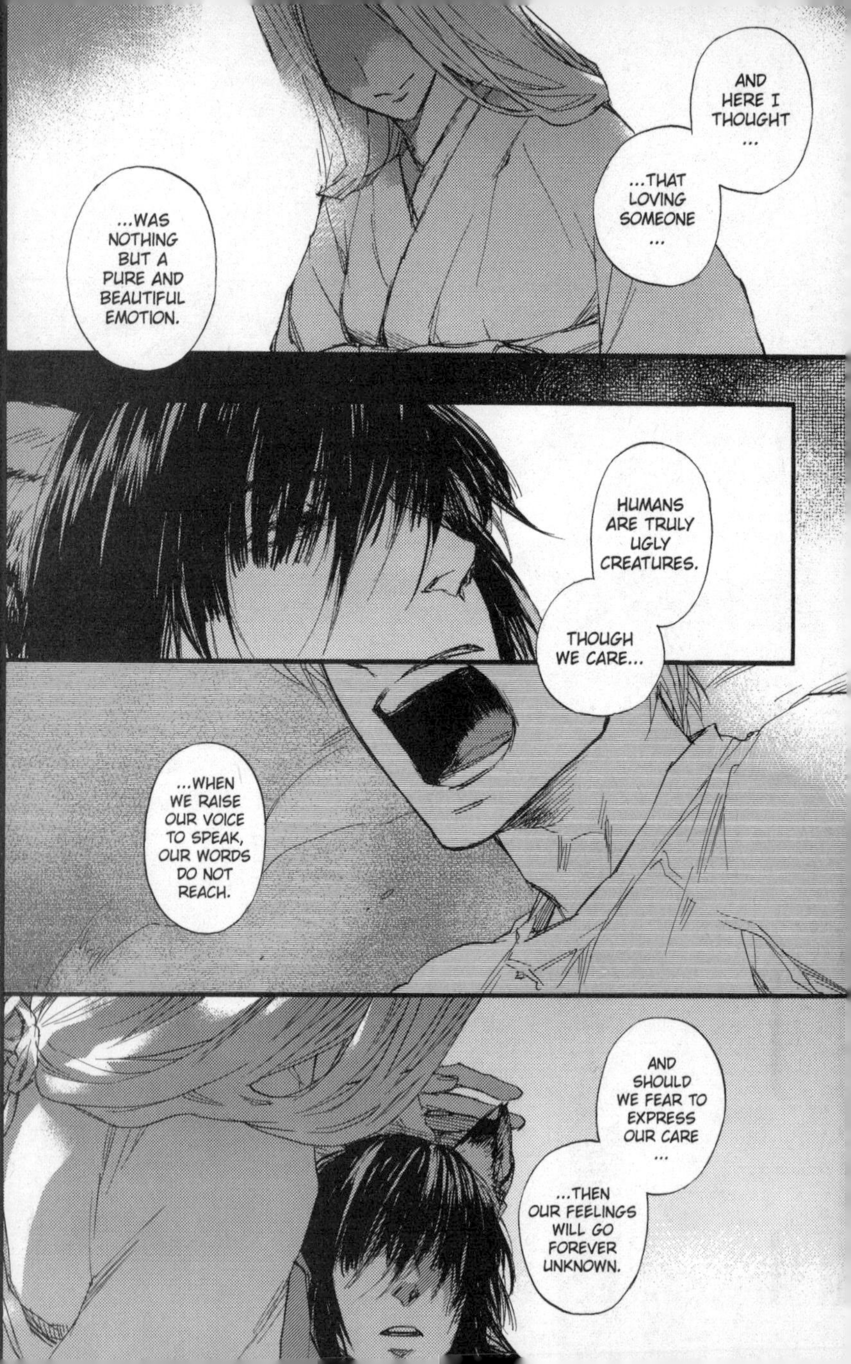
AND HERE I THOUGHT ...
...THAT LOVING SOMEONE ...
...WAS NOTHING BUT A PURE AND BEAUTIFUL EMOTION.
HUMANS ARE TRULY UGLY CREATURES.
THOUGH WE CARE...
...WHEN WE RAISE OUR VOICE TO SPEAK, OUR WORDS DO NOT REACH.
AND SHOULD WE FEAR TO EXPRESS OUR CARE ...
...THEN OUR FEELINGS WILL GO FOREVER UNKNOWN.

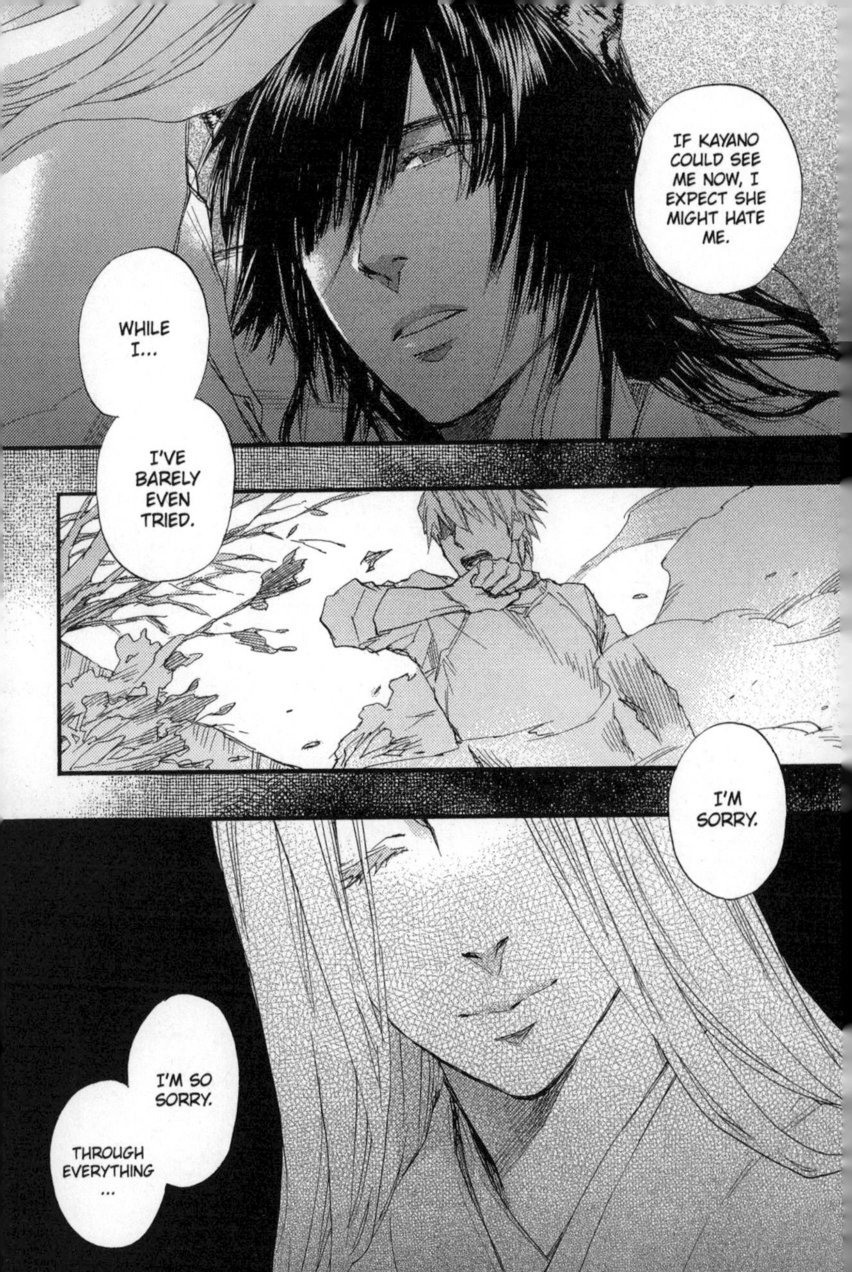
IF KAYANO COULD SEE ME NOW, I EXPECT SHE MIGHT HATE ME.
WHILE I...
I'VE BARELY EVEN TRIED.
I'M SORRY.
I'M SO SORRY.
THROUGH EVERYTHING ...

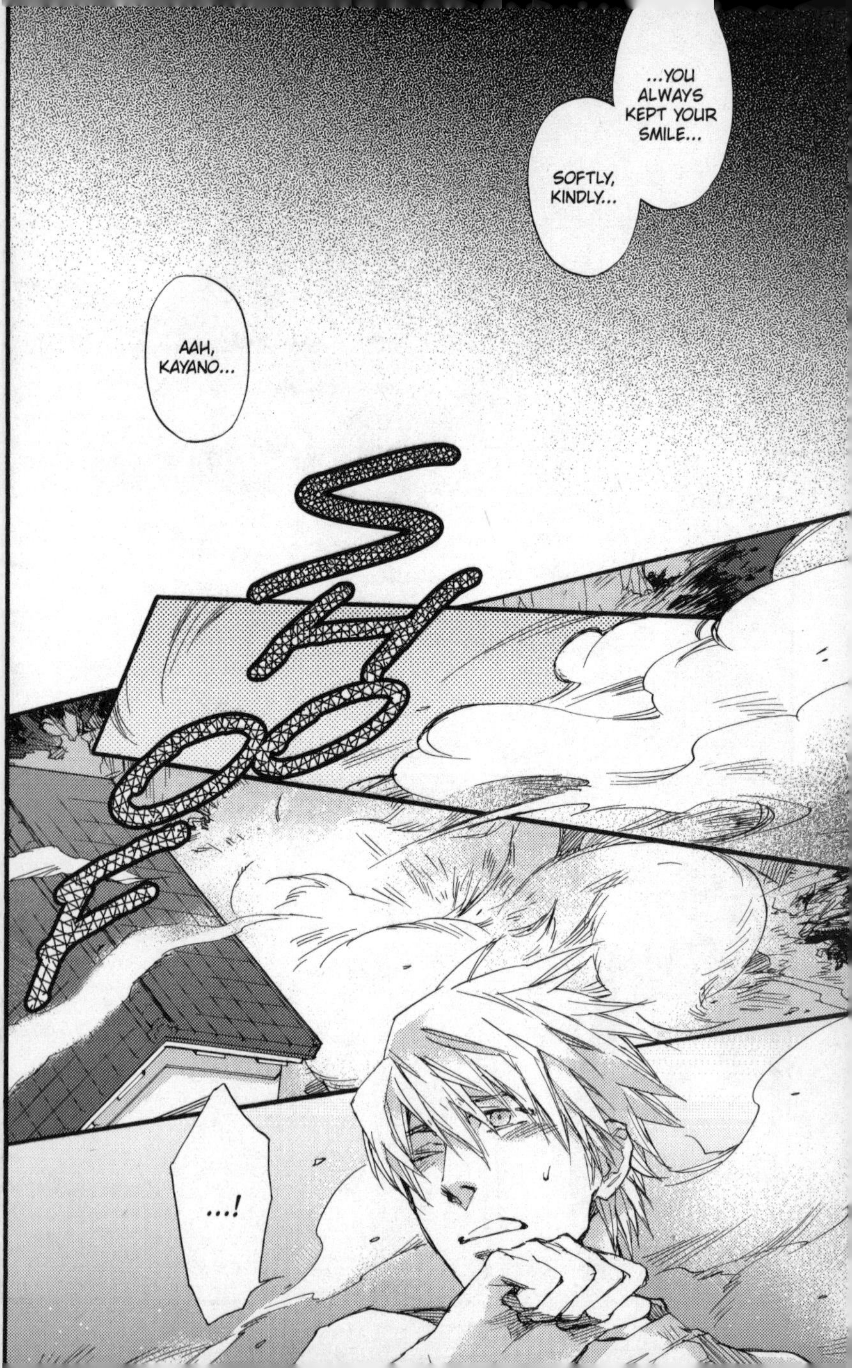
...YOU ALWAYS KEPT YOUR SMILE...
SOFTLY, KINDLY...
AAH, KAYANO...
SHOOP
...!

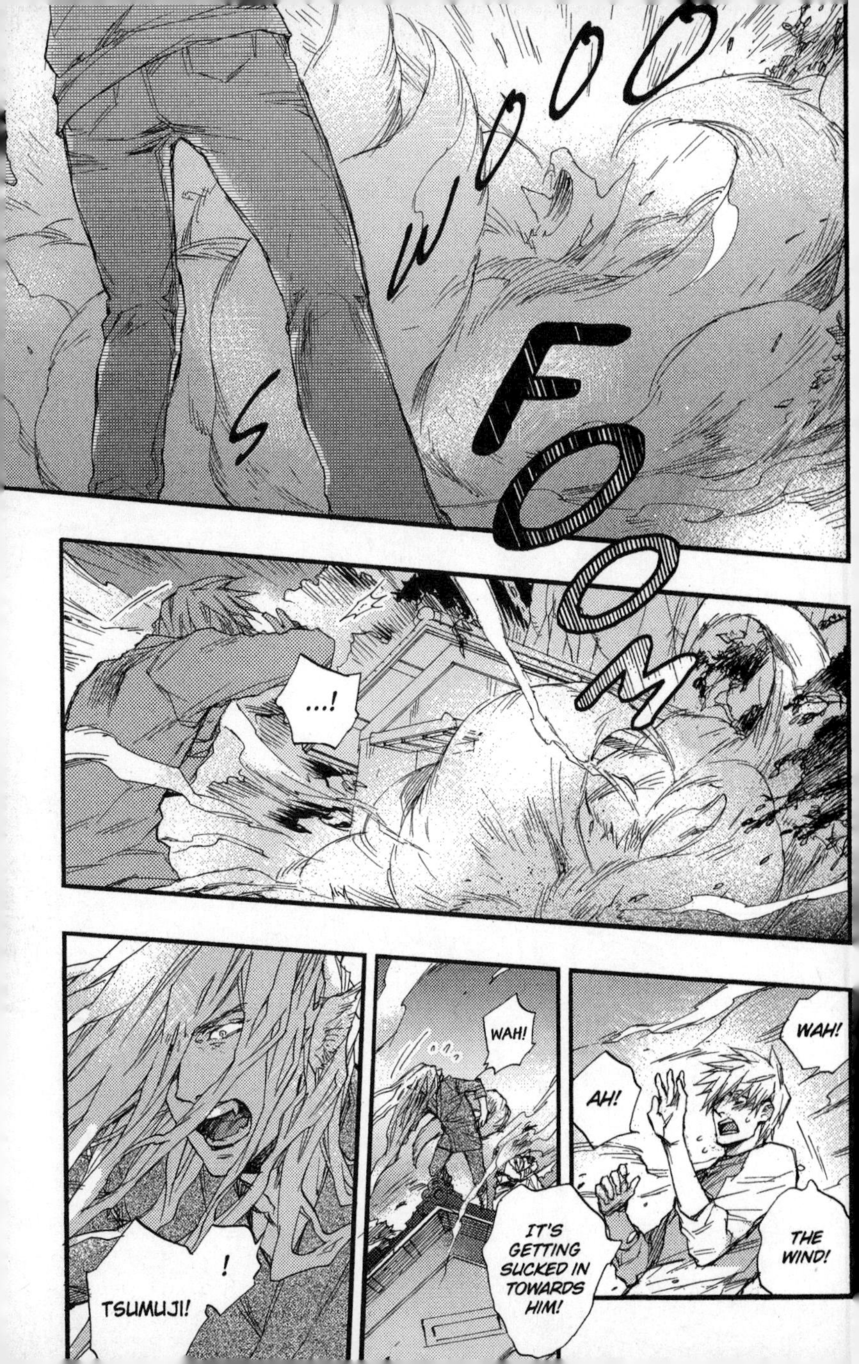
SWOOOO
FOOM
...!
WAH!
AH!
THE WIND!
WAH!
IT'S GETTING SUCKED IN TOWARDS HIM!
!
TSUMUJI!

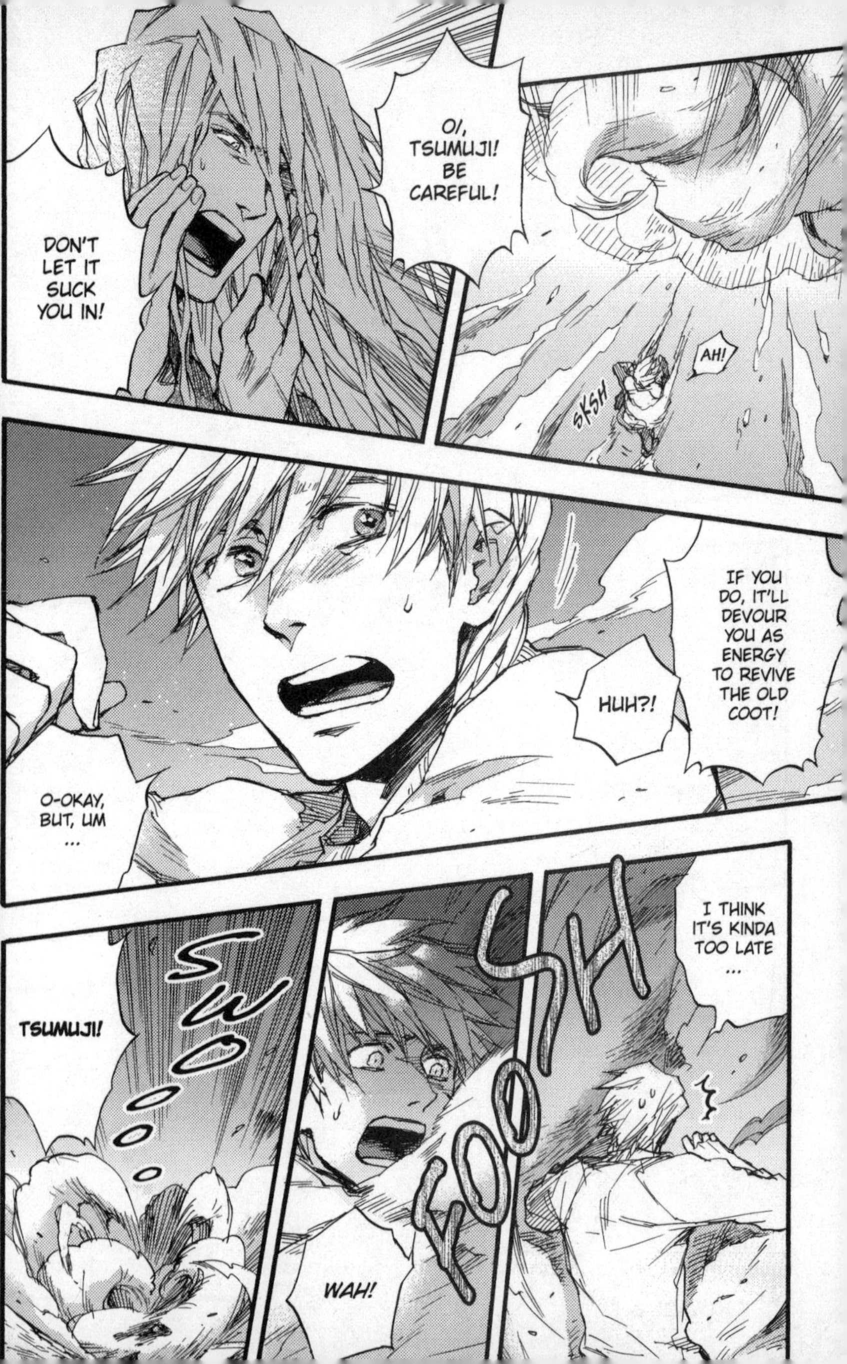
AH!
SKSH
OI, TSUMUJI! BE CAREFUL!
DON'T LET IT SUCK YOU IN!
IF YOU DO, IT'LL DEVOUR YOU AS ENERGY TO REVIVE THE OLD COOT!
HUH?!
O-OKAY, BUT, UM ...
I THINK IT'S KINDA TOO LATE ...
FOOOSH
WAH!
SWOOOOO
TSUMUJI!

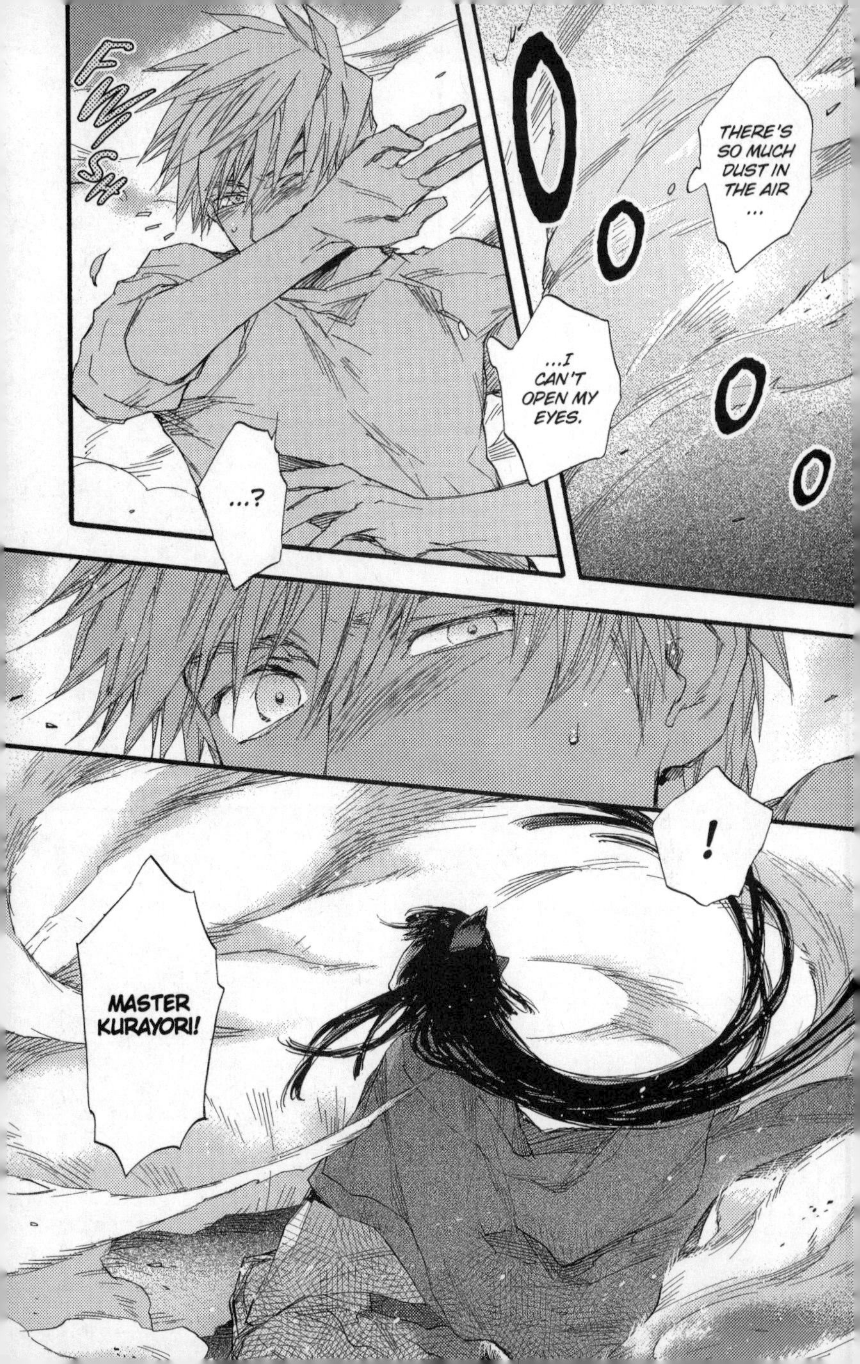
OOOO
THERE'S SO MUCH DUST IN THE AIR ...
...I CAN'T OPEN MY EYES.
FWISH
...?
!
MASTER KURAYORI!

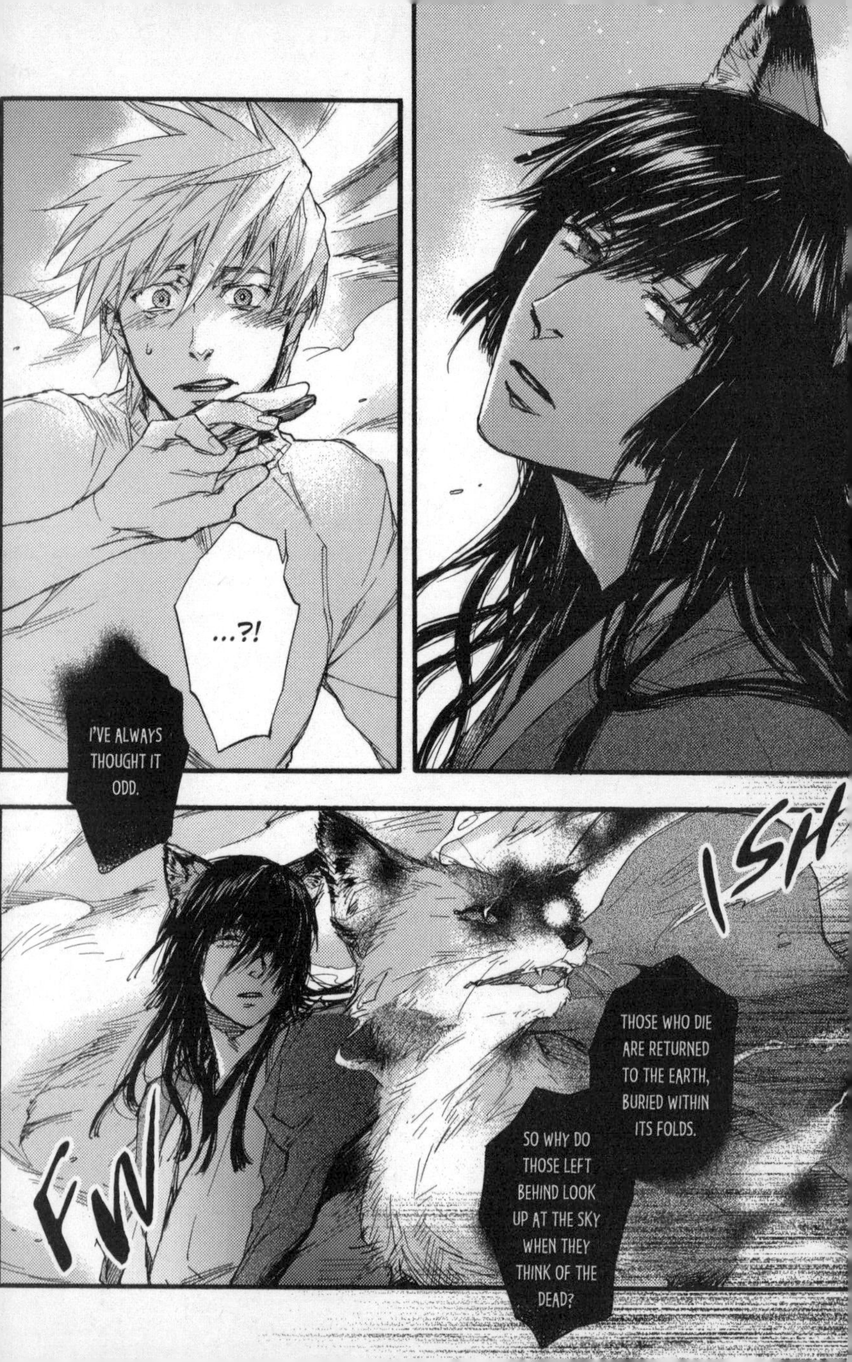
...?!
I'VE ALWAYS THOUGHT IT ODD.
ISH
THOSE WHO DIE ARE RETURNED TO THE EARTH, BURIED WITHIN ITS FOLDS.
SO WHY DO THOSE LEFT BEHIND LOOK UP AT THE SKY WHEN THEY THINK OF THE DEAD?
FW

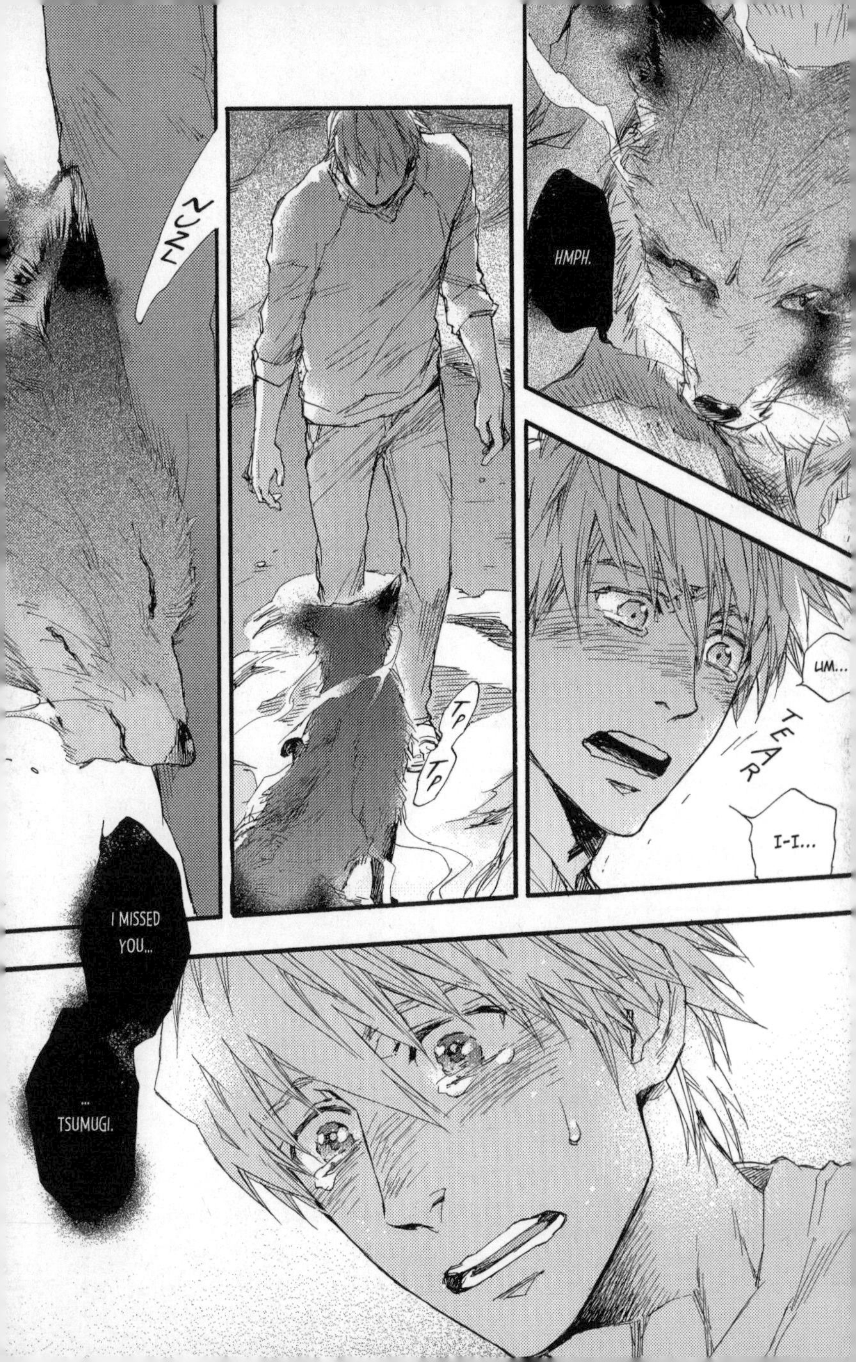
HMPH.
UM...
TEAR
I-I...
Tp Tp
I MISSED YOU...
... TSUMUGI.

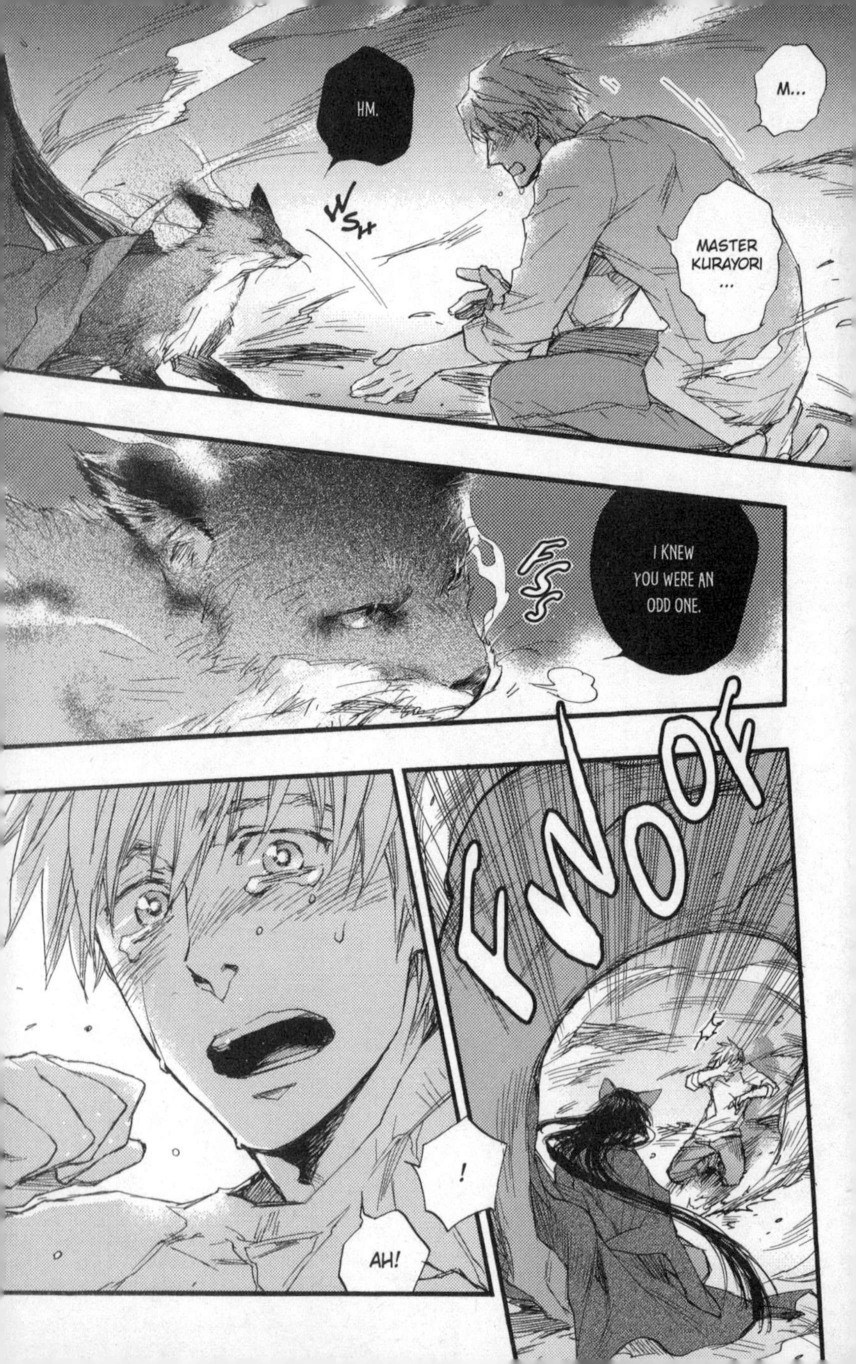
M...
MASTER KURAYORI ...
HM.
WSH
I KNEW YOU WERE AN ODD ONE.
FSS
FWOOF
!
AH!

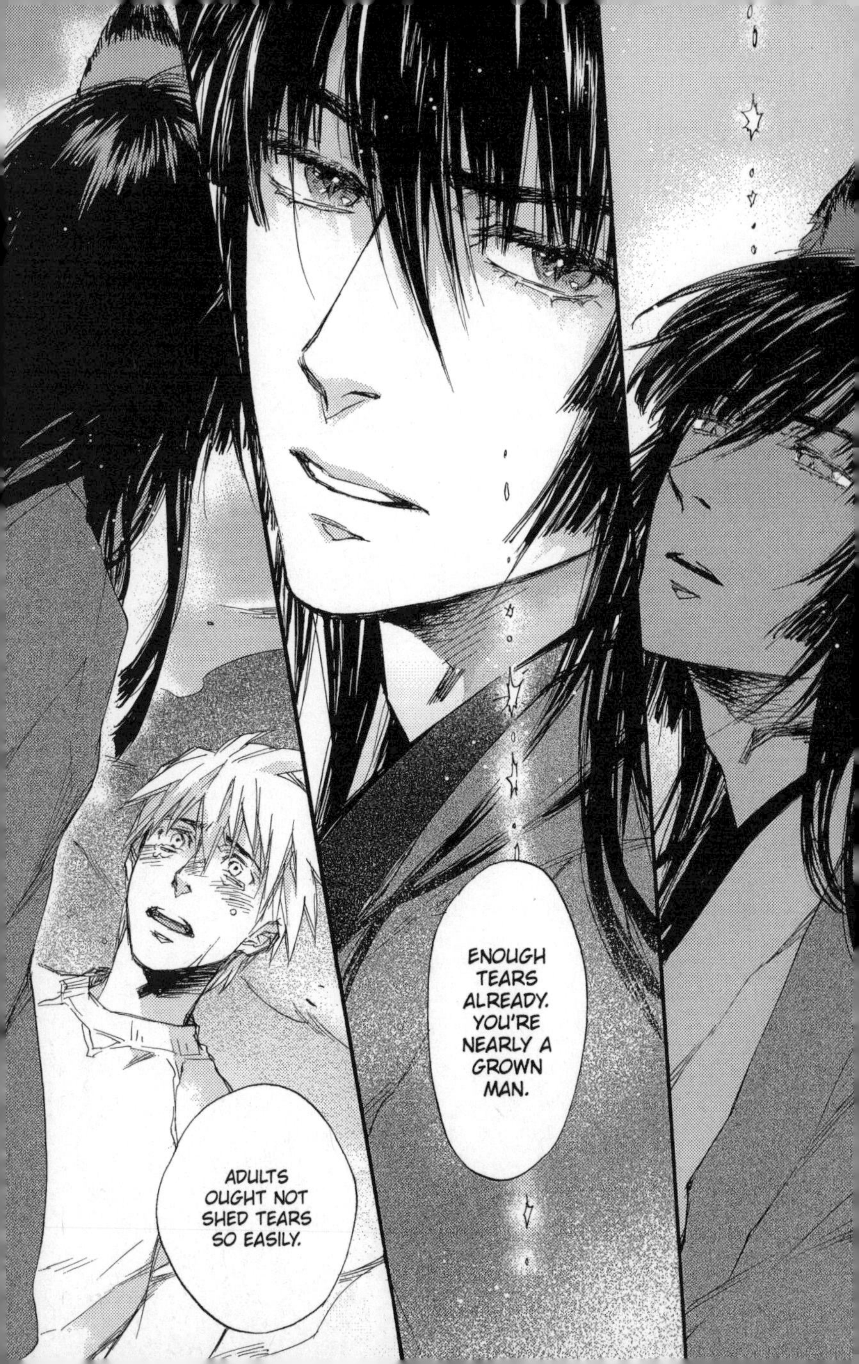
ENOUGH TEARS ALREADY. YOU'RE NEARLY A GROWN MAN.
ADULTS OUGHT NOT SHED TEARS SO EASILY.

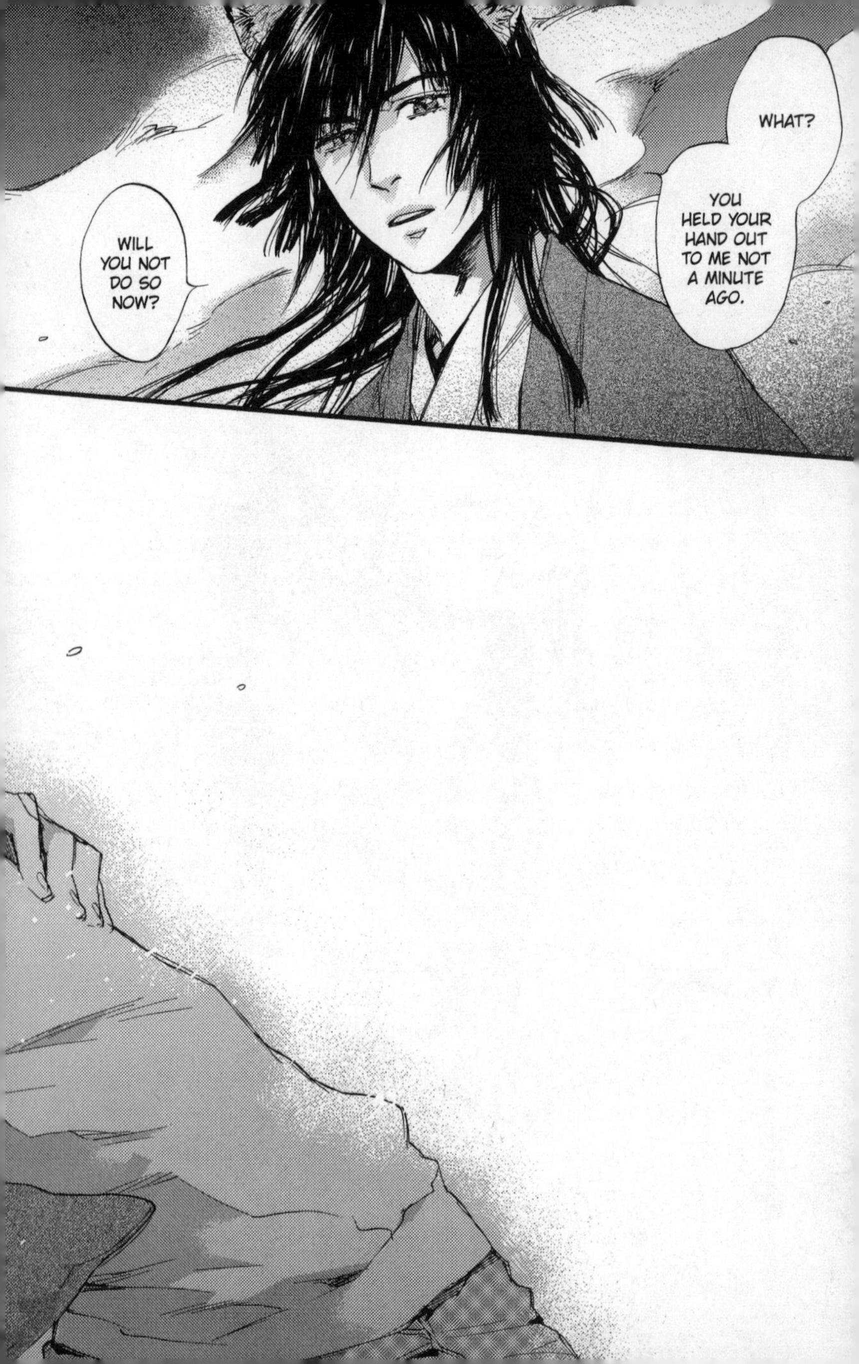
WHAT?
YOU HELD YOUR HAND OUT TO ME NOT A MINUTE AGO.
WILL YOU NOT DO SO NOW?

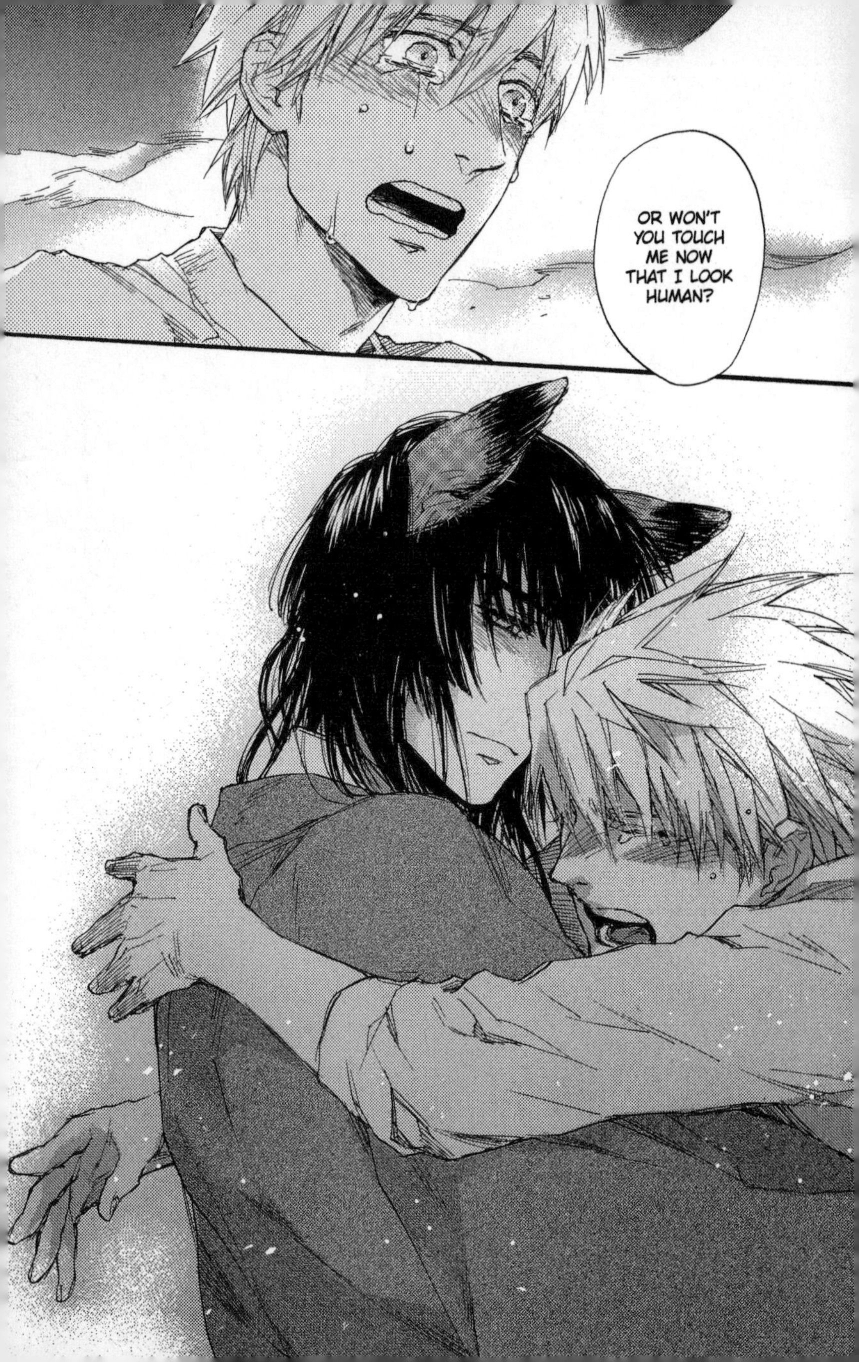
OR WON'T YOU TOUCH ME NOW THAT I LOOK HUMAN?

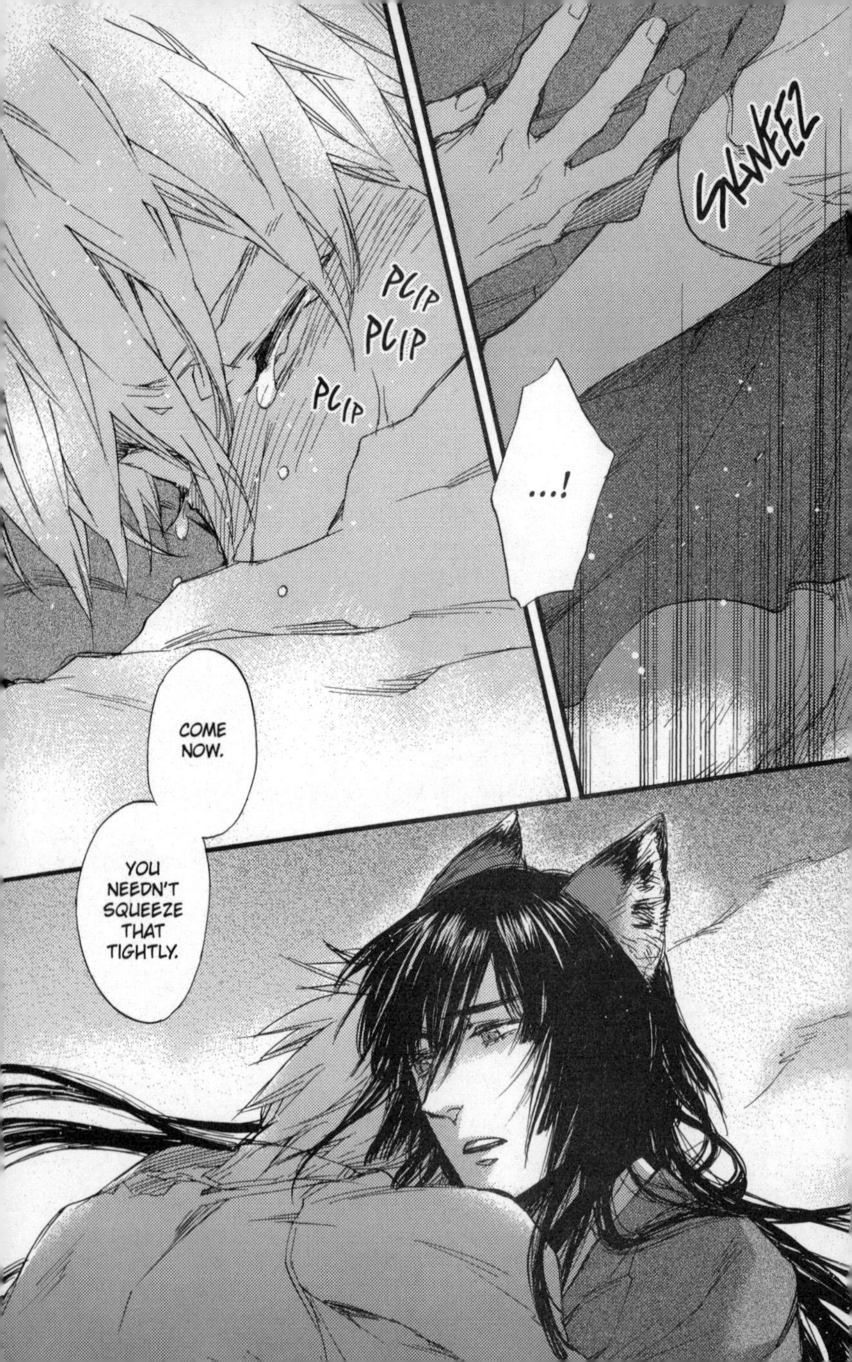
SKWEEZ
...!
PLIP
PLIP
PLIP
COME NOW.
YOU NEEDN'T SQUEEZE THAT TIGHTLY.

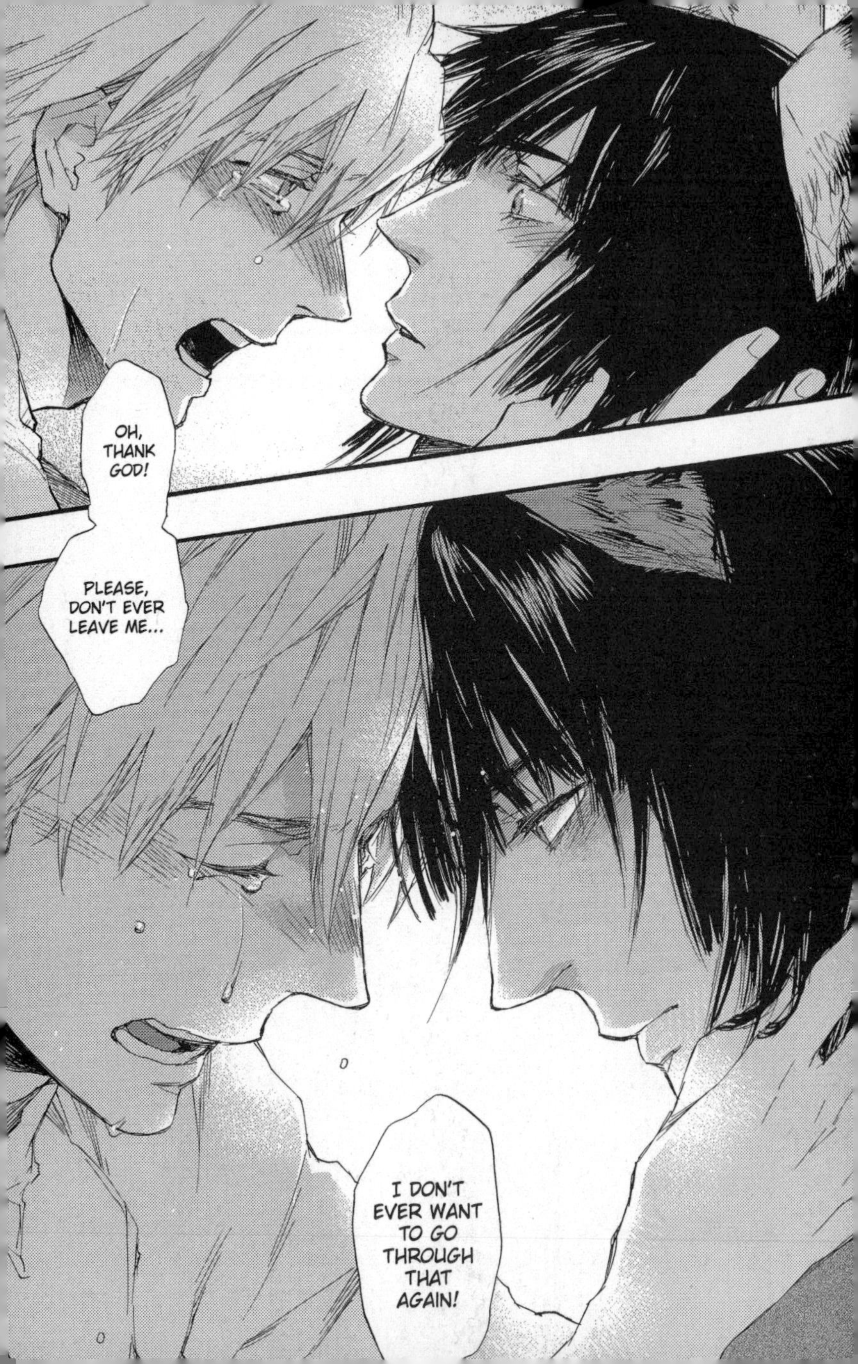
OH, THANK GOD!
PLEASE, DON'T EVER LEAVE ME...
I DON'T EVER WANT TO GO THROUGH THAT AGAIN!

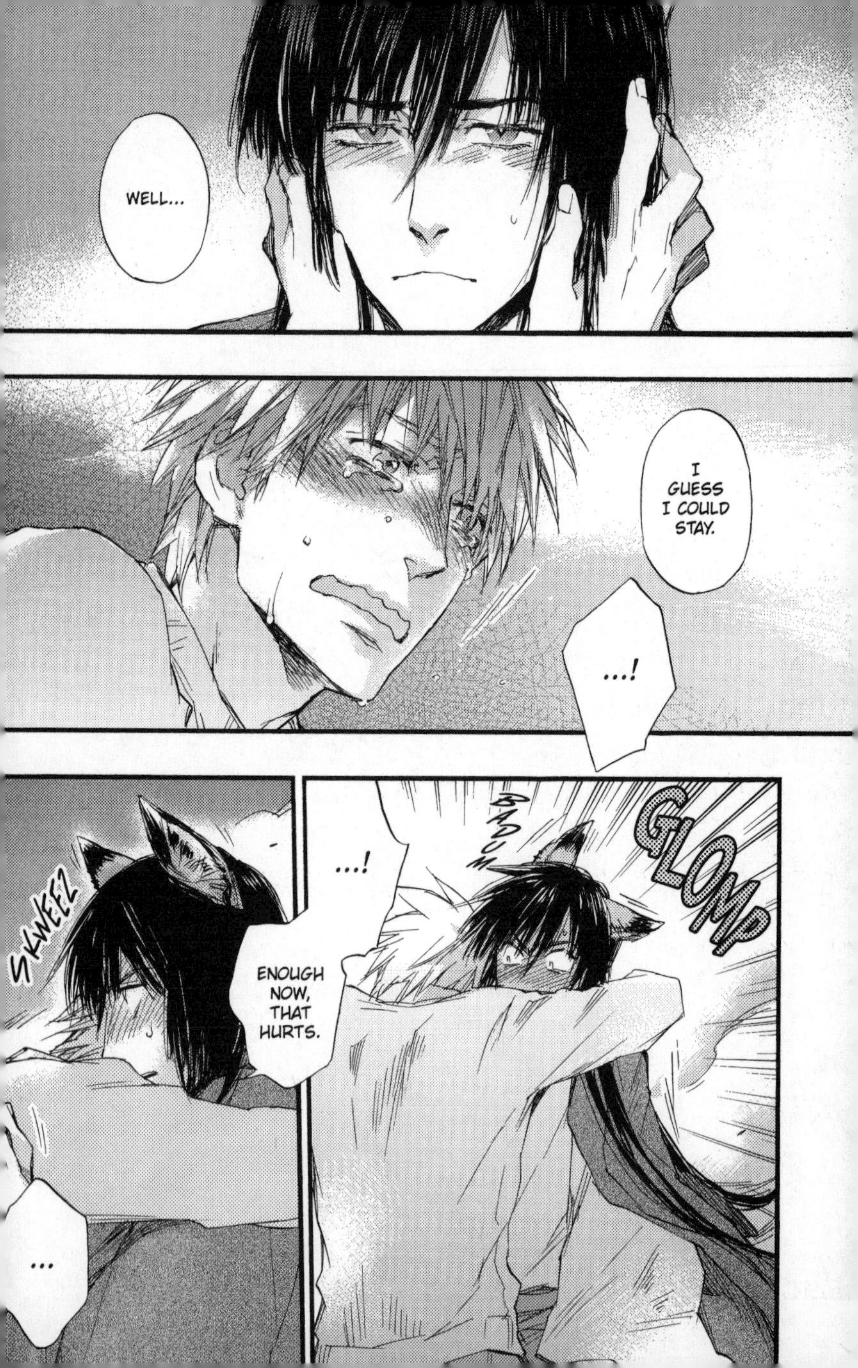
WELL...
I GUESS I COULD STAY.
...!
GLOMP
BADUMP
...!
ENOUGH NOW, THAT HURTS.
SKWEEZ
...

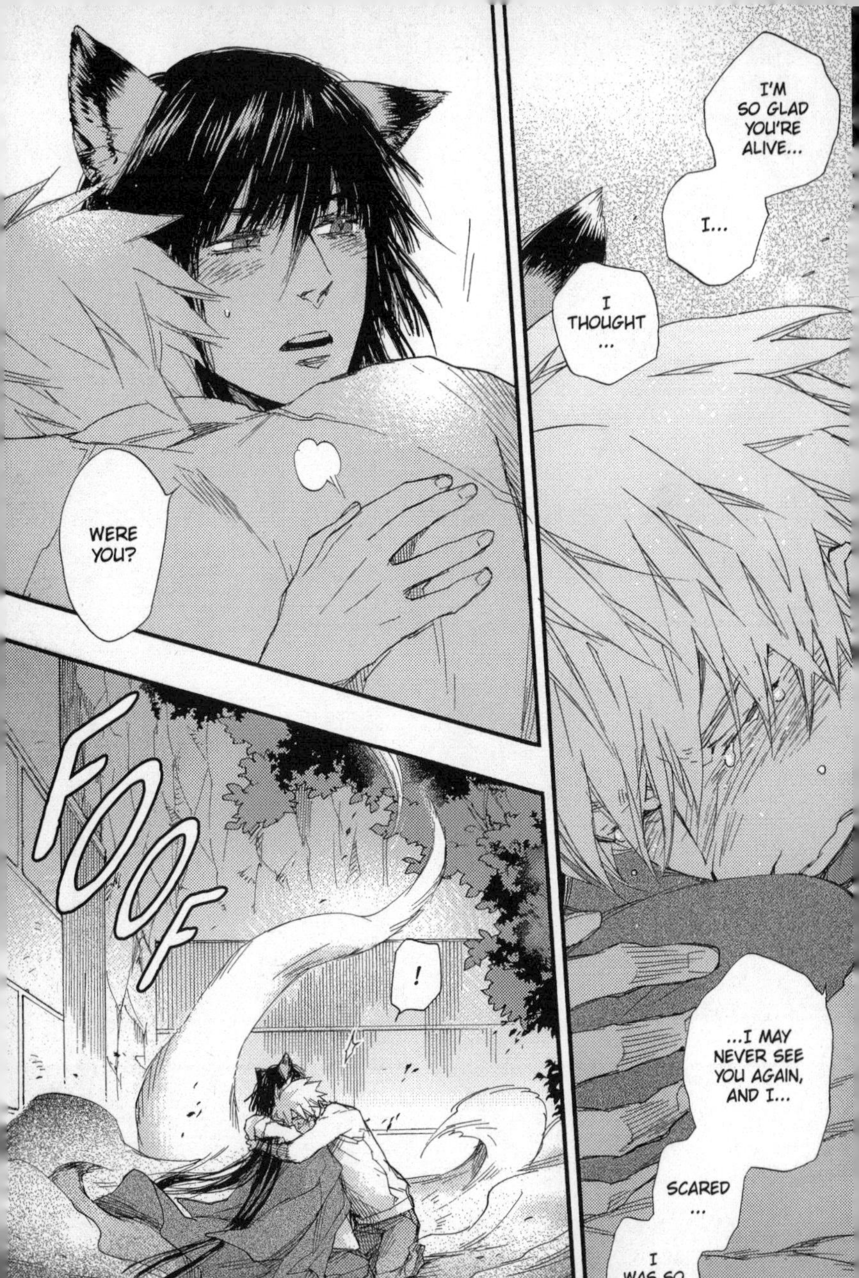
I'M SO GLAD YOU'RE ALIVE...
I...
I THOUGHT ...
...I MAY NEVER SEE YOU AGAIN, AND I...
SCARED ...
I WAS SO SCARED ...
WERE YOU?
FOOF
!

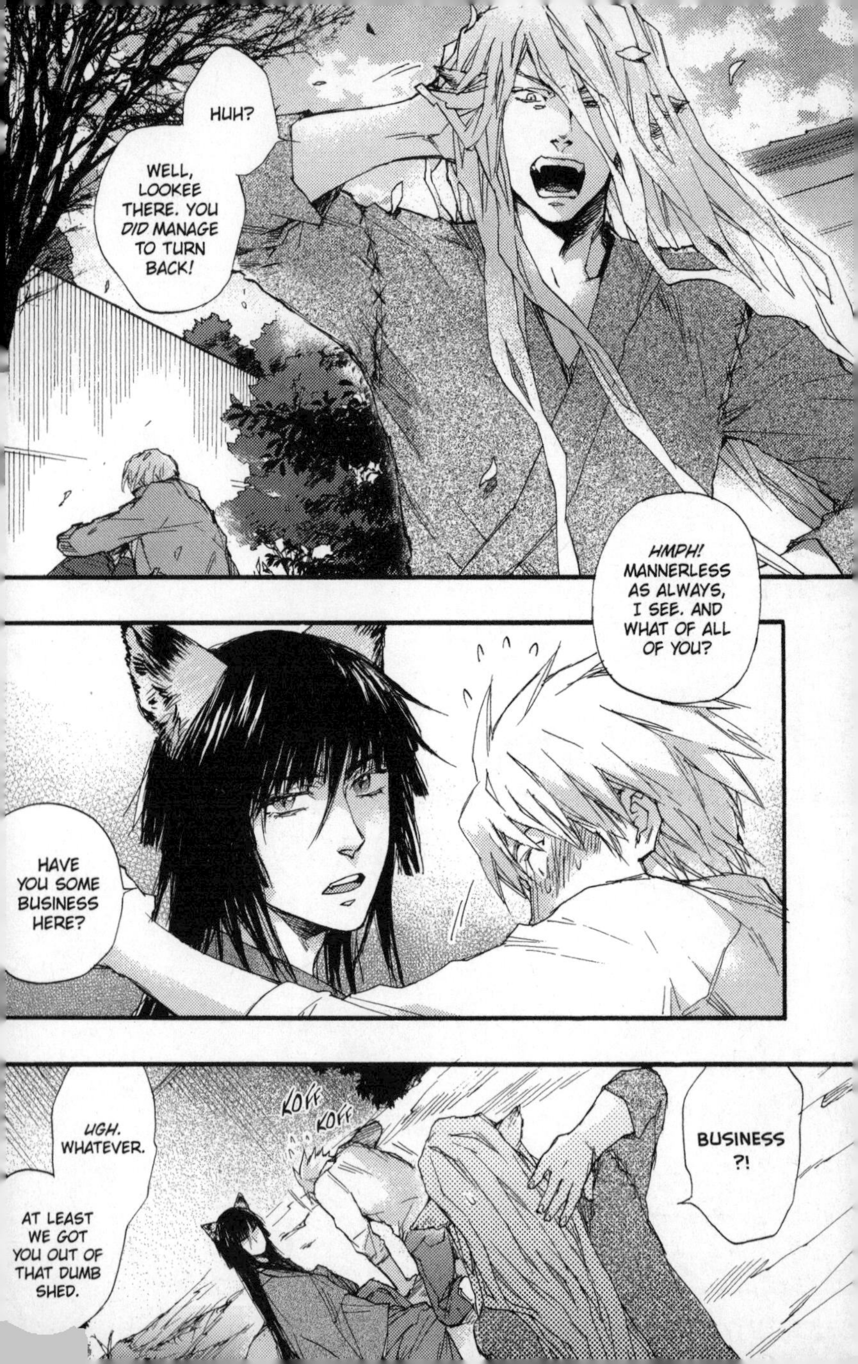
HUH?
WELL, LOOKEE THERE. YOU *DID* MANAGE TO TURN BACK!
HMPH! MANNERLESS AS ALWAYS, I SEE. AND WHAT OF ALL OF YOU?
HAVE YOU SOME BUSINESS HERE?
BUSINESS ?!
KOFF KOFF
UGH. WHATEVER.
AT LEAST WE GOT YOU OUT OF THAT DUMB SHED.

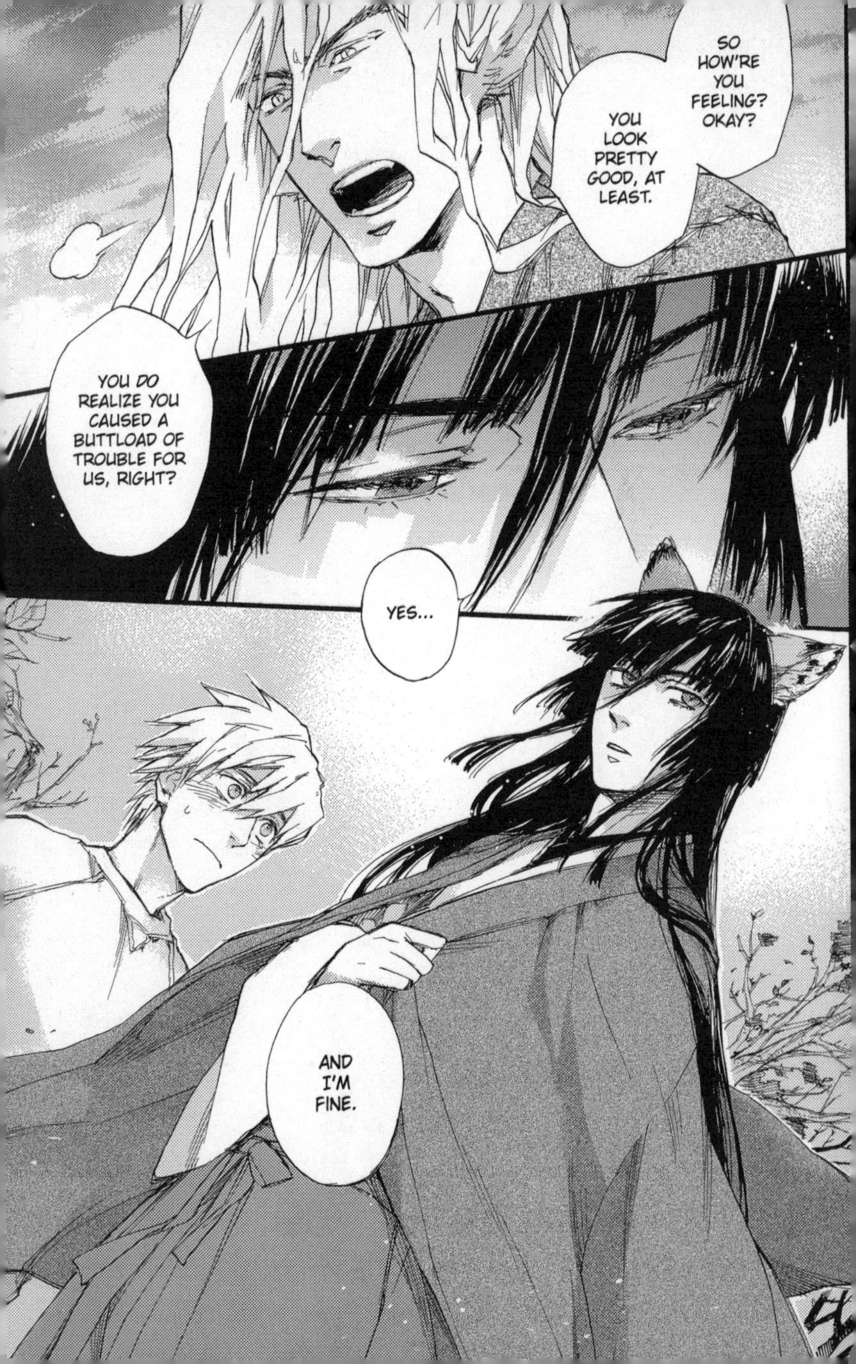
SO HOW'RE YOU FEELING? OKAY?
YOU LOOK PRETTY GOOD, AT LEAST.
YOU DO REALIZE YOU CAUSED A BUTTLOAD OF TROUBLE FOR US, RIGHT?
YES...
AND I'M FINE.

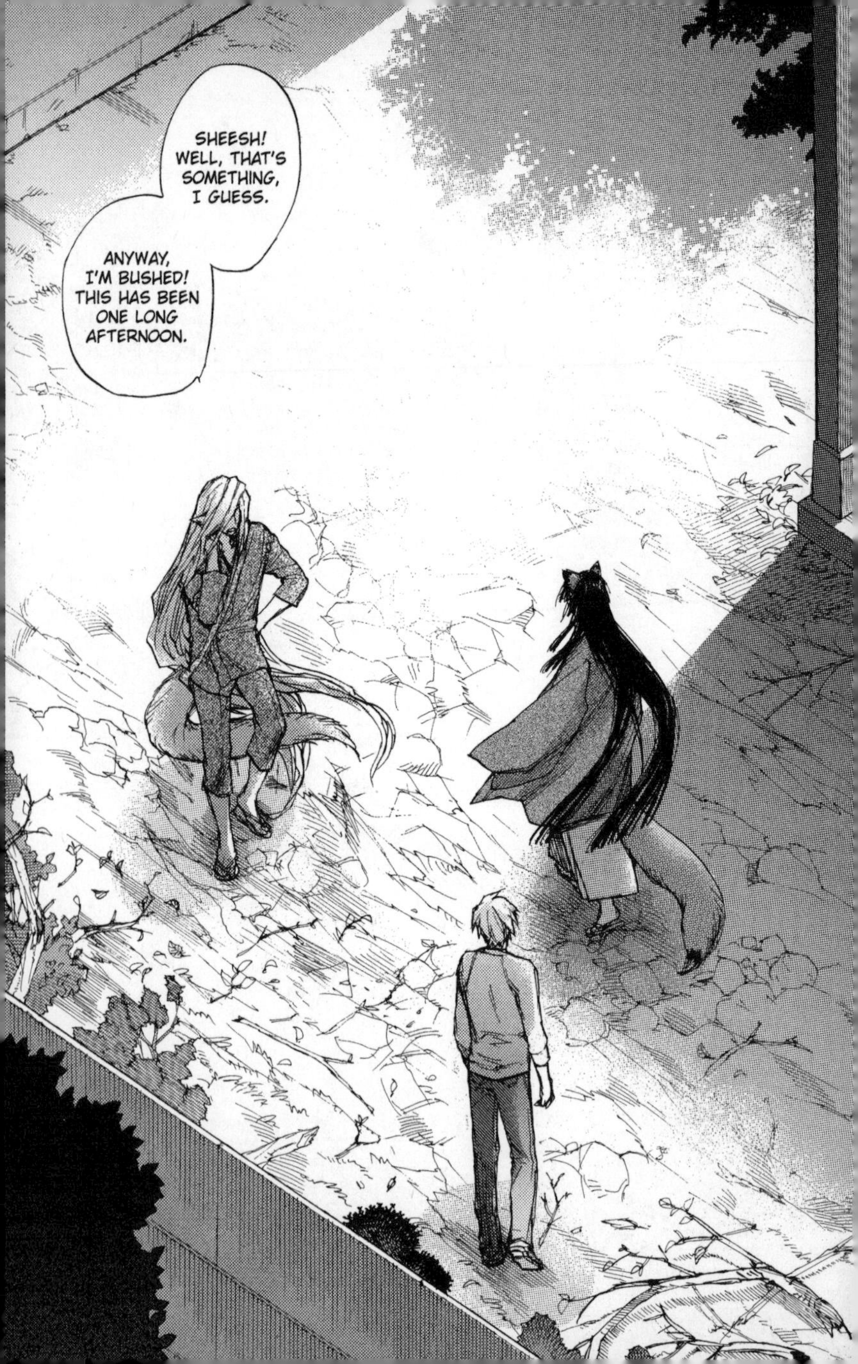
SHEESH! WELL, THAT'S SOMETHING, I GUESS.
ANYWAY, I'M BUSHED! THIS HAS BEEN ONE LONG AFTERNOON.

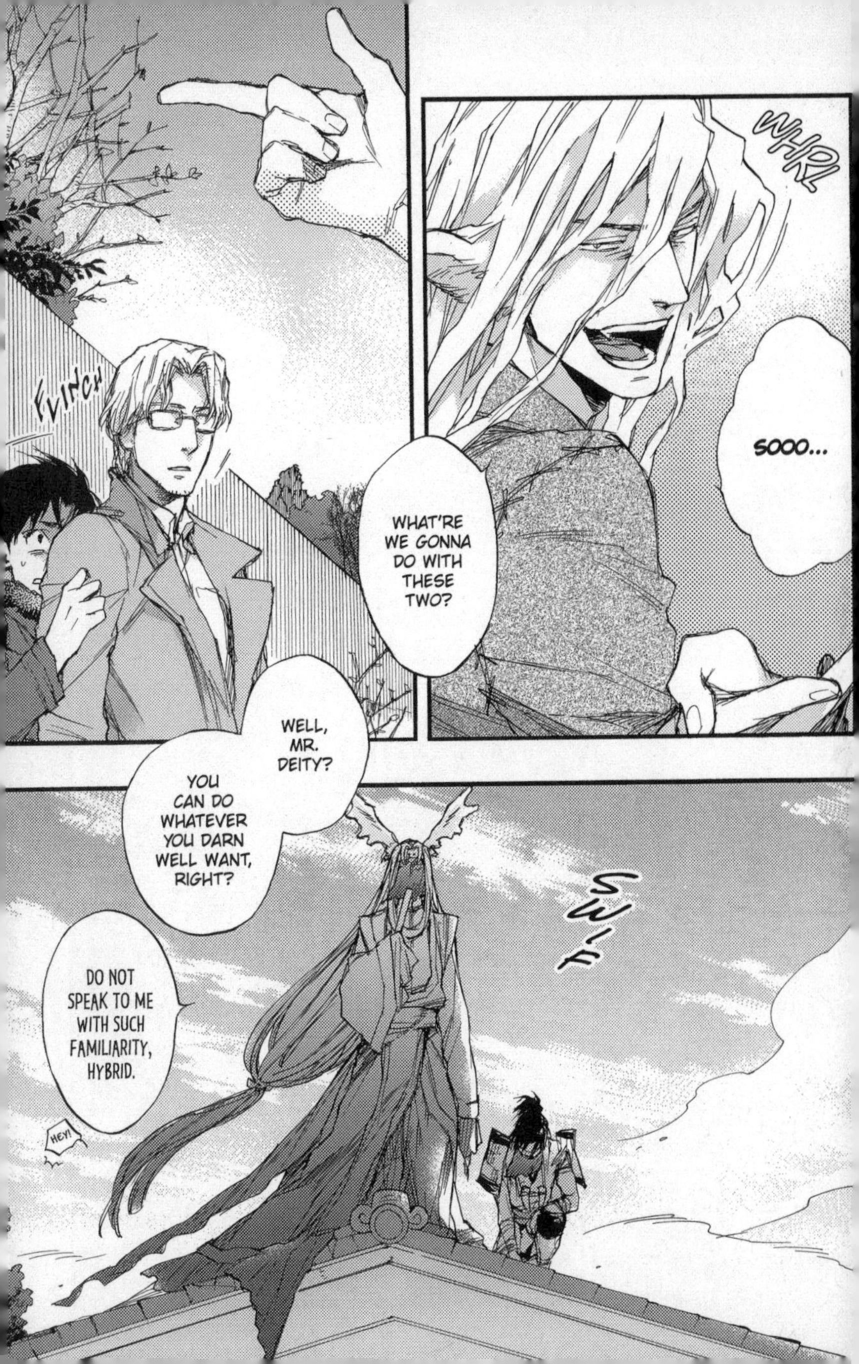
WHRL
SOOO...
WHAT'RE WE GONNA DO WITH THESE TWO?
FLINCH
WELL, MR. DEITY?
YOU CAN DO WHATEVER YOU DARN WELL WANT, RIGHT?
SWIF
DO NOT SPEAK TO ME WITH SUCH FAMILIARITY, HYBRID.
HEY!

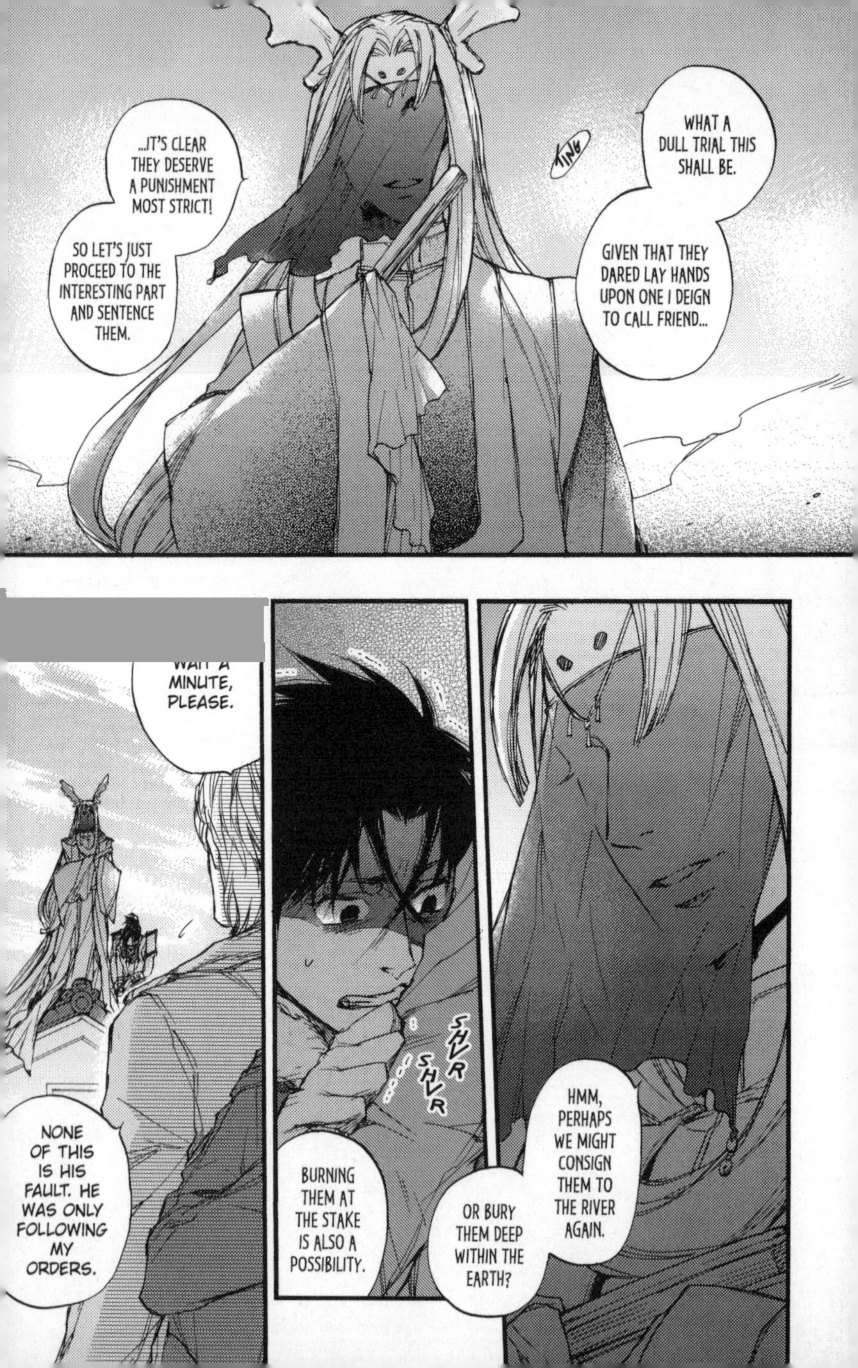
WHAT A DULL TRIAL THIS SHALL BE.
TING
GIVEN THAT THEY DARED LAY HANDS UPON ONE I DEIGN TO CALL FRIEND...
...IT'S CLEAR THEY DESERVE A PUNISHMENT MOST STRICT!
SO LET'S JUST PROCEED TO THE INTERESTING PART AND SENTENCE THEM.
HMM, PERHAPS WE MIGHT CONSIGN THEM TO THE RIVER AGAIN.
OR BURY THEM DEEP WITHIN THE EARTH?
SHVR SHVR
BURNING THEM AT THE STAKE IS ALSO A POSSIBILITY.
WAIT A MINUTE, PLEASE.
NONE OF THIS IS HIS FAULT. HE WAS ONLY FOLLOWING MY ORDERS.

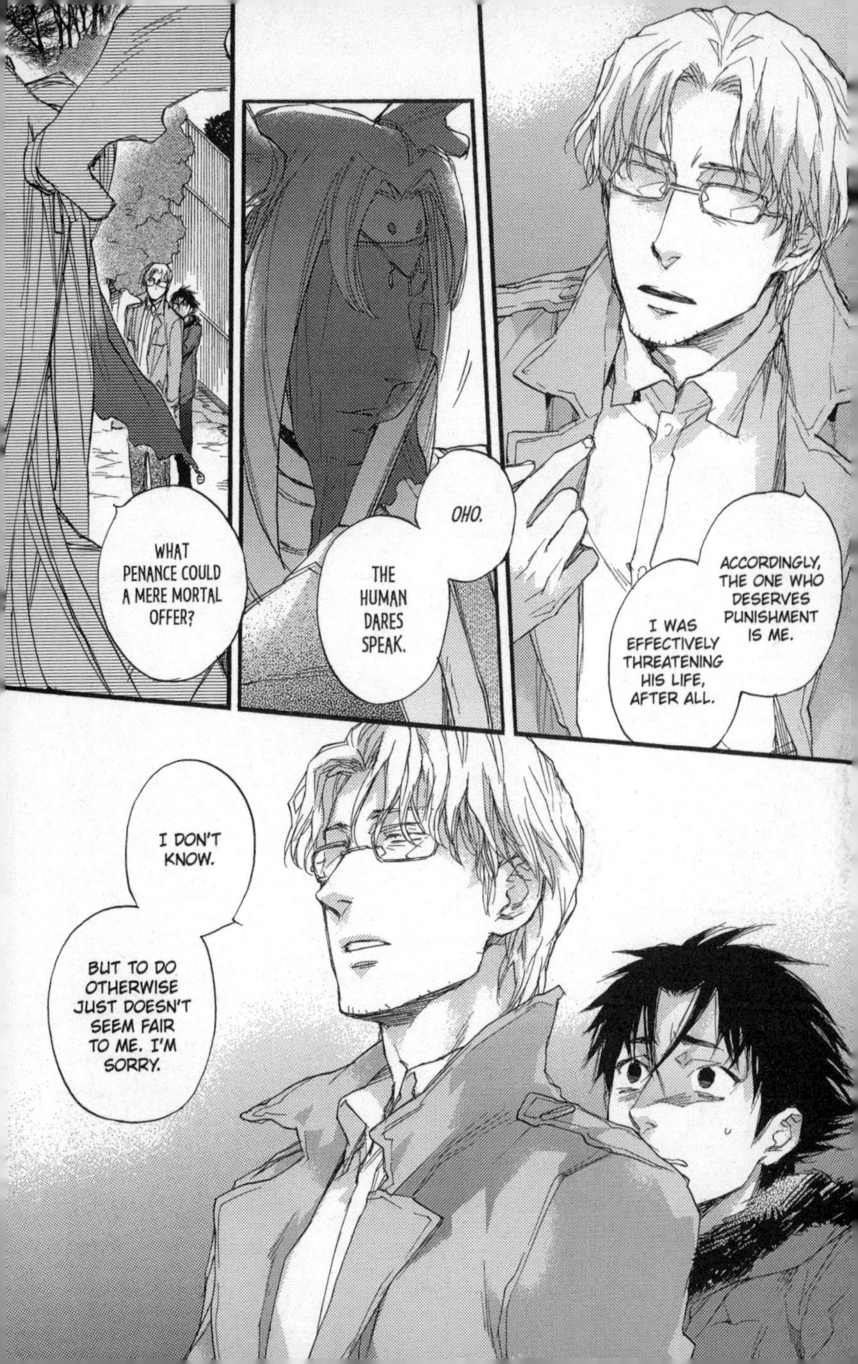
ACCORDINGLY, THE ONE WHO DESERVES PUNISHMENT IS ME.
I WAS EFFECTIVELY THREATENING HIS LIFE, AFTER ALL.
OHO.
THE HUMAN DARES SPEAK.
WHAT PENANCE COULD A MERE MORTAL OFFER?
I DON'T KNOW.
BUT TO DO OTHERWISE JUST DOESN'T SEEM FAIR TO ME. I'M SORRY.

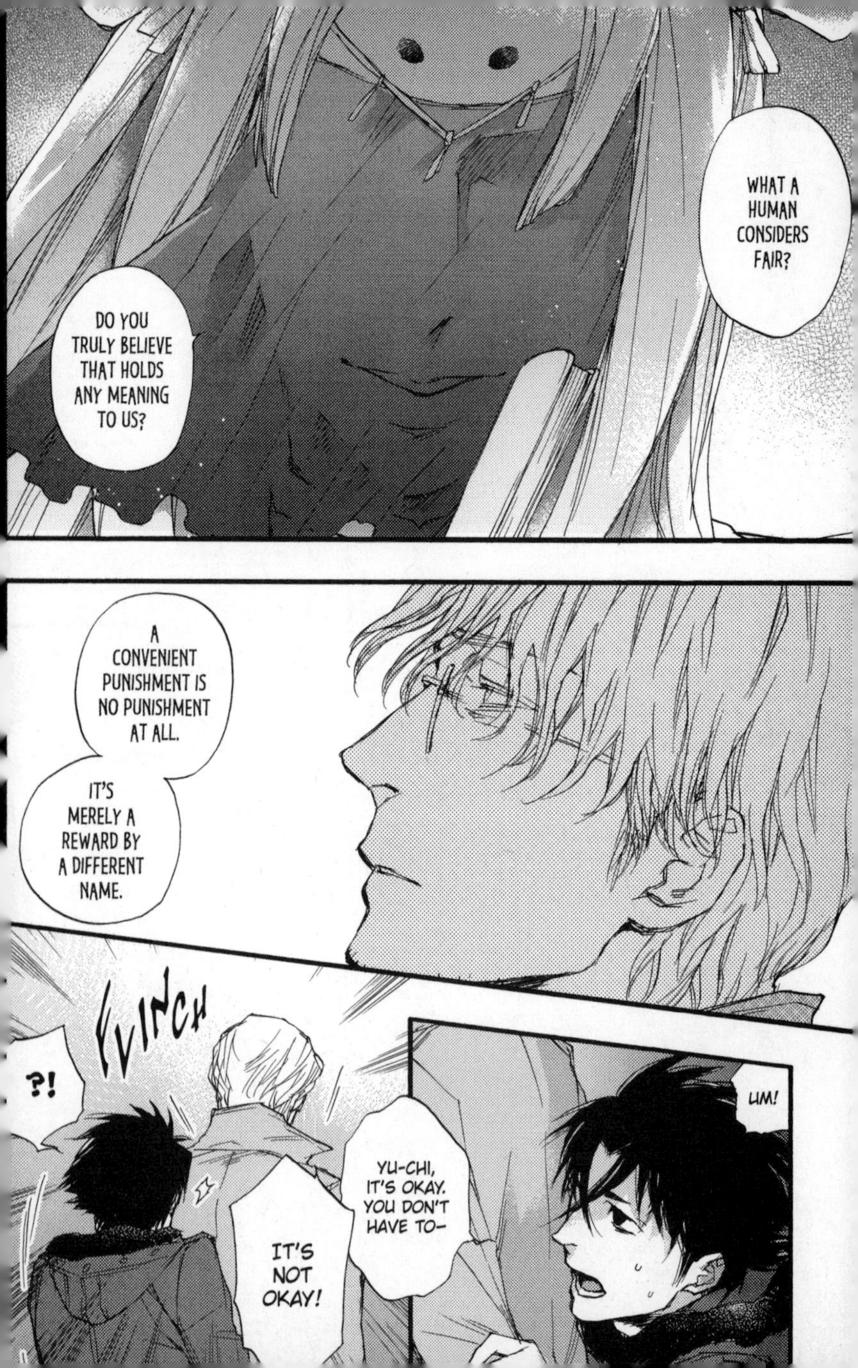
WHAT A HUMAN CONSIDERS FAIR?
DO YOU TRULY BELIEVE THAT HOLDS ANY MEANING TO US?
A CONVENIENT PUNISHMENT IS NO PUNISHMENT AT ALL.
IT'S MERELY A REWARD BY A DIFFERENT NAME.
UM!
YU-CHI, IT'S OKAY. YOU DON'T HAVE TO–
FLINCH
?!
IT'S NOT OKAY!

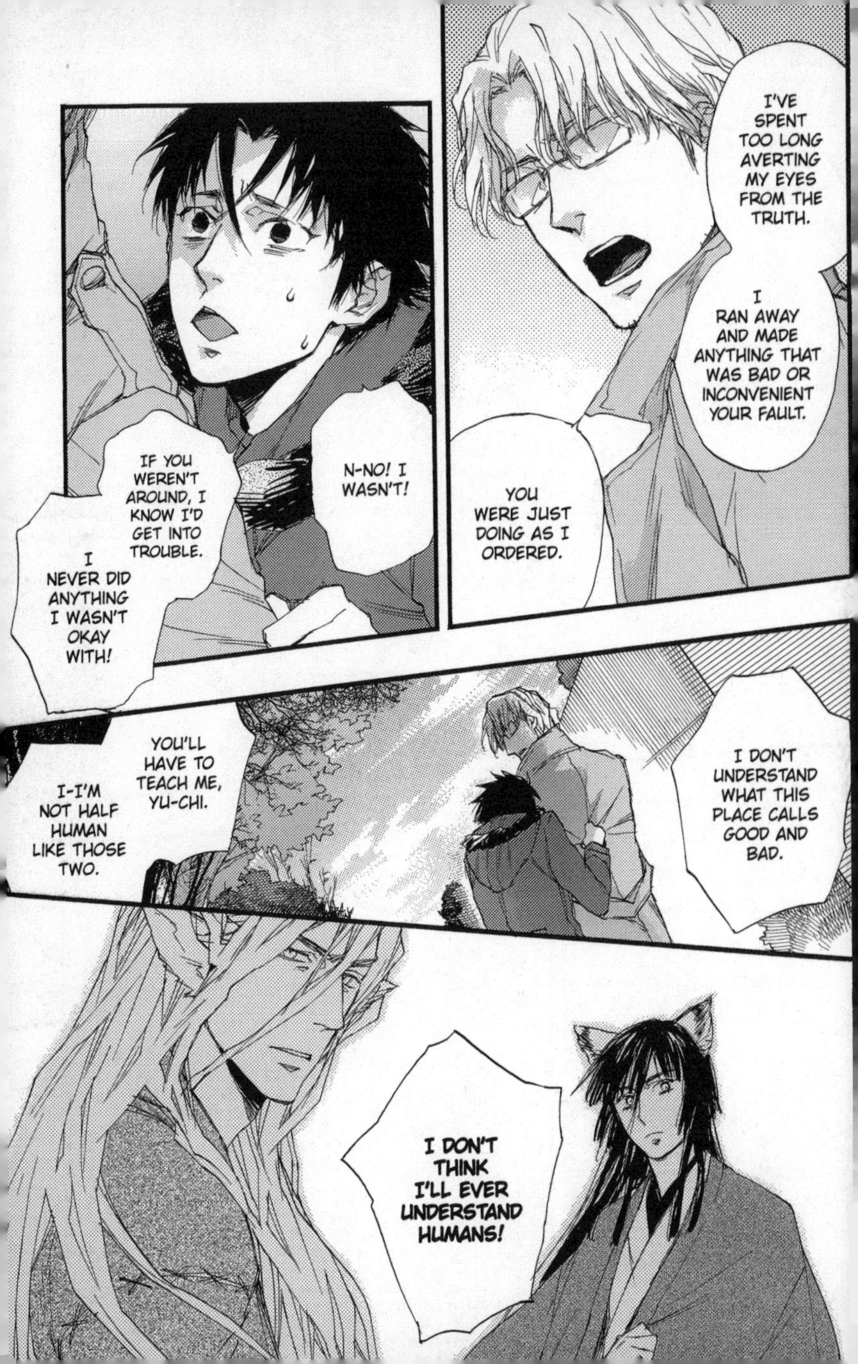
I'VE SPENT TOO LONG AVERTING MY EYES FROM THE TRUTH.
I RAN AWAY AND MADE ANYTHING THAT WAS BAD OR INCONVENIENT YOUR FAULT.
YOU WERE JUST DOING AS I ORDERED.
N-NO! I WASN'T!
IF YOU WEREN'T AROUND, I KNOW I'D GET INTO TROUBLE.
I NEVER DID ANYTHING I WASN'T OKAY WITH!
I DON'T UNDERSTAND WHAT THIS PLACE CALLS GOOD AND BAD.
YOU'LL HAVE TO TEACH ME, YU-CHI.
I-I'M NOT HALF HUMAN LIKE THOSE TWO.
I DON'T THINK I'LL EVER UNDERSTAND HUMANS!

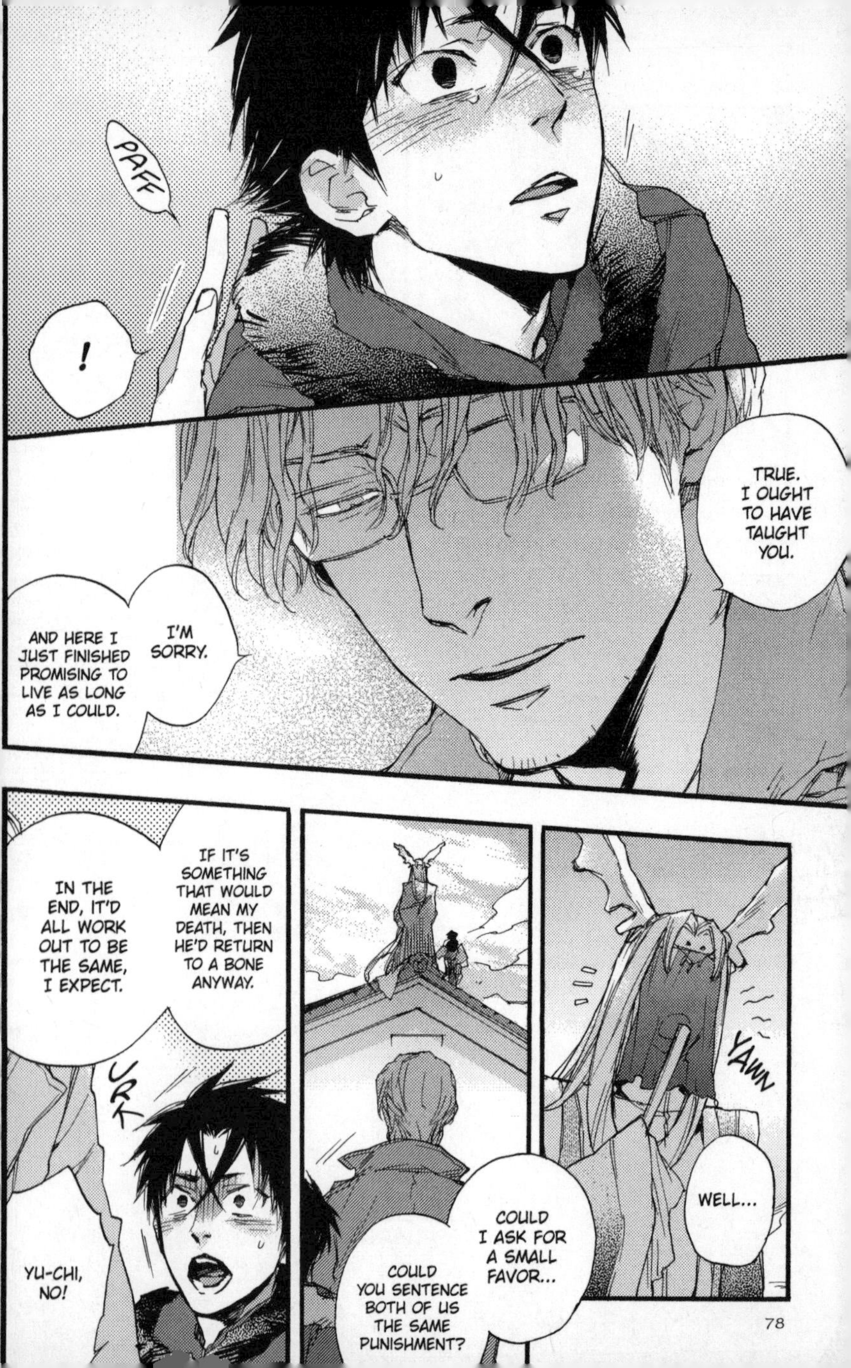
PAFF
!
TRUE. I OUGHT TO HAVE TAUGHT YOU.
I'M SORRY.
AND HERE I JUST FINISHED PROMISING TO LIVE AS LONG AS I COULD.
YAWN
WELL...
COULD I ASK FOR A SMALL FAVOR...
COULD YOU SENTENCE BOTH OF US THE SAME PUNISHMENT?
IF IT'S SOMETHING THAT WOULD MEAN MY DEATH, THEN HE'D RETURN TO A BONE ANYWAY.
IN THE END, IT'D ALL WORK OUT TO BE THE SAME, I EXPECT.
URK
YU-CHI, NO!

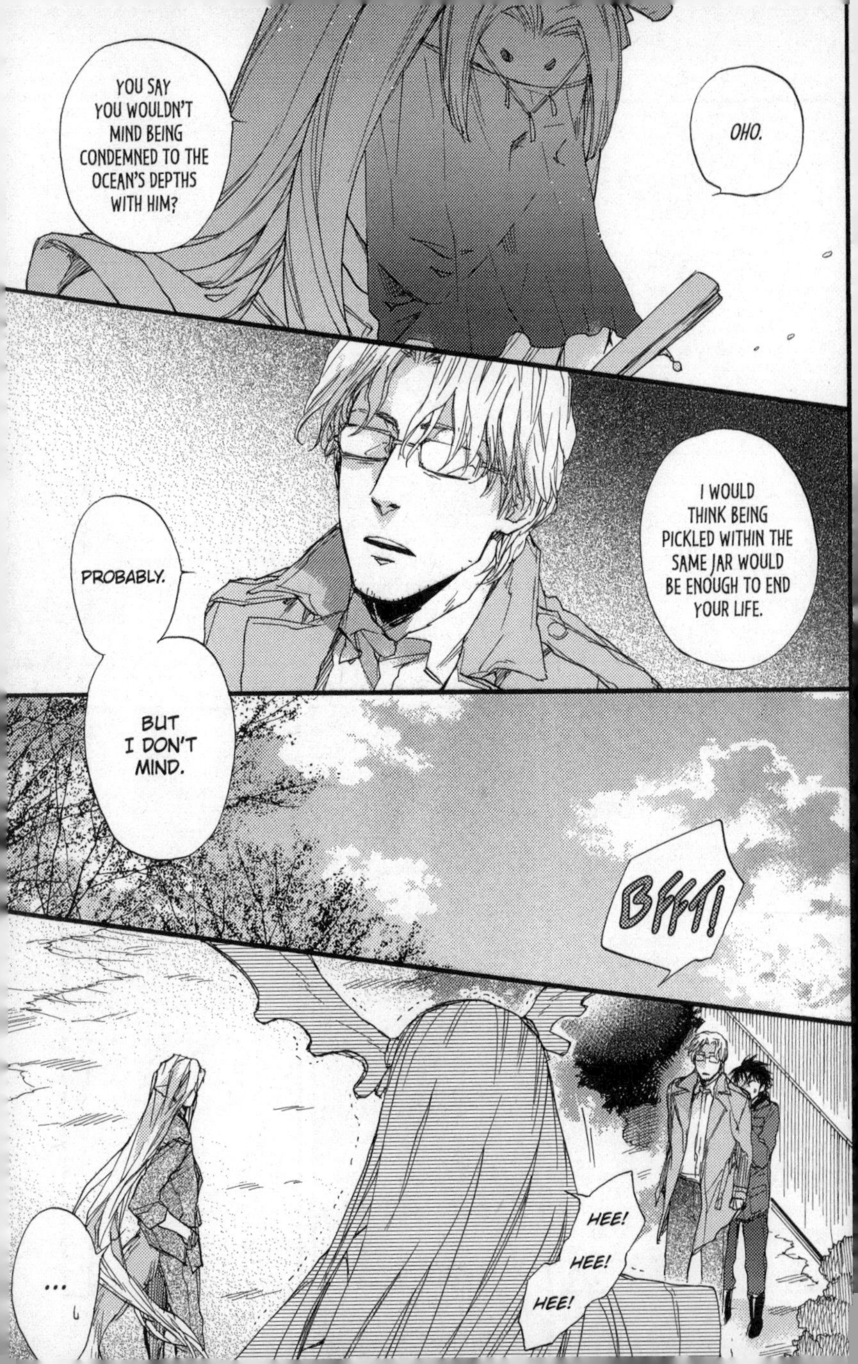
OHO.
YOU SAY YOU WOULDN'T MIND BEING CONDEMNED TO THE OCEAN'S DEPTHS WITH HIM?
I WOULD THINK BEING PICKLED WITHIN THE SAME JAR WOULD BE ENOUGH TO END YOUR LIFE.
PROBABLY.
BUT I DON'T MIND.
BFFT!
HEE! HEE! HEE!
...

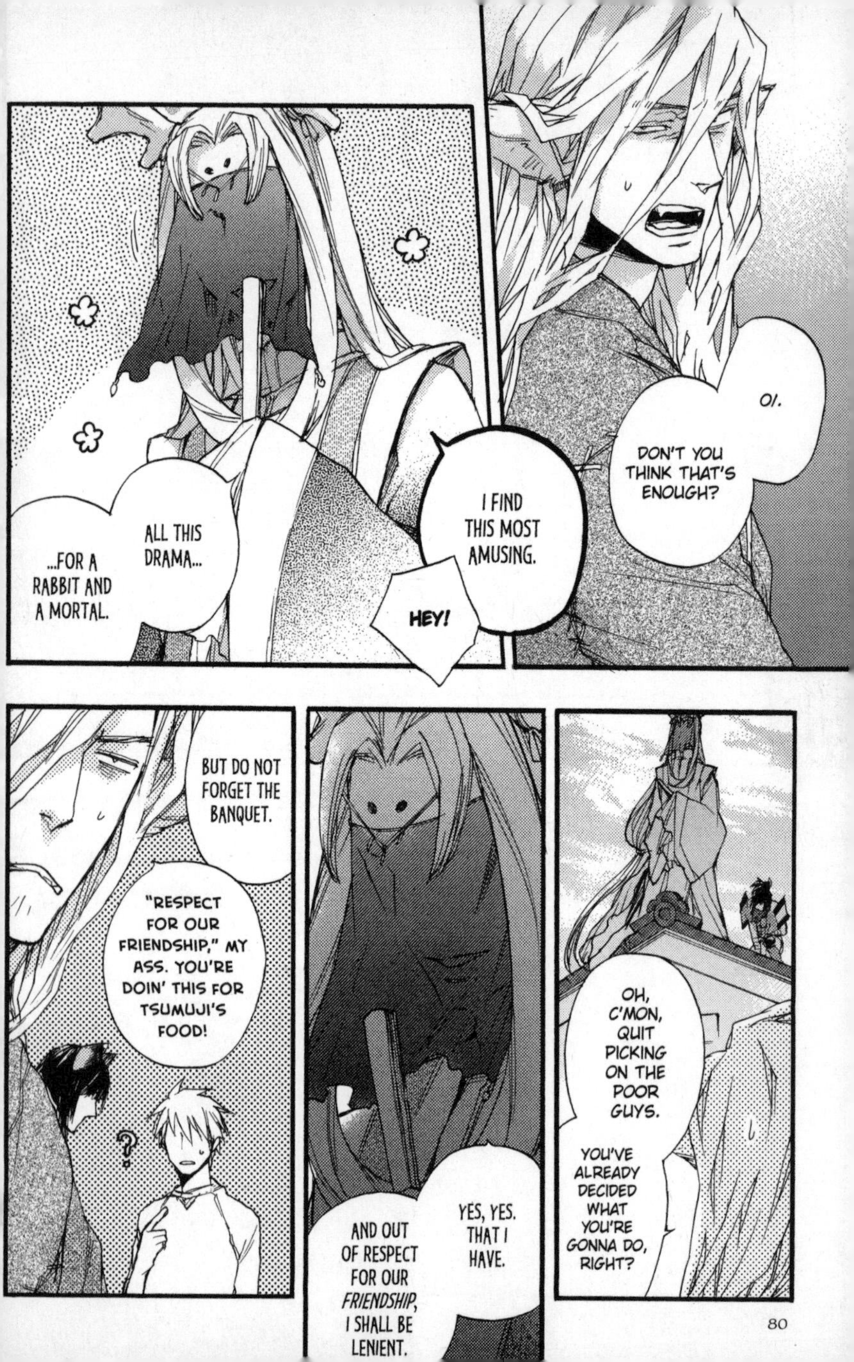
OI.
DON'T YOU THINK THAT'S ENOUGH?
I FIND THIS MOST AMUSING.
HEY!
ALL THIS DRAMA...
...FOR A RABBIT AND A MORTAL.
OH, C'MON, QUIT PICKING ON THE POOR GUYS.
YOU'VE ALREADY DECIDED WHAT YOU'RE GONNA DO, RIGHT?
YES, YES. THAT I HAVE.
AND OUT OF RESPECT FOR OUR *FRIENDSHIP*, I SHALL BE LENIENT.
BUT DO NOT FORGET THE BANQUET.
"RESPECT FOR OUR FRIENDSHIP," MY ASS. YOU'RE DOIN' THIS FOR TSUMUJI'S FOOD!

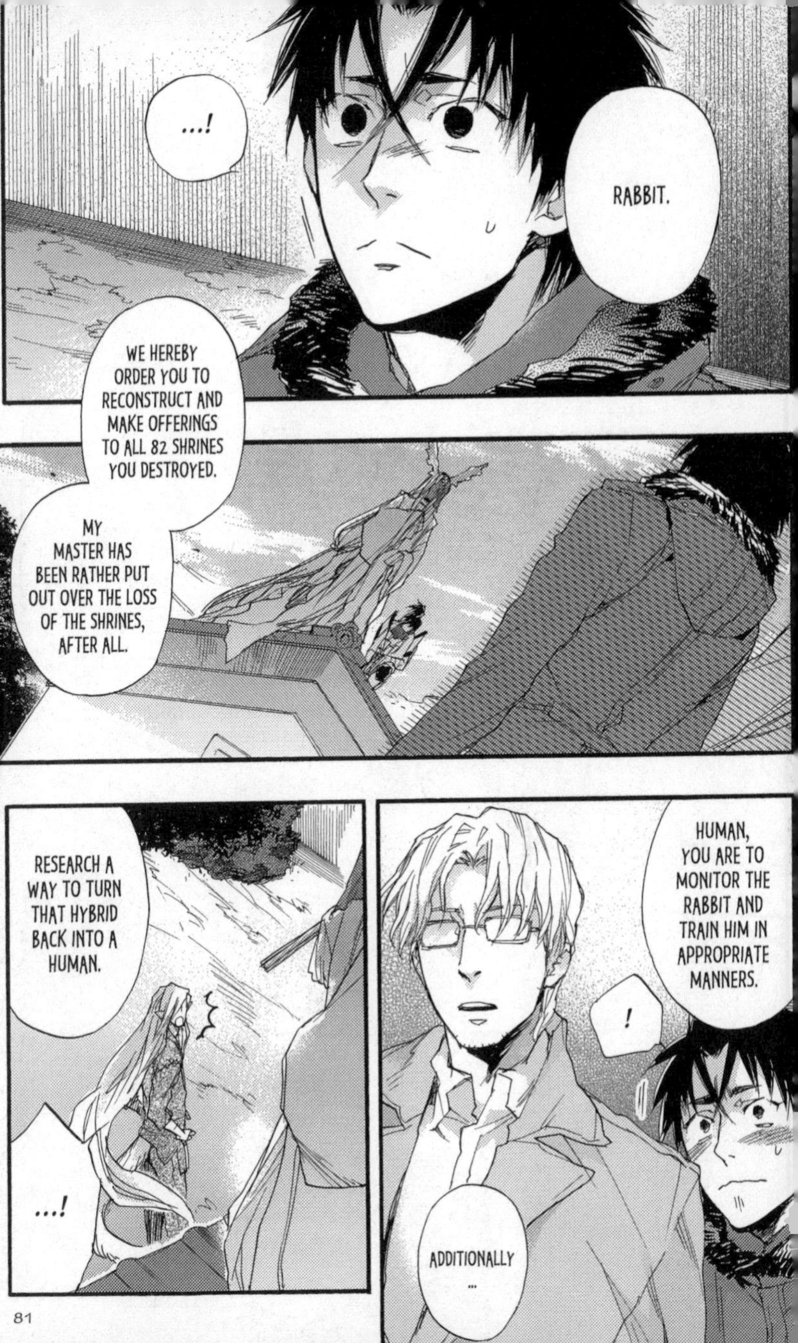
RABBIT.
...!
WE HEREBY ORDER YOU TO RECONSTRUCT AND MAKE OFFERINGS TO ALL 82 SHRINES YOU DESTROYED.
MY MASTER HAS BEEN RATHER PUT OUT OVER THE LOSS OF THE SHRINES, AFTER ALL.
HUMAN, YOU ARE TO MONITOR THE RABBIT AND TRAIN HIM IN APPROPRIATE MANNERS.
!
ADDITIONALLY ...
RESEARCH A WAY TO TURN THAT HYBRID BACK INTO A HUMAN.
...!

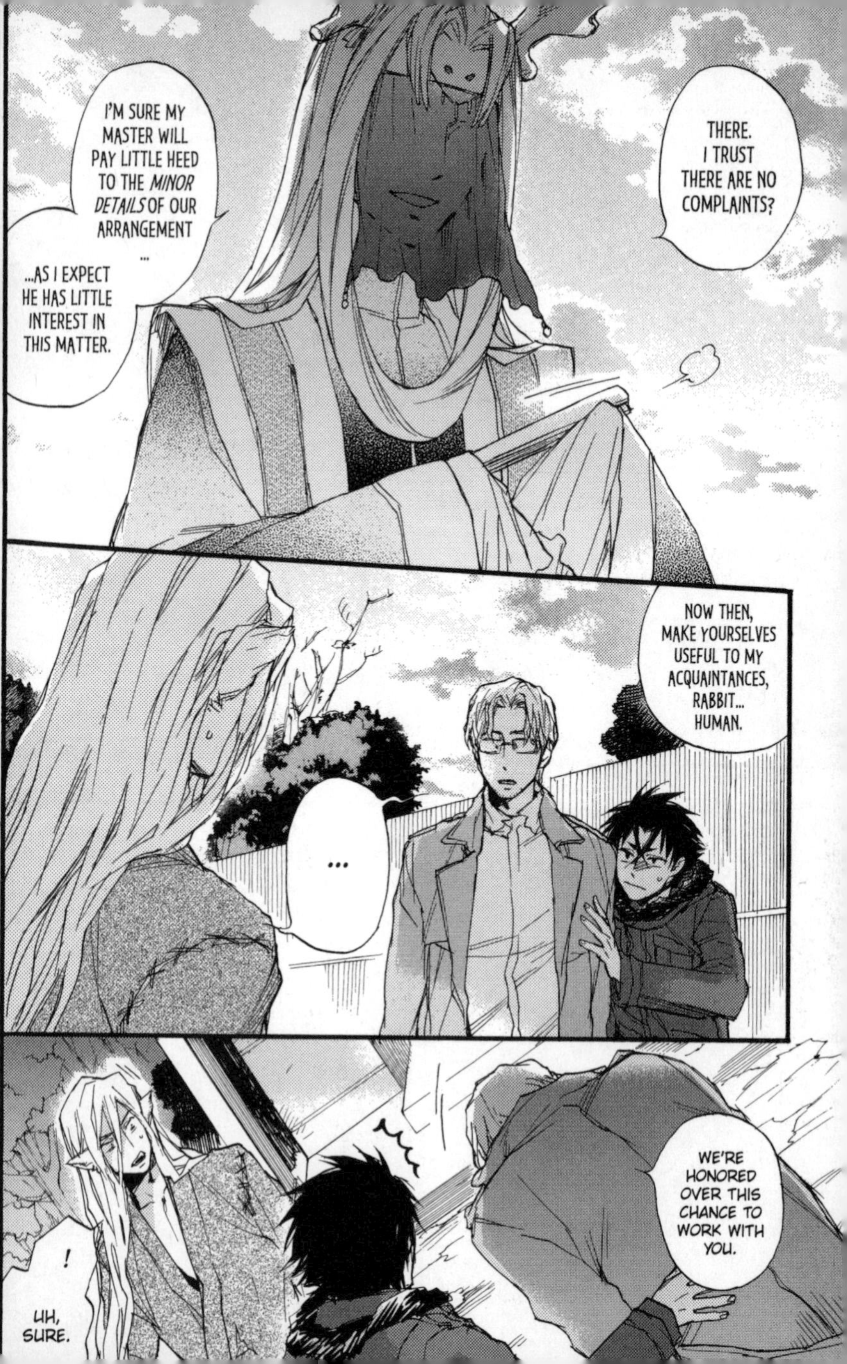
THERE. I TRUST THERE ARE NO COMPLAINTS?
I'M SURE MY MASTER WILL PAY LITTLE HEED TO THE *MINOR DETAILS* OF OUR ARRANGEMENT ...
...AS I EXPECT HE HAS LITTLE INTEREST IN THIS MATTER.
NOW THEN, MAKE YOURSELVES USEFUL TO MY ACQUAINTANCES, RABBIT... HUMAN.
...
WE'RE HONORED OVER THIS CHANCE TO WORK WITH YOU.
!
UH, SURE.

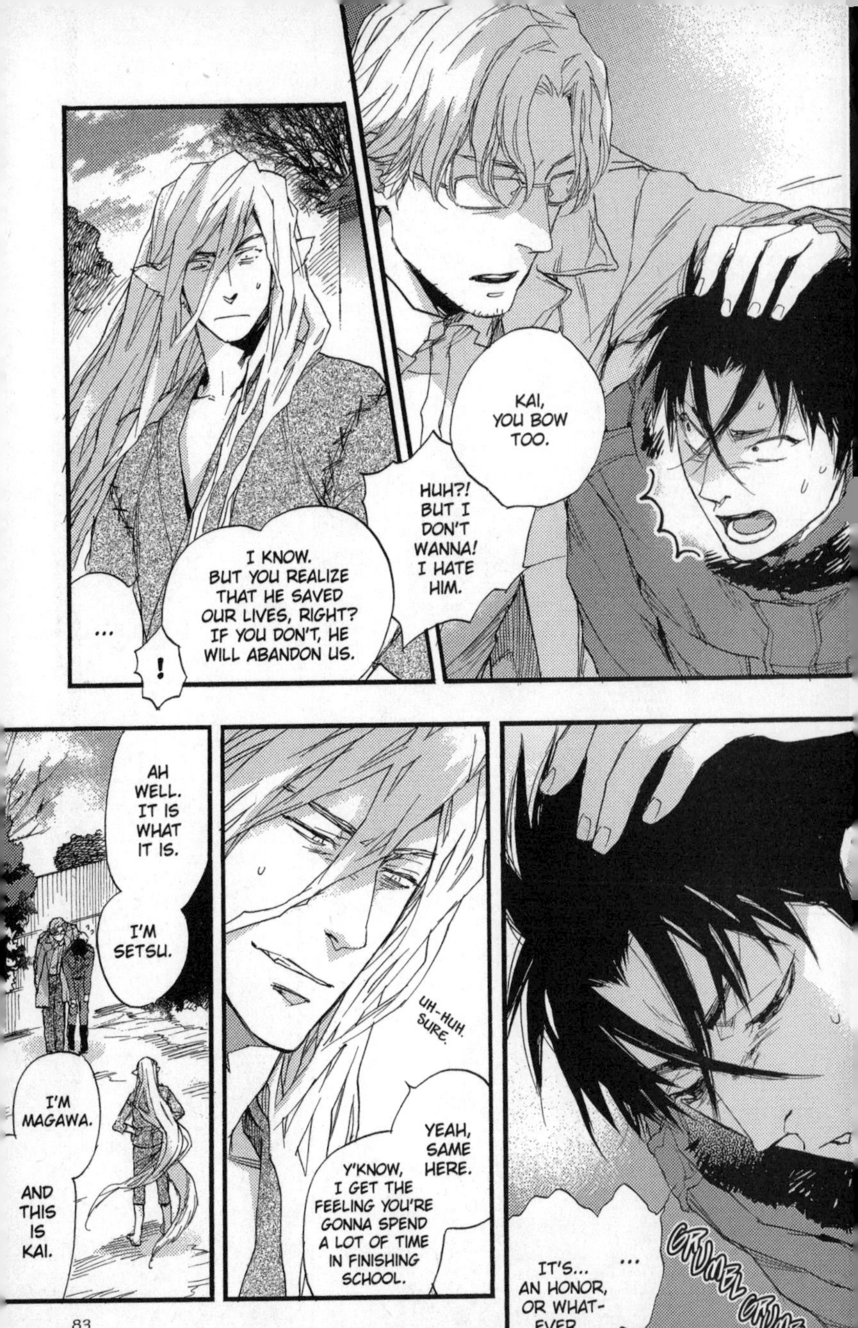
KAI, YOU BOW TOO.
HUH?! BUT I DON'T WANNA! I HATE HIM.
I KNOW. BUT YOU REALIZE THAT HE SAVED OUR LIVES, RIGHT? IF YOU DON'T, HE WILL ABANDON US.
...
!
...
IT'S... AN HONOR, OR WHAT-EVER...
UH-HUH. SURE.
YEAH, SAME HERE.
Y'KNOW, I GET THE FEELING YOU'RE GONNA SPEND A LOT OF TIME IN FINISHING SCHOOL.
AH WELL. IT IS WHAT IT IS.
I'M SETSU.
I'M MAGAWA.
AND THIS IS KAI.

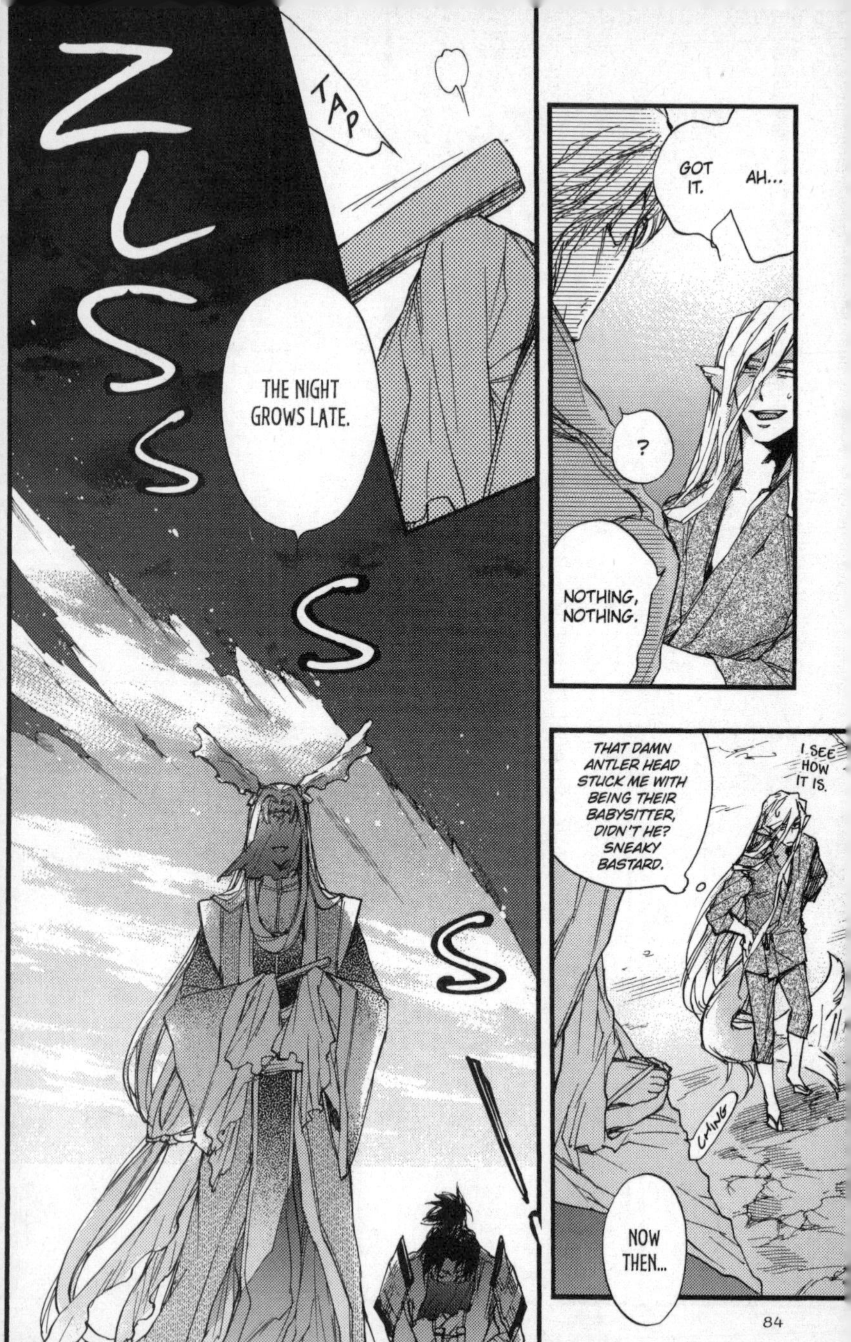
AH...
GOT IT.
?
NOTHING, NOTHING.
I SEE HOW IT IS.
THAT DAMN ANTLER HEAD STUCK ME WITH BEING THEIR BABYSITTER, DIDN'T HE? SNEAKY BASTARD.
CHING
NOW THEN...
TAP
THE NIGHT GROWS LATE.
ZUSSSSS

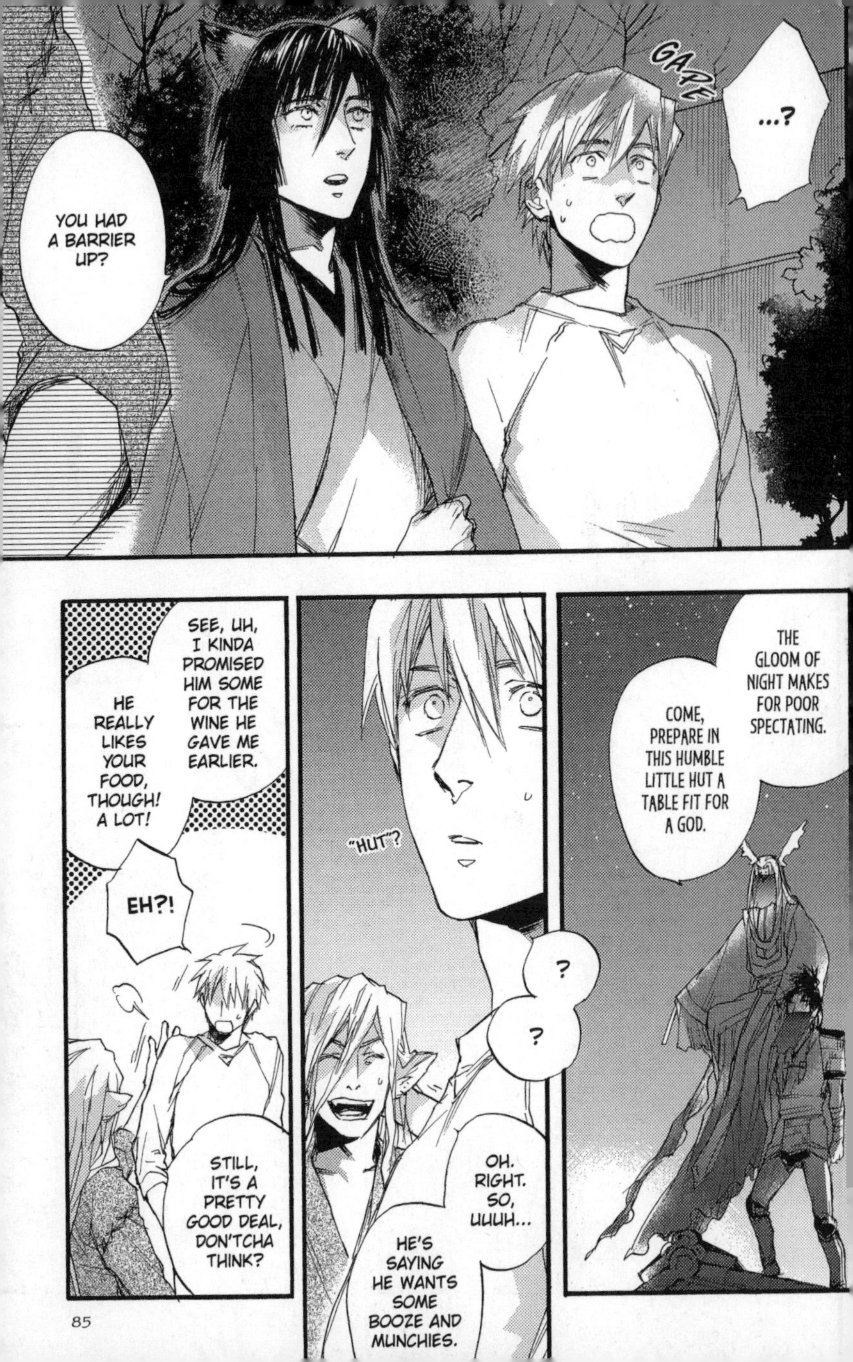
GAPE
...?
YOU HAD A BARRIER UP?
THE GLOOM OF NIGHT MAKES FOR POOR SPECTATING.
COME, PREPARE IN THIS HUMBLE LITTLE HUT A TABLE FIT FOR A GOD.
"HUT"?
?
?
OH. RIGHT. SO, UUUH...
HE'S SAYING HE WANTS SOME BOOZE AND MUNCHIES.
SEE, UH, I KINDA PROMISED HIM SOME FOR THE WINE HE GAVE ME EARLIER.
HE REALLY LIKES YOUR FOOD, THOUGH! A LOT!
EH?!
STILL, IT'S A PRETTY GOOD DEAL, DON'TCHA THINK?

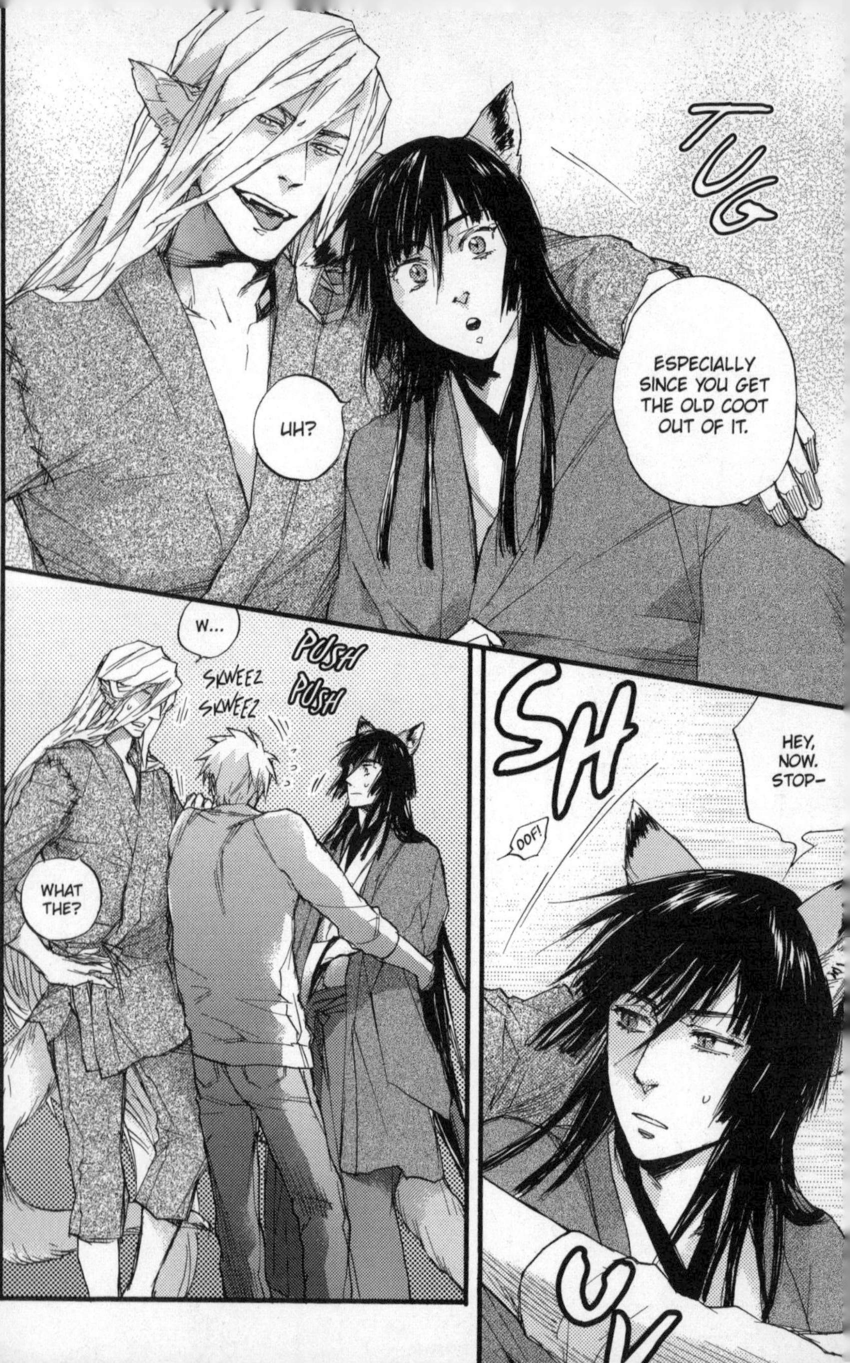
TUG
ESPECIALLY SINCE YOU GET THE OLD COOT OUT OF IT.
UH?
SH
HEY, NOW. STOP—
OOF!
UV
W...
PUSH PUSH
SKWEEZ SKWEEZ
WHAT THE?

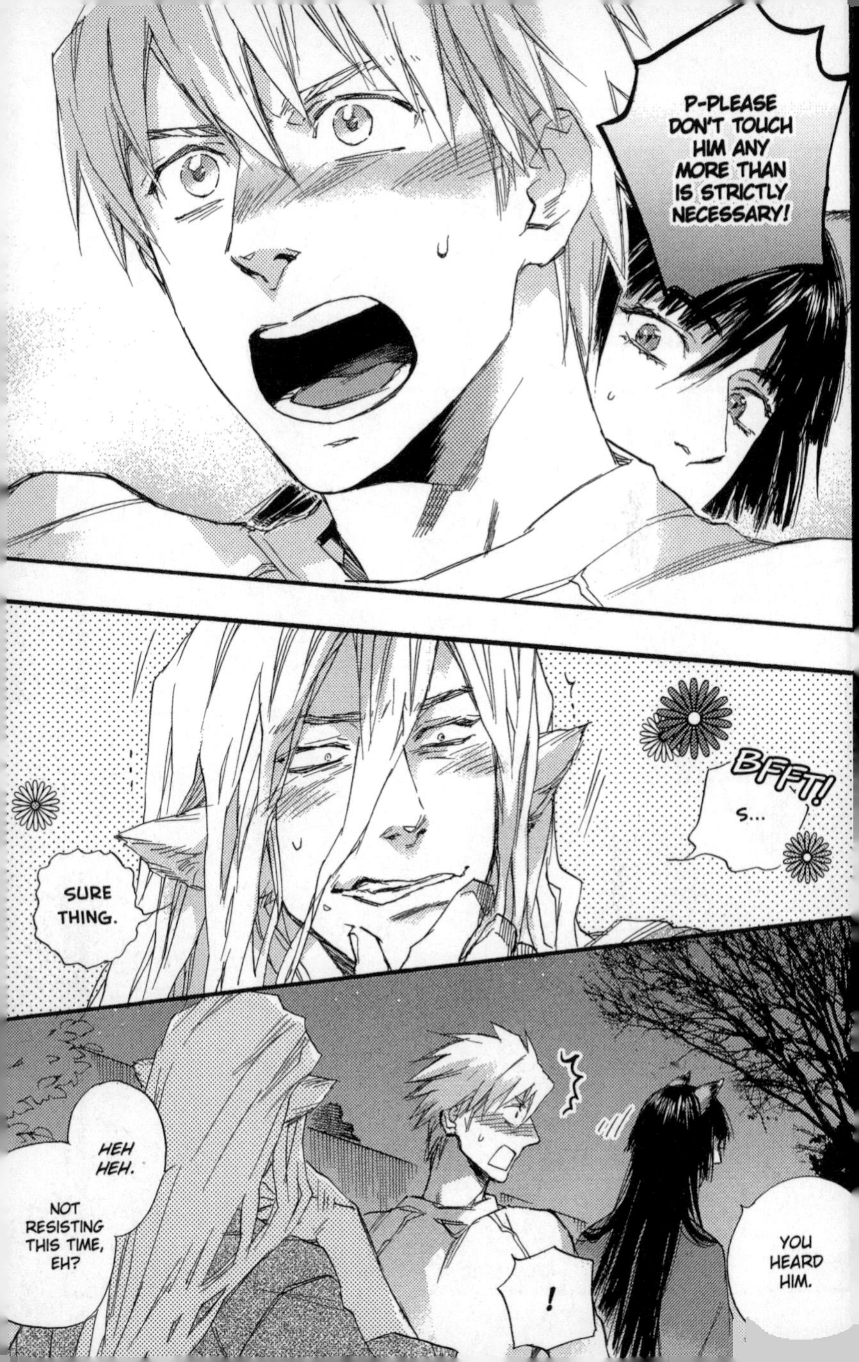
P-PLEASE DON'T TOUCH HIM ANY MORE THAN IS STRICTLY NECESSARY!
BFFT!
S...
SURE THING.
YOU HEARD HIM.
!
HEH HEH.
NOT RESISTING THIS TIME, EH?

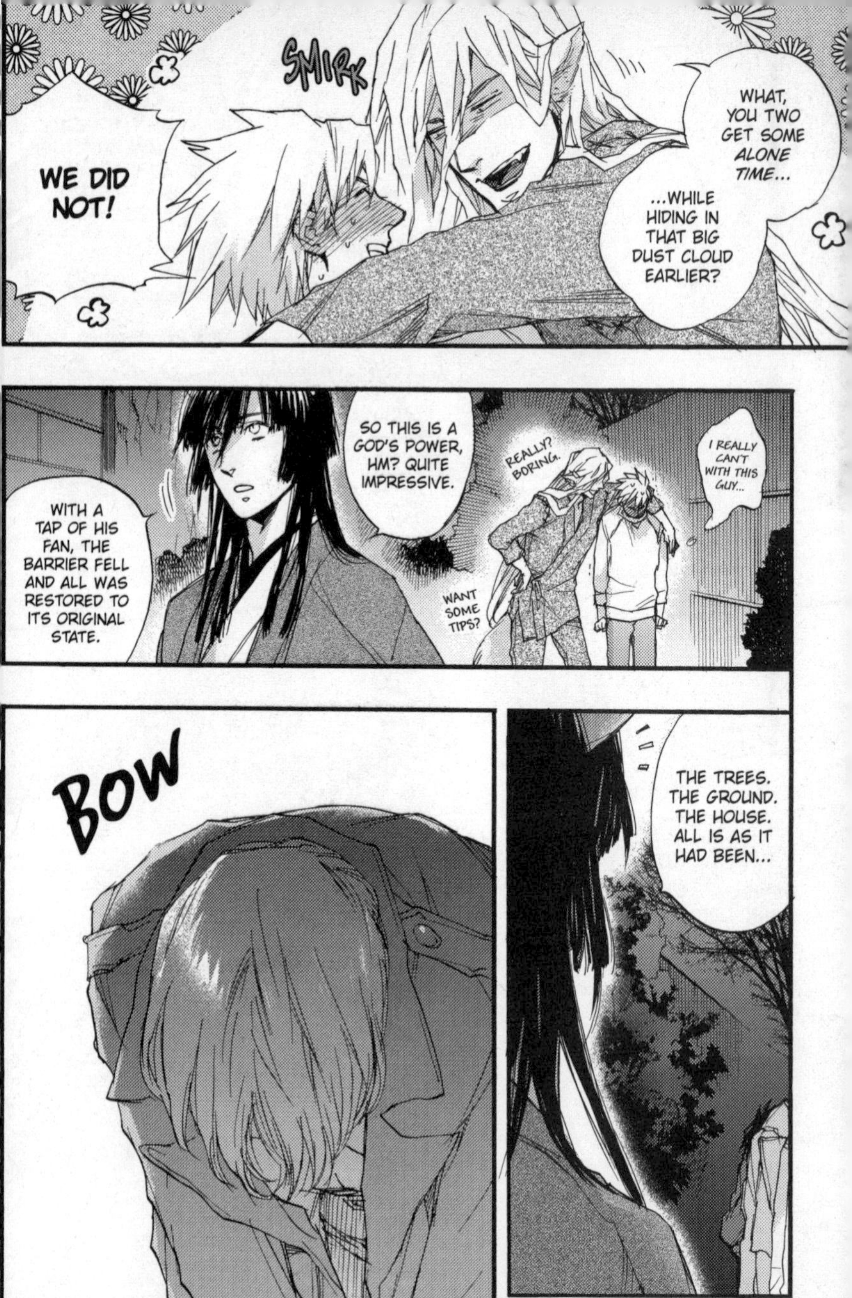
WHAT, YOU TWO GET SOME ALONE TIME...
...WHILE HIDING IN THAT BIG DUST CLOUD EARLIER?
SMIRK
WE DID NOT!
I REALLY CAN'T WITH THIS GUY...
REALLY? BORING.
WANT SOME TIPS?
SO THIS IS A GOD'S POWER, HM? QUITE IMPRESSIVE.
WITH A TAP OF HIS FAN, THE BARRIER FELL AND ALL WAS RESTORED TO ITS ORIGINAL STATE.
THE TREES. THE GROUND. THE HOUSE. ALL IS AS IT HAD BEEN...
BOW

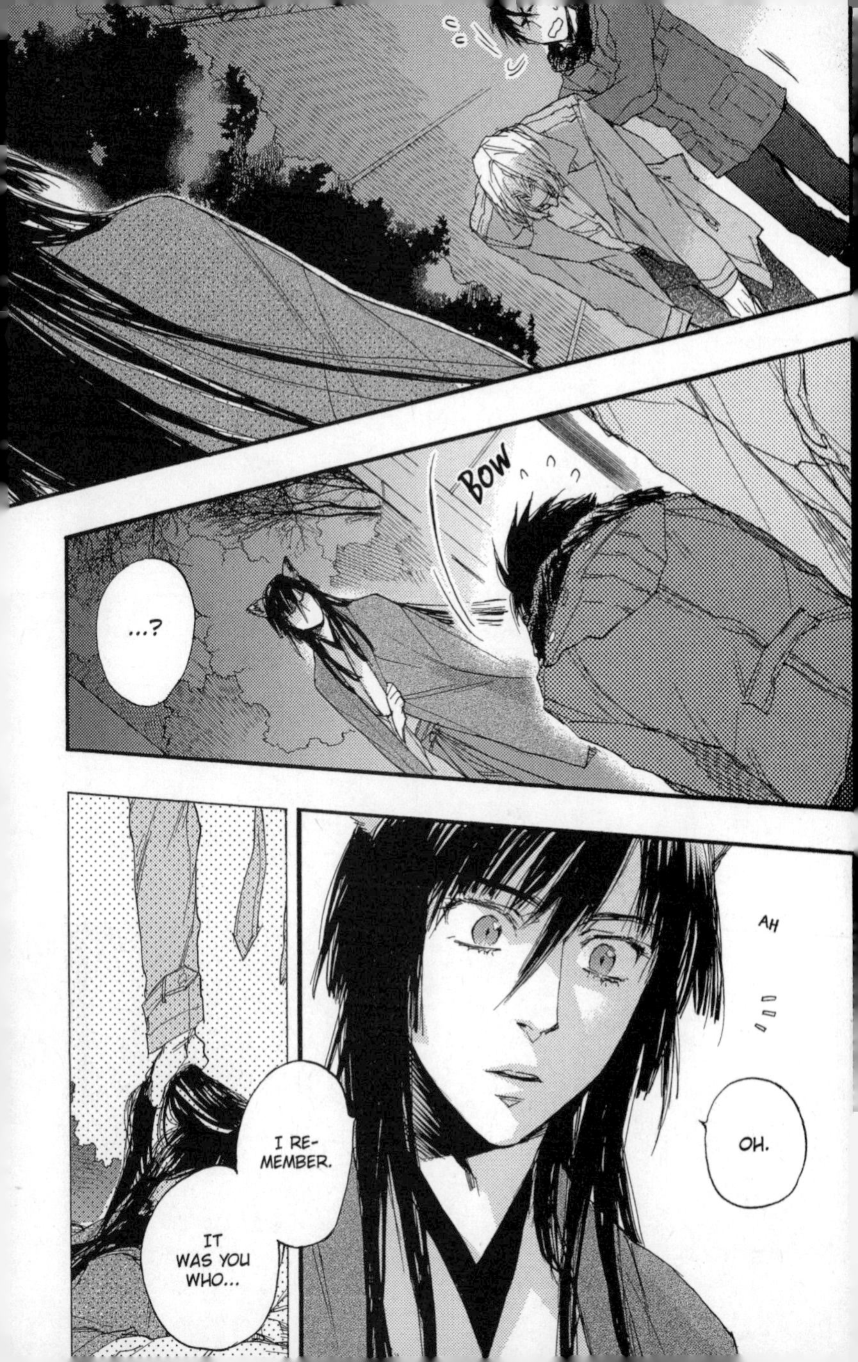
BOW
...?
AH
OH.
I RE-MEMBER.
IT WAS YOU WHO...

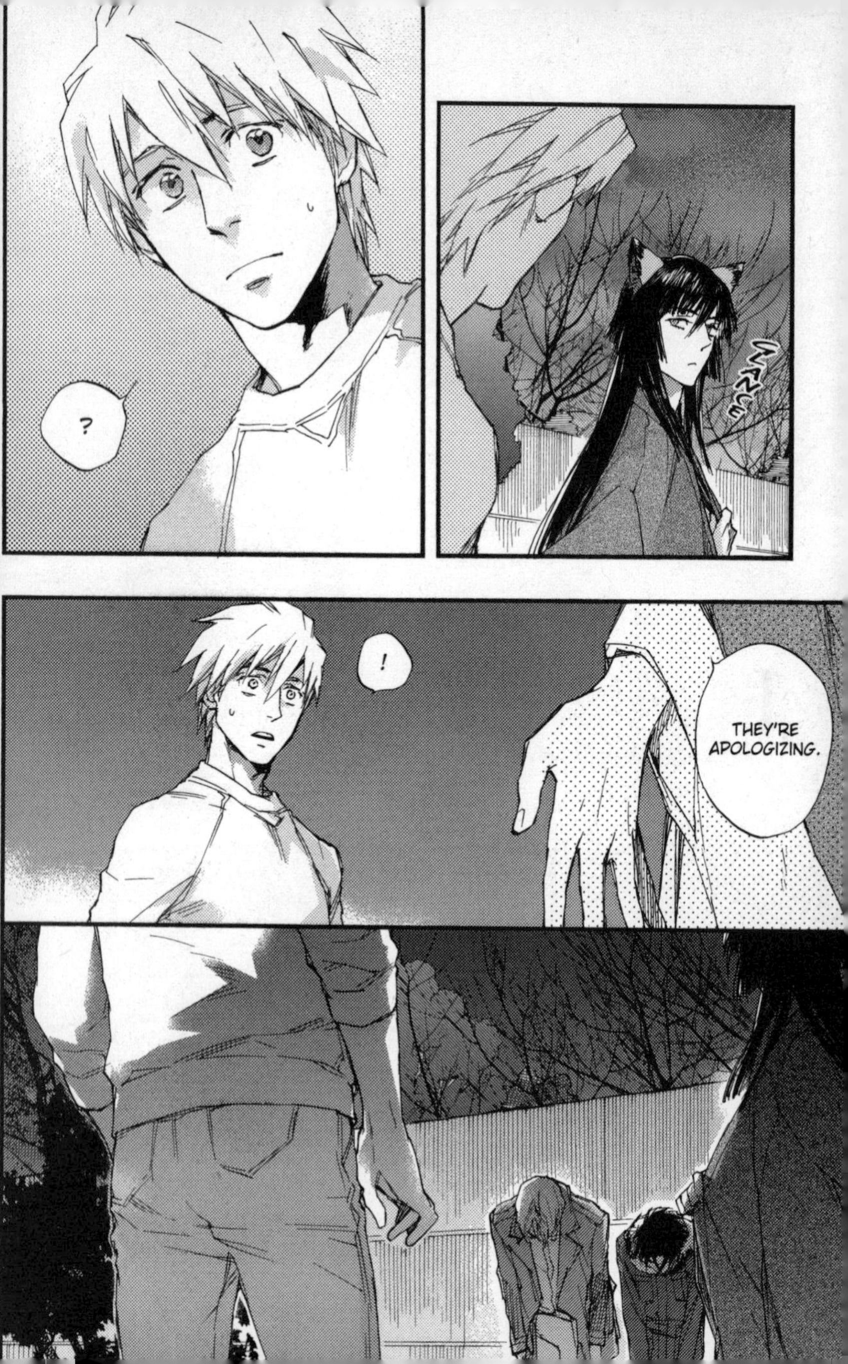
GLANCE
?
THEY'RE APOLOGIZING.
!

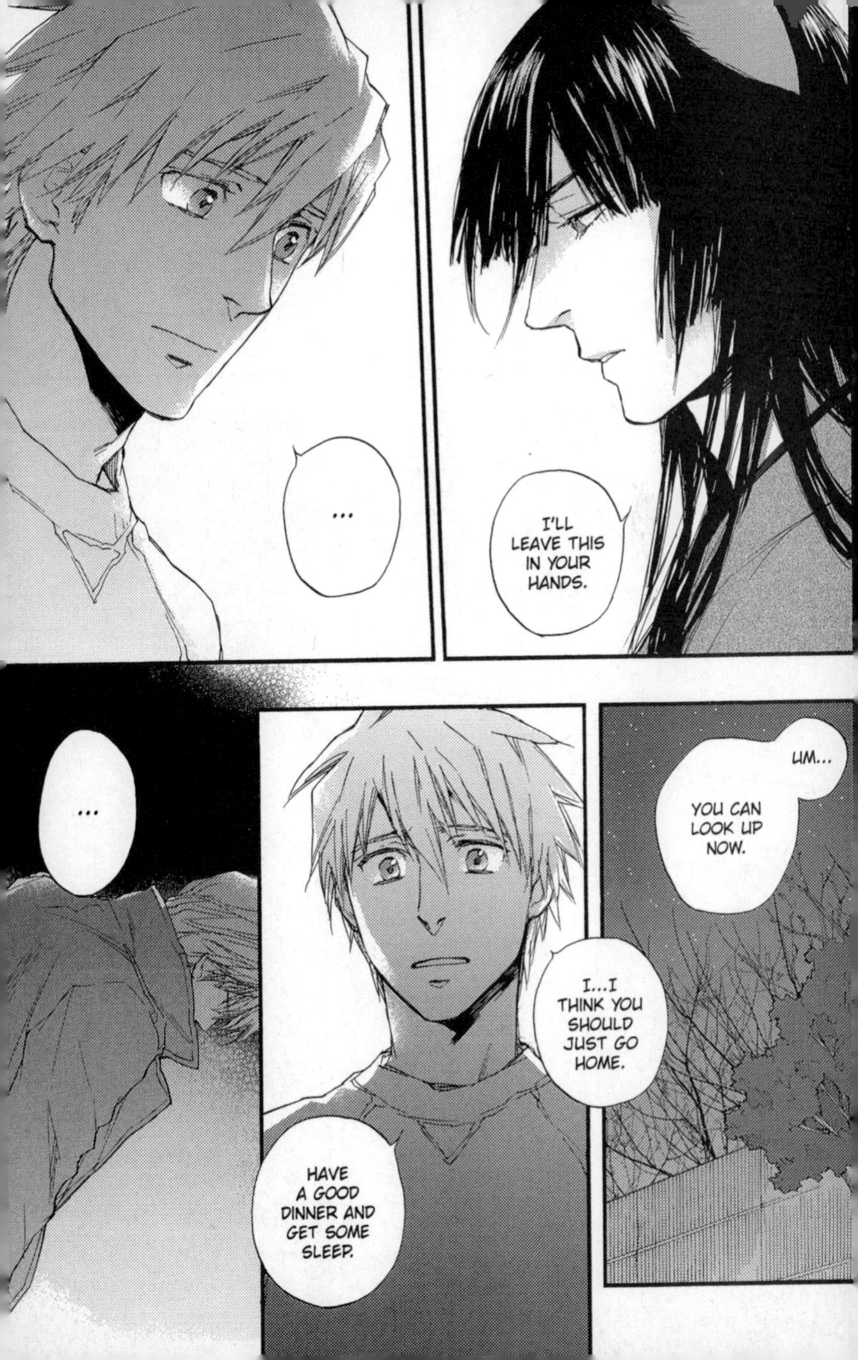
I'LL LEAVE THIS IN YOUR HANDS.
...
UM...
YOU CAN LOOK UP NOW.
I...I THINK YOU SHOULD JUST GO HOME.
HAVE A GOOD DINNER AND GET SOME SLEEP.
...

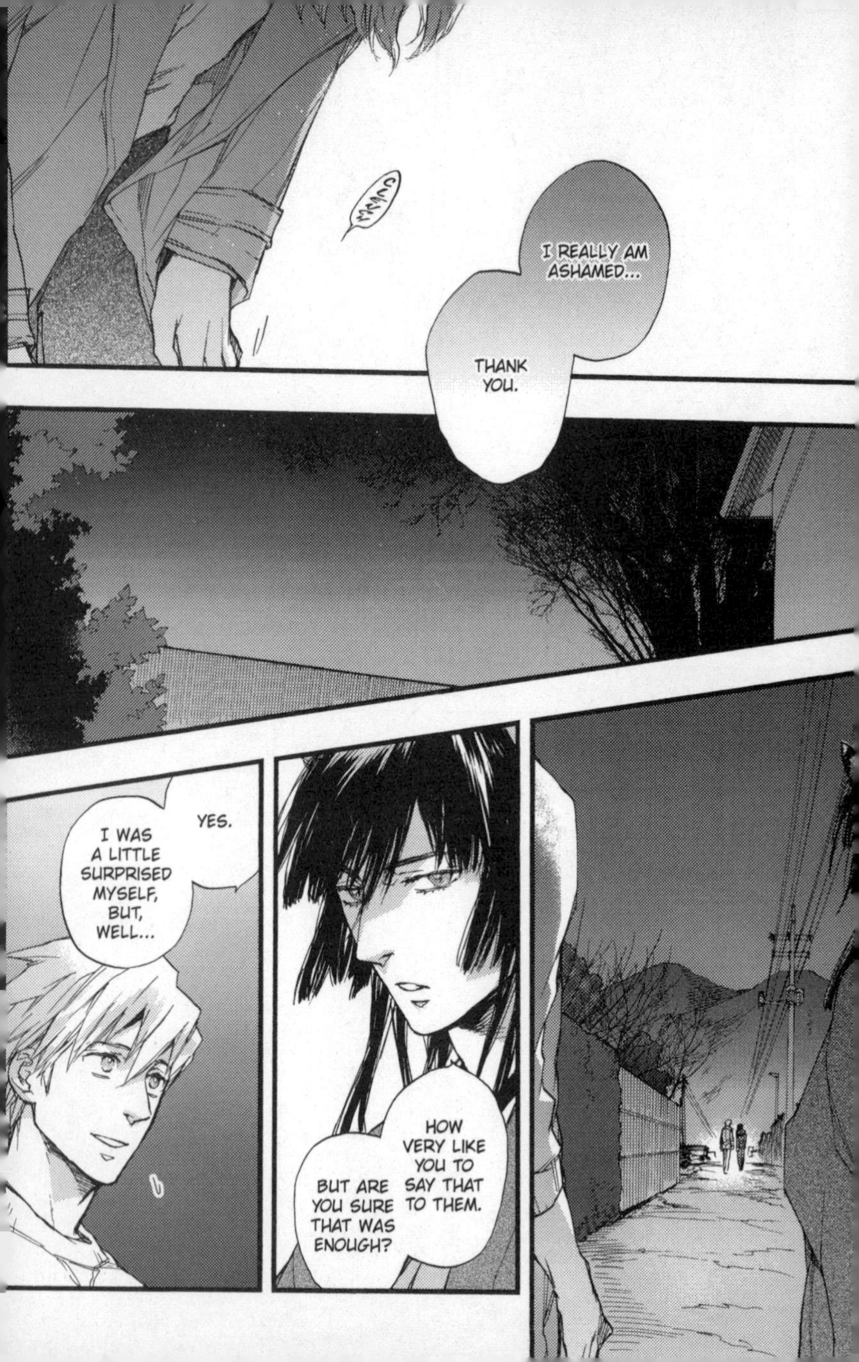
I REALLY AM ASHAMED...
THANK YOU.
HOW VERY LIKE YOU TO SAY THAT TO THEM.
BUT ARE YOU SURE THAT WAS ENOUGH?
YES.
I WAS A LITTLE SURPRISED MYSELF, BUT, WELL...

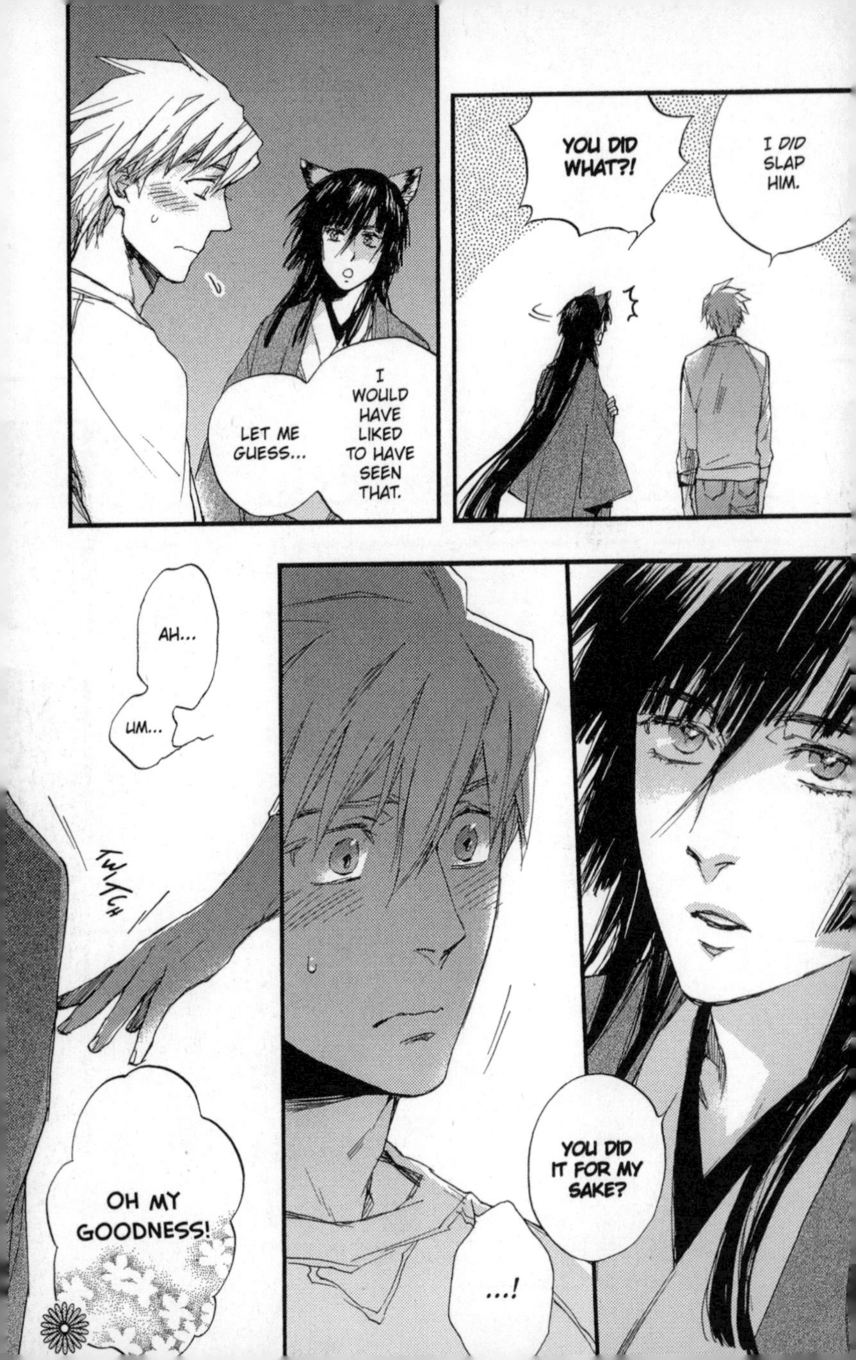
I DID SLAP HIM.
YOU DID WHAT?!
I WOULD HAVE LIKED TO HAVE SEEN THAT.
LET ME GUESS...
YOU DID IT FOR MY SAKE?
...!
AH...
UM...
TWITCH
OH MY GOODNESS!

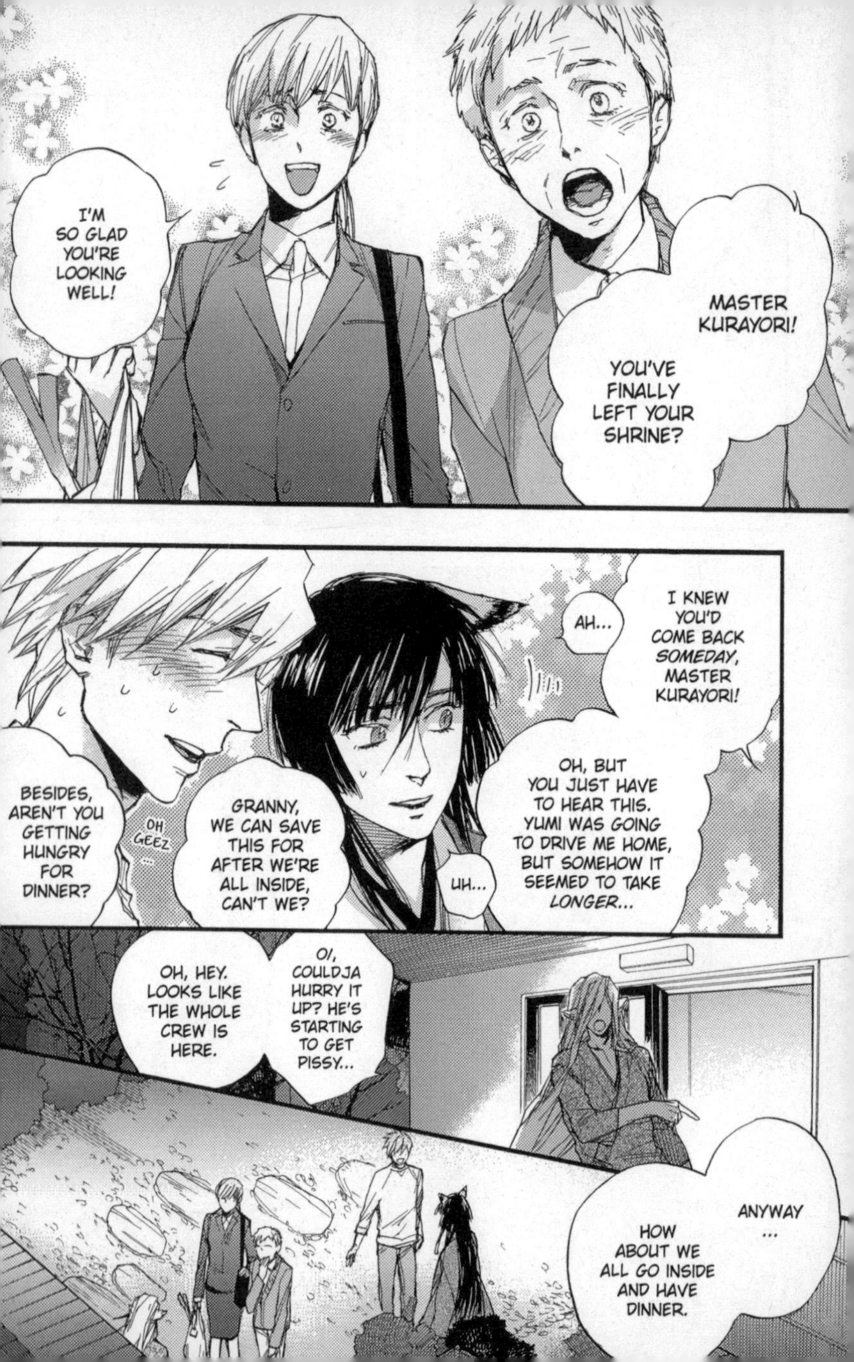
MASTER KURAYORI!
YOU'VE FINALLY LEFT YOUR SHRINE?
I'M SO GLAD YOU'RE LOOKING WELL!
I KNEW YOU'D COME BACK *SOMEDAY*, MASTER KURAYORI!
AH...
OH, BUT YOU JUST HAVE TO HEAR THIS. YUMI WAS GOING TO DRIVE ME HOME, BUT SOMEHOW IT SEEMED TO TAKE *LONGER*...
UH...
GRANNY, WE CAN SAVE THIS FOR AFTER WE'RE ALL INSIDE, CAN'T WE?
OH GEEZ...
BESIDES, AREN'T YOU GETTING HUNGRY FOR DINNER?
OI, COULDJA HURRY IT UP? HE'S STARTING TO GET PISSY...
OH, HEY. LOOKS LIKE THE WHOLE CREW IS HERE.
ANYWAY...
HOW ABOUT WE ALL GO INSIDE AND HAVE DINNER.

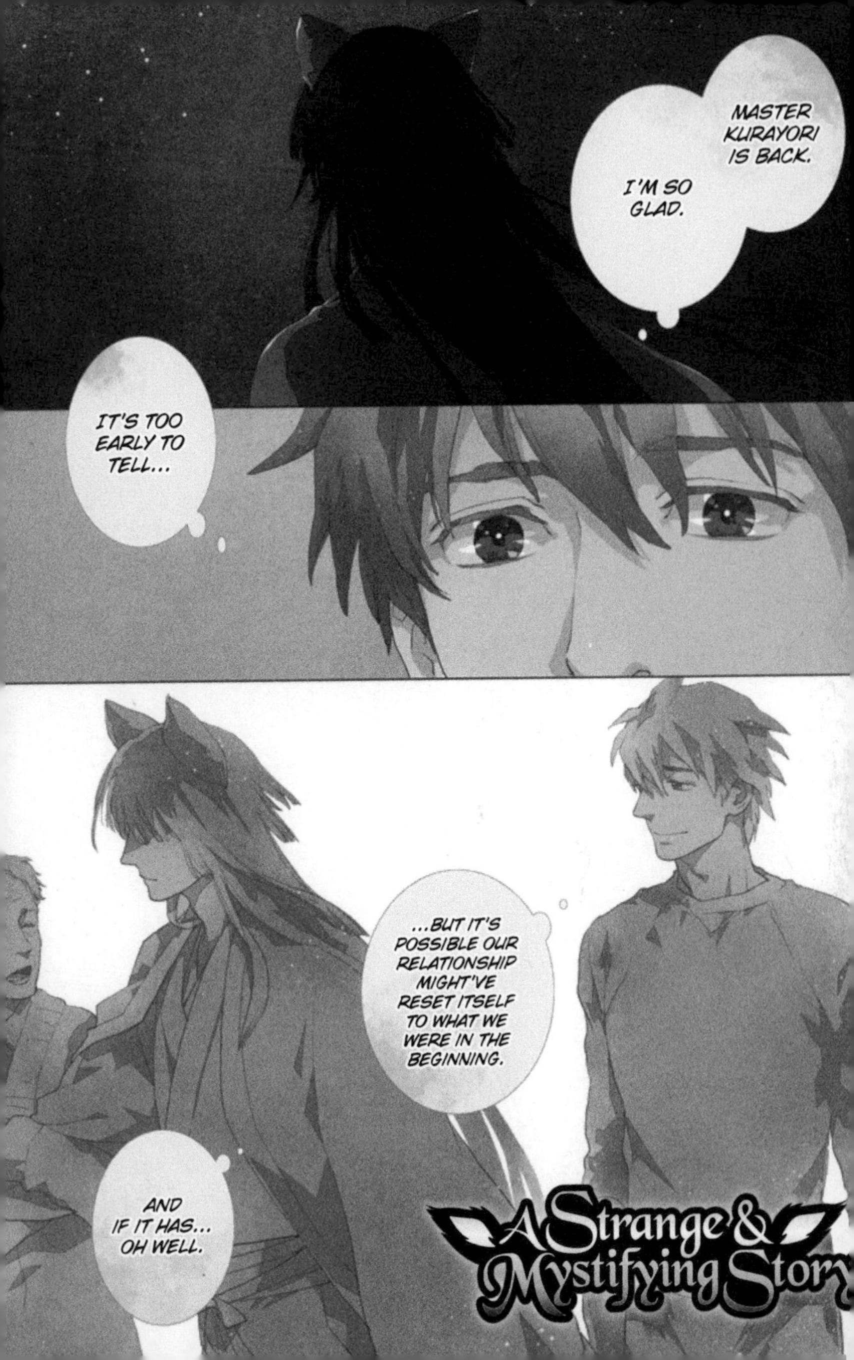
MASTER KURAYORI IS BACK.
I'M SO GLAD.
IT'S TOO EARLY TO TELL...
...BUT IT'S POSSIBLE OUR RELATIONSHIP MIGHT'VE RESET ITSELF TO WHAT WE WERE IN THE BEGINNING.
AND IF IT HAS... OH WELL.
A Strange & Mystifying Story

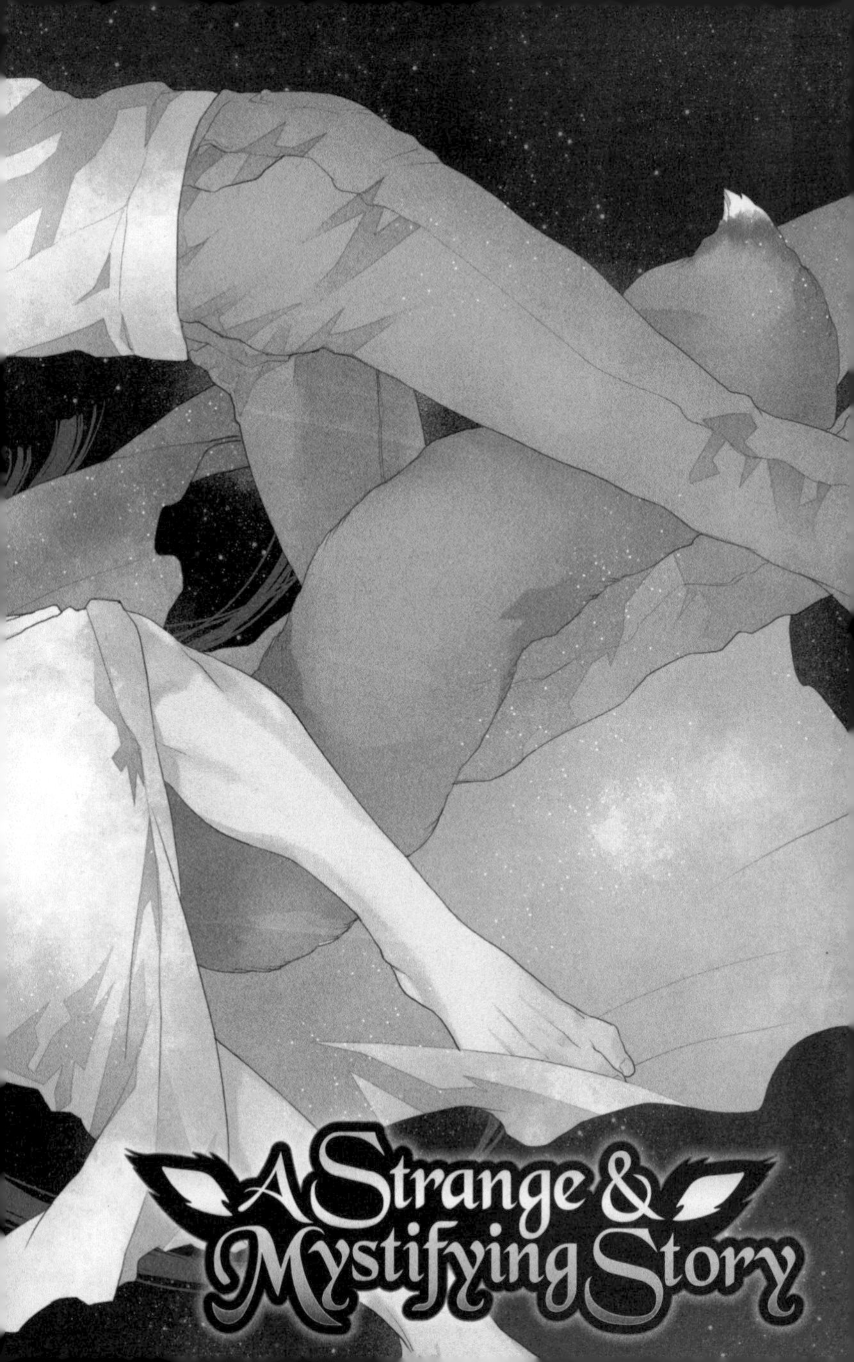
A Strange &
Mystifying Story

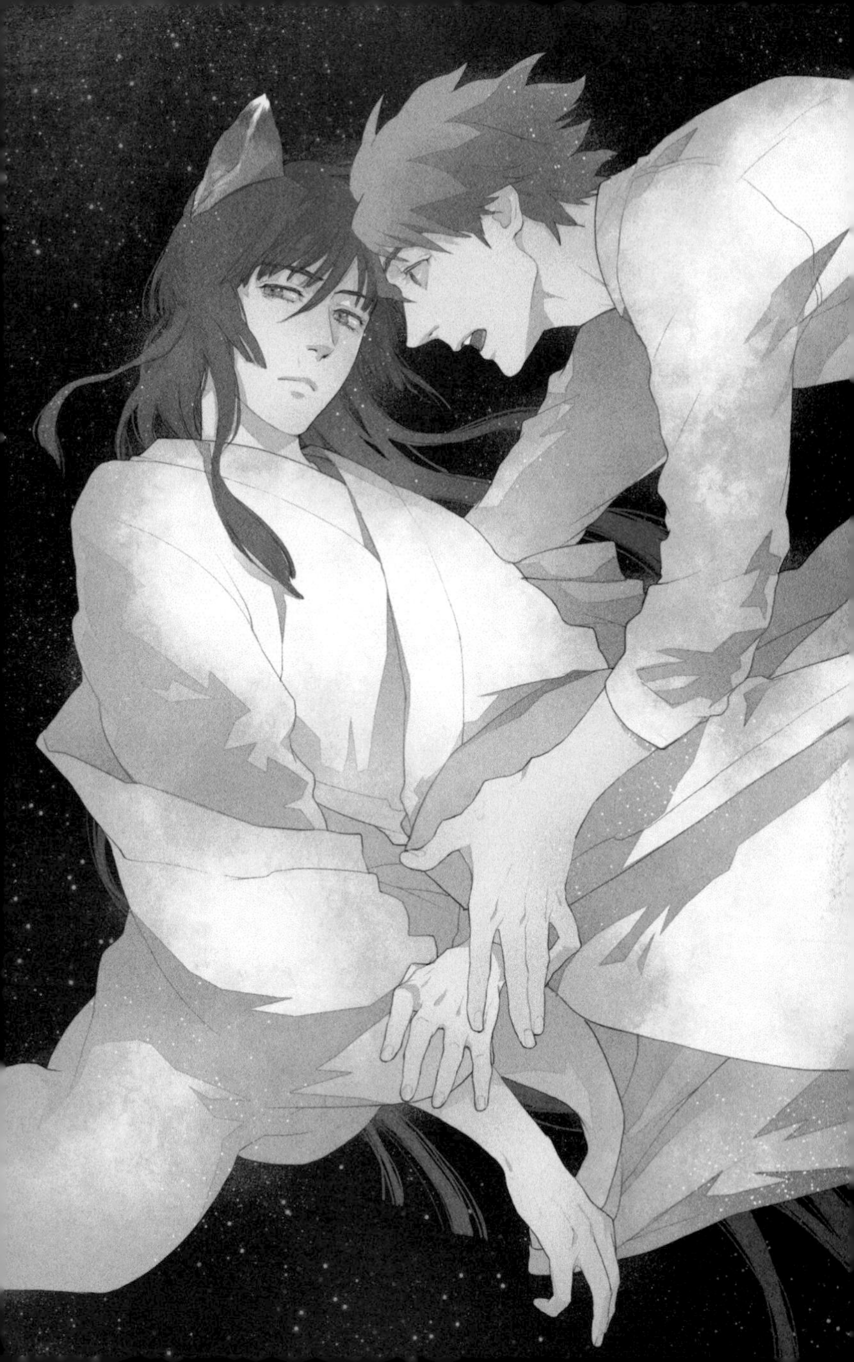

A Strange & Mystifying Story

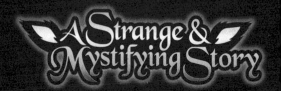

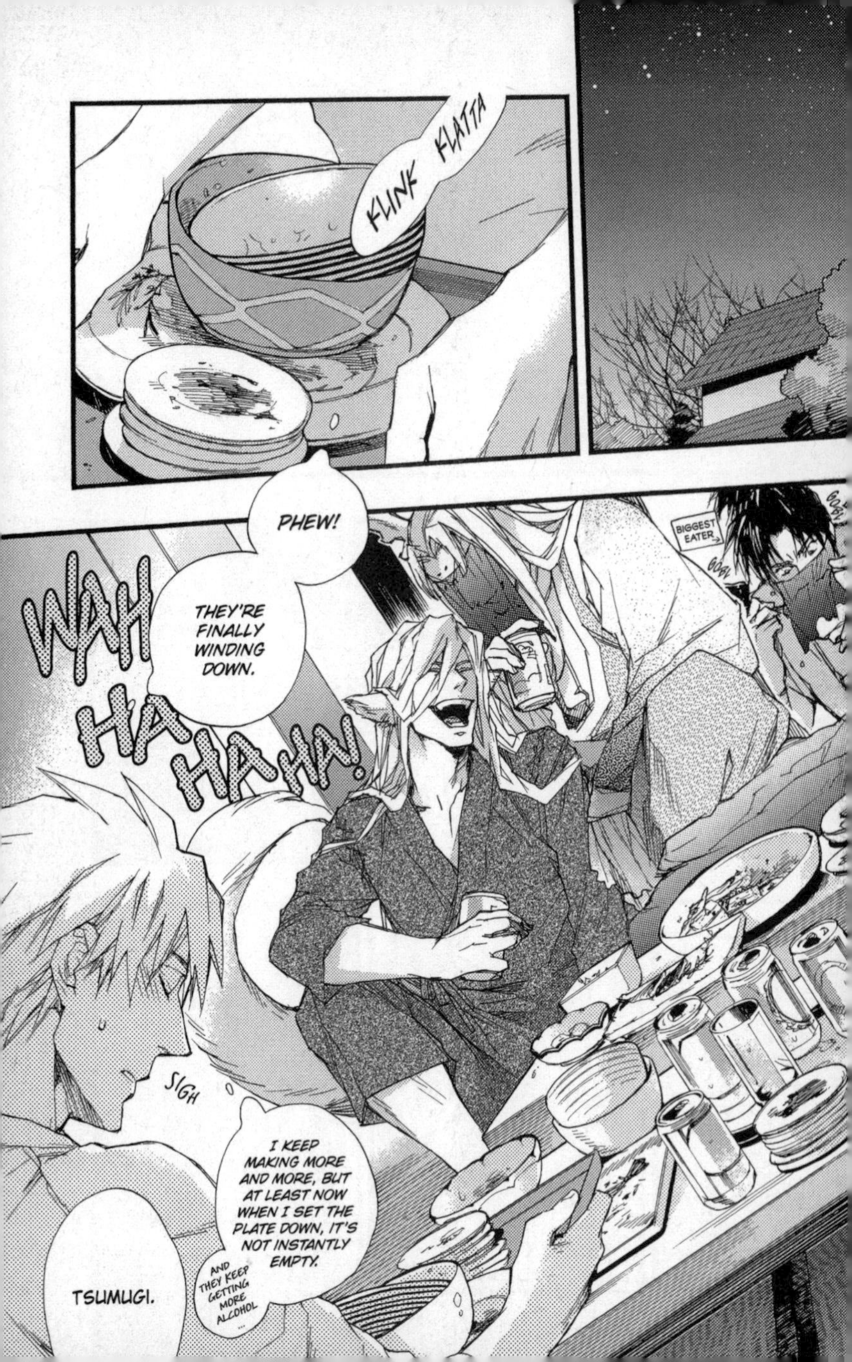
KLINK KLATTA
GOBL
GOBL
BIGGEST EATER
PHEW!
THEY'RE FINALLY WINDING DOWN.
WAH HA HA HA!
SIGH
I KEEP MAKING MORE AND MORE, BUT AT LEAST NOW WHEN I SET THE PLATE DOWN, IT'S NOT INSTANTLY EMPTY.
AND THEY KEEP GETTING MORE ALCOHOL...
TSUMUGI.

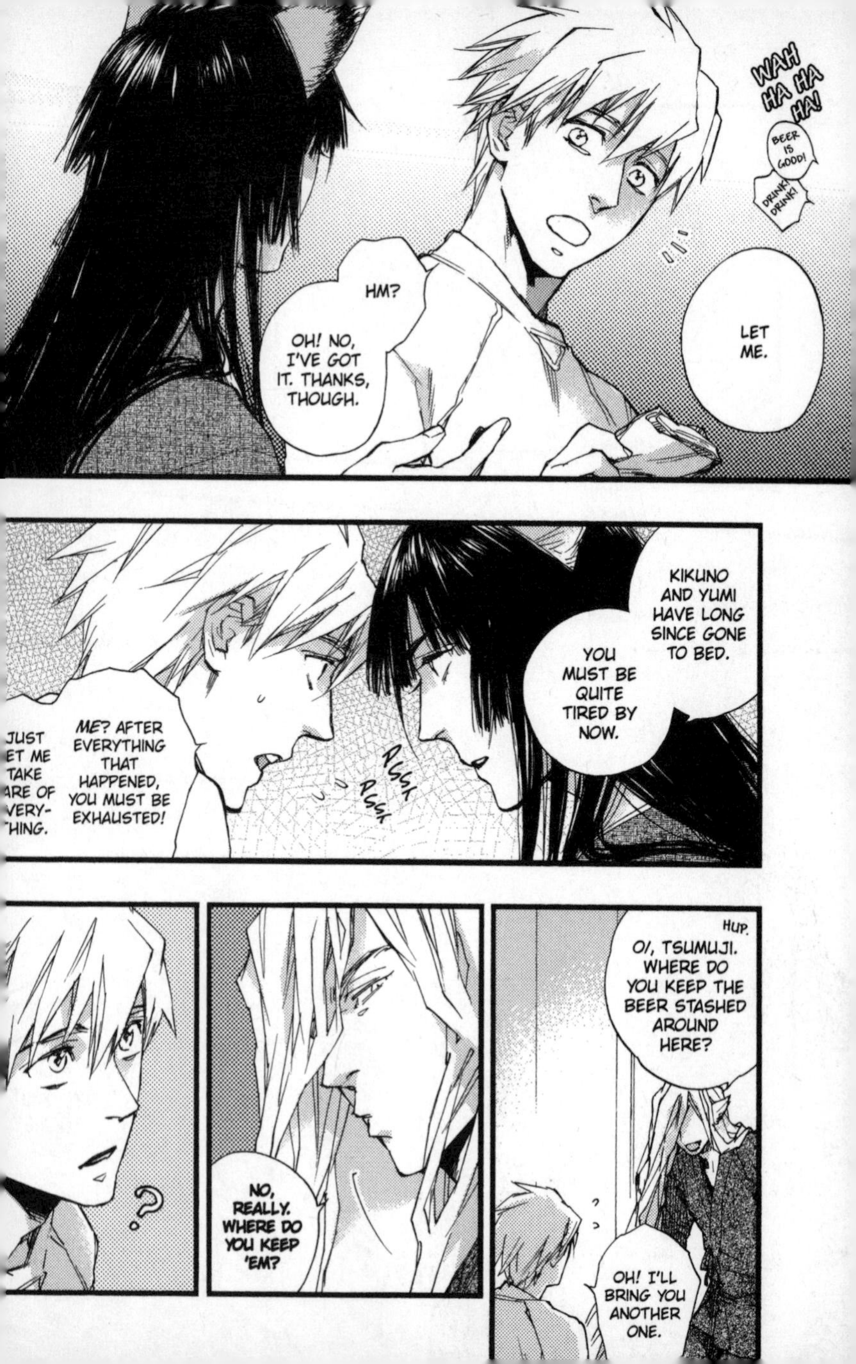
WAH HA HA HA!
BEER IS GOOD!
DRINK! DRINK!
LET ME.
HM?
OH! NO, I'VE GOT IT. THANKS, THOUGH.
KIKUNO AND YUMI HAVE LONG SINCE GONE TO BED.
YOU MUST BE QUITE TIRED BY NOW.
RSSK RSSK
ME? AFTER EVERYTHING THAT HAPPENED, YOU MUST BE EXHAUSTED!
JUST ET ME TAKE ARE OF VERY- THING.
HUP.
OI, TSUMUJI. WHERE DO YOU KEEP THE BEER STASHED AROUND HERE?
OH! I'LL BRING YOU ANOTHER ONE.
NO, REALLY. WHERE DO YOU KEEP 'EM?
?

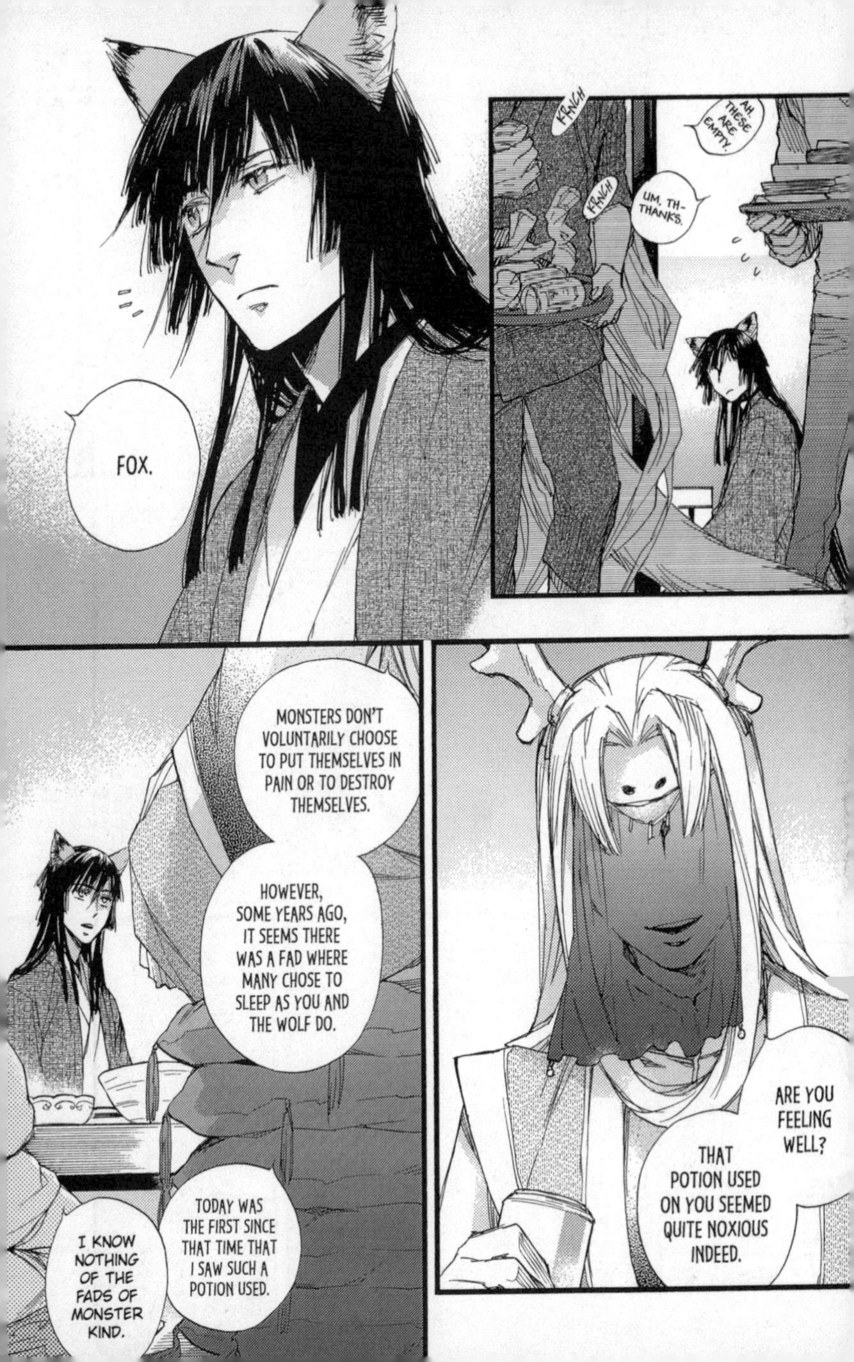
AH, THESE ARE EMPTY.
KRNCH
UM, TH-THANKS.
KRNCH
FOX.
ARE YOU FEELING WELL?
THAT POTION USED ON YOU SEEMED QUITE NOXIOUS INDEED.
MONSTERS DON'T VOLUNTARILY CHOOSE TO PUT THEMSELVES IN PAIN OR TO DESTROY THEMSELVES.
HOWEVER, SOME YEARS AGO, IT SEEMS THERE WAS A FAD WHERE MANY CHOSE TO SLEEP AS YOU AND THE WOLF DO.
TODAY WAS THE FIRST SINCE THAT TIME THAT I SAW SUCH A POTION USED.
I KNOW NOTHING OF THE FADS OF MONSTER KIND.

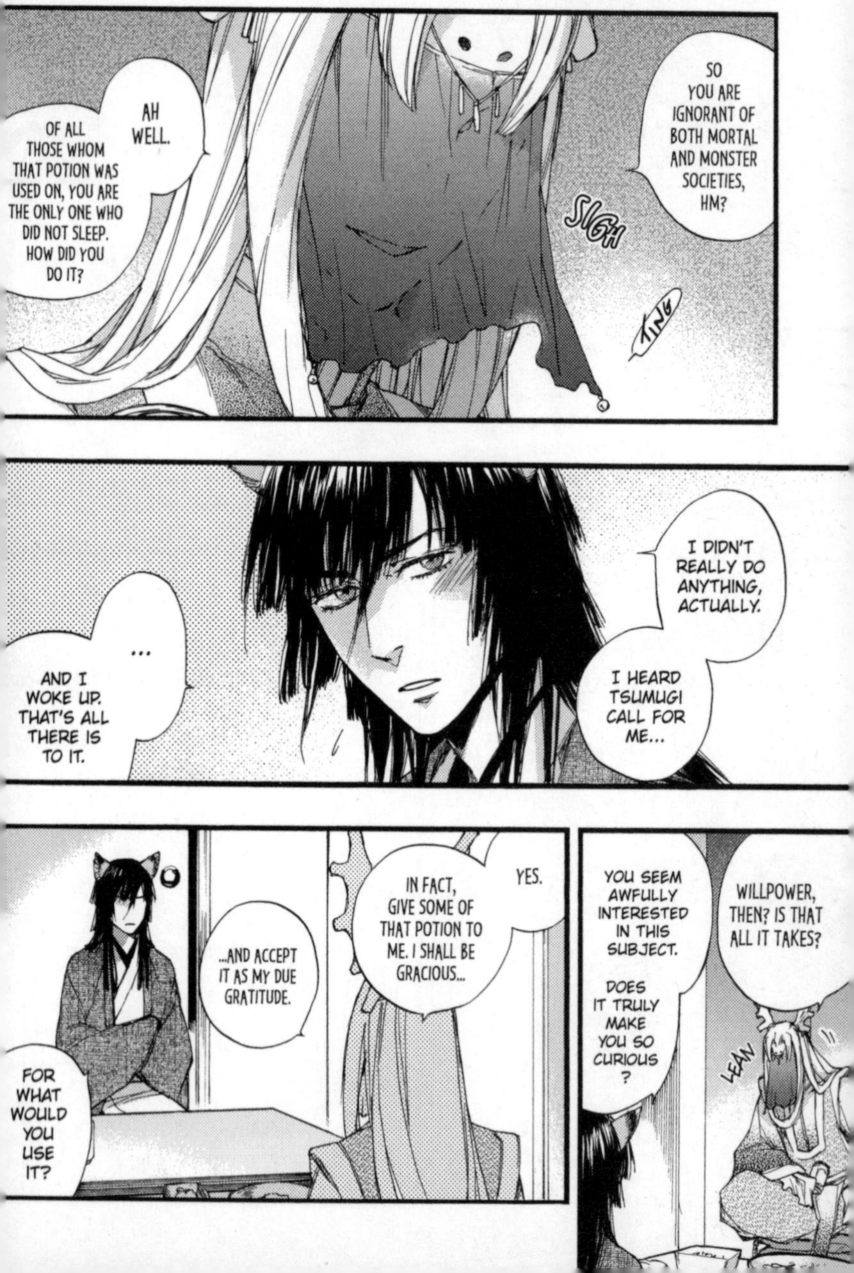
SO YOU ARE IGNORANT OF BOTH MORTAL AND MONSTER SOCIETIES, HM?
SIGH
TING
AH WELL.
OF ALL THOSE WHOM THAT POTION WAS USED ON, YOU ARE THE ONLY ONE WHO DID NOT SLEEP. HOW DID YOU DO IT?
I DIDN'T REALLY DO ANYTHING, ACTUALLY.
I HEARD TSUMUGI CALL FOR ME...
...
AND I WOKE UP. THAT'S ALL THERE IS TO IT.
WILLPOWER, THEN? IS THAT ALL IT TAKES?
LEAN
YOU SEEM AWFULLY INTERESTED IN THIS SUBJECT.
DOES IT TRULY MAKE YOU SO CURIOUS?
YES.
IN FACT, GIVE SOME OF THAT POTION TO ME. I SHALL BE GRACIOUS...
...AND ACCEPT IT AS MY DUE GRATITUDE.
FOR WHAT WOULD YOU USE IT?

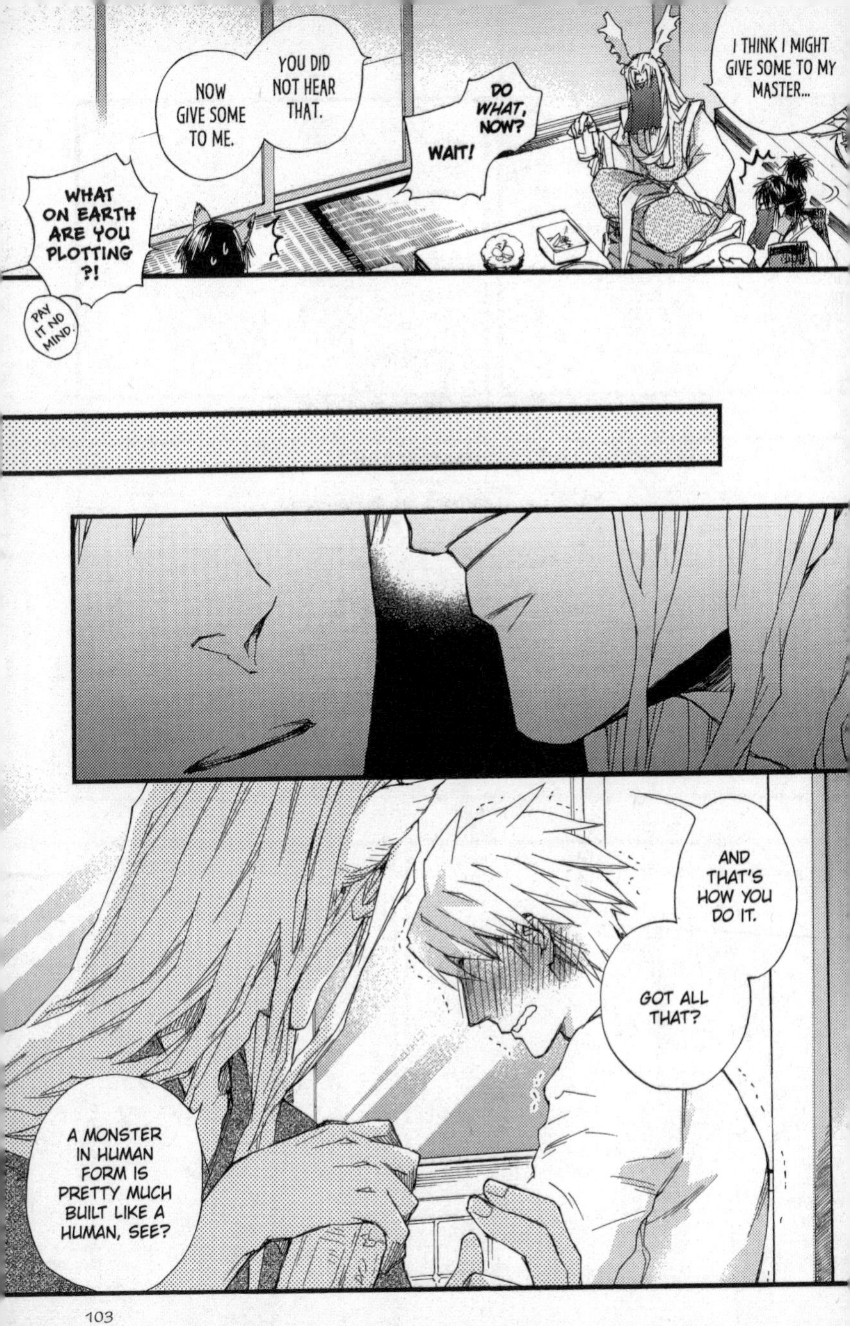
I THINK I MIGHT GIVE SOME TO MY MASTER...
DO WHAT, NOW?
WAIT!
YOU DID NOT HEAR THAT.
NOW GIVE SOME TO ME.
WHAT ON EARTH ARE YOU PLOTTING ?!
PAY IT NO MIND.
AND THAT'S HOW YOU DO IT.
GOT ALL THAT?
A MONSTER IN HUMAN FORM IS PRETTY MUCH BUILT LIKE A HUMAN, SEE?

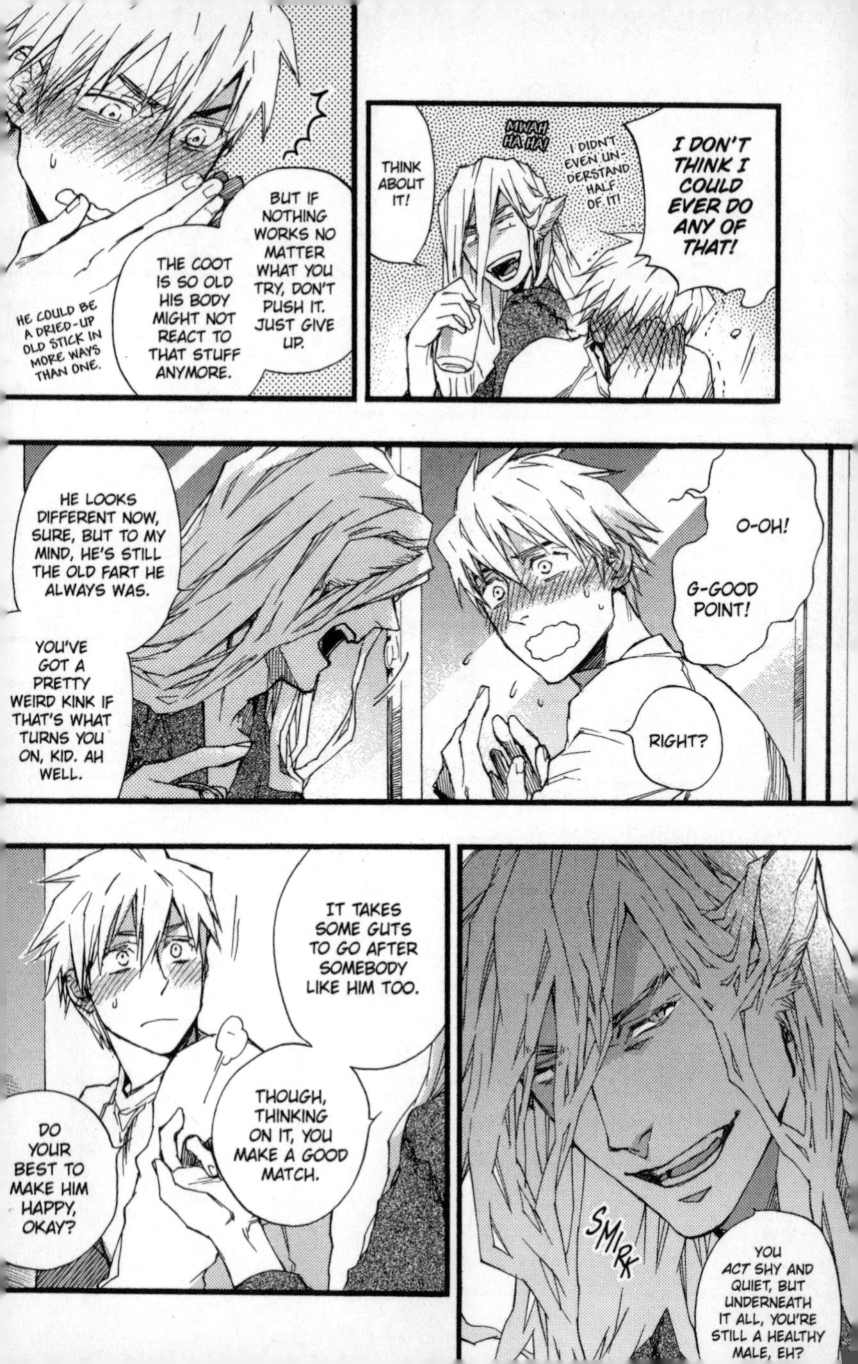
I DON'T THINK I COULD EVER DO ANY OF THAT!
I DIDN'T EVEN UNDERSTAND HALF OF IT!
MWAH HA HA!
THINK ABOUT IT!
BUT IF NOTHING WORKS NO MATTER WHAT YOU TRY, DON'T PUSH IT. JUST GIVE UP.
THE COOT IS SO OLD HIS BODY MIGHT NOT REACT TO THAT STUFF ANYMORE.
HE COULD BE A DRIED-UP OLD STICK IN MORE WAYS THAN ONE.
O-OH!
G-GOOD POINT!
RIGHT?
HE LOOKS DIFFERENT NOW, SURE, BUT TO MY MIND, HE'S STILL THE OLD FART HE ALWAYS WAS.
YOU'VE GOT A PRETTY WEIRD KINK IF THAT'S WHAT TURNS YOU ON, KID. AH WELL.
SMIRK
YOU ACT SHY AND QUIET, BUT UNDERNEATH IT ALL, YOU'RE STILL A HEALTHY MALE, EH?
IT TAKES SOME GUTS TO GO AFTER SOMEBODY LIKE HIM TOO.
THOUGH, THINKING ON IT, YOU MAKE A GOOD MATCH.
DO YOUR BEST TO MAKE HIM HAPPY, OKAY?

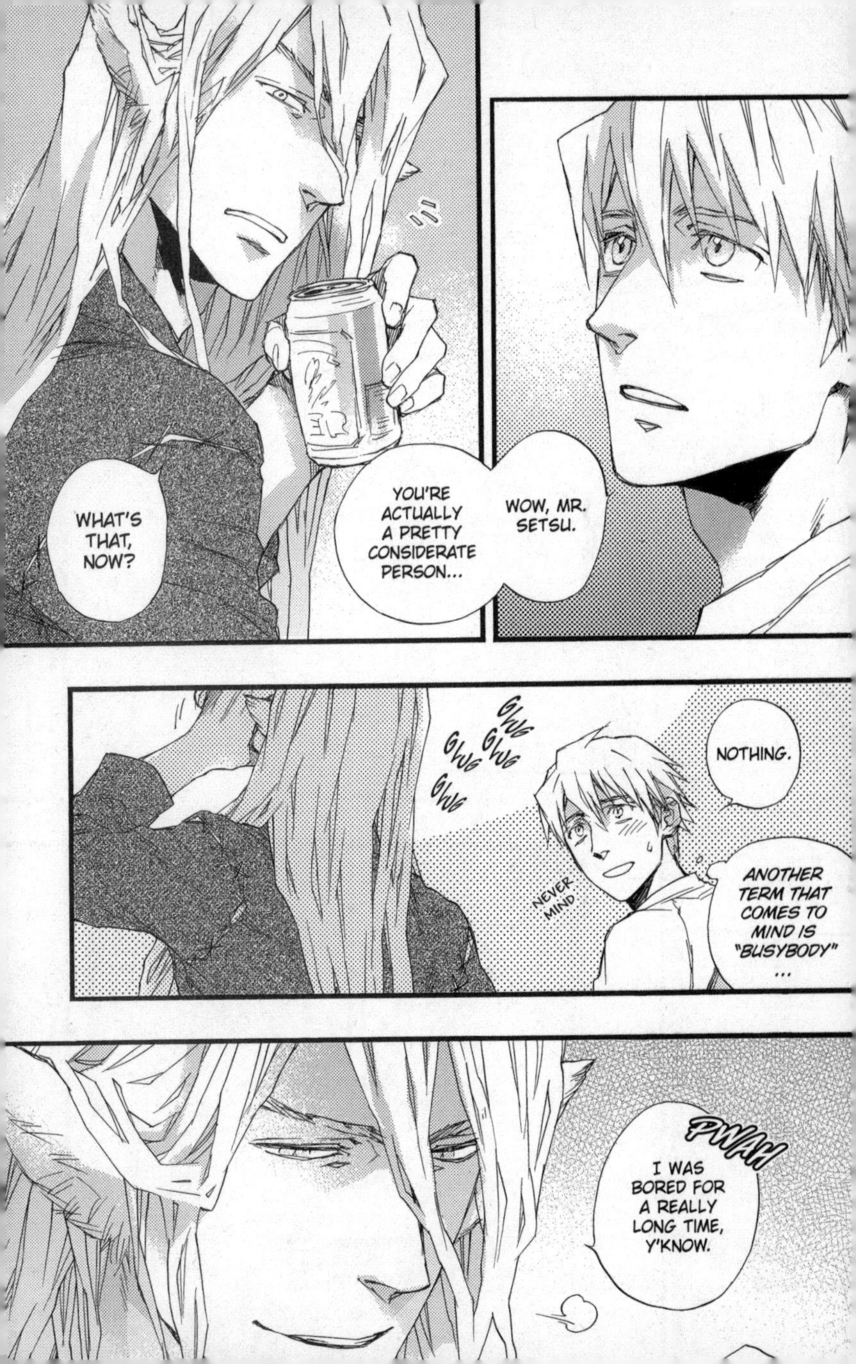
WOW, MR. SETSU.
YOU'RE ACTUALLY A PRETTY CONSIDERATE PERSON...
WHAT'S THAT, NOW?
NOTHING.
GLUG GLUG GLUG GLUG
ANOTHER TERM THAT COMES TO MIND IS "BUSYBODY"...
NEVER MIND
PWAH
I WAS BORED FOR A REALLY LONG TIME, Y'KNOW.

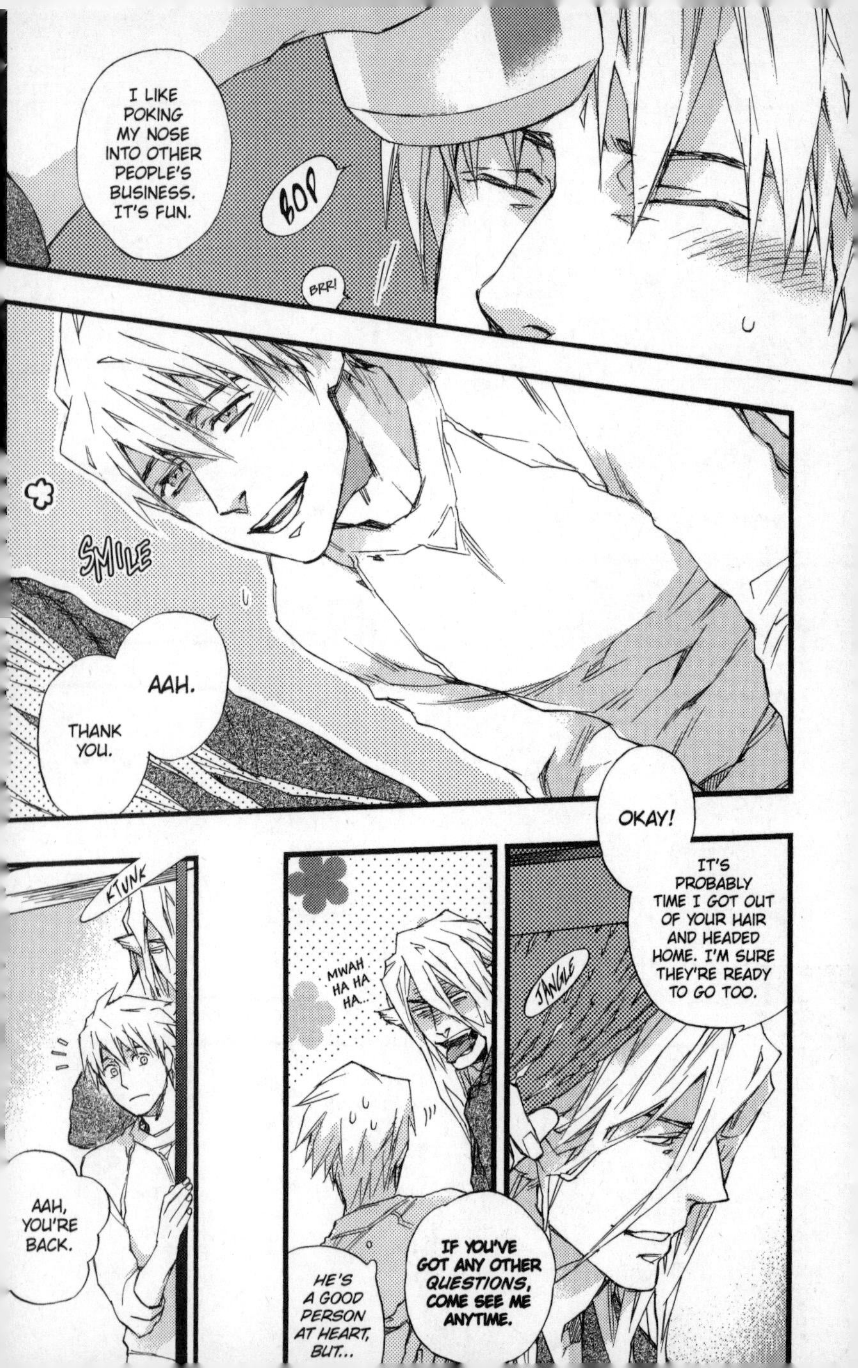
I LIKE POKING MY NOSE INTO OTHER PEOPLE'S BUSINESS. IT'S FUN.
BOP
BRR!
SMILE
AAH.
THANK YOU.
OKAY!
IT'S PROBABLY TIME I GOT OUT OF YOUR HAIR AND HEADED HOME. I'M SURE THEY'RE READY TO GO TOO.
JANGLE
IF YOU'VE GOT ANY OTHER QUESTIONS, COME SEE ME ANYTIME.
MWAH HA HA HA...
HE'S A GOOD PERSON AT HEART, BUT...
KTUNK
AAH, YOU'RE BACK.

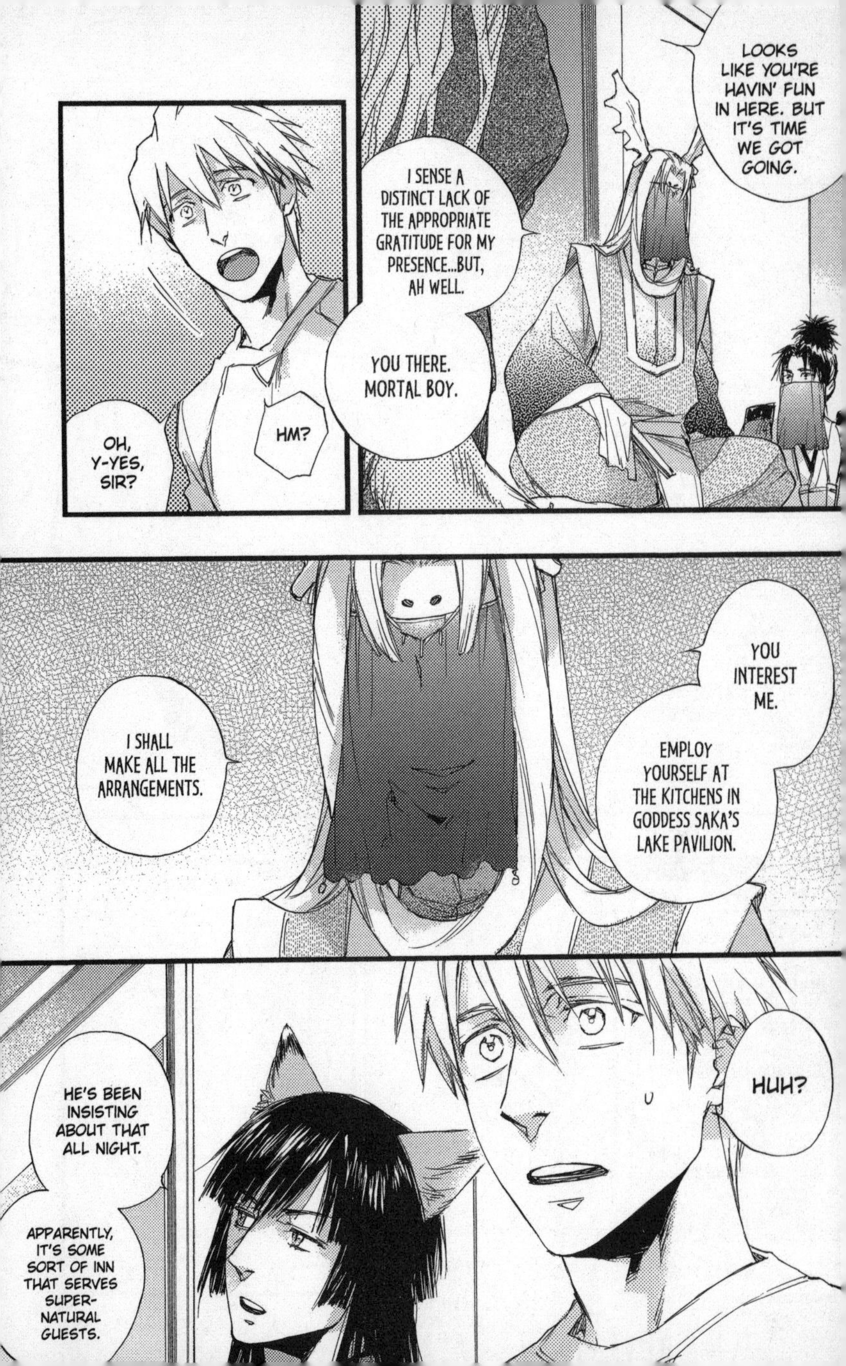
LOOKS LIKE YOU'RE HAVIN' FUN IN HERE. BUT IT'S TIME WE GOT GOING.
I SENSE A DISTINCT LACK OF THE APPROPRIATE GRATITUDE FOR MY PRESENCE...BUT, AH WELL.
YOU THERE. MORTAL BOY.
HM?
OH, Y-YES, SIR?
YOU INTEREST ME.
EMPLOY YOURSELF AT THE KITCHENS IN GODDESS SAKA'S LAKE PAVILION.
I SHALL MAKE ALL THE ARRANGEMENTS.
HUH?
HE'S BEEN INSISTING ABOUT THAT ALL NIGHT.
APPARENTLY, IT'S SOME SORT OF INN THAT SERVES SUPER-NATURAL GUESTS.

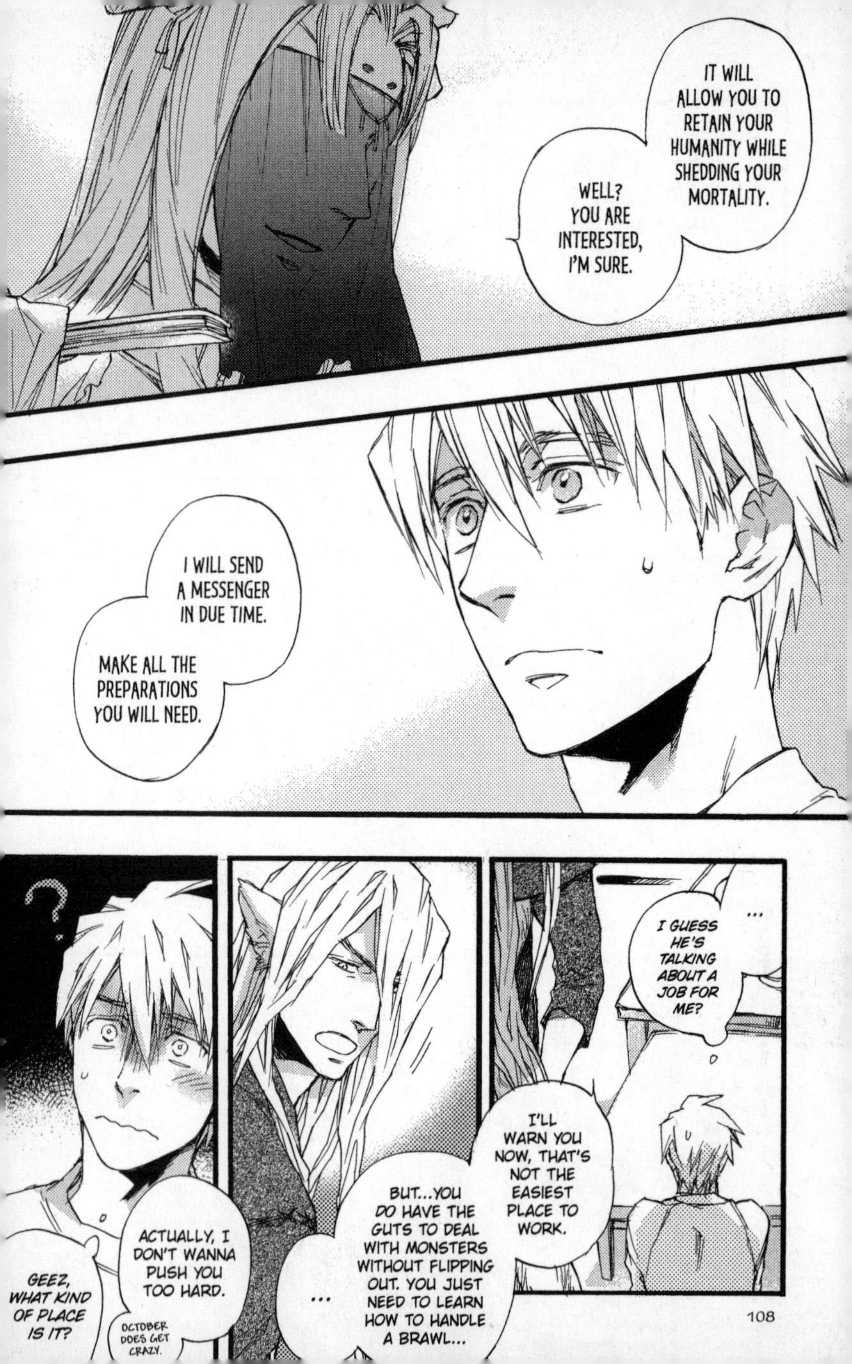
IT WILL ALLOW YOU TO RETAIN YOUR HUMANITY WHILE SHEDDING YOUR MORTALITY.
WELL? YOU ARE INTERESTED, I'M SURE.
I WILL SEND A MESSENGER IN DUE TIME.
MAKE ALL THE PREPARATIONS YOU WILL NEED.
...
I GUESS HE'S TALKING ABOUT A JOB FOR ME?
I'LL WARN YOU NOW, THAT'S NOT THE EASIEST PLACE TO WORK.
BUT...YOU DO HAVE THE GUTS TO DEAL WITH MONSTERS WITHOUT FLIPPING OUT. YOU JUST NEED TO LEARN HOW TO HANDLE A BRAWL...
...
?
ACTUALLY, I DON'T WANNA PUSH YOU TOO HARD.
OCTOBER DOES GET CRAZY.
GEEZ, WHAT KIND OF PLACE IS IT?

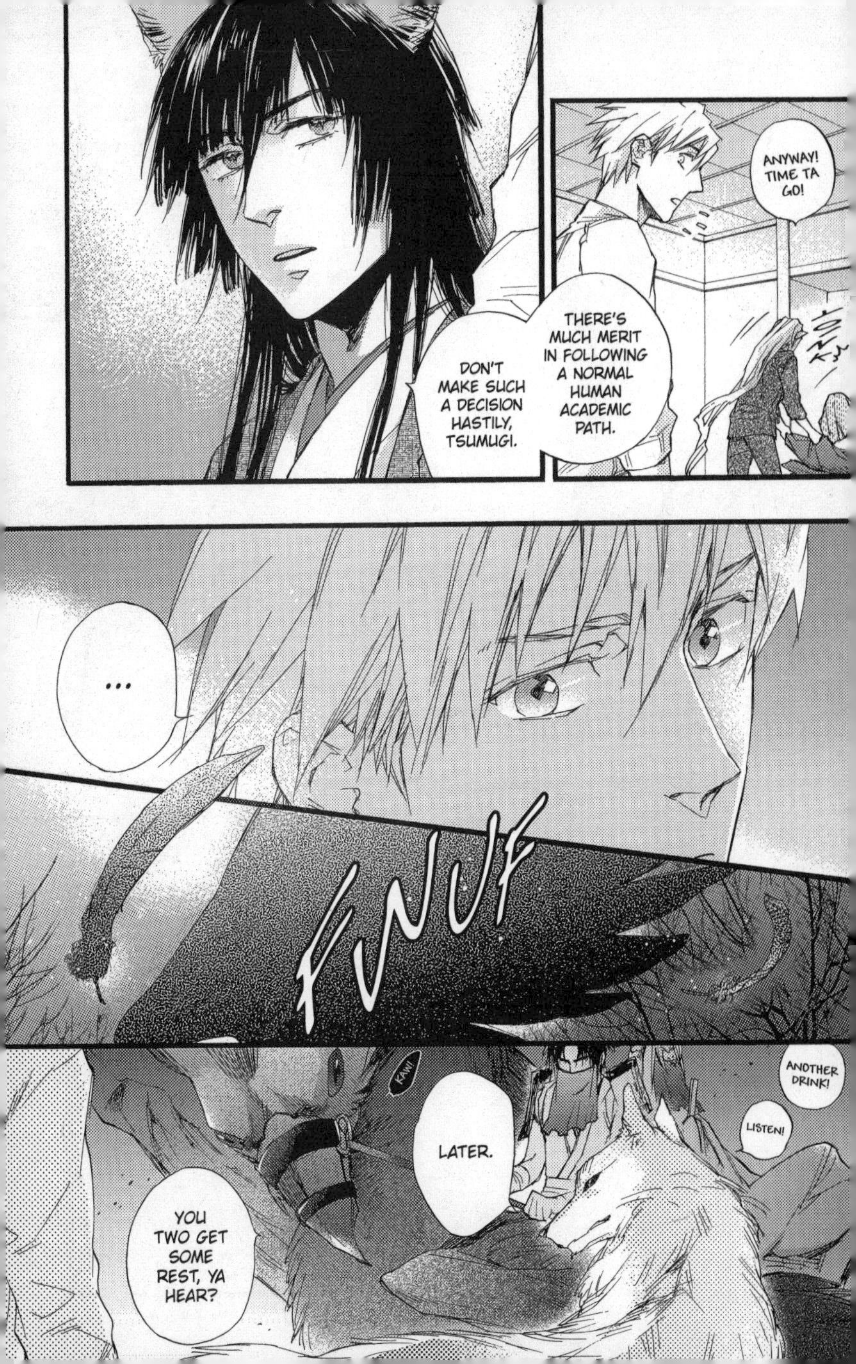
ANYWAY! TIME TA GO!
THERE'S MUCH MERIT IN FOLLOWING A NORMAL HUMAN ACADEMIC PATH.
DON'T MAKE SUCH A DECISION HASTILY, TSUMUGI.
...
FWUF
ANOTHER DRINK!
LISTEN!
KAW!
LATER.
YOU TWO GET SOME REST, YA HEAR?

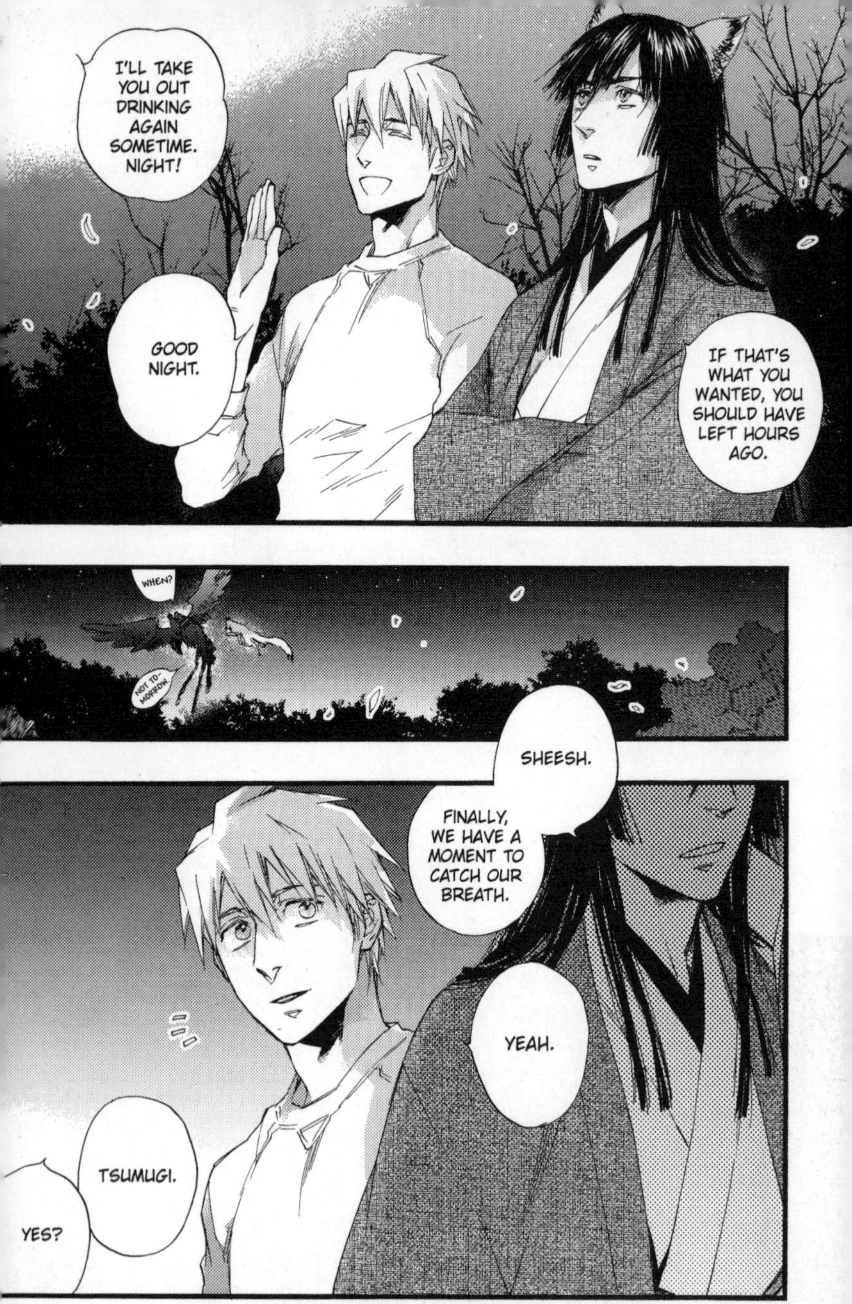
I'LL TAKE YOU OUT DRINKING AGAIN SOMETIME. NIGHT!
GOOD NIGHT.
IF THAT'S WHAT YOU WANTED, YOU SHOULD HAVE LEFT HOURS AGO.
WHEN?
NOT TO-MORROW.
SHEESH.
FINALLY, WE HAVE A MOMENT TO CATCH OUR BREATH.
YEAH.
TSUMUGI.
YES?

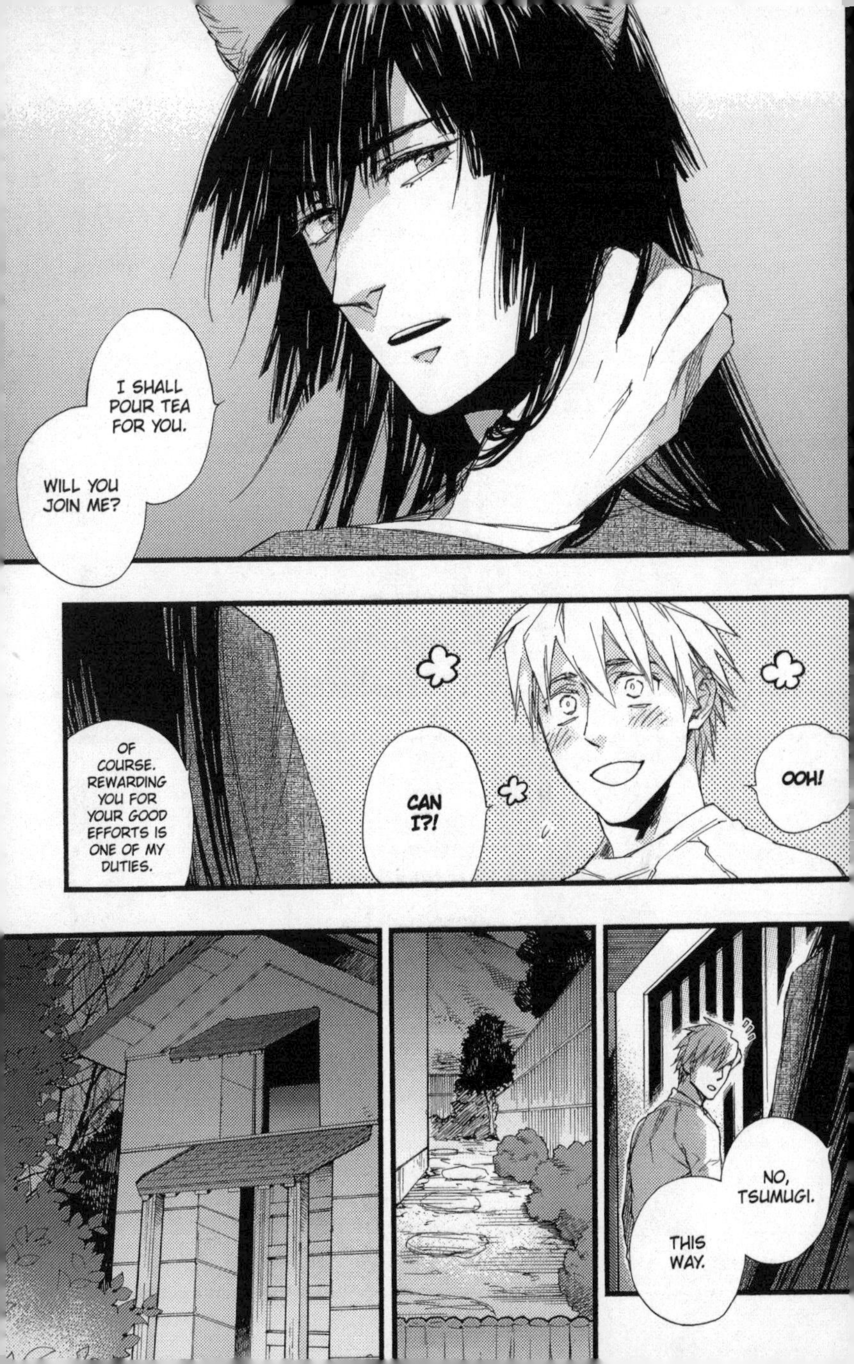
I SHALL POUR TEA FOR YOU.
WILL YOU JOIN ME?
OOH!
CAN I?!
OF COURSE. REWARDING YOU FOR YOUR GOOD EFFORTS IS ONE OF MY DUTIES.
NO, TSUMUGI.
THIS WAY.

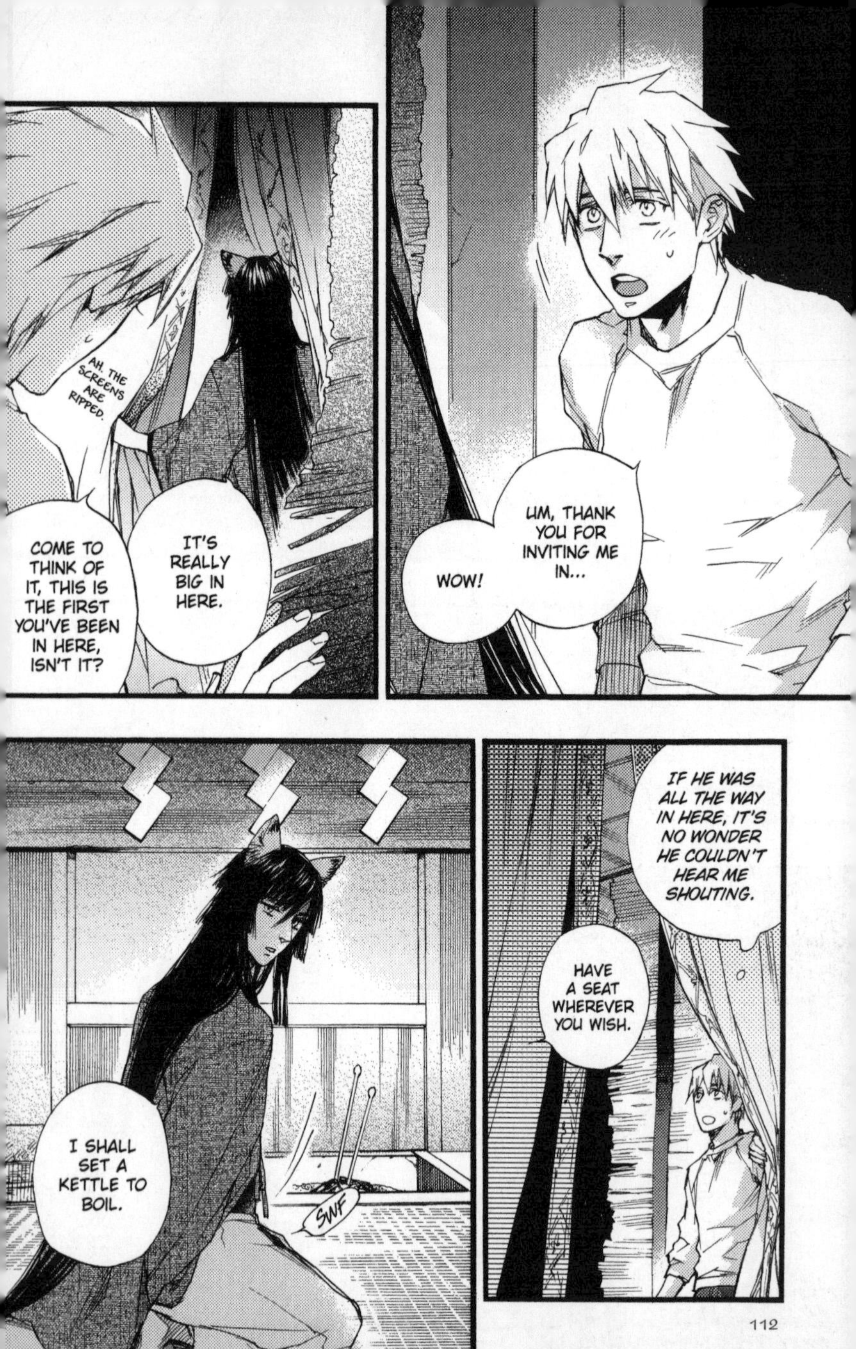
UM, THANK YOU FOR INVITING ME IN...
WOW!
AH. THE SCREENS ARE RIPPED.
IT'S REALLY BIG IN HERE.
COME TO THINK OF IT, THIS IS THE FIRST YOU'VE BEEN IN HERE, ISN'T IT?
IF HE WAS ALL THE WAY IN HERE, IT'S NO WONDER HE COULDN'T HEAR ME SHOUTING.
HAVE A SEAT WHEREVER YOU WISH.
I SHALL SET A KETTLE TO BOIL.
SWF

BOY, THE ATMOSPHERE IN HERE IS REALLY OLD-FASHIONED.

OH, UM, THANKS.

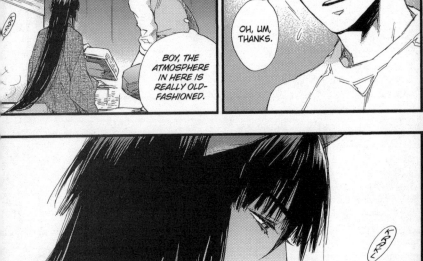

IT'S NICE... BUT IT'S QUITE DARK.

HOW MUCH TIME HAS HE SPENT ALONE IN HERE?

AND FOR HOW MANY GENERATIONS?

...

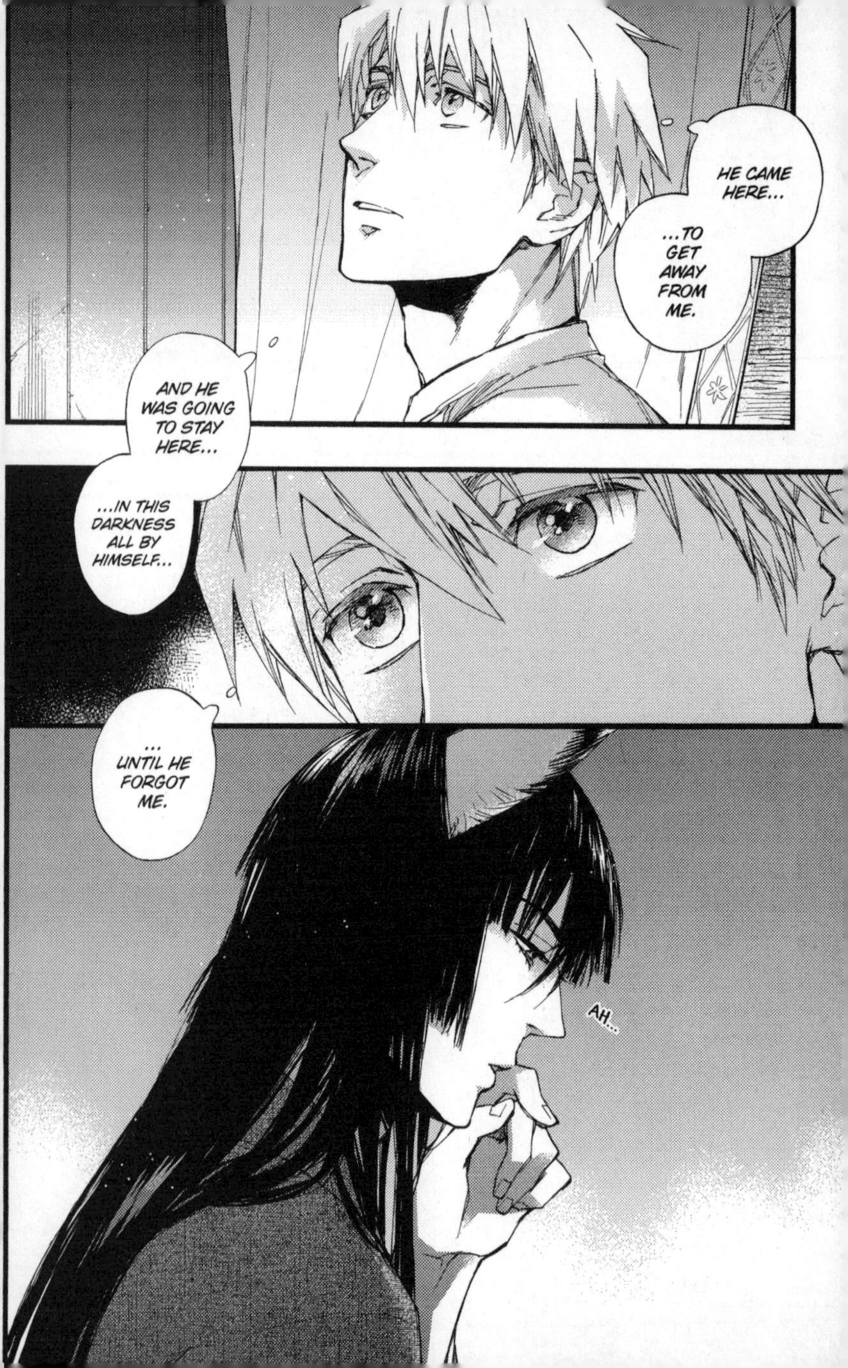
HE CAME HERE...
...TO GET AWAY FROM ME.
AND HE WAS GOING TO STAY HERE...
...IN THIS DARKNESS ALL BY HIMSELF...
... UNTIL HE FORGOT ME.
AH...

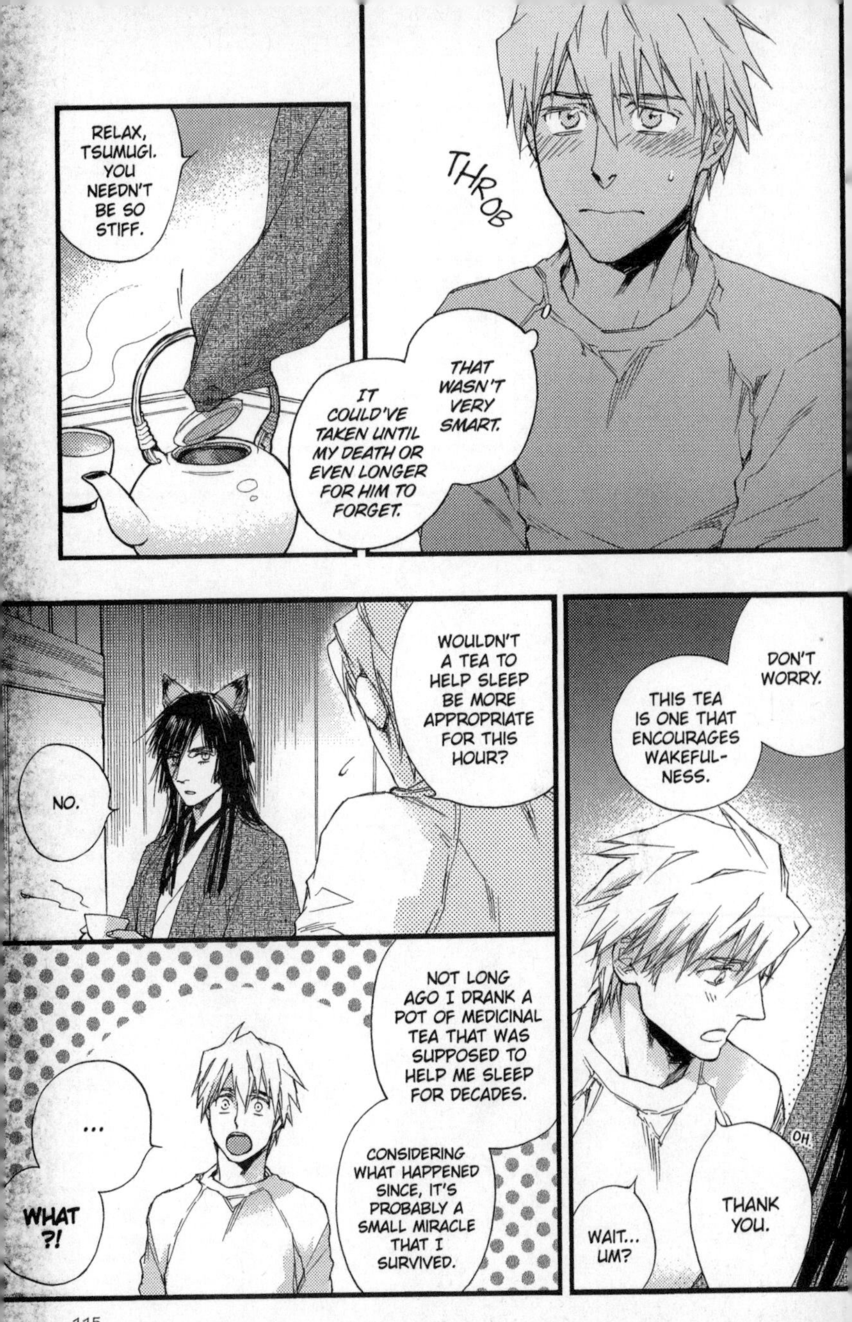
THROB
THAT WASN'T VERY SMART.
IT COULD'VE TAKEN UNTIL MY DEATH OR EVEN LONGER FOR HIM TO FORGET.
RELAX, TSUMUGI. YOU NEEDN'T BE SO STIFF.
DON'T WORRY.
THIS TEA IS ONE THAT ENCOURAGES WAKEFUL-NESS.
OH.
THANK YOU.
WAIT... UM?
WOULDN'T A TEA TO HELP SLEEP BE MORE APPROPRIATE FOR THIS HOUR?
NO.
NOT LONG AGO I DRANK A POT OF MEDICINAL TEA THAT WAS SUPPOSED TO HELP ME SLEEP FOR DECADES.
CONSIDERING WHAT HAPPENED SINCE, IT'S PROBABLY A SMALL MIRACLE THAT I SURVIVED.
...
WHAT ?!

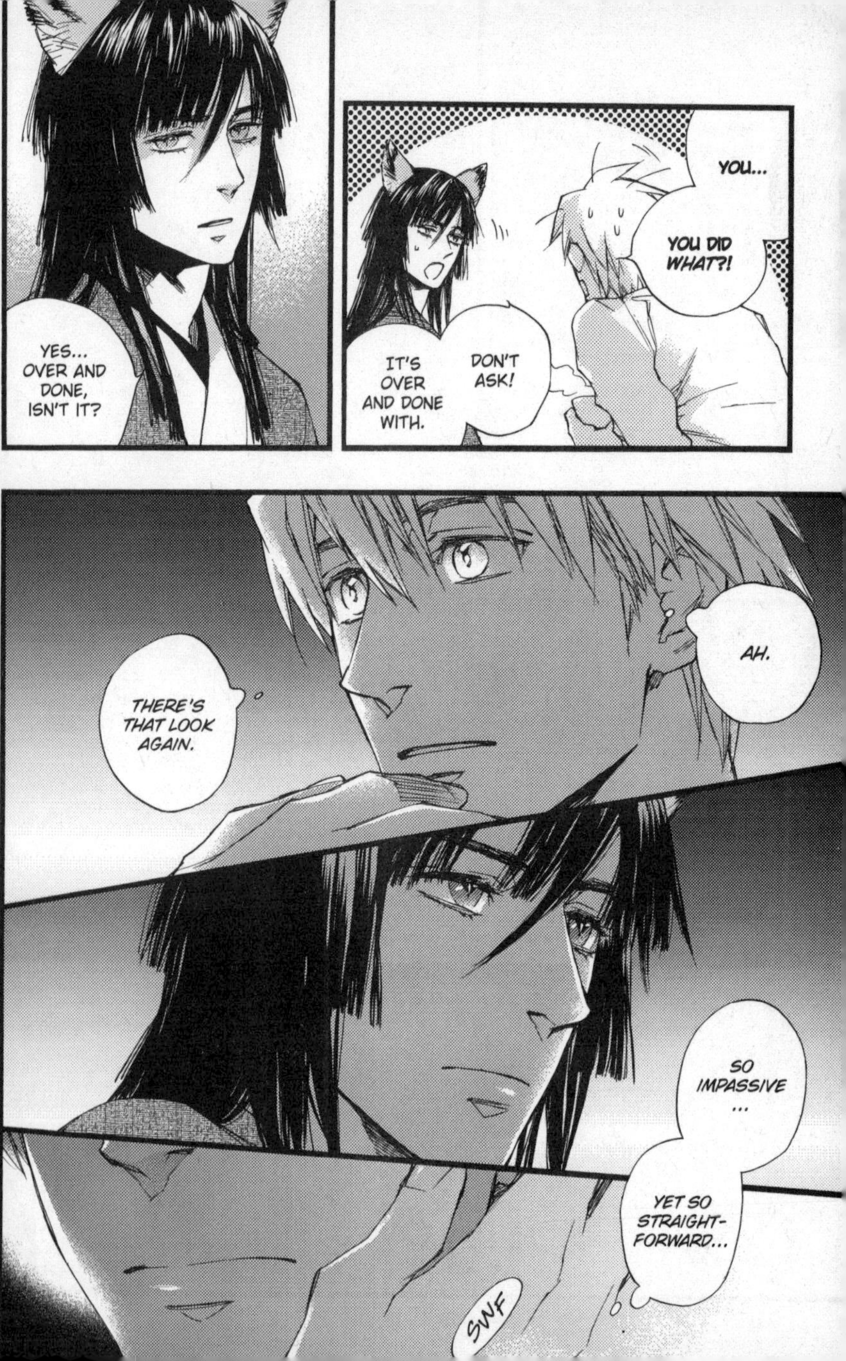
YOU...
YOU DID WHAT?!
DON'T ASK!
IT'S OVER AND DONE WITH.
YES... OVER AND DONE, ISN'T IT?
AH.
THERE'S THAT LOOK AGAIN.
SO IMPASSIVE...
YET SO STRAIGHT-FORWARD...
SNF

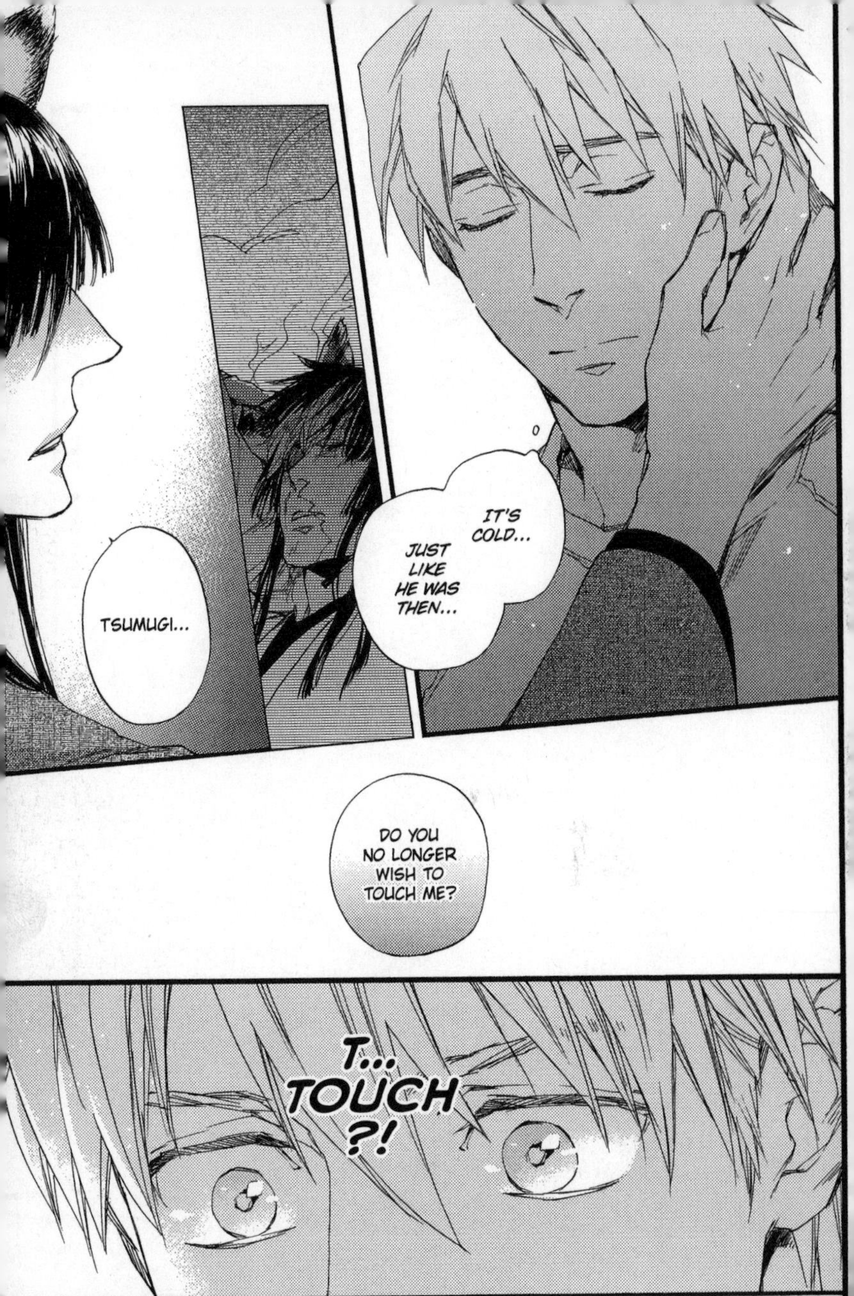
IT'S COLD... JUST LIKE HE WAS THEN...
TSUMUGI...
DO YOU NO LONGER WISH TO TOUCH ME?
T... TOUCH ?!

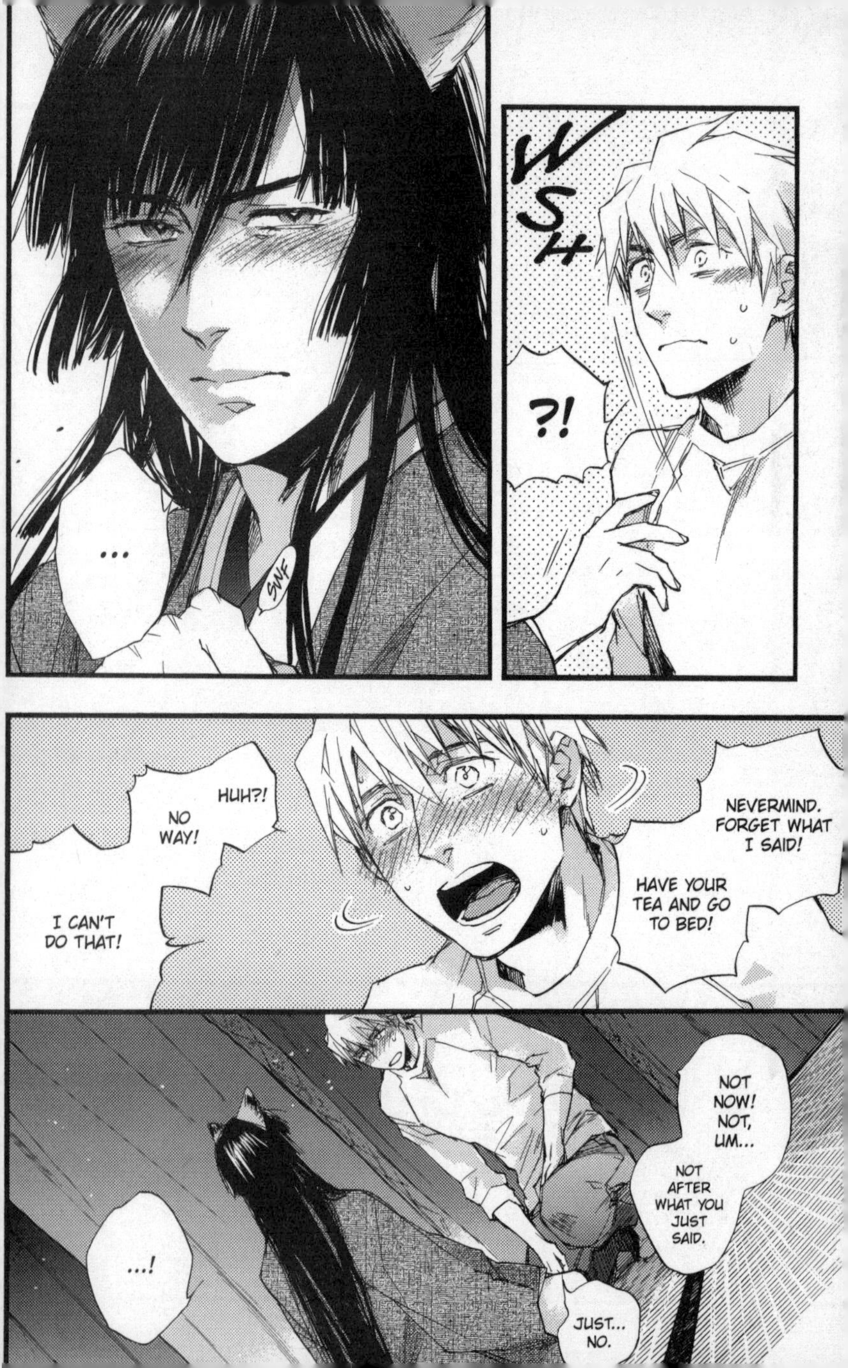
WSH
?!
SNF
...
NEVERMIND. FORGET WHAT I SAID!
HAVE YOUR TEA AND GO TO BED!
HUH?!
NO WAY!
I CAN'T DO THAT!
NOT NOW! NOT, UM...
NOT AFTER WHAT YOU JUST SAID.
JUST... NO.
...!

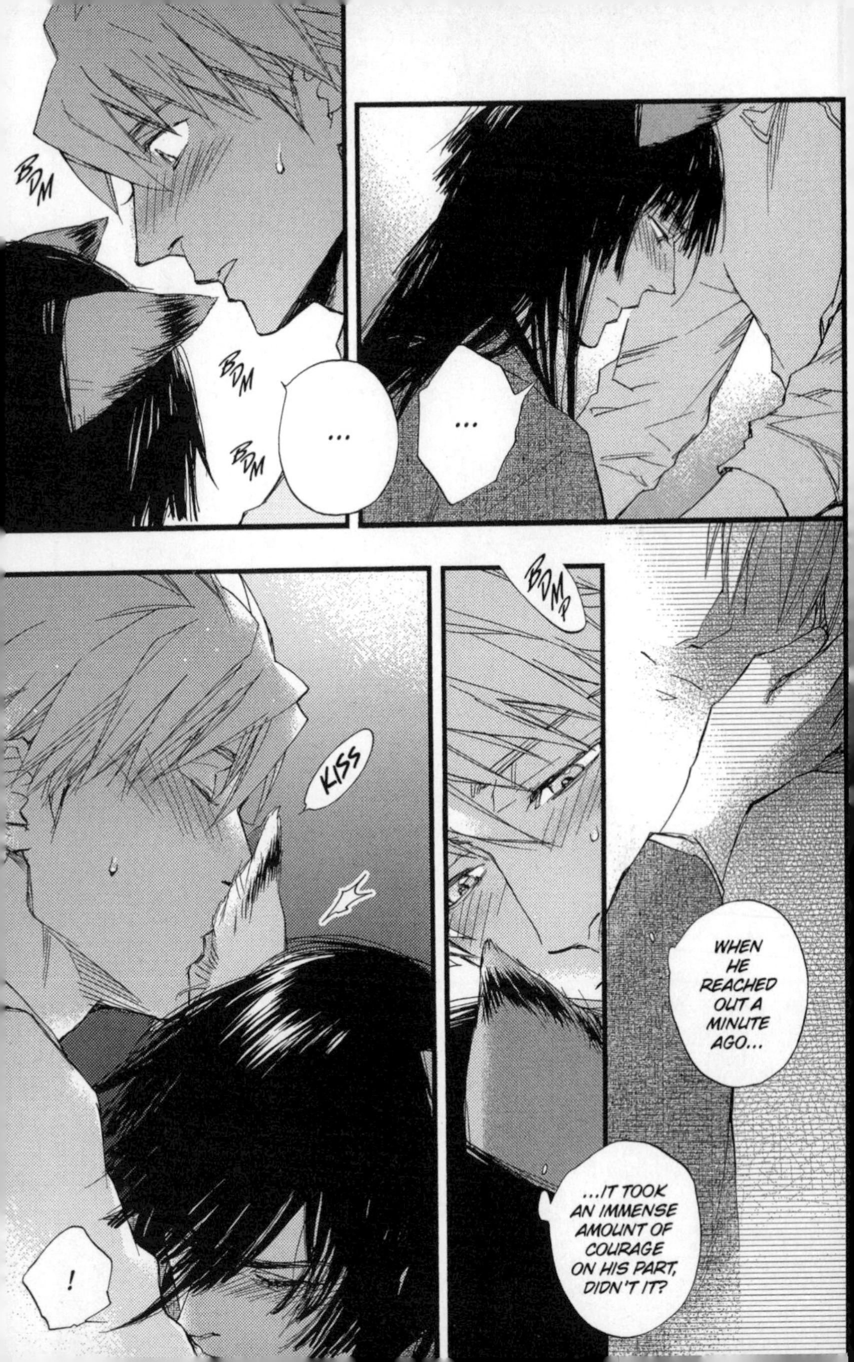
...
BDM
BDM
BDM
...
WHEN HE REACHED OUT A MINUTE AGO...
...IT TOOK AN IMMENSE AMOUNT OF COURAGE ON HIS PART, DIDN'T IT?
BDMP
KISS
!

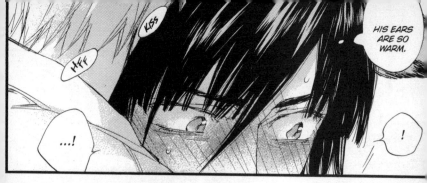

HFF

KISS

...!

HIS EARS ARE SO WARM.

!

TUG

WELCOME HOME, MASTER KURAYORI.

!

SNUGL

THEY AREN'T VERY REASSURING, ARE THEY?

THESE WEAK HUMAN ARMS OF MINE.

PHEW.

ER... THANK YOU.

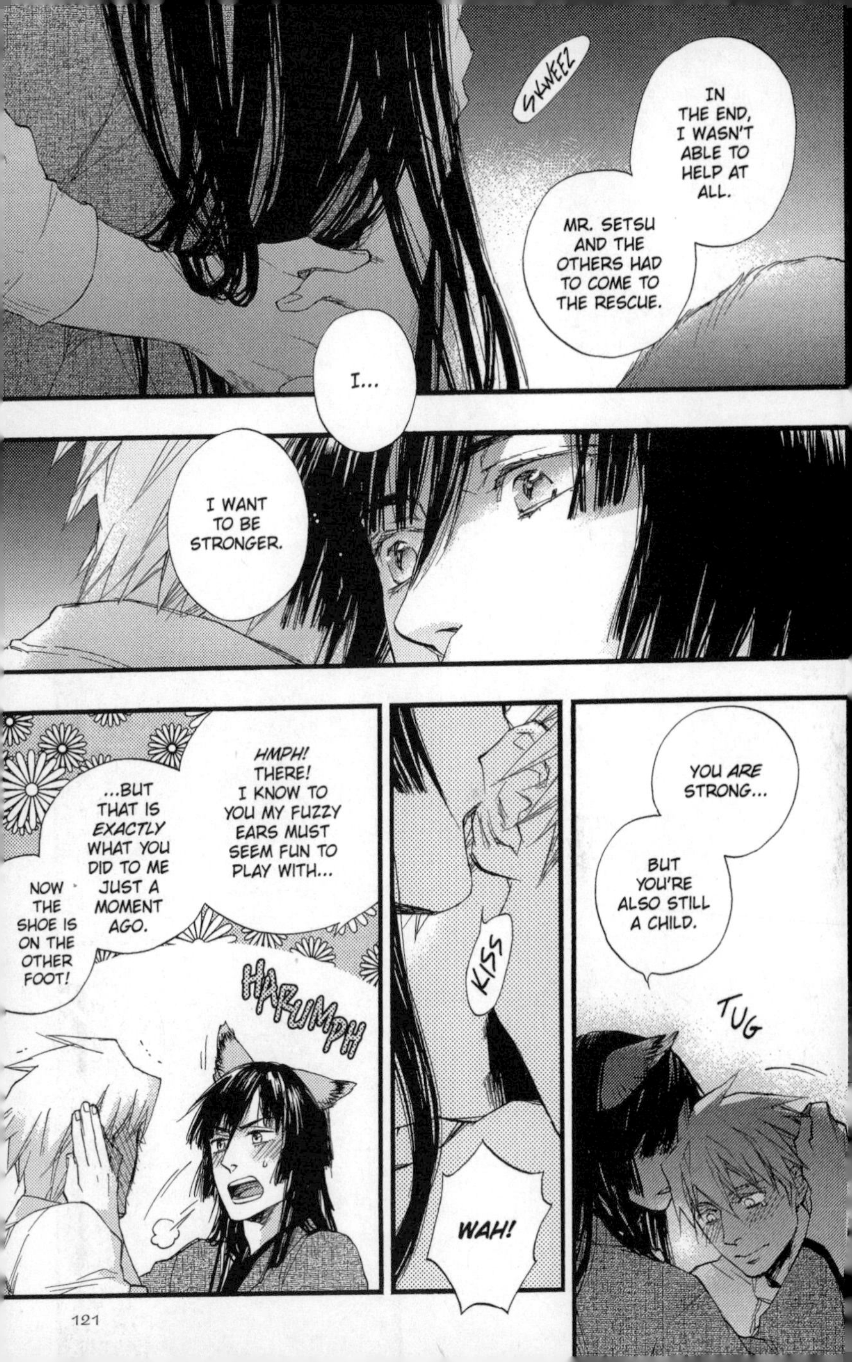
SKWEEZ
IN THE END, I WASN'T ABLE TO HELP AT ALL.
MR. SETSU AND THE OTHERS HAD TO COME TO THE RESCUE.
I...
I WANT TO BE STRONGER.
YOU *ARE* STRONG...
BUT YOU'RE ALSO STILL A CHILD.
TUG
KISS
WAH!
HMPH! THERE! I KNOW TO YOU MY FUZZY EARS MUST SEEM FUN TO PLAY WITH...
...BUT THAT IS *EXACTLY* WHAT YOU DID TO ME JUST A MOMENT AGO.
NOW THE SHOE IS ON THE OTHER FOOT!
HARUMPH

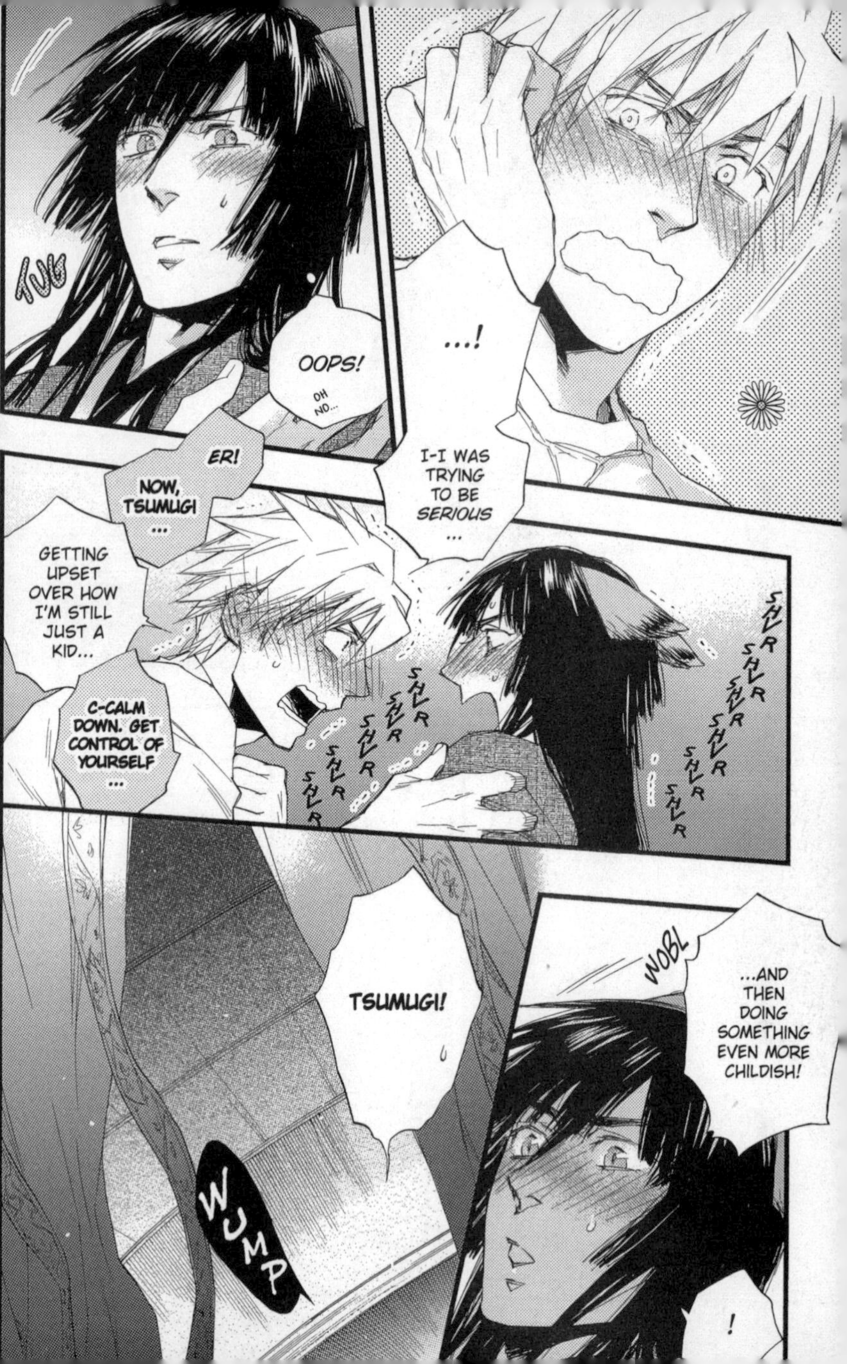
...!
TUG
OOPS!
OH NO...
I-I WAS TRYING TO BE SERIOUS...
ER!
NOW, TSUMUGI...
GETTING UPSET OVER HOW I'M STILL JUST A KID...
C-CALM DOWN. GET CONTROL OF YOURSELF...
SHLR SHLR SHLR SHLR
SHLR SHLR SHLR SHLR SHLR SHLR
WOBL
...AND THEN DOING SOMETHING EVEN MORE CHILDISH!
!
TSUMUGI!
WUMP

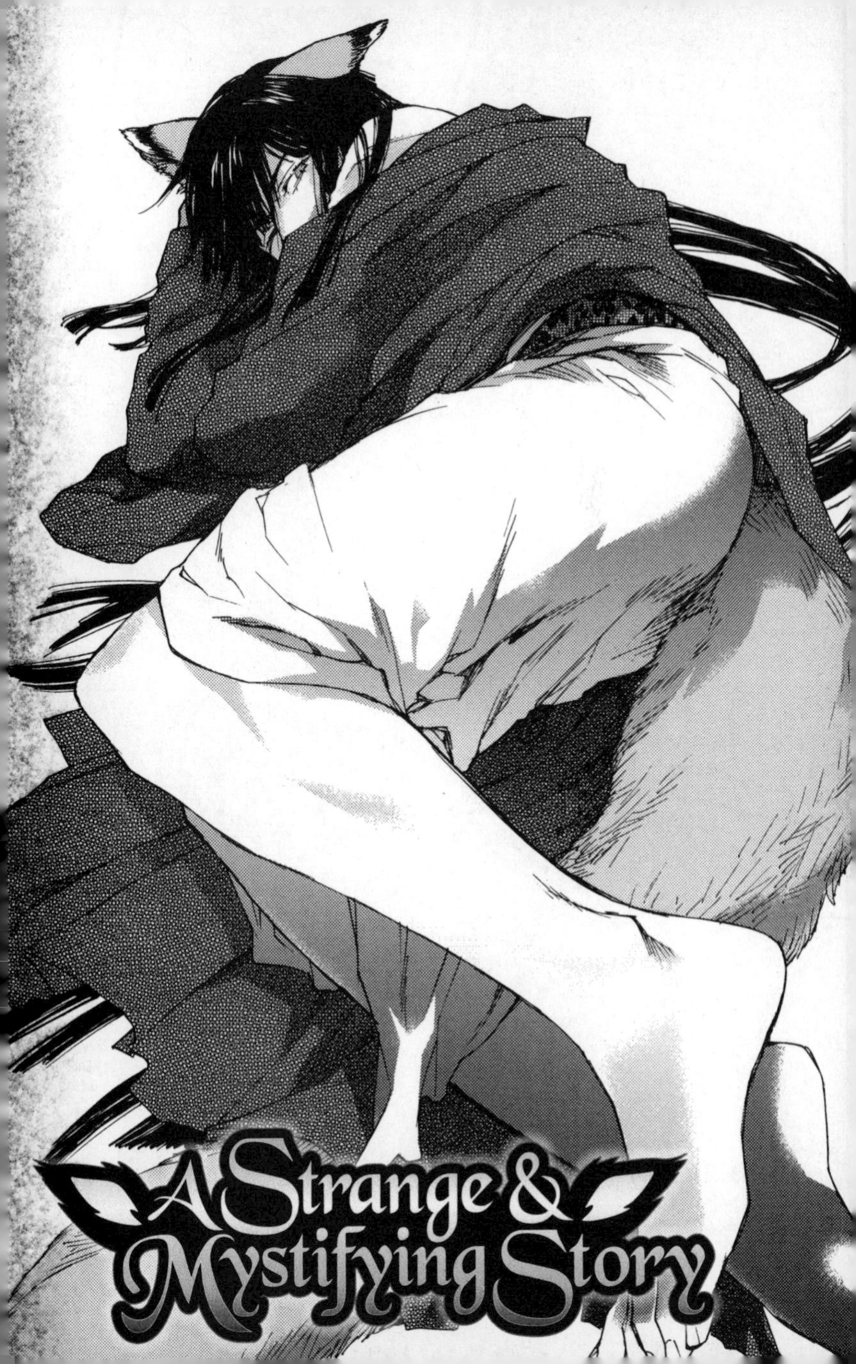
A Strange &
Mystifying Story

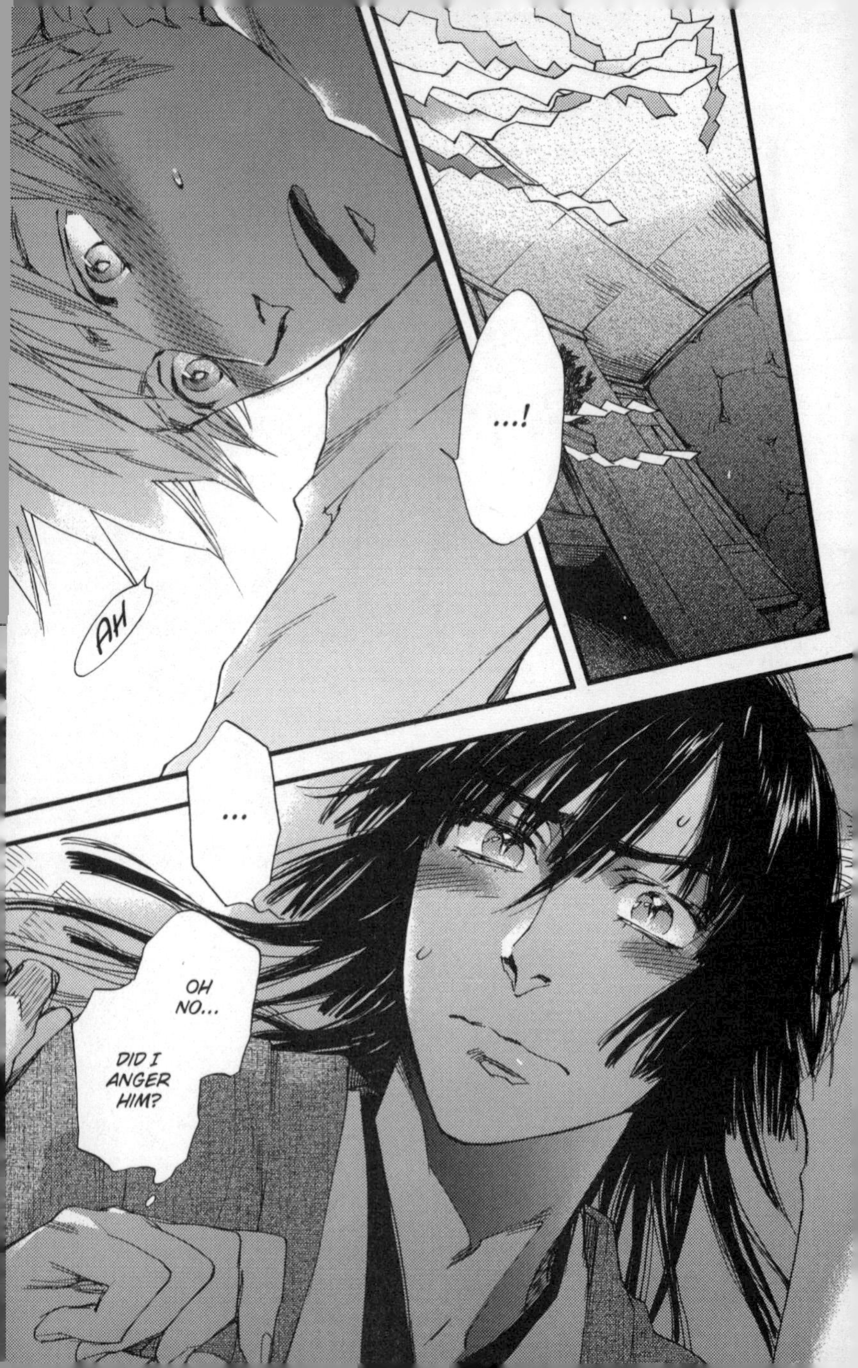
...!
AH
...
OH NO...
DID I ANGER HIM?

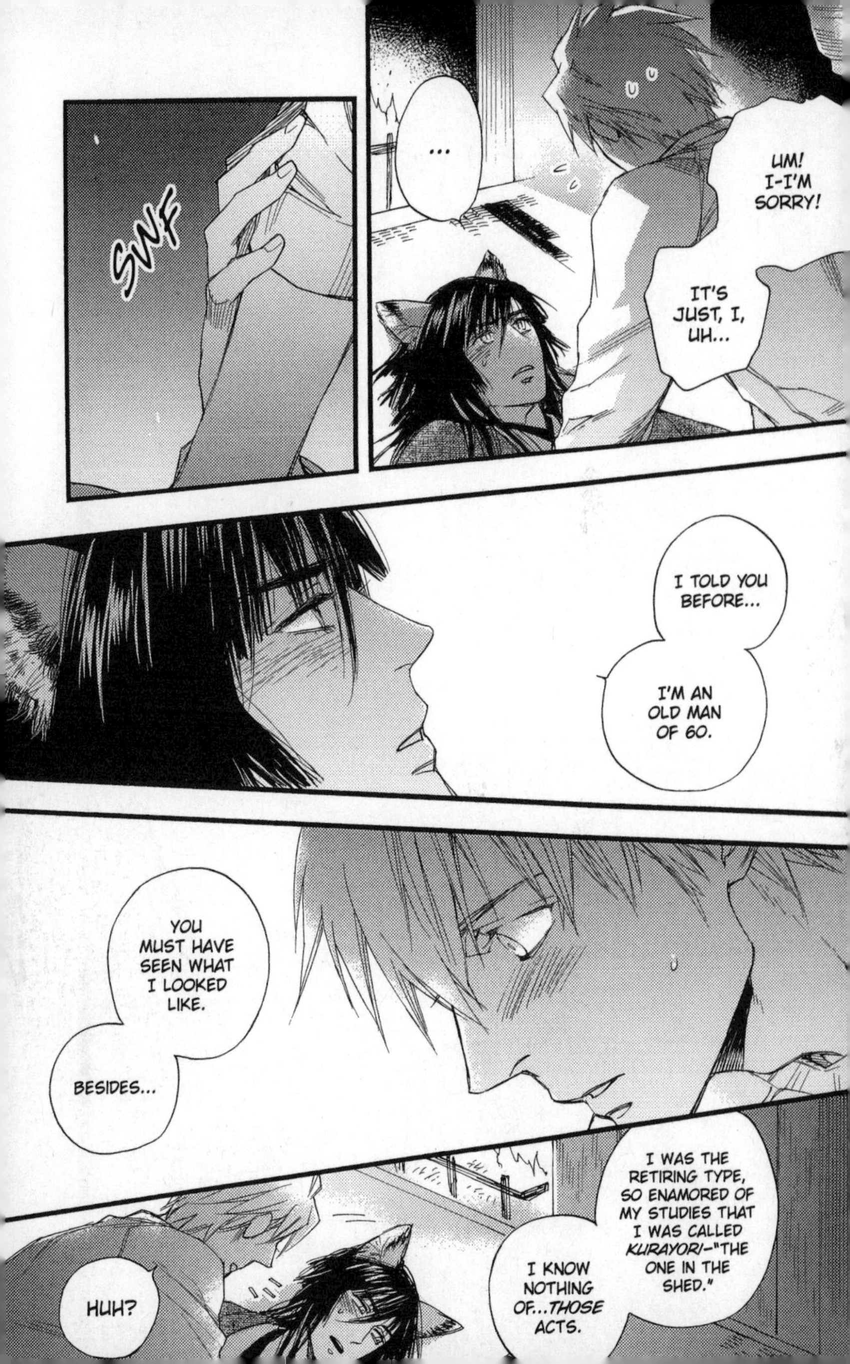
UM! I-I'M SORRY!
IT'S JUST, I, UH...
...
SNF
I TOLD YOU BEFORE...
I'M AN OLD MAN OF 60.
YOU MUST HAVE SEEN WHAT I LOOKED LIKE.
BESIDES...
I WAS THE RETIRING TYPE, SO ENAMORED OF MY STUDIES THAT I WAS CALLED *KURAYORI*—"THE ONE IN THE SHED."
I KNOW NOTHING OF...*THOSE* ACTS.
HUH?

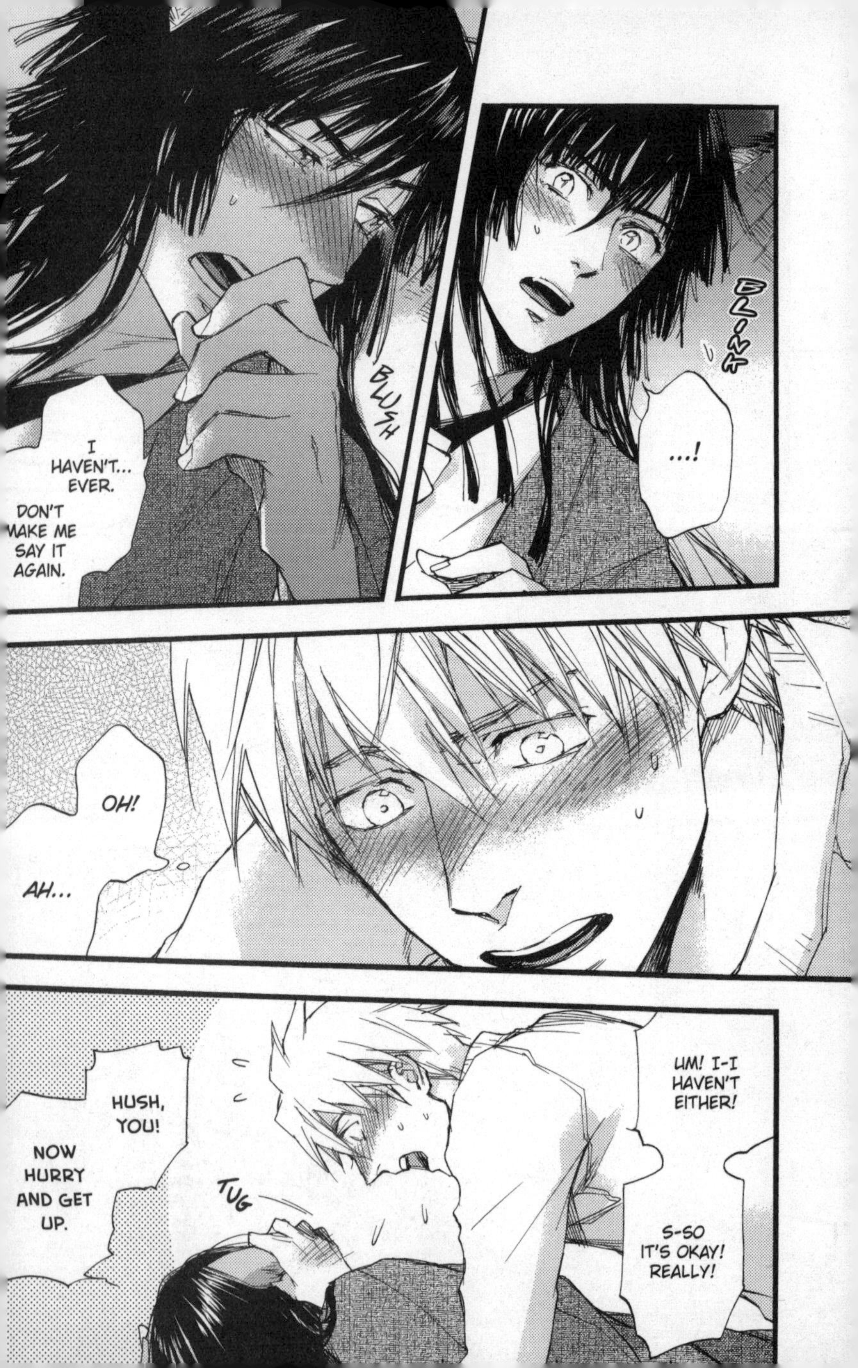
BLINK
...!
BLUSH
I HAVEN'T... EVER.
DON'T MAKE ME SAY IT AGAIN.
OH!
AH...
UM! I-I HAVEN'T EITHER!
S-SO IT'S OKAY! REALLY!
TUG
HUSH, YOU!
NOW HURRY AND GET UP.

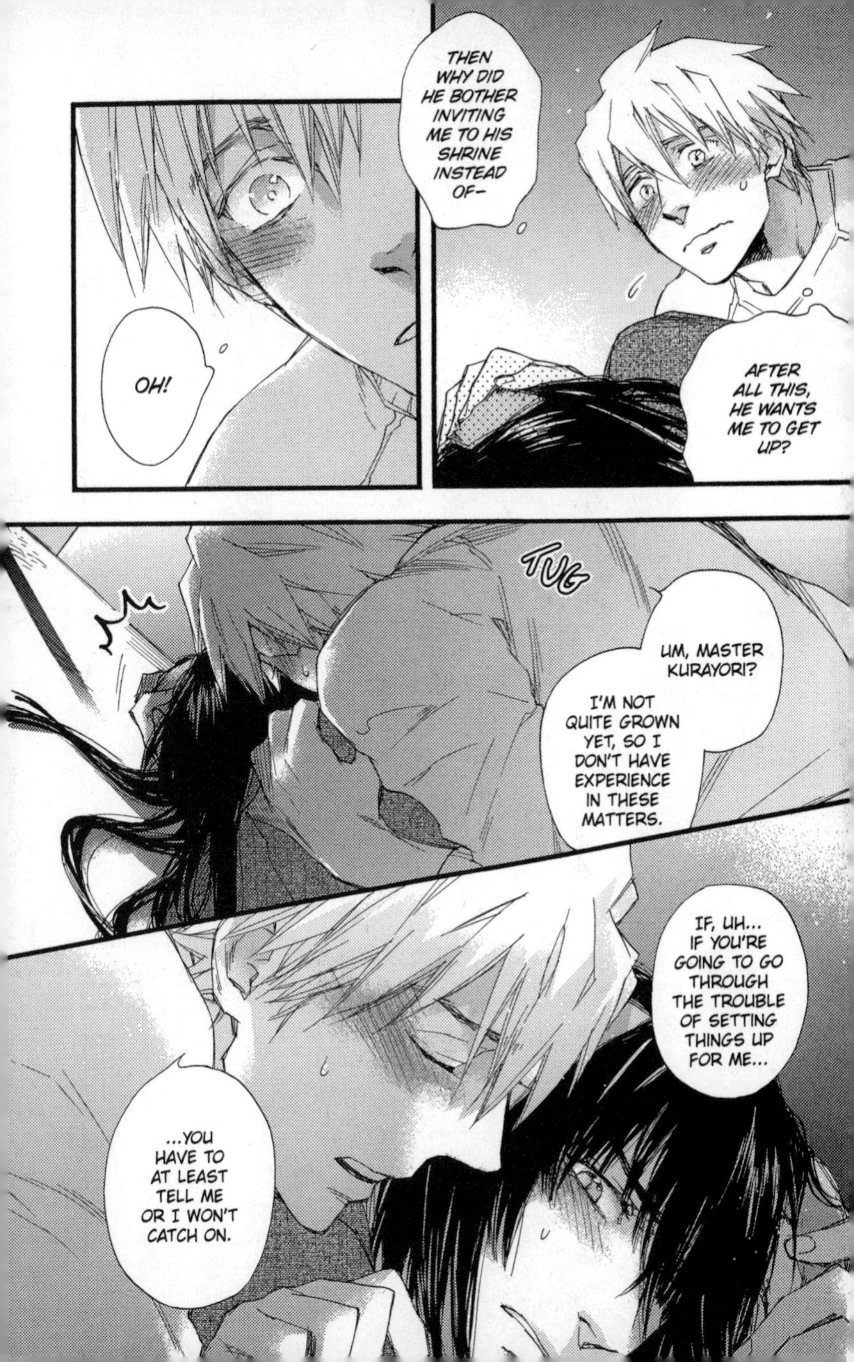
AFTER ALL THIS, HE WANTS ME TO GET UP?
THEN WHY DID HE BOTHER INVITING ME TO HIS SHRINE INSTEAD OF–
OH!
TUG
UM, MASTER KURAYORI?
I'M NOT QUITE GROWN YET, SO I DON'T HAVE EXPERIENCE IN THESE MATTERS.
IF, UH... IF YOU'RE GOING TO GO THROUGH THE TROUBLE OF SETTING THINGS UP FOR ME...
...YOU HAVE TO AT LEAST TELL ME OR I WON'T CATCH ON.

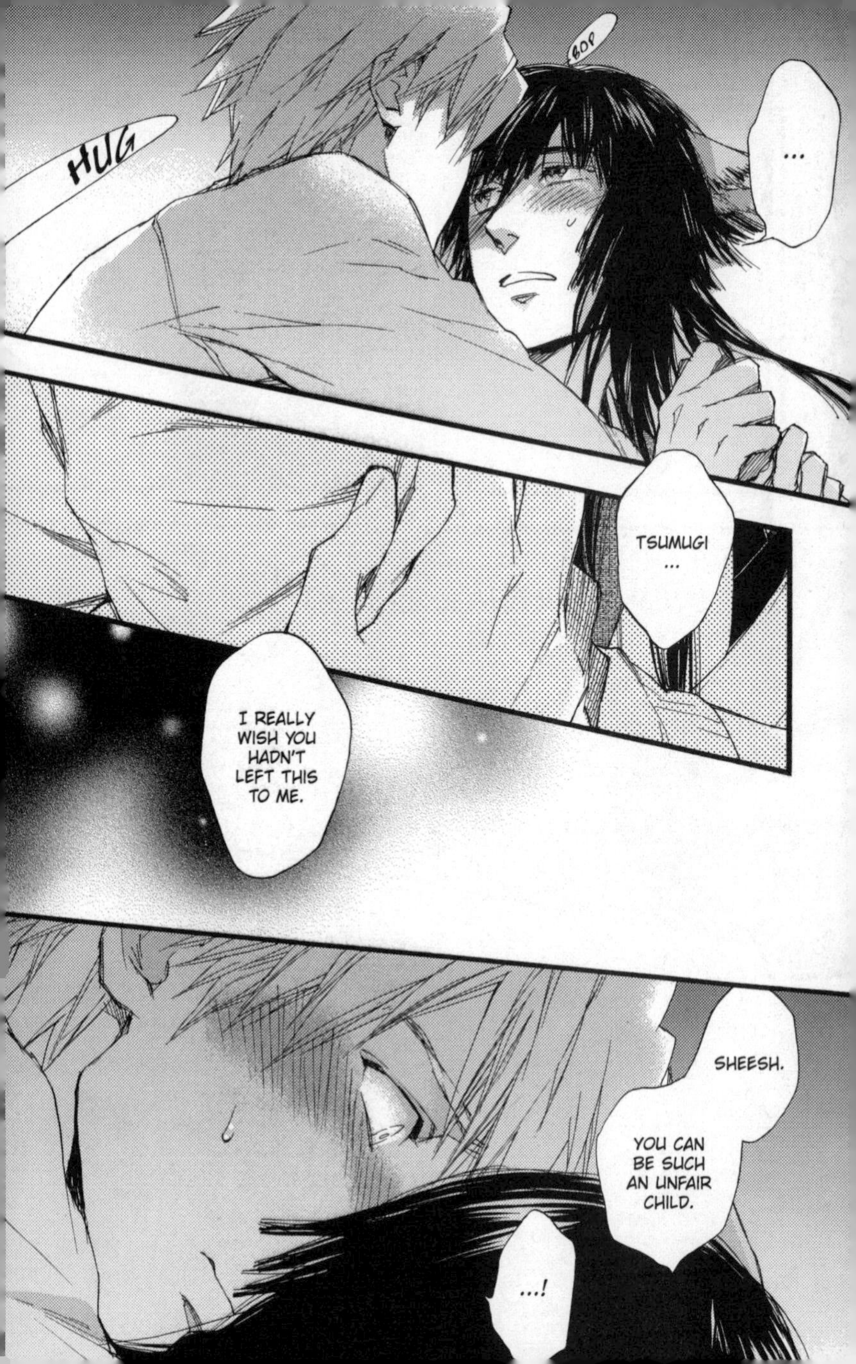
...
BOP
HUG
TSUMUGI ...
I REALLY WISH YOU HADN'T LEFT THIS TO ME.
SHEESH.
YOU CAN BE SUCH AN UNFAIR CHILD.
...!

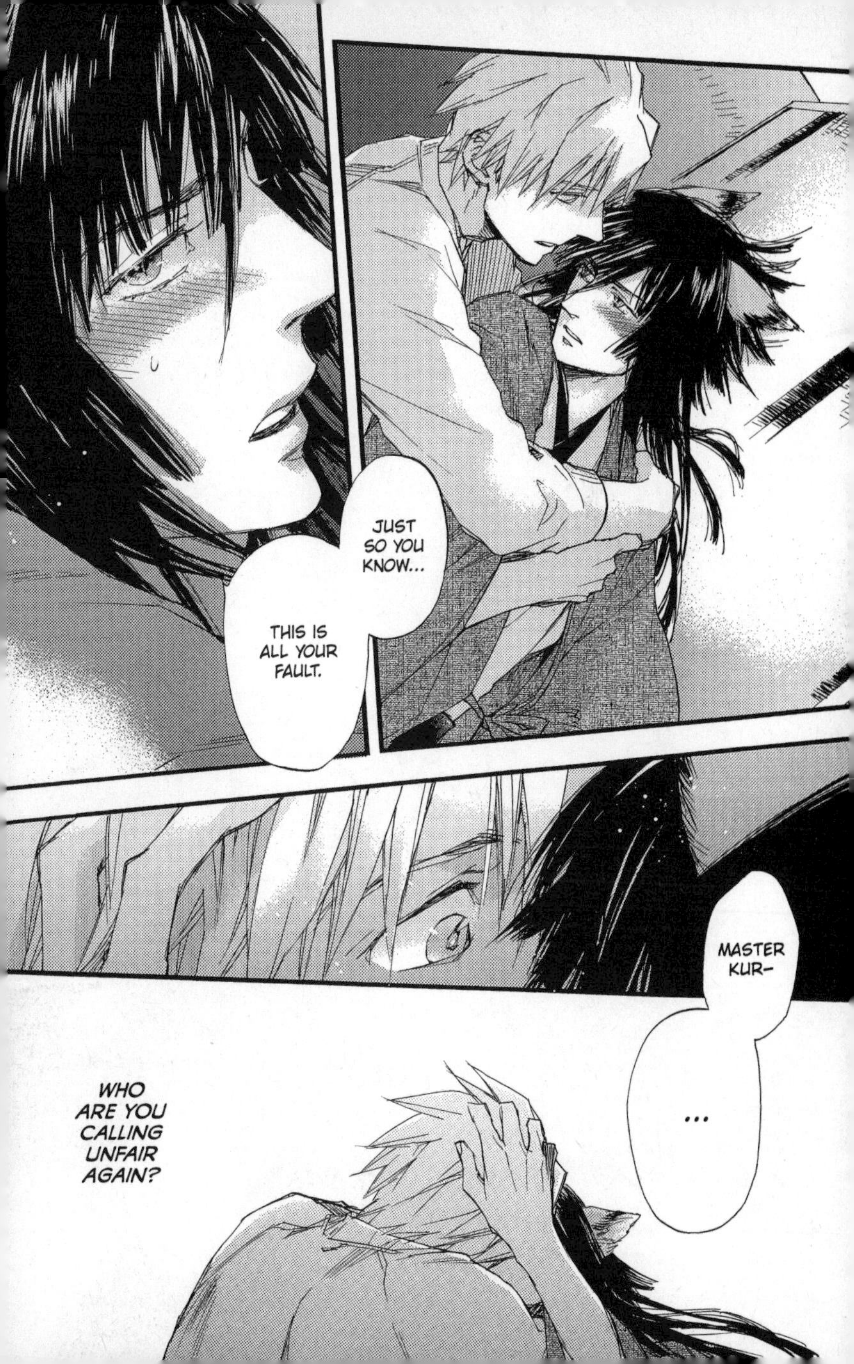
JUST SO YOU KNOW...
THIS IS ALL YOUR FAULT.
MASTER KUR-
...
WHO ARE YOU CALLING UNFAIR AGAIN?

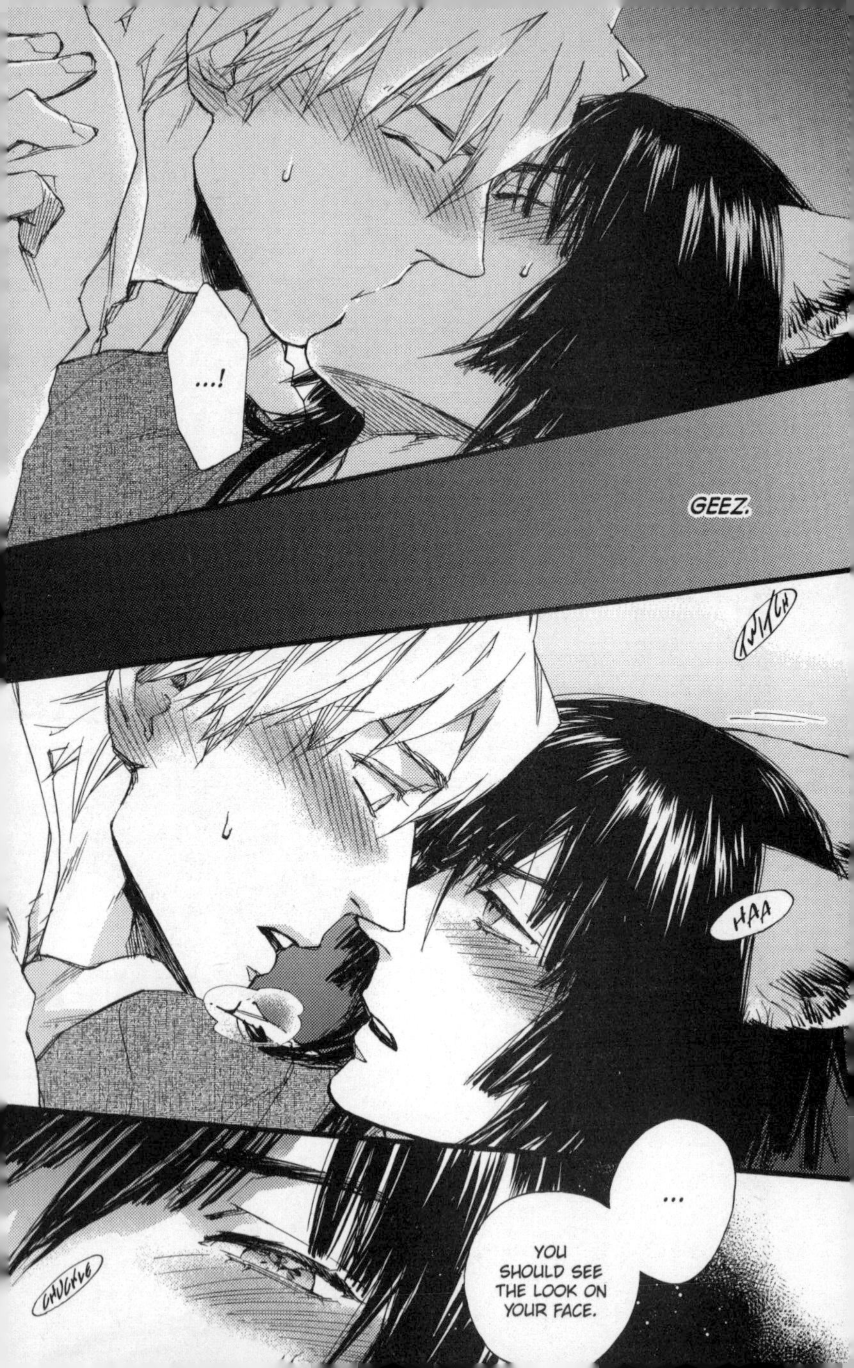
...!
GEEZ.
TWITCH
HAA
...
YOU SHOULD SEE THE LOOK ON YOUR FACE.
CHUCKLE

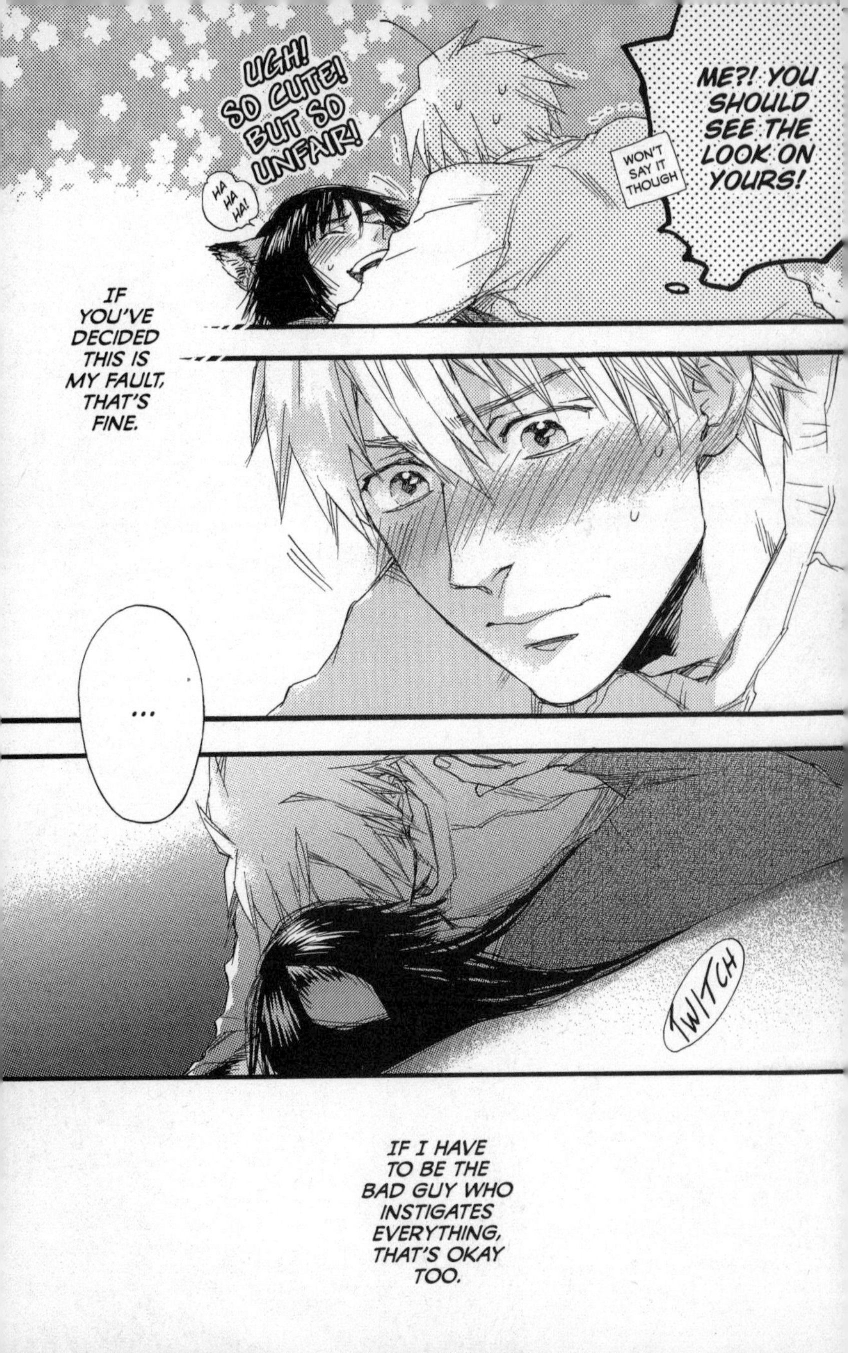
ME?! YOU SHOULD SEE THE LOOK ON YOURS!
WON'T SAY IT THOUGH
UGH! SO CUTE! BUT SO UNFAIR!
HA HA HA!
IF YOU'VE DECIDED THIS IS MY FAULT, THAT'S FINE.
...
TWITCH
IF I HAVE TO BE THE BAD GUY WHO INSTIGATES EVERYTHING, THAT'S OKAY TOO.

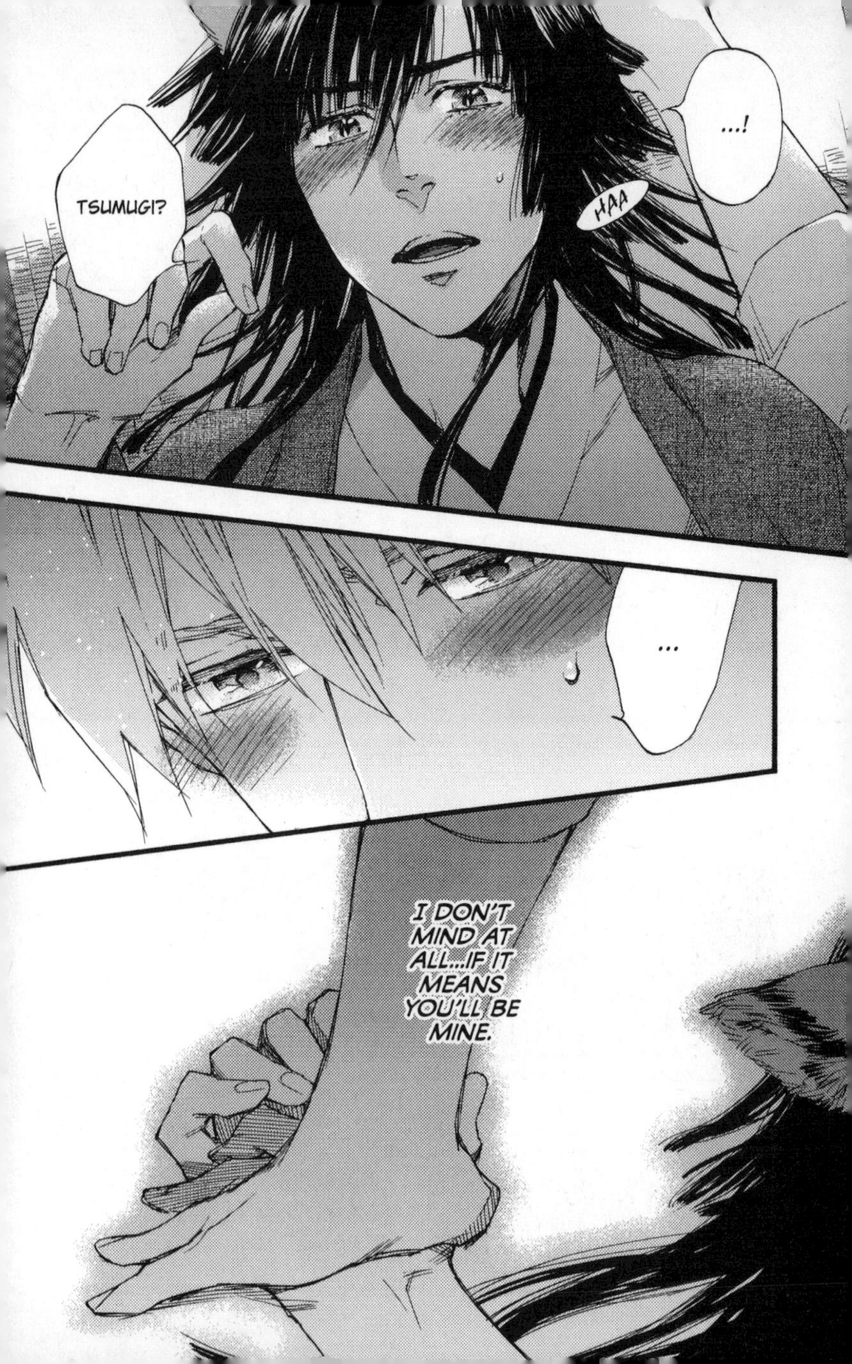
...!
HAA
TSUMUGI?
...
I DON'T MIND AT ALL...IF IT MEANS YOU'LL BE MINE.

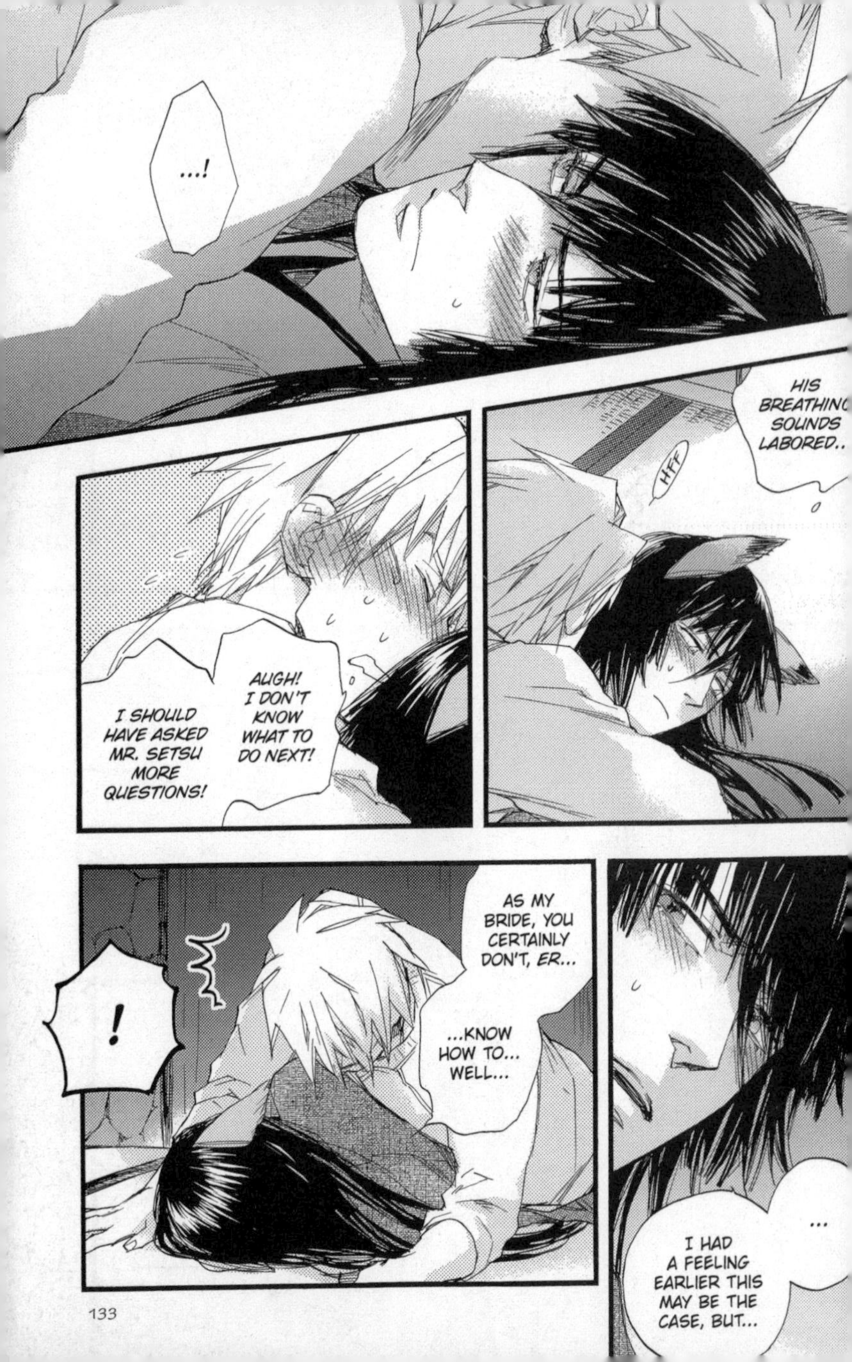
...!
HIS BREATHING SOUNDS LABORED...
HFF
AUGH! I DON'T KNOW WHAT TO DO NEXT!
I SHOULD HAVE ASKED MR. SETSU MORE QUESTIONS!
...
I HAD A FEELING EARLIER THIS MAY BE THE CASE, BUT...
AS MY BRIDE, YOU CERTAINLY DON'T, ER...
...KNOW HOW TO... WELL...
!

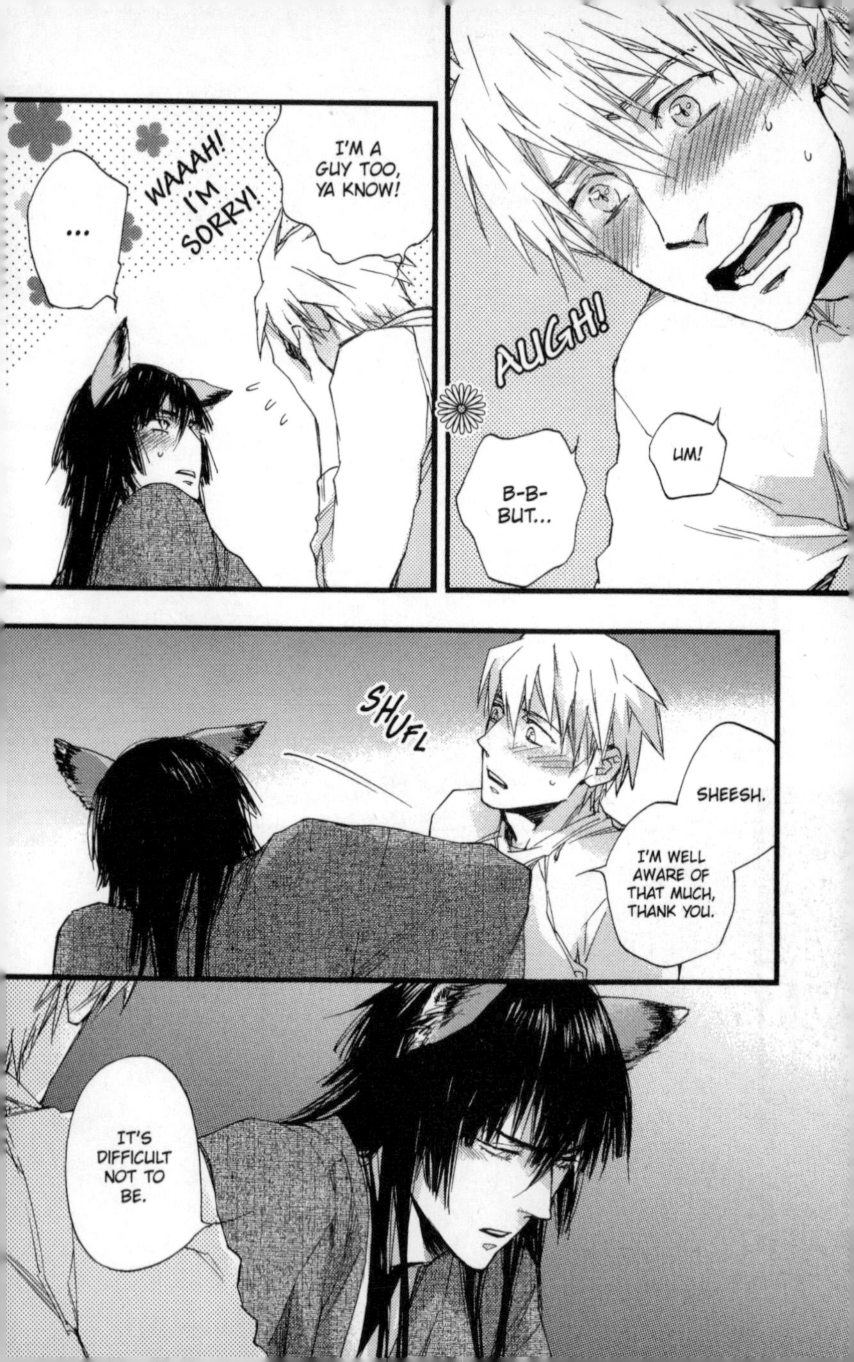
AUGH!
UM!
B-B-BUT...
I'M A GUY TOO, YA KNOW!
WAAAH! I'M SORRY!
...
SHEESH.
I'M WELL AWARE OF THAT MUCH, THANK YOU.
SHUFL
IT'S DIFFICULT NOT TO BE.

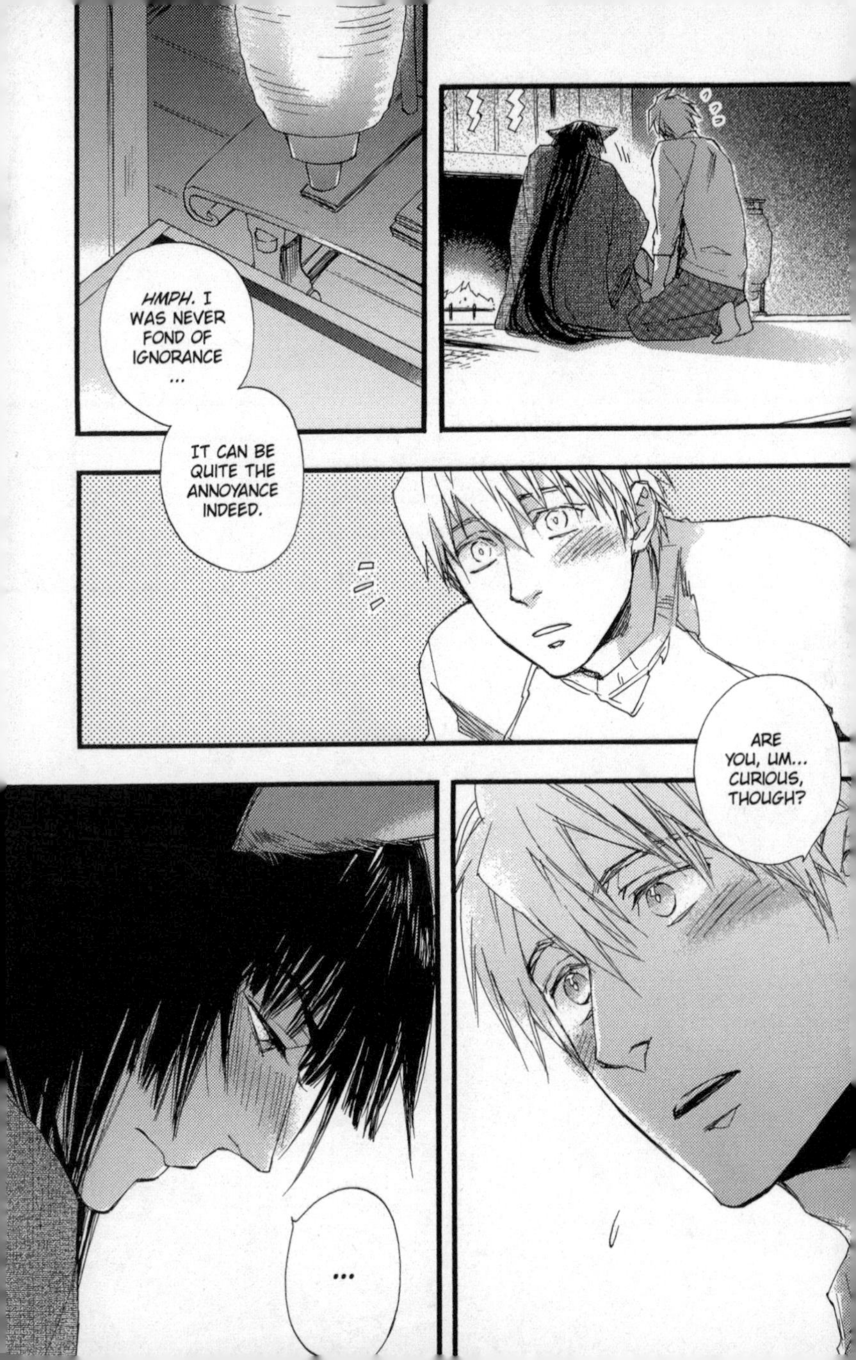
HMPH. I WAS NEVER FOND OF IGNORANCE...
IT CAN BE QUITE THE ANNOYANCE INDEED.
ARE YOU, UM... CURIOUS, THOUGH?
...

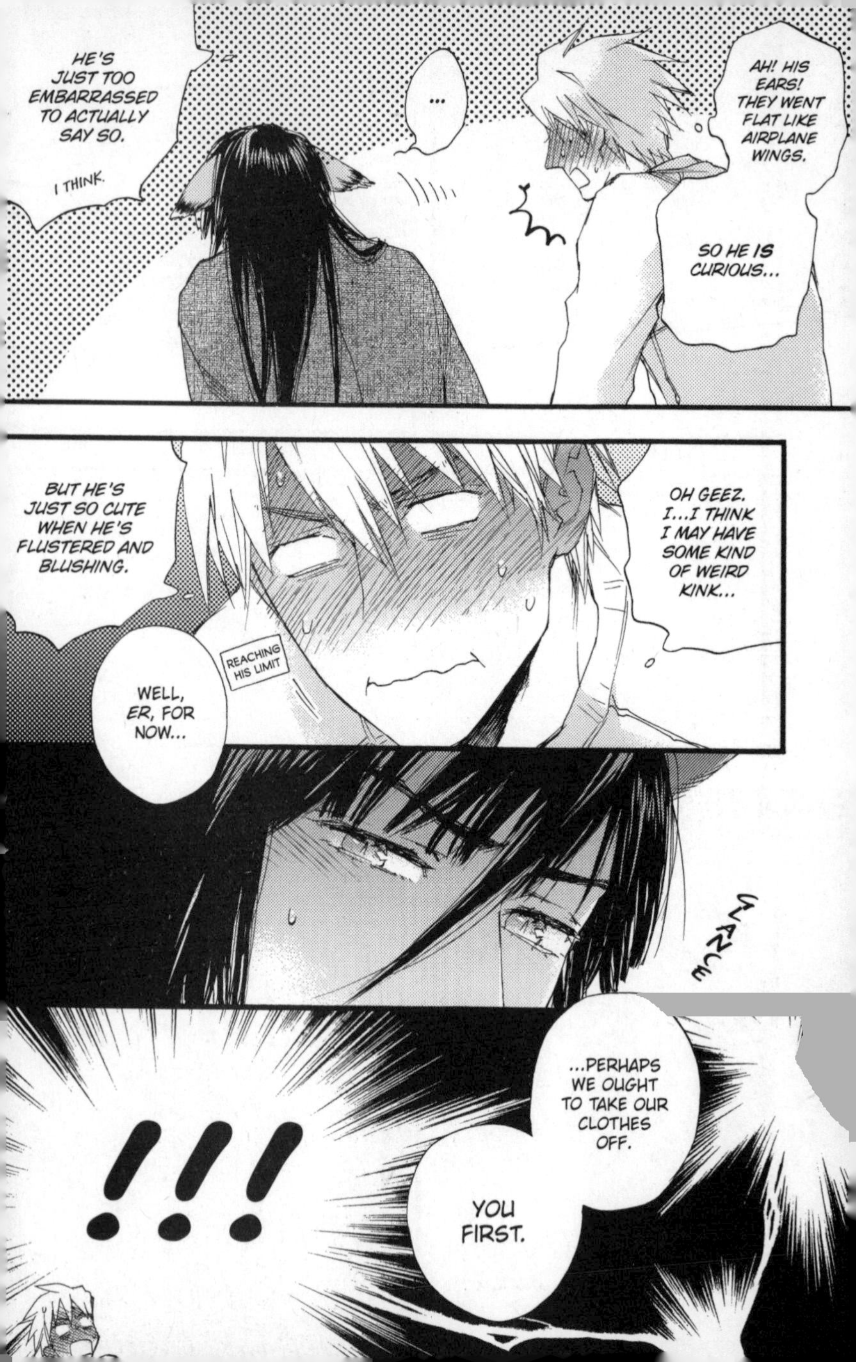
AH! HIS EARS! THEY WENT FLAT LIKE AIRPLANE WINGS.
SO HE IS CURIOUS...
...
HE'S JUST TOO EMBARRASSED TO ACTUALLY SAY SO.
I THINK.
OH GEEZ. I...I THINK I MAY HAVE SOME KIND OF WEIRD KINK...
BUT HE'S JUST SO CUTE WHEN HE'S FLUSTERED AND BLUSHING.
REACHING HIS LIMIT
WELL, ER, FOR NOW...
WINCE
...PERHAPS WE OUGHT TO TAKE OUR CLOTHES OFF.
YOU FIRST.
!!!

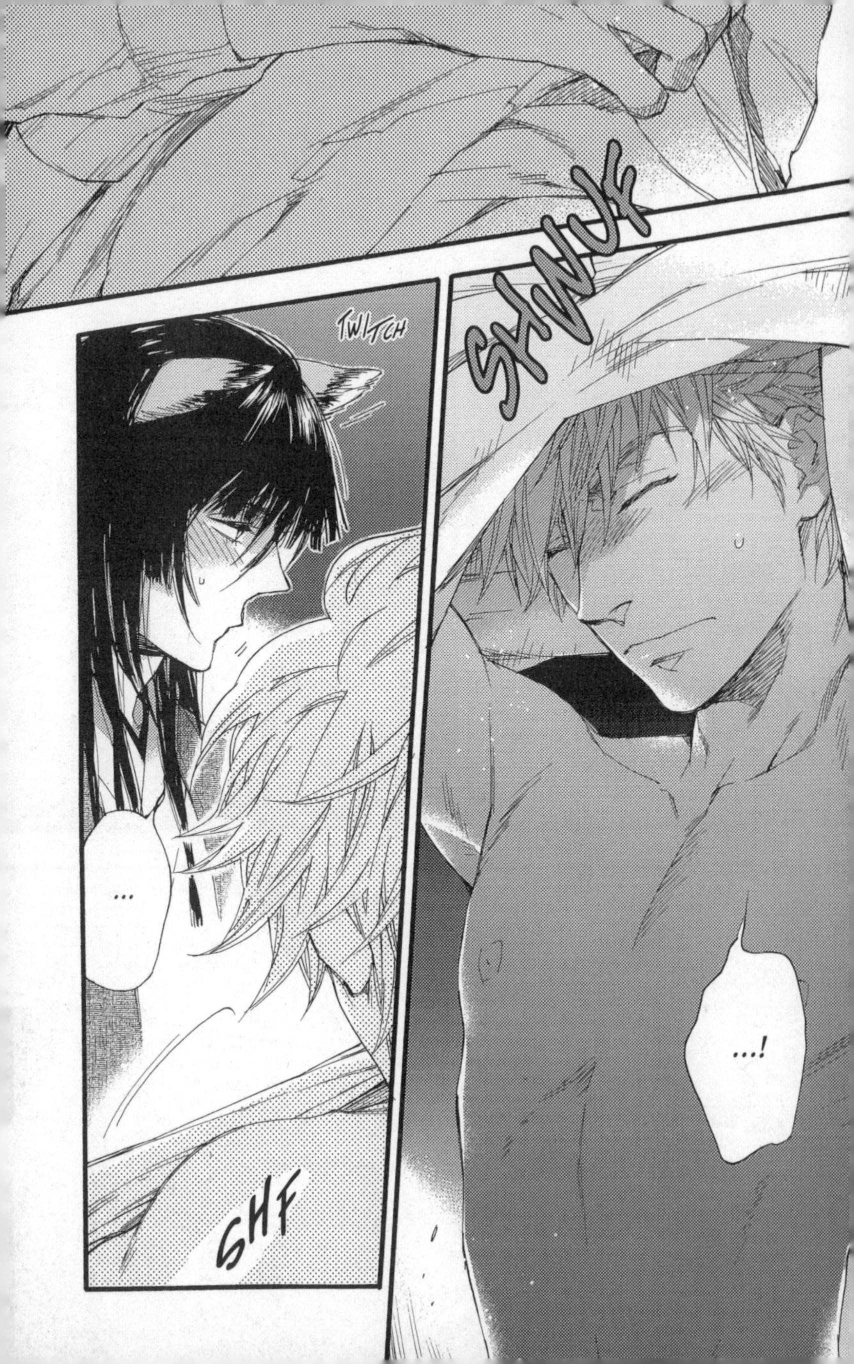
SHWUF
TWITCH
...!
...
SHF

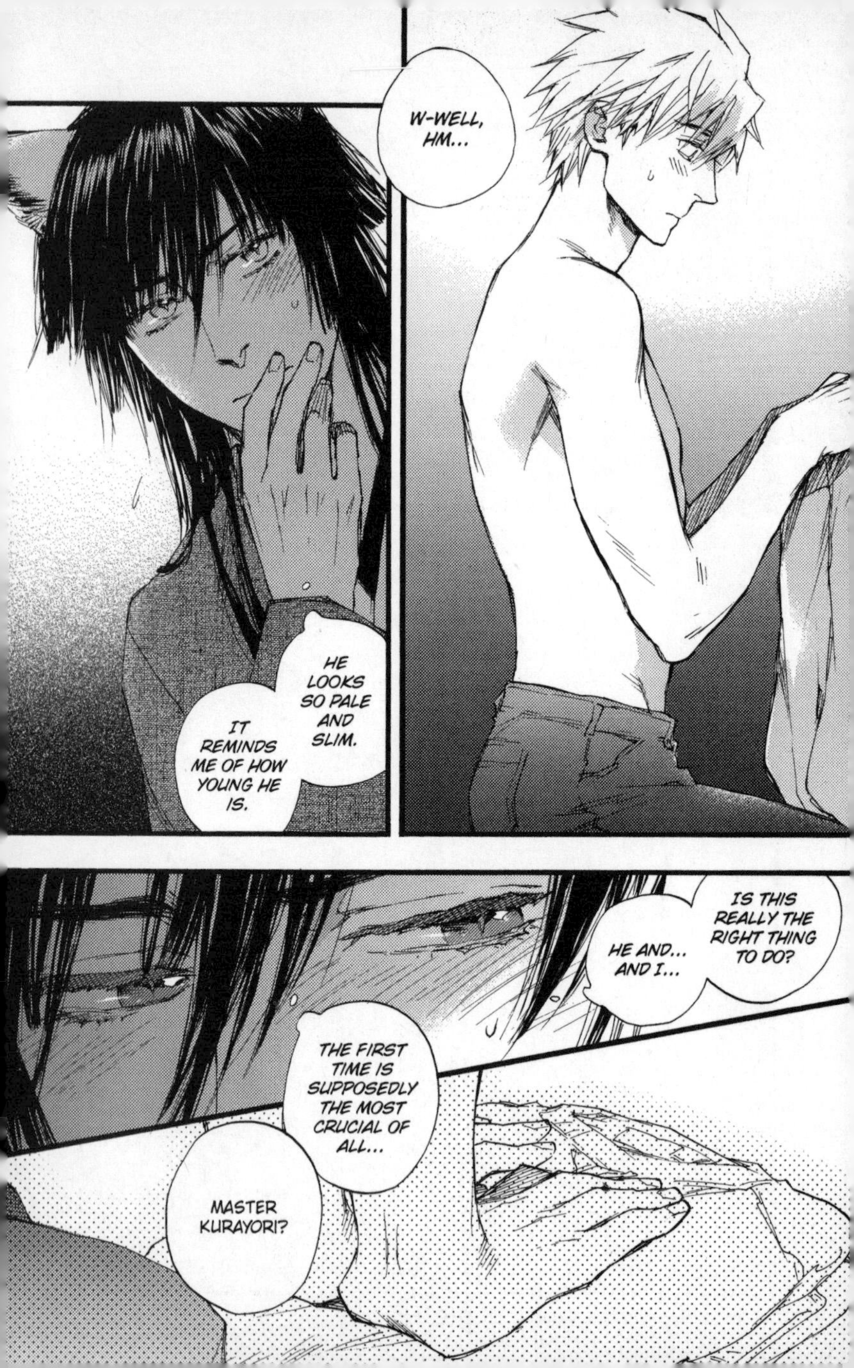
W-WELL, HM...
HE LOOKS SO PALE AND SLIM.
IT REMINDS ME OF HOW YOUNG HE IS.
IS THIS REALLY THE RIGHT THING TO DO?
HE AND... AND I...
THE FIRST TIME IS SUPPOSEDLY THE MOST CRUCIAL OF ALL...
MASTER KURAYORI?

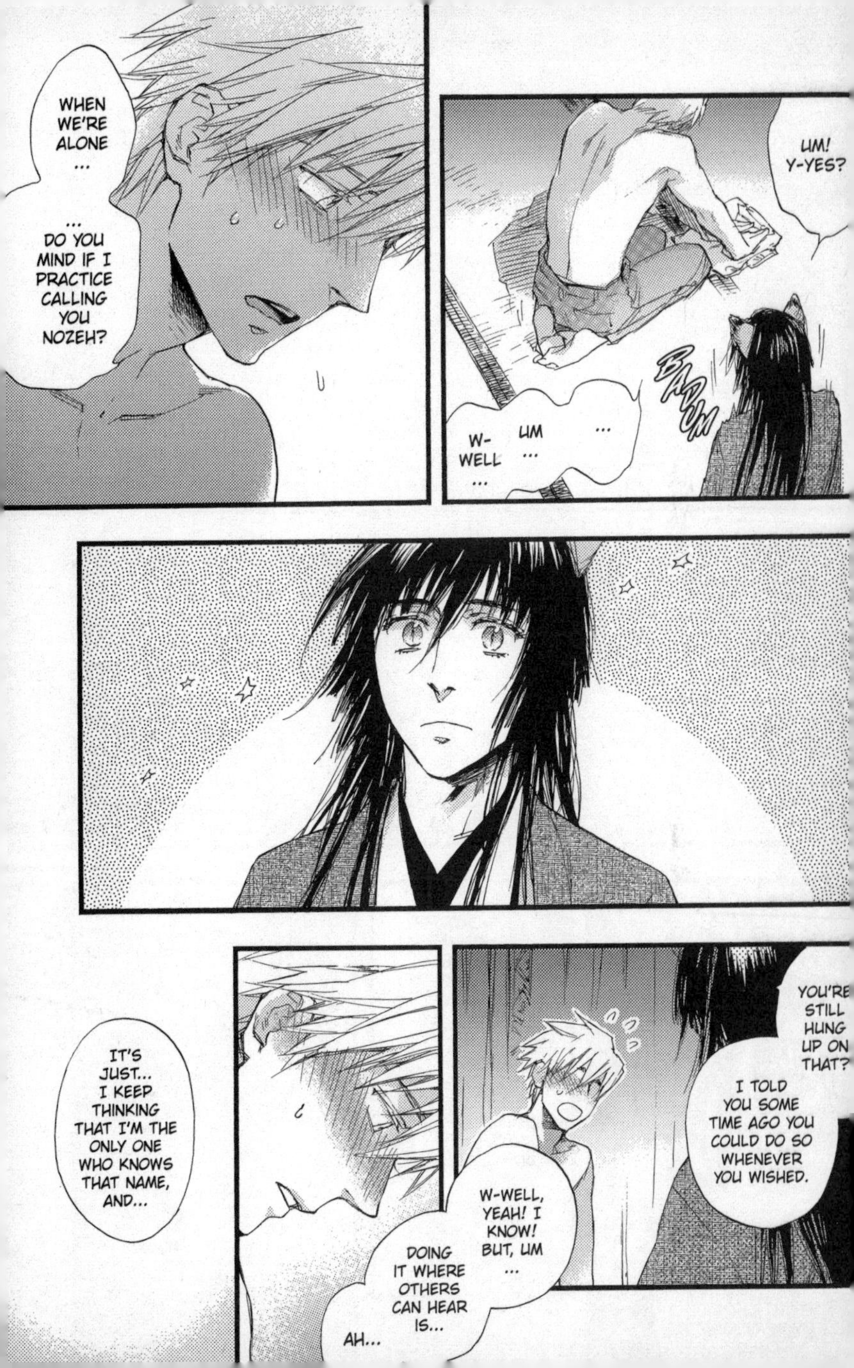
UM! Y-YES?
BADUM
W-WELL... UM... ...
WHEN WE'RE ALONE... ...DO YOU MIND IF I PRACTICE CALLING YOU NOZEH?
YOU'RE STILL HUNG UP ON THAT?
I TOLD YOU SOME TIME AGO YOU COULD DO SO WHENEVER YOU WISHED.
W-WELL, YEAH! I KNOW! BUT, UM...
DOING IT WHERE OTHERS CAN HEAR IS... AH...
IT'S JUST... I KEEP THINKING THAT I'M THE ONLY ONE WHO KNOWS THAT NAME, AND...

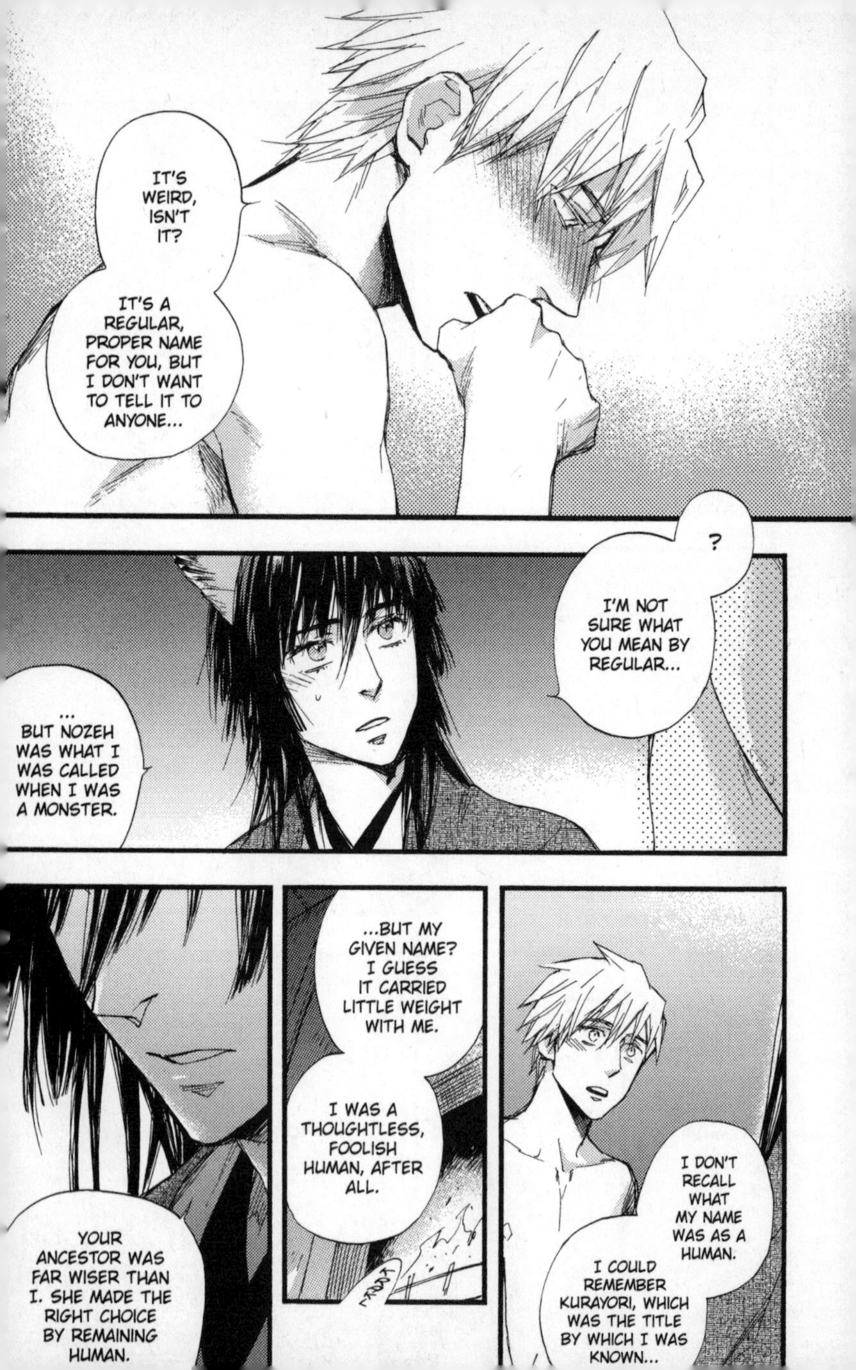
IT'S WEIRD, ISN'T IT?
IT'S A REGULAR, PROPER NAME FOR YOU, BUT I DON'T WANT TO TELL IT TO ANYONE...
?
I'M NOT SURE WHAT YOU MEAN BY REGULAR...
... BUT NOZEH WAS WHAT I WAS CALLED WHEN I WAS A MONSTER.
I DON'T RECALL WHAT MY NAME WAS AS A HUMAN.
I COULD REMEMBER KURAYORI, WHICH WAS THE TITLE BY WHICH I WAS KNOWN...
...BUT MY GIVEN NAME? I GUESS IT CARRIED LITTLE WEIGHT WITH ME.
I WAS A THOUGHTLESS, FOOLISH HUMAN, AFTER ALL.
YOUR ANCESTOR WAS FAR WISER THAN I. SHE MADE THE RIGHT CHOICE BY REMAINING HUMAN.

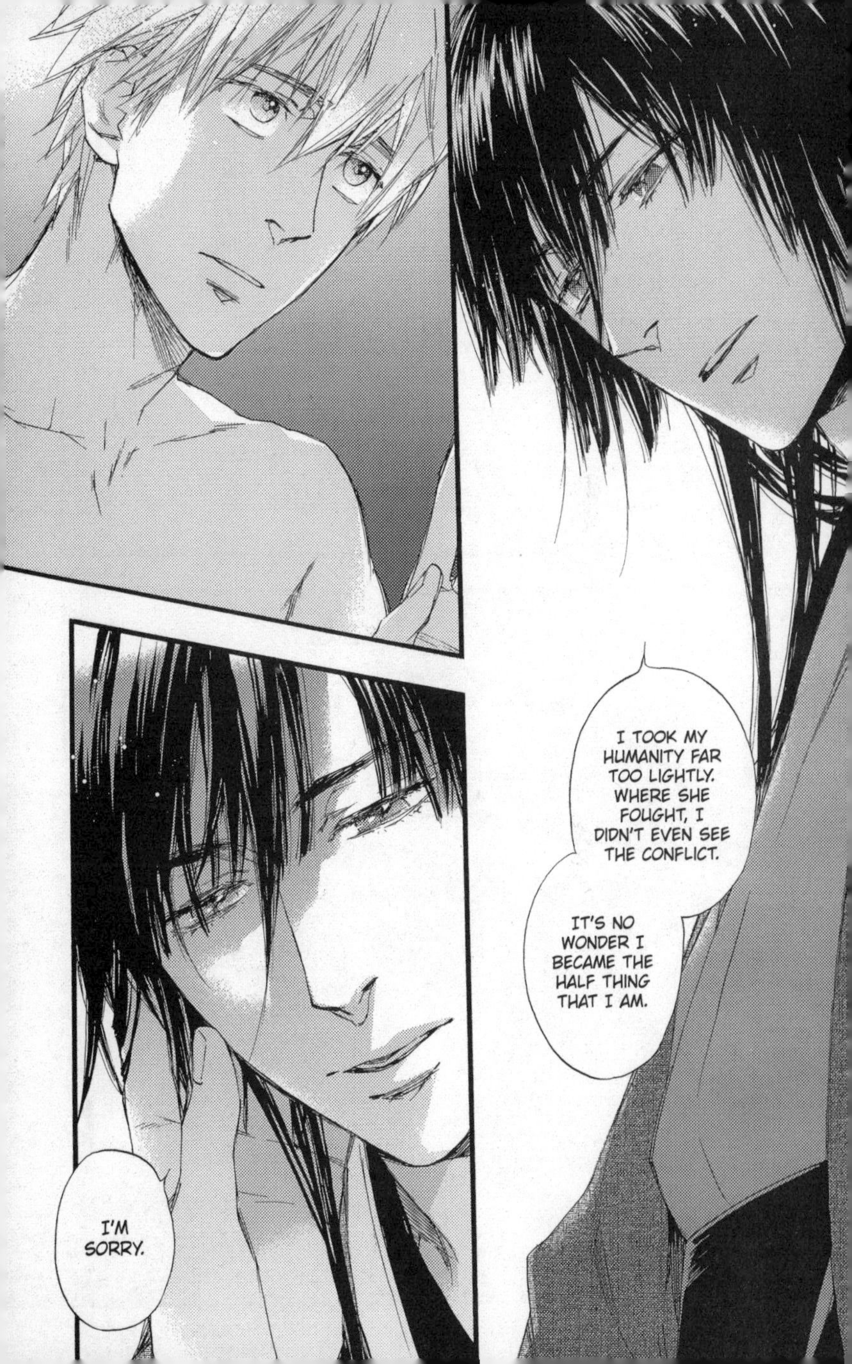
I TOOK MY HUMANITY FAR TOO LIGHTLY. WHERE SHE FOUGHT, I DIDN'T EVEN SEE THE CONFLICT.
IT'S NO WONDER I BECAME THE HALF THING THAT I AM.
I'M SORRY.

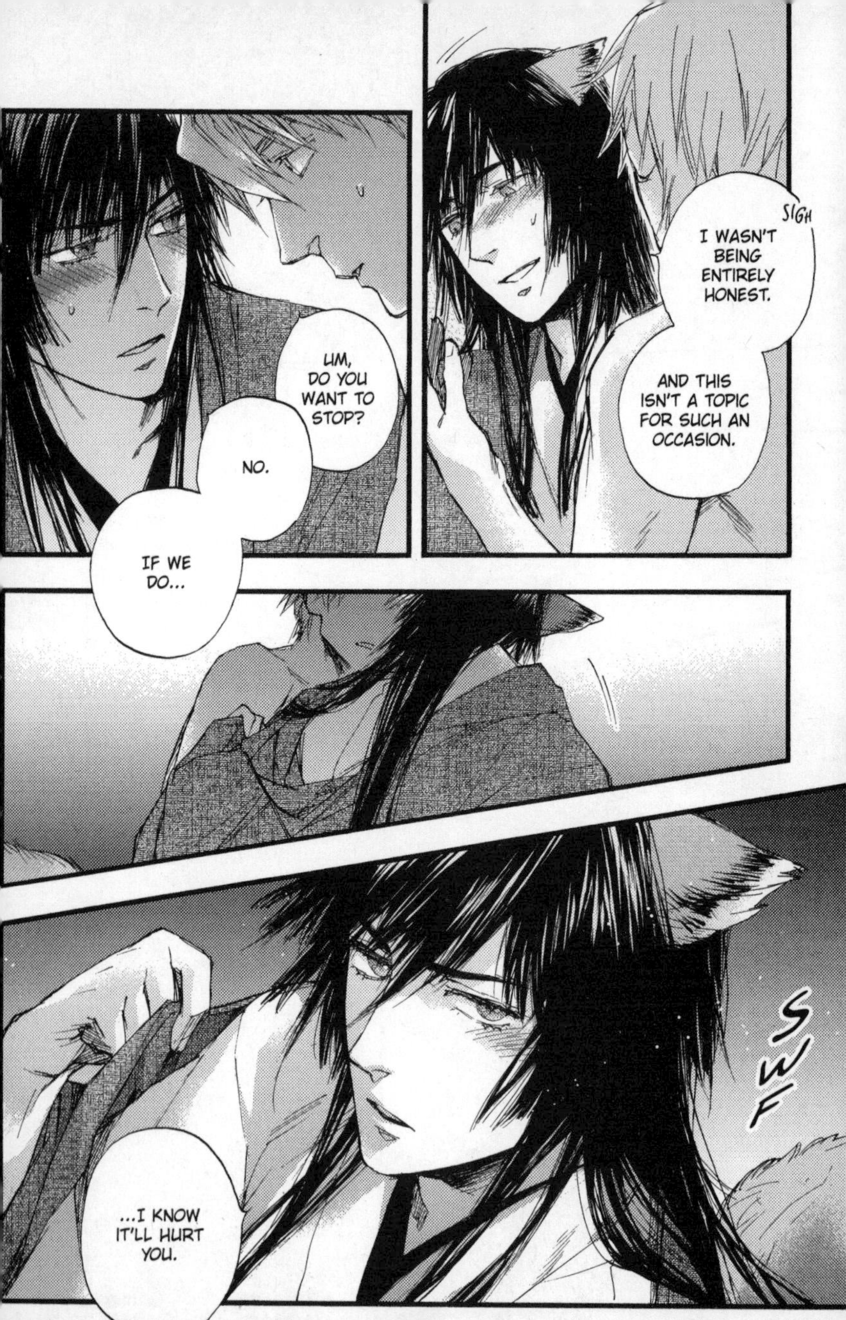
SIGH
I WASN'T BEING ENTIRELY HONEST.
AND THIS ISN'T A TOPIC FOR SUCH AN OCCASION.
UM, DO YOU WANT TO STOP?
NO.
IF WE DO...
SWF
...I KNOW IT'LL HURT YOU.

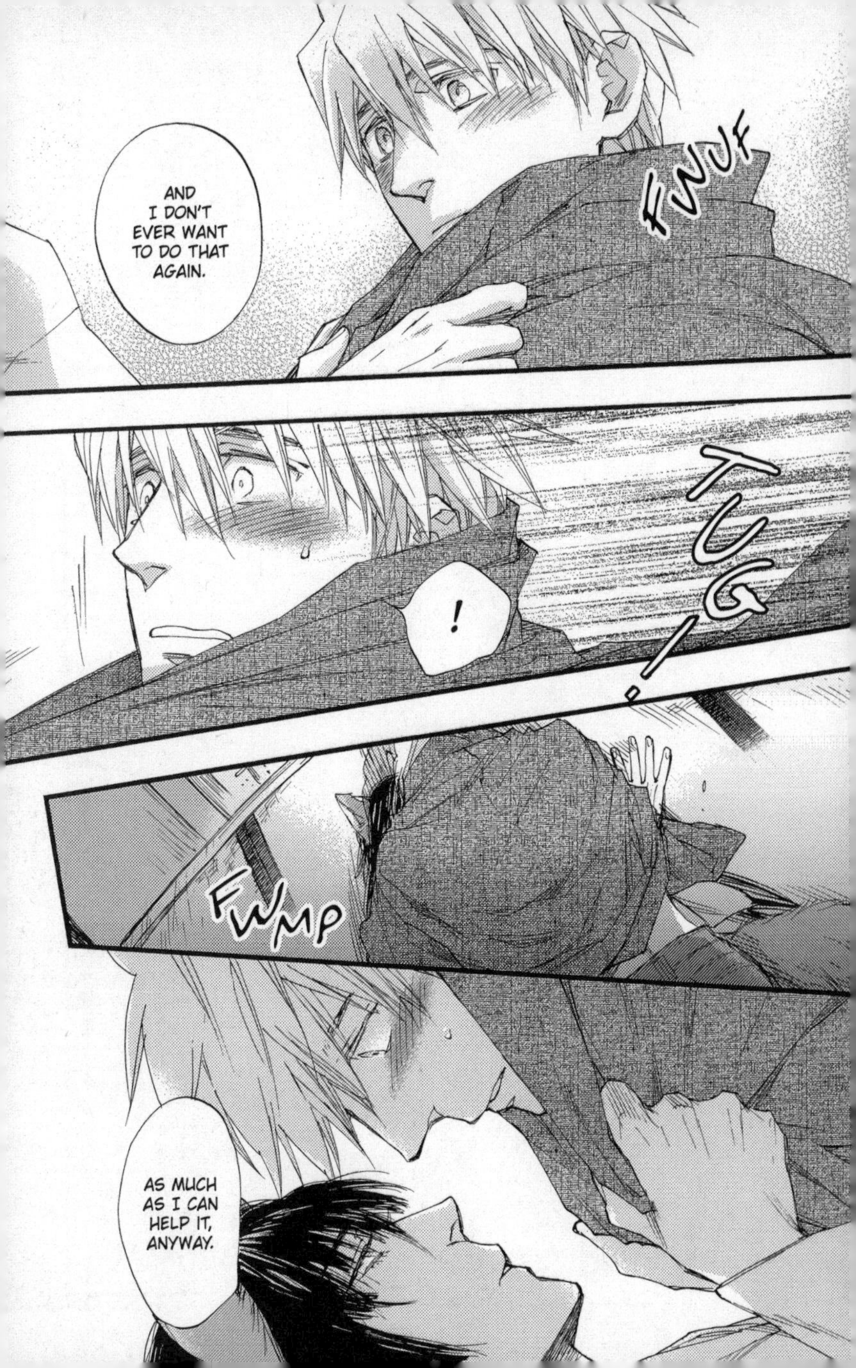
FWUF
AND I DON'T EVER WANT TO DO THAT AGAIN.
TUG!!
!
FWMP
AS MUCH AS I CAN HELP IT, ANYWAY.

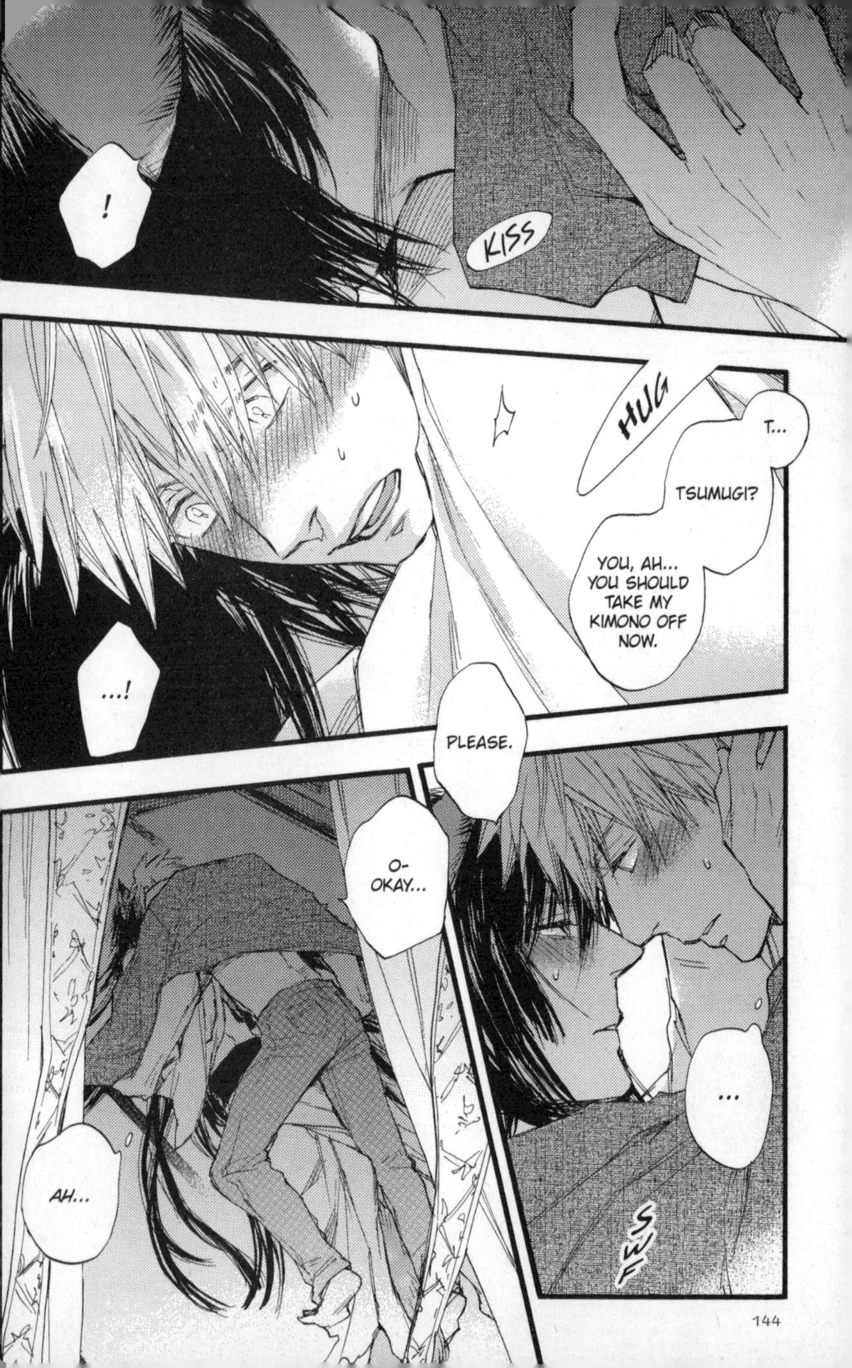
KISS
!
HUG
T...
TSUMUGI?
YOU, AH... YOU SHOULD TAKE MY KIMONO OFF NOW.
...!
PLEASE.
...
SWF
O-OKAY...
AH...

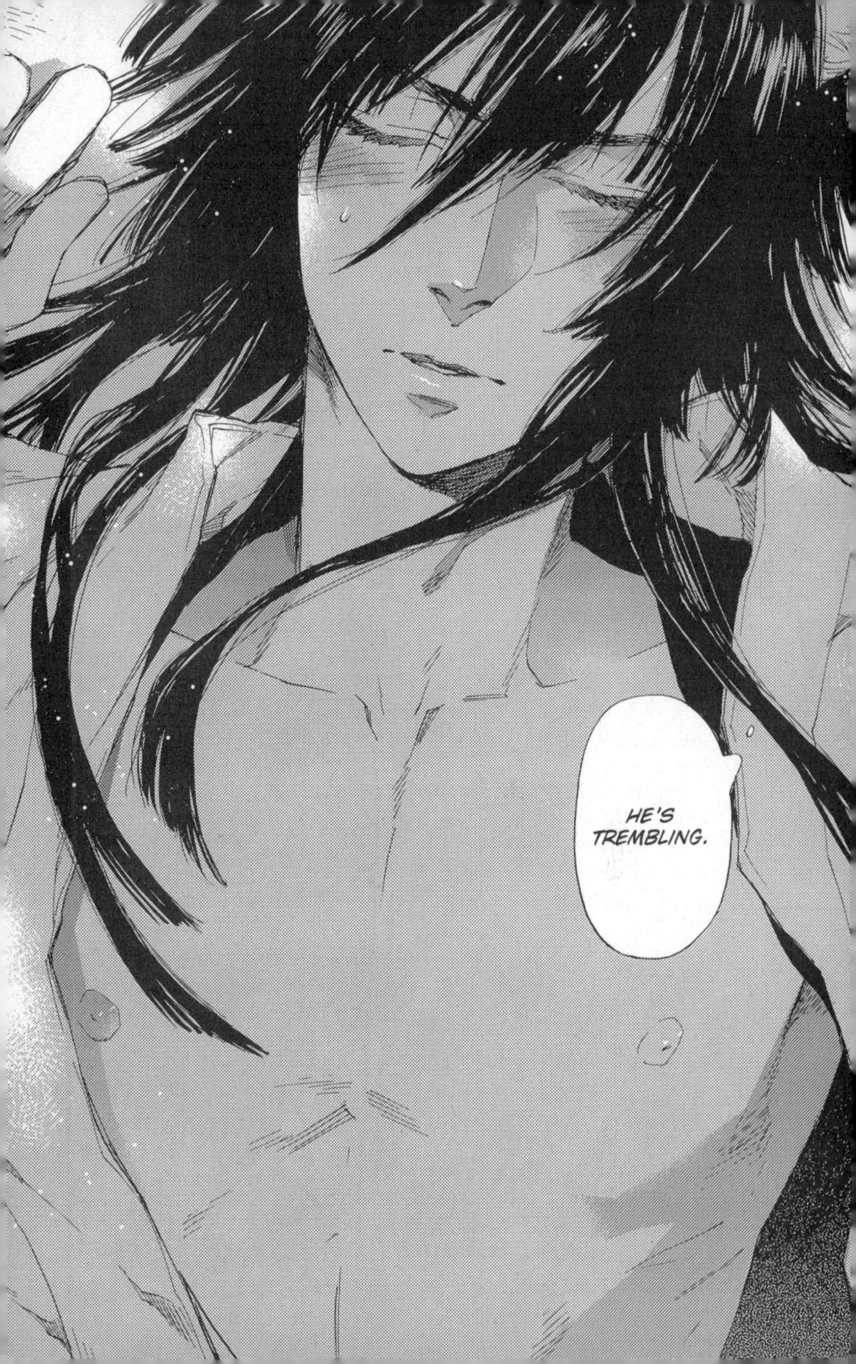
HE'S TREMBLING.

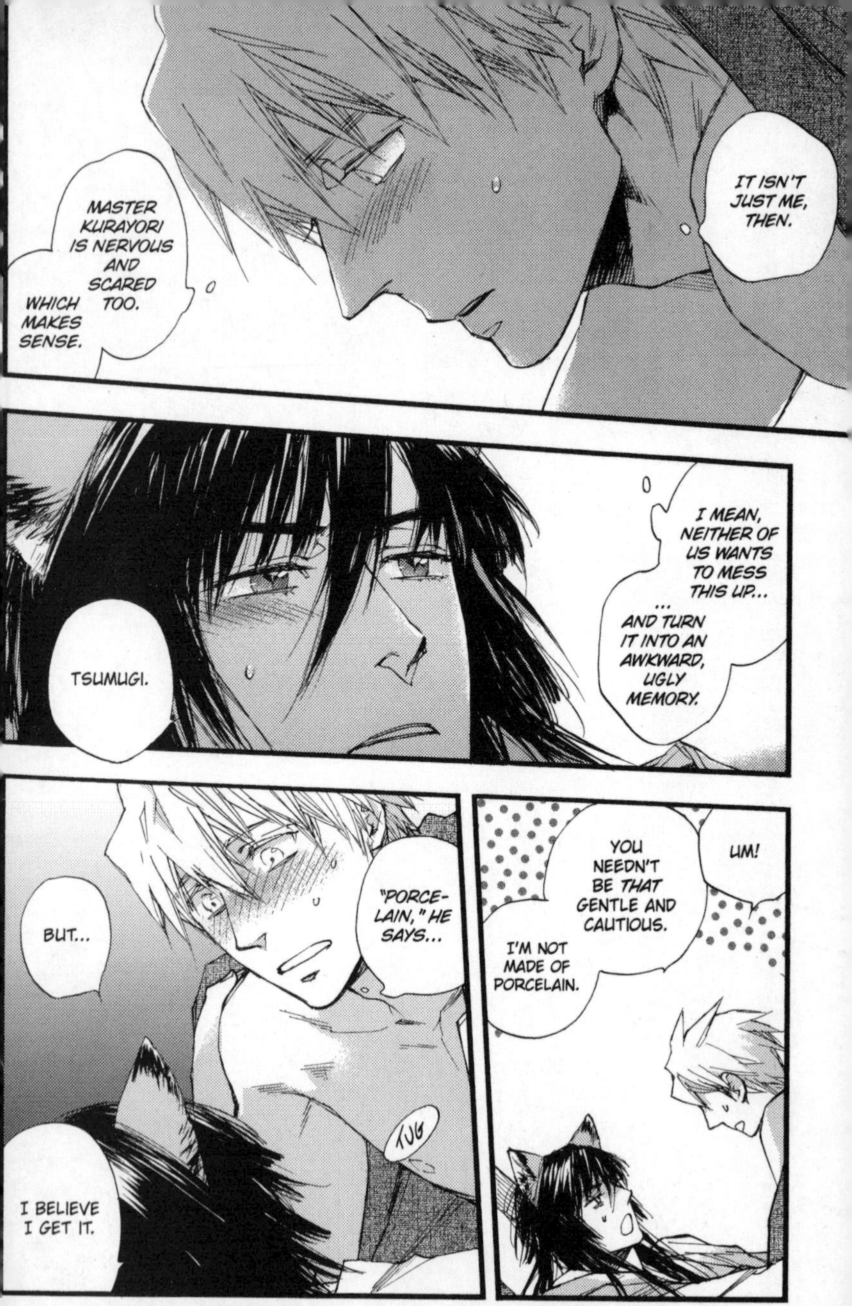
IT ISN'T JUST ME, THEN.
MASTER KURAYORI IS NERVOUS AND SCARED TOO.
WHICH MAKES SENSE.
I MEAN, NEITHER OF US WANTS TO MESS THIS UP...
...AND TURN IT INTO AN AWKWARD, UGLY MEMORY.
TSUMUGI.
UM!
YOU NEEDN'T BE *THAT* GENTLE AND CAUTIOUS.
I'M NOT MADE OF PORCELAIN.
"PORCE-LAIN," HE SAYS...
BUT...
TUG
I BELIEVE I GET IT.

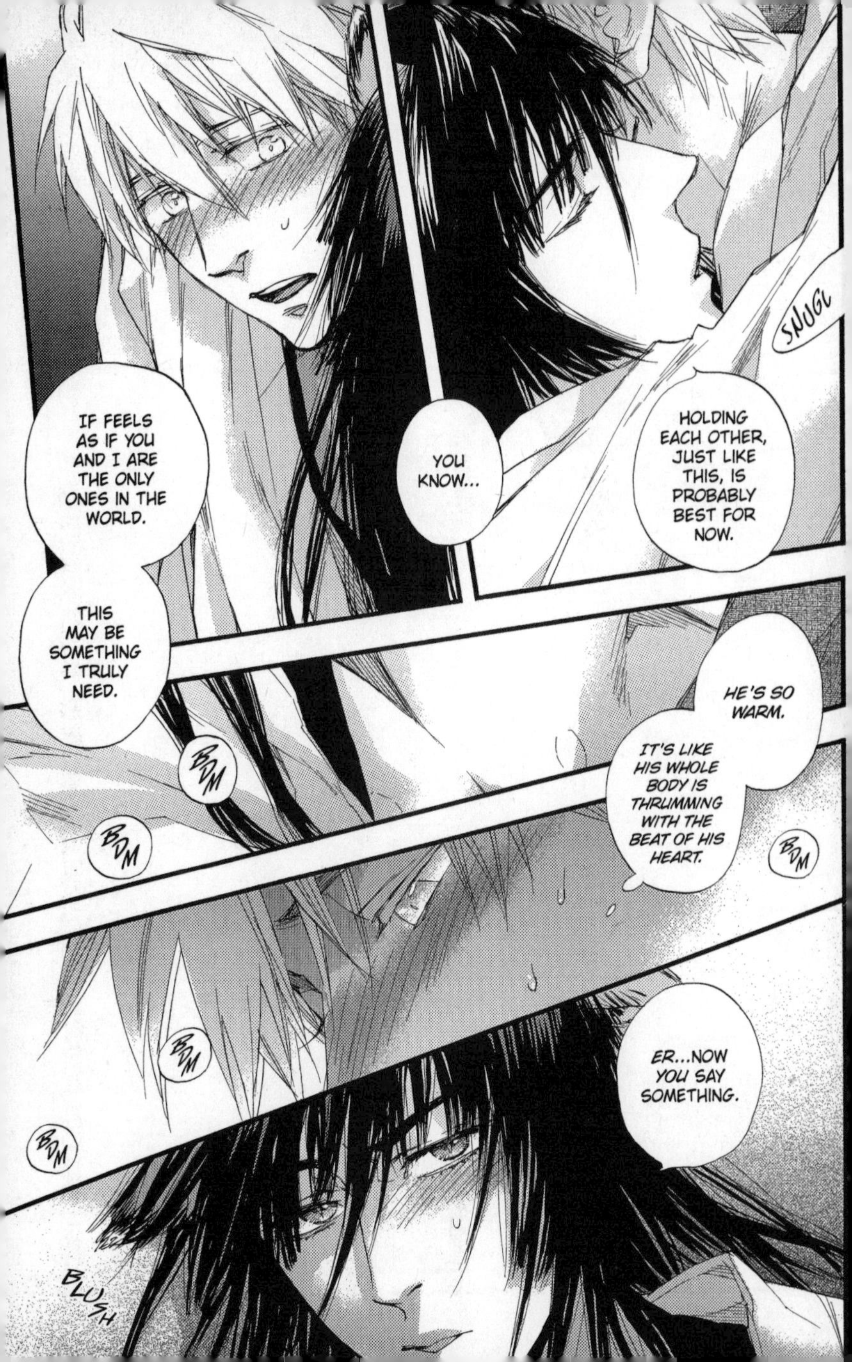
SNUGL
HOLDING EACH OTHER, JUST LIKE THIS, IS PROBABLY BEST FOR NOW.
YOU KNOW...
IF FEELS AS IF YOU AND I ARE THE ONLY ONES IN THE WORLD.
THIS MAY BE SOMETHING I TRULY NEED.
HE'S SO WARM.
IT'S LIKE HIS WHOLE BODY IS THRUMMING WITH THE BEAT OF HIS HEART.
BDM
BDM
BDM
ER...NOW YOU SAY SOMETHING.
BDM
BDM
BLUSH

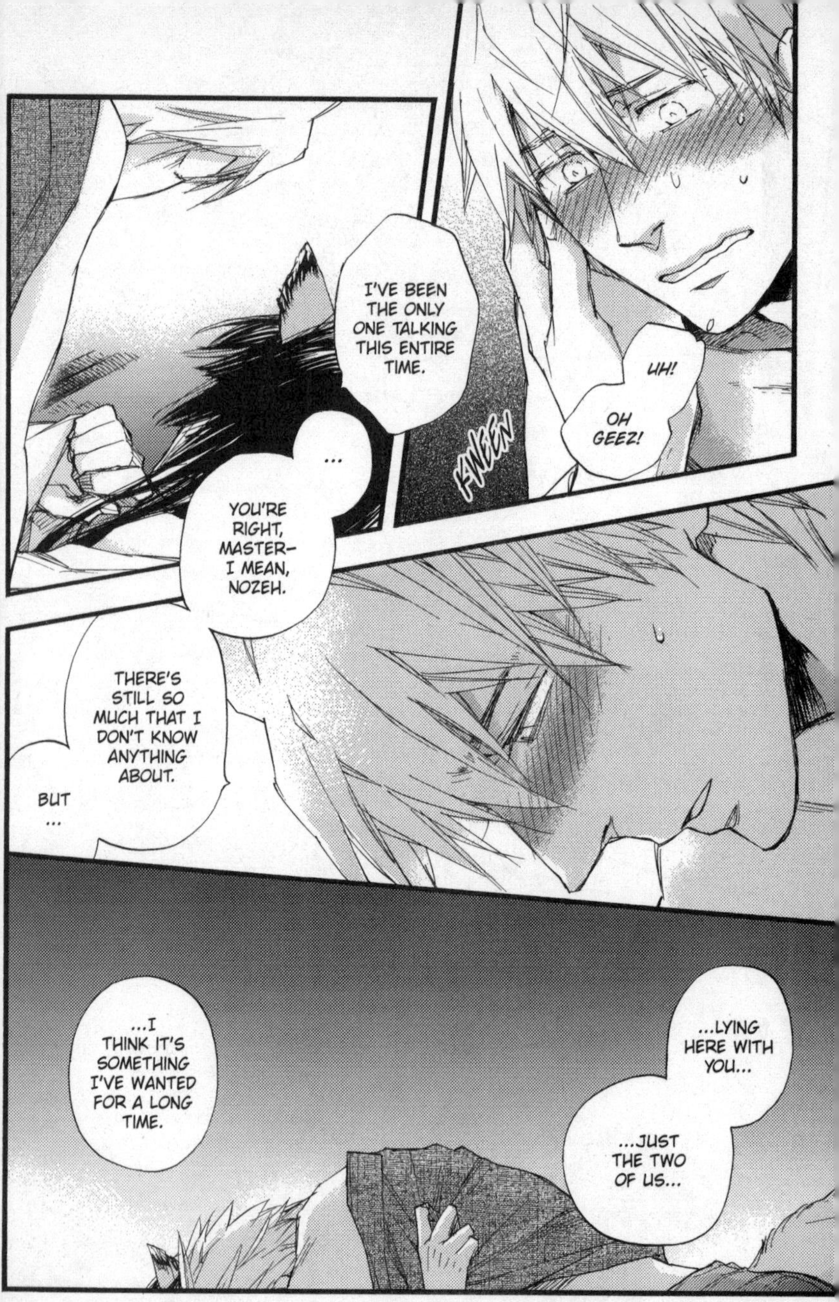
UH!
OH GEEZ!
KWEEN
I'VE BEEN THE ONLY ONE TALKING THIS ENTIRE TIME.
...
YOU'RE RIGHT, MASTER– I MEAN, NOZEH.
THERE'S STILL SO MUCH THAT I DON'T KNOW ANYTHING ABOUT.
BUT ...
...LYING HERE WITH YOU...
...JUST THE TWO OF US...
...I THINK IT'S SOMETHING I'VE WANTED FOR A LONG TIME.

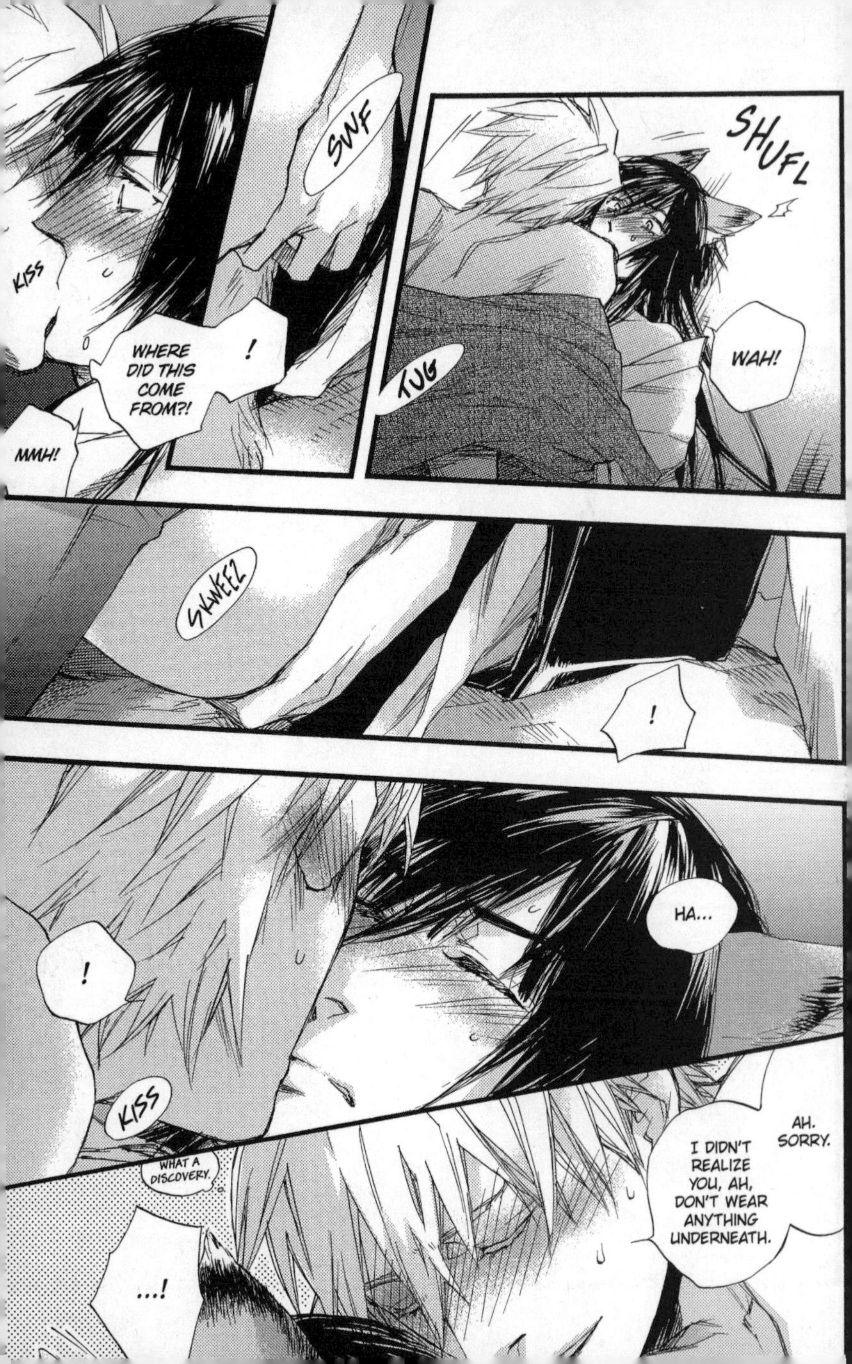
SHUFL
WAH!
TUG
SNF
!
WHERE DID THIS COME FROM?!
KISS
MMH!
SKWEEZ
!
HA...
!
KISS
AH. SORRY.
I DIDN'T REALIZE YOU, AH, DON'T WEAR ANYTHING UNDERNEATH.
WHAT A DISCOVERY.
...!

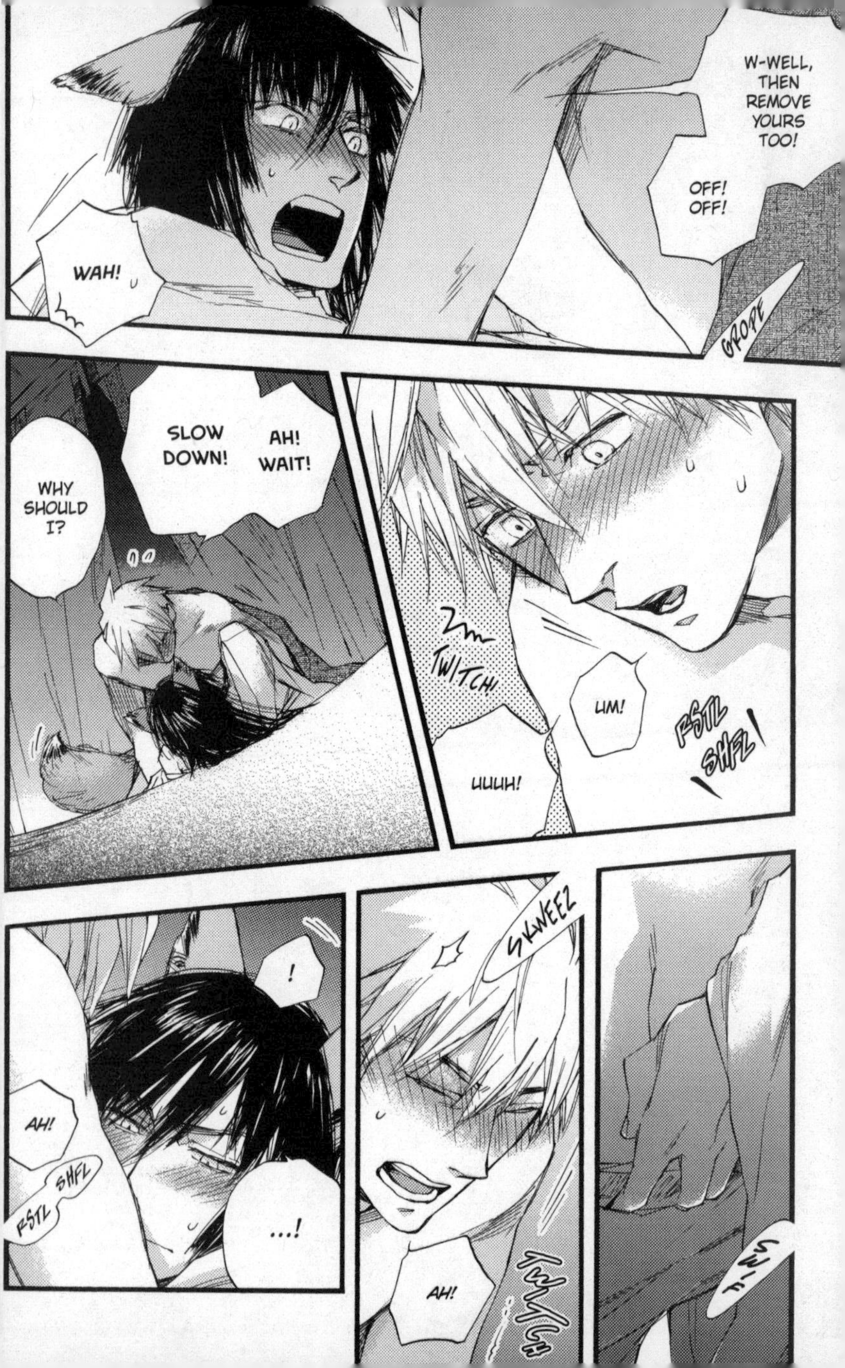
W-WELL, THEN REMOVE YOURS TOO!
OFF! OFF!
GROPE
WAH!
TWITCH
UM!
RSTL SHFL
UUUH!
AH! WAIT!
SLOW DOWN!
WHY SHOULD I?
SWIF
SKWEEZ
TWITCH
AH!
!
AH!
RSTL SHFL
...!

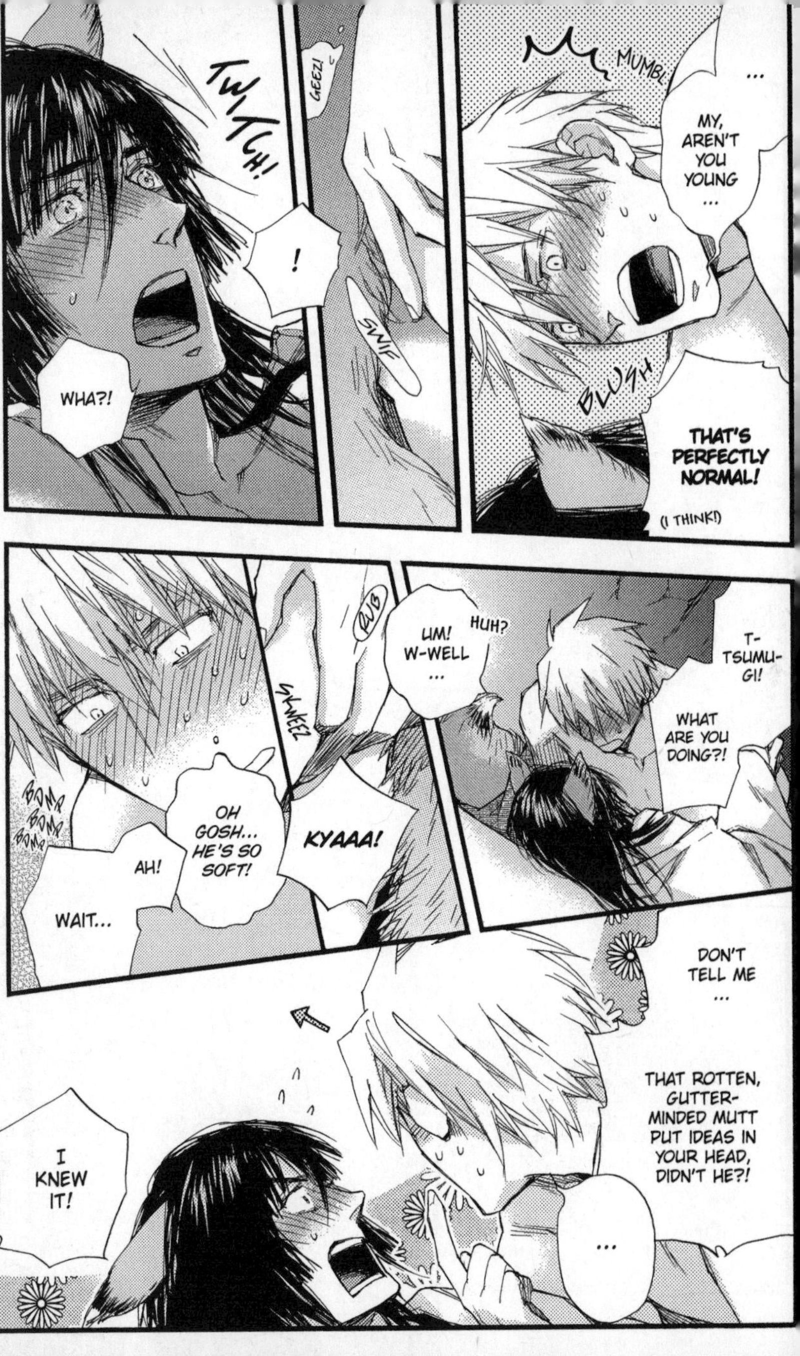
MUMBL
...
MY, AREN'T YOU YOUNG ...
BLUSH
THAT'S PERFECTLY NORMAL!
(I THINK!)
GEEZ!
SWIF
TWITCH!
!
WHA?!
T-TSUMUGI!
WHAT ARE YOU DOING?!
HUH?
UM! W-WELL ...
RUB
SKWEEZ
KYAAA!
OH GOSH... HE'S SO SOFT!
AH!
WAIT...
BOMP BOMP BOMP
DON'T TELL ME ...
THAT ROTTEN, GUTTER-MINDED MUTT PUT IDEAS IN YOUR HEAD, DIDN'T HE?!
...
I KNEW IT!

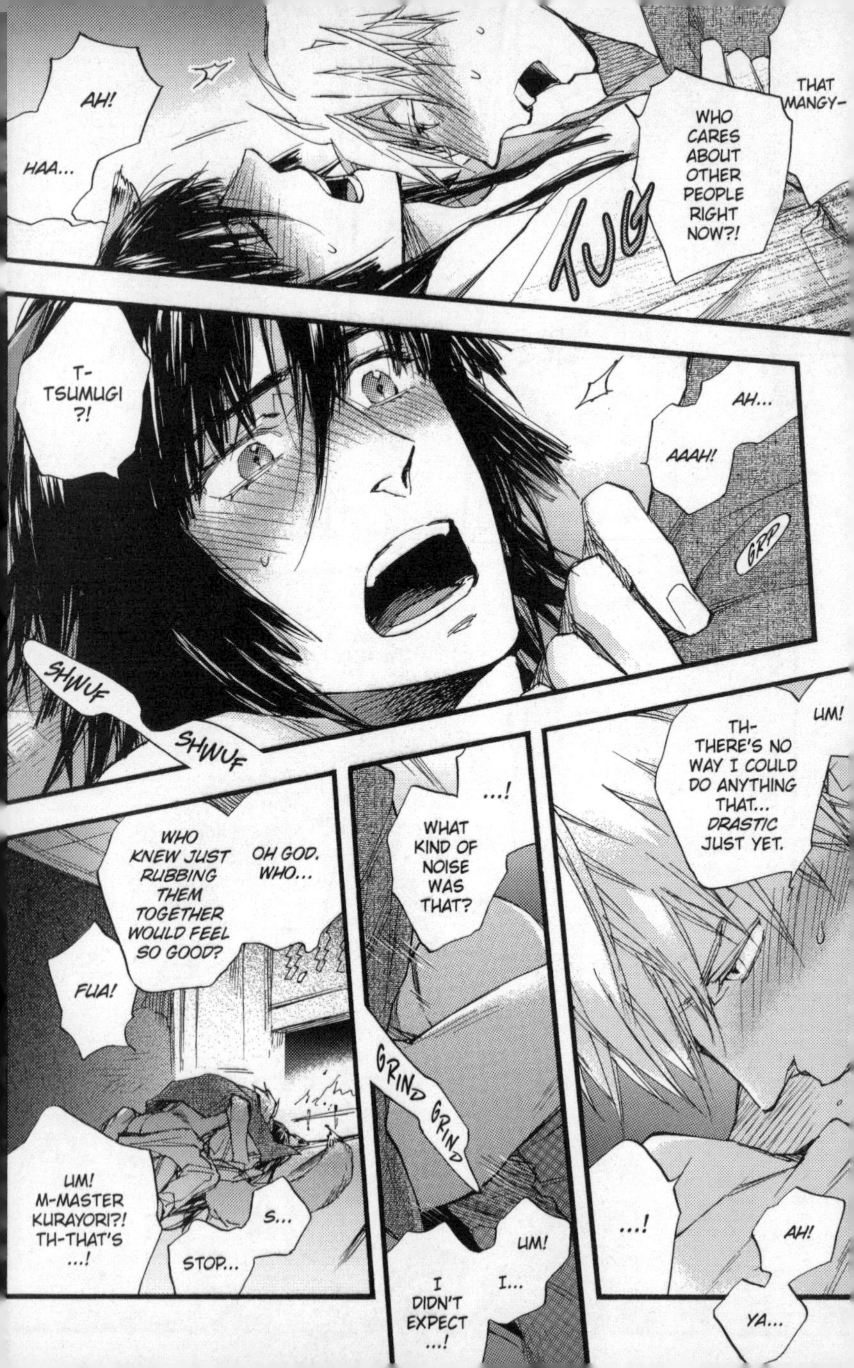
THAT MANGY-
WHO CARES ABOUT OTHER PEOPLE RIGHT NOW?!
TUG
AH!
HAA...
AH...
AAAH!
GRP
T-TSUMUGI?!
SHWUF
SHWUF
UM!
TH- THERE'S NO WAY I COULD DO ANYTHING THAT... DRASTIC JUST YET.
AH!
...!
YA...
...!
WHAT KIND OF NOISE WAS THAT?
GRIND GRIND
UM!
I...
I DIDN'T EXPECT ...!
OH GOD. WHO...
WHO KNEW JUST RUBBING THEM TOGETHER WOULD FEEL SO GOOD?
FUA!
S...
STOP...
UM! M-MASTER KURAYORI?! TH-THAT'S ...!

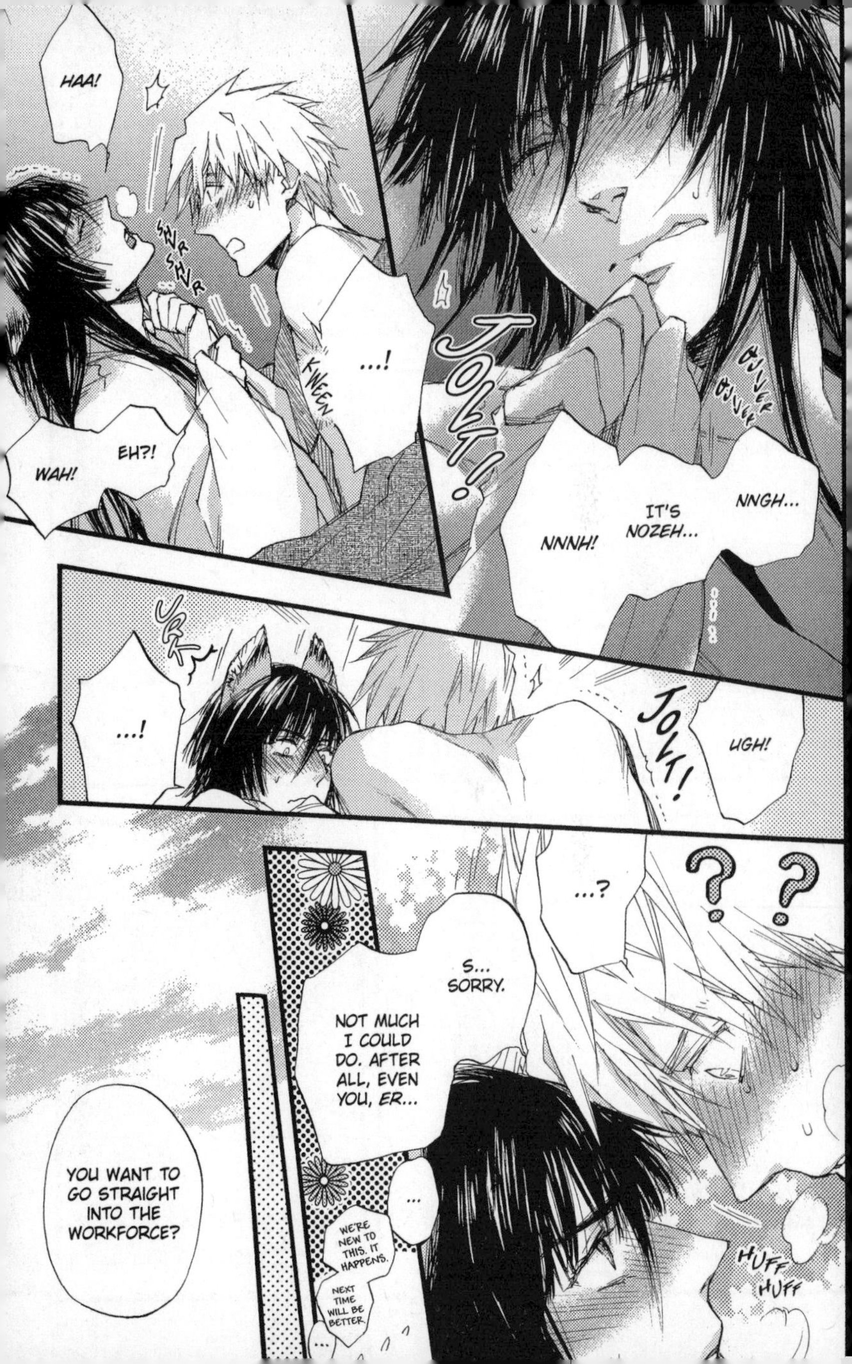
JOLT!!
QUIVER QUIVER
NNGH...
IT'S NOZEH...
NNNH!
HAA!
SHVR SHVR
...!
KWEEN
EH?!
WAH!
UGH!
JOLT!
...!
URK
? ?
...?
S... SORRY.
NOT MUCH I COULD DO. AFTER ALL, EVEN YOU, ER...
...
WE'RE NEW TO THIS. IT HAPPENS.
NEXT TIME WILL BE BETTER.
HUFF HUFF
YOU WANT TO GO STRAIGHT INTO THE WORKFORCE?

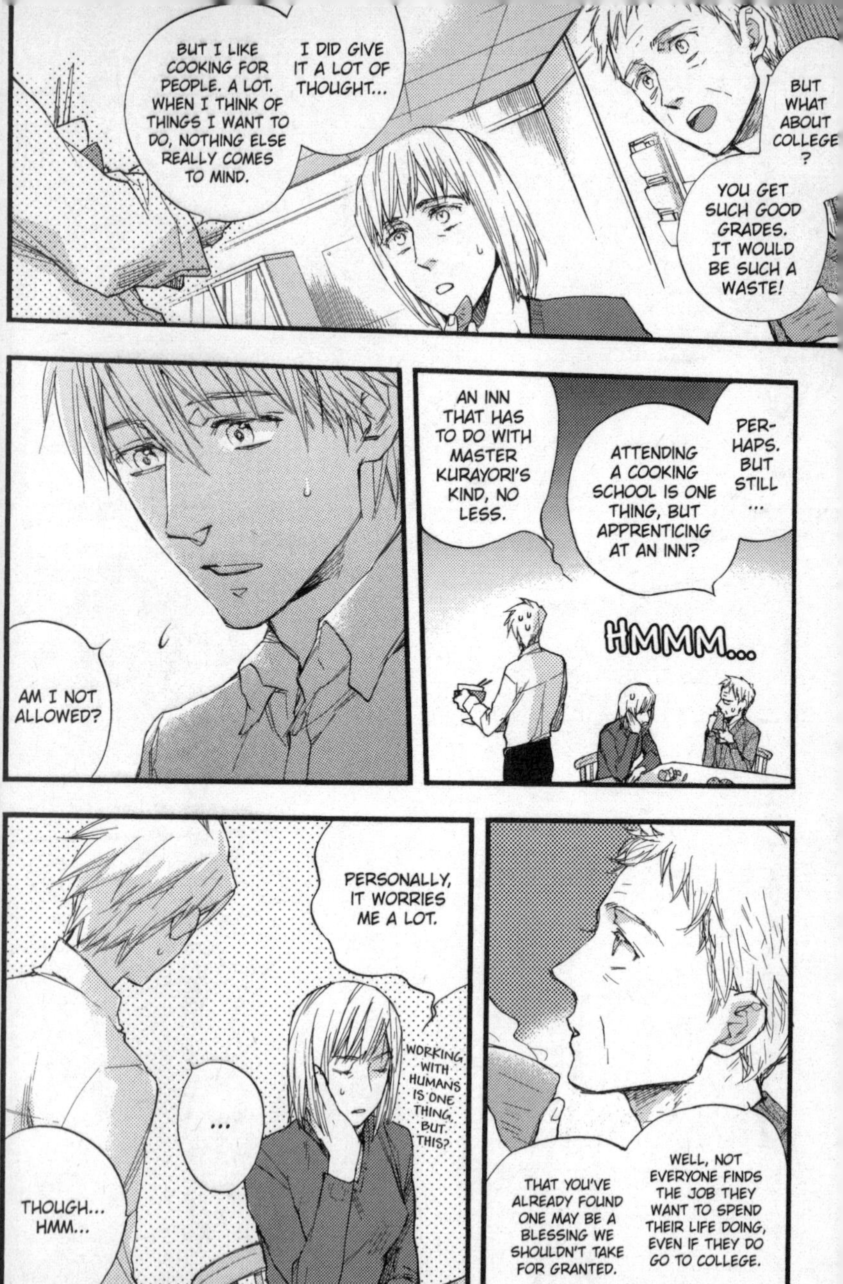
BUT WHAT ABOUT COLLEGE?
YOU GET SUCH GOOD GRADES. IT WOULD BE SUCH A WASTE!
I DID GIVE IT A LOT OF THOUGHT...
BUT I LIKE COOKING FOR PEOPLE. A LOT. WHEN I THINK OF THINGS I WANT TO DO, NOTHING ELSE REALLY COMES TO MIND.
PER-HAPS. BUT STILL...
ATTENDING A COOKING SCHOOL IS ONE THING, BUT APPRENTICING AT AN INN?
AN INN THAT HAS TO DO WITH MASTER KURAYORI'S KIND, NO LESS.
HMMM...
AM I NOT ALLOWED?
WELL, NOT EVERYONE FINDS THE JOB THEY WANT TO SPEND THEIR LIFE DOING, EVEN IF THEY DO GO TO COLLEGE.
THAT YOU'VE ALREADY FOUND ONE MAY BE A BLESSING WE SHOULDN'T TAKE FOR GRANTED.
PERSONALLY, IT WORRIES ME A LOT.
WORKING WITH HUMANS IS ONE THING, BUT THIS?
...
THOUGH... HMM...

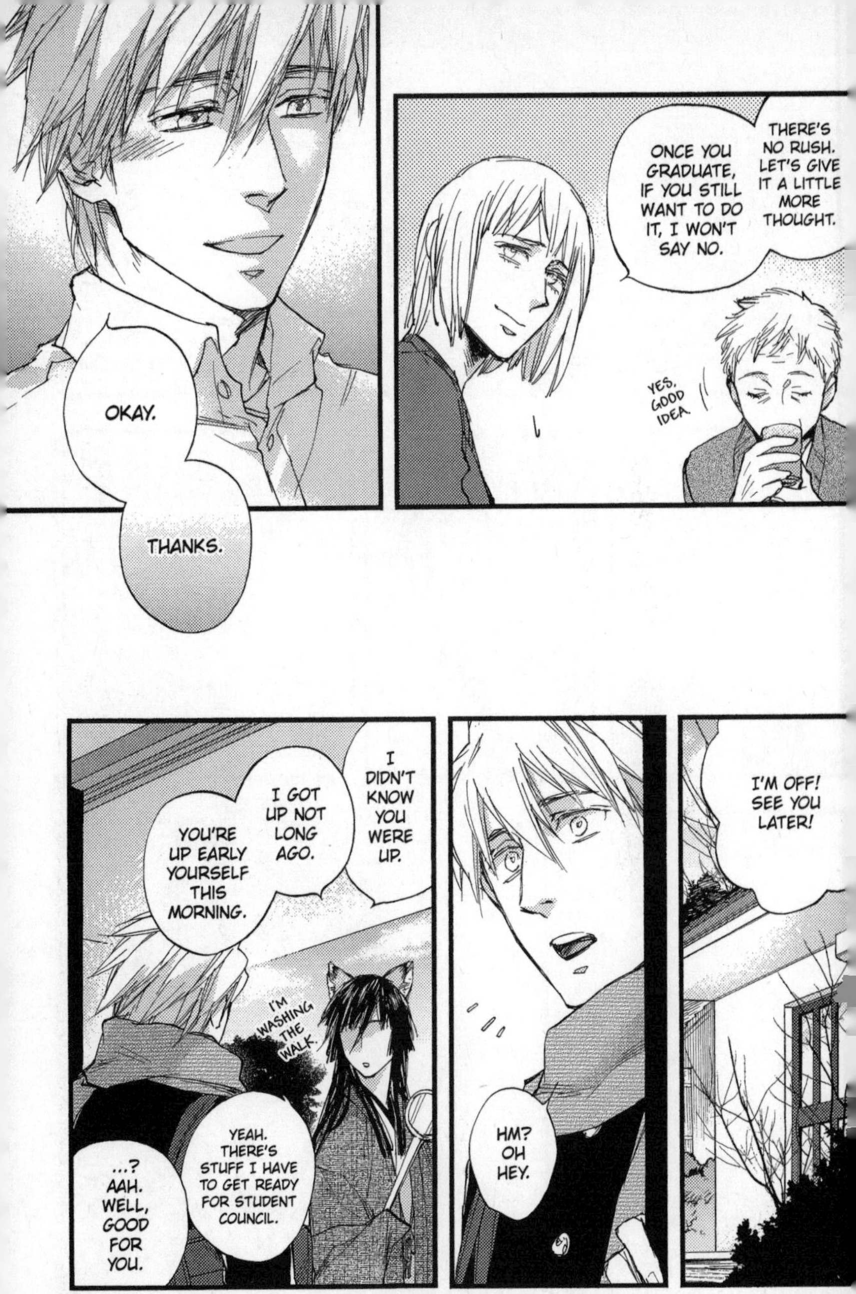
THERE'S NO RUSH. LET'S GIVE IT A LITTLE MORE THOUGHT.
ONCE YOU GRADUATE, IF YOU STILL WANT TO DO IT, I WON'T SAY NO.
YES, GOOD IDEA.
OKAY.
THANKS.
I'M OFF! SEE YOU LATER!
HM? OH HEY.
I DIDN'T KNOW YOU WERE UP.
I GOT UP NOT LONG AGO.
YOU'RE UP EARLY YOURSELF THIS MORNING.
I'M WASHING THE WALK.
YEAH. THERE'S STUFF I HAVE TO GET READY FOR STUDENT COUNCIL.
...? AAH. WELL, GOOD FOR YOU.

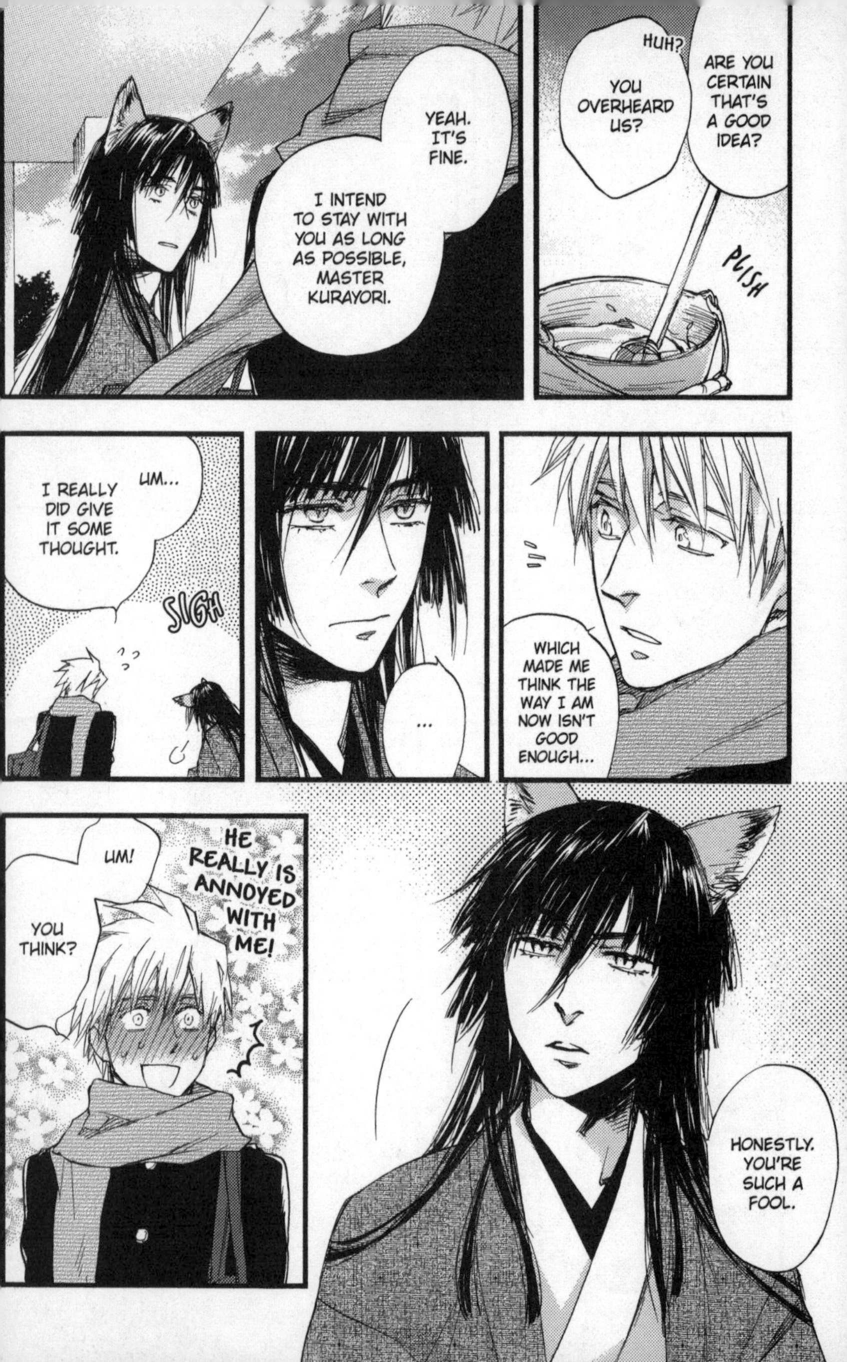
ARE YOU CERTAIN THAT'S A GOOD IDEA?
HUH?
YOU OVERHEARD US?
PLISH
YEAH. IT'S FINE.
I INTEND TO STAY WITH YOU AS LONG AS POSSIBLE, MASTER KURAYORI.
WHICH MADE ME THINK THE WAY I AM NOW ISN'T GOOD ENOUGH...
...
UM...
I REALLY DID GIVE IT SOME THOUGHT.
SIGH
HONESTLY. YOU'RE SUCH A FOOL.
HE REALLY IS ANNOYED WITH ME!
UM!
YOU THINK?

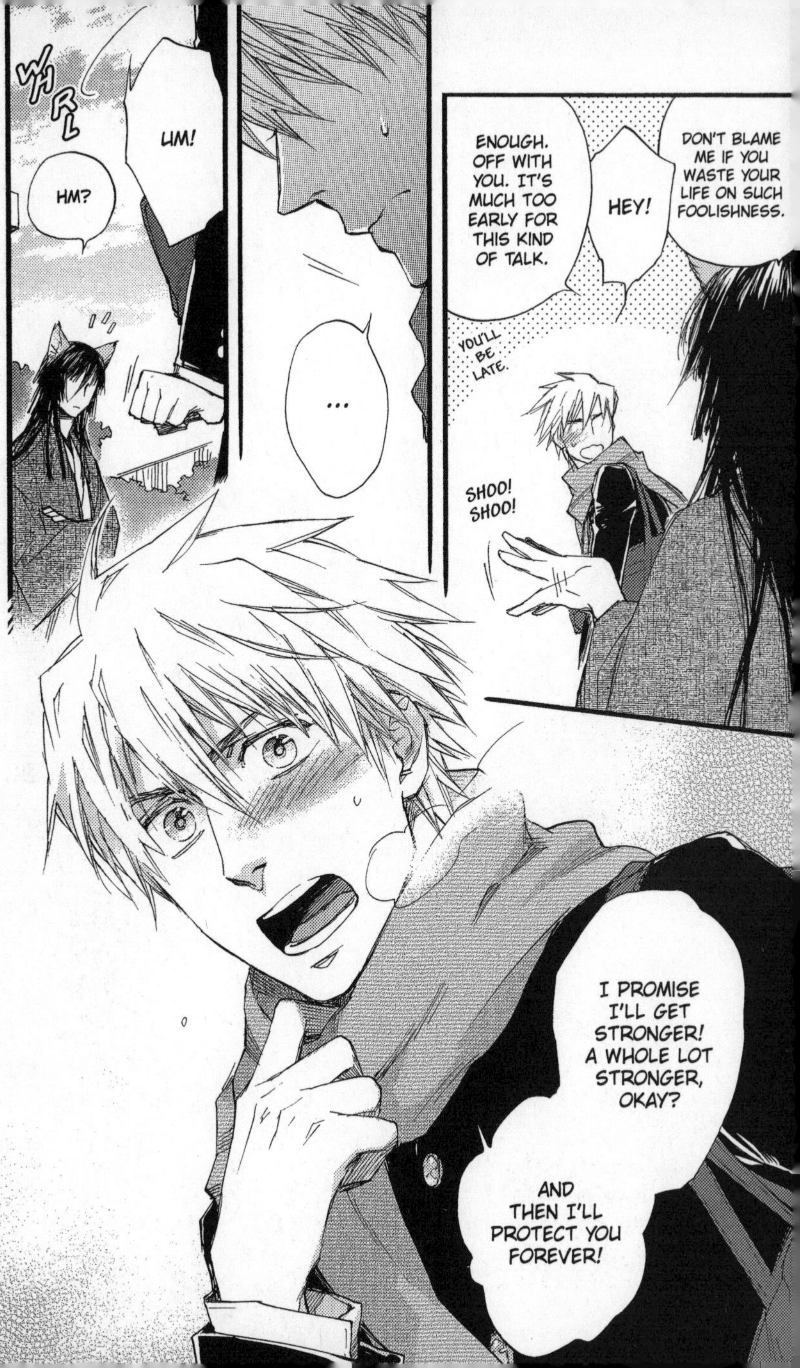
DON'T BLAME ME IF YOU WASTE YOUR LIFE ON SUCH FOOLISHNESS.
HEY!
ENOUGH. OFF WITH YOU. IT'S MUCH TOO EARLY FOR THIS KIND OF TALK.
YOU'LL BE LATE.
SHOO! SHOO!
...
UM!
WHRL
HM?
I PROMISE I'LL GET STRONGER! A WHOLE LOT STRONGER, OKAY?
AND THEN I'LL PROTECT YOU FOREVER!

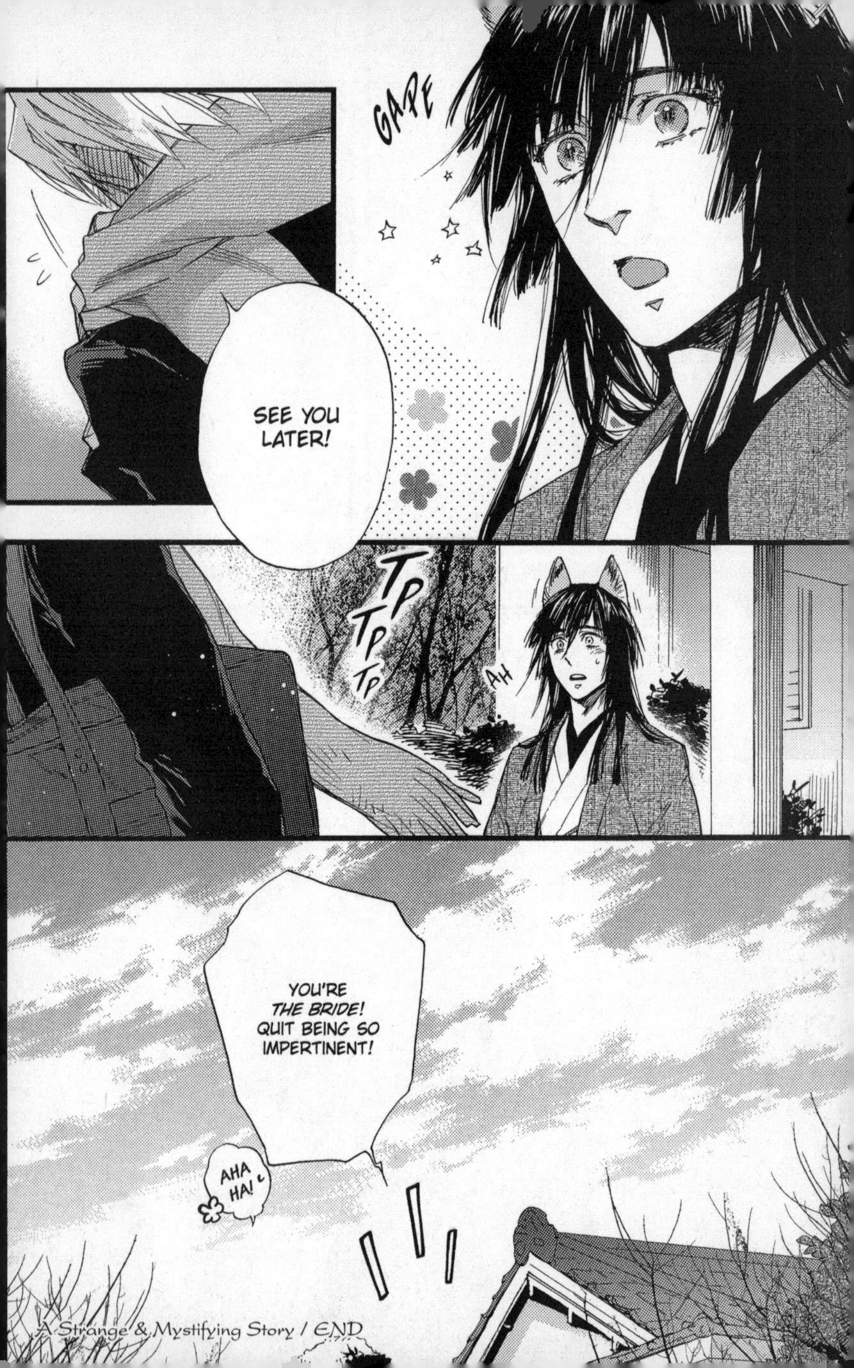
GAPE
SEE YOU LATER!
AH
TP TP TP
YOU'RE THE BRIDE! QUIT BEING SO IMPERTINENT!
AHA HA!
A Strange & Mystifying Story / END

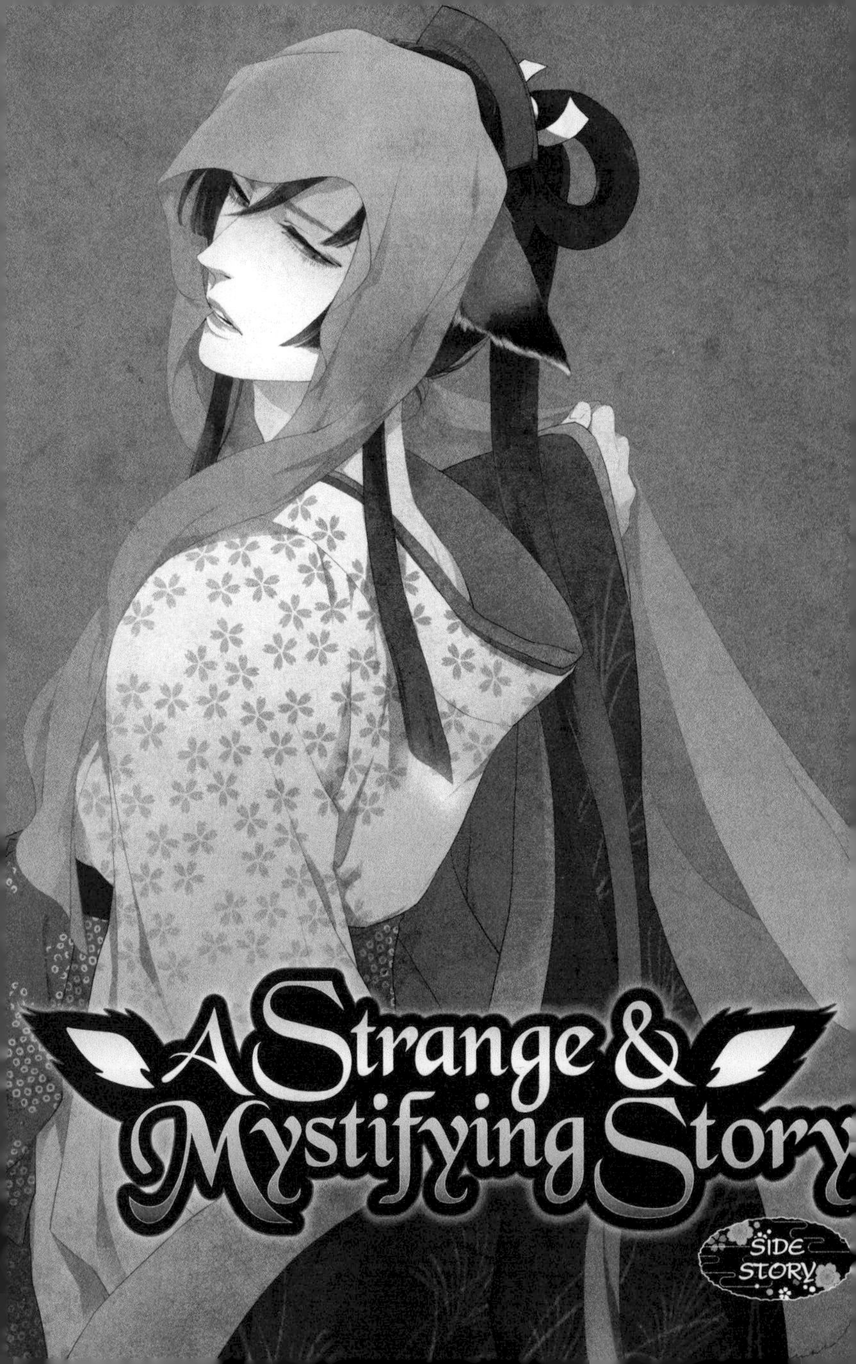
A Strange & Mystifying Story
SIDE STORY

A Strange & Mystifying Story

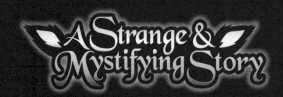

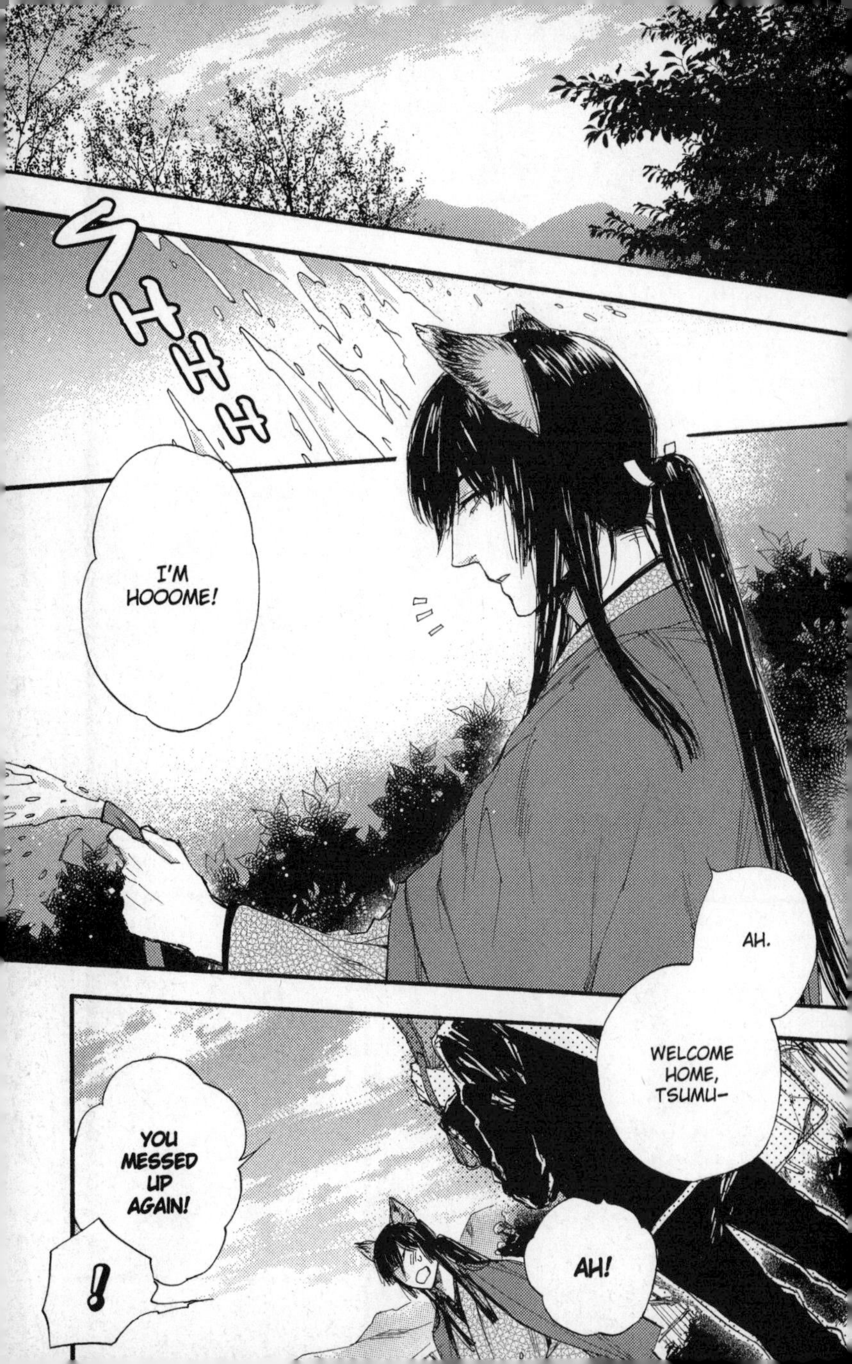
I'M HOOOME!
AH.
WELCOME HOME, TSUMU-
YOU MESSED UP AGAIN!
AH!
!

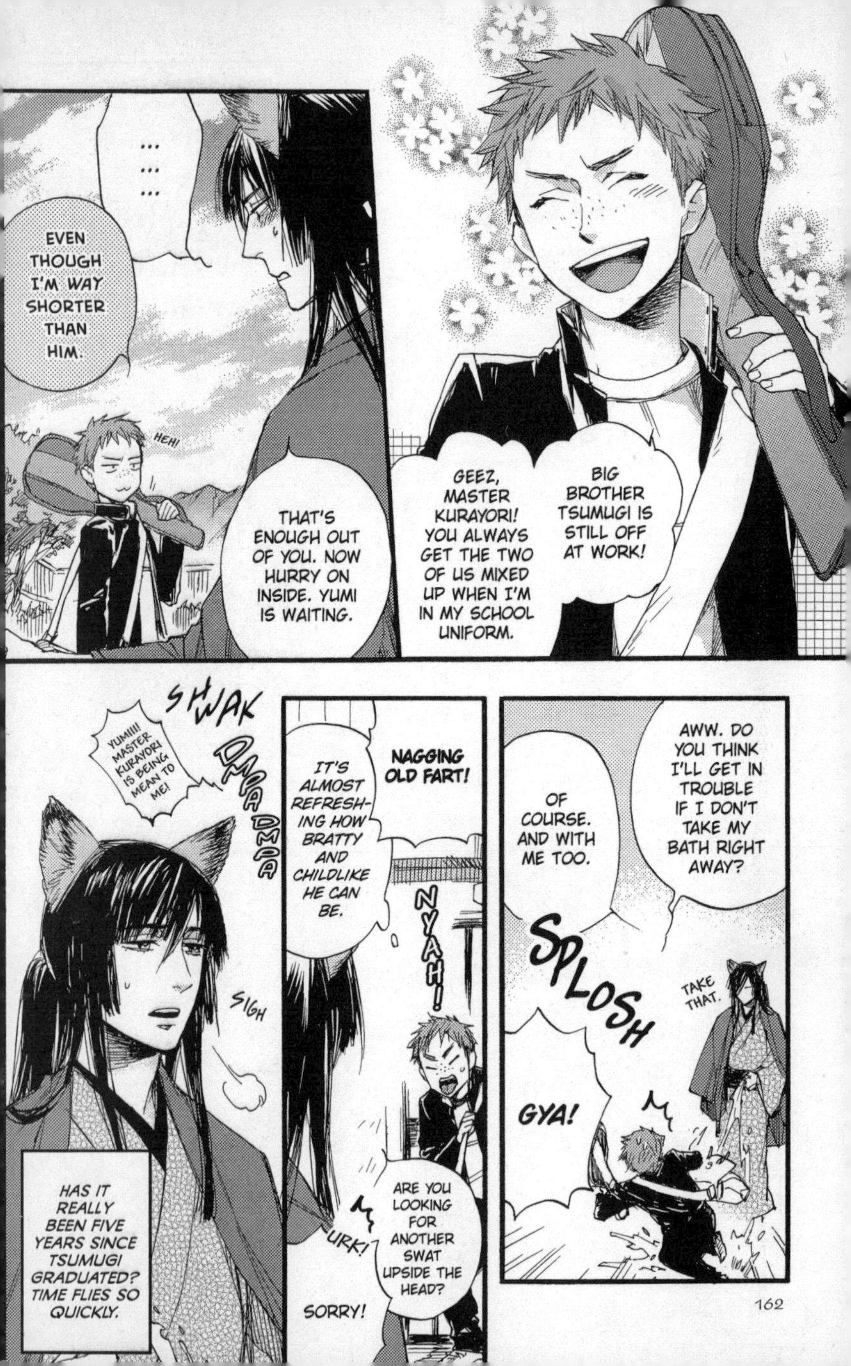
BIG BROTHER TSUMUGI IS STILL OFF AT WORK!
GEEZ, MASTER KURAYORI! YOU ALWAYS GET THE TWO OF US MIXED UP WHEN I'M IN MY SCHOOL UNIFORM.
...
...
...
EVEN THOUGH I'M WAY SHORTER THAN HIM.
HEH!
THAT'S ENOUGH OUT OF YOU. NOW HURRY ON INSIDE. YUMI IS WAITING.
AWW. DO YOU THINK I'LL GET IN TROUBLE IF I DON'T TAKE MY BATH RIGHT AWAY?
OF COURSE. AND WITH ME TOO.
SPLOSH
TAKE THAT.
GYA!
NAGGING OLD FART!
IT'S ALMOST REFRESHING HOW BRATTY AND CHILDLIKE HE CAN BE.
NYAH!
ARE YOU LOOKING FOR ANOTHER SWAT UPSIDE THE HEAD?
URK!
SORRY!
SHWAK
YUMIII! MASTER KURAYORI IS BEING MEAN TO ME!
DMPA DMPA
SIGH
HAS IT REALLY BEEN FIVE YEARS SINCE TSUMUGI GRADUATED? TIME FLIES SO QUICKLY.

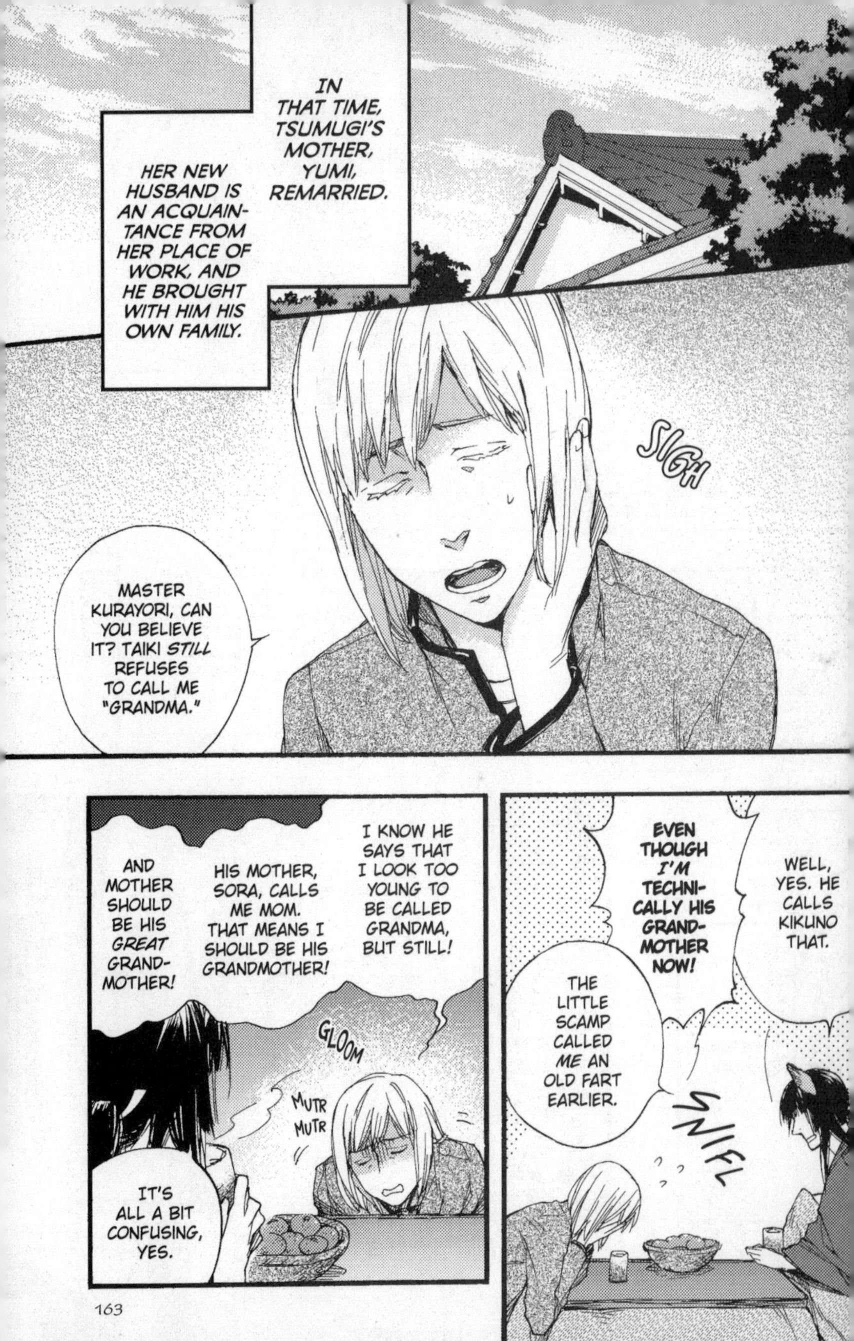
IN THAT TIME, TSUMUGI'S MOTHER, YUMI, REMARRIED.
HER NEW HUSBAND IS AN ACQUAIN-TANCE FROM HER PLACE OF WORK, AND HE BROUGHT WITH HIM HIS OWN FAMILY.
SIGH
MASTER KURAYORI, CAN YOU BELIEVE IT? TAIKI *STILL* REFUSES TO CALL ME "GRANDMA."
WELL, YES. HE CALLS KIKUNO THAT.
EVEN THOUGH *I'M* TECHNI-CALLY HIS GRAND-MOTHER NOW!
THE LITTLE SCAMP CALLED *ME* AN OLD FART EARLIER.
SNIFL
I KNOW HE SAYS THAT I LOOK TOO YOUNG TO BE CALLED GRANDMA, BUT STILL!
HIS MOTHER, SORA, CALLS ME MOM. THAT MEANS I SHOULD BE HIS GRANDMOTHER!
AND MOTHER SHOULD BE HIS *GREAT* GRAND-MOTHER!
GLOOM
MUTR MUTR
IT'S ALL A BIT CONFUSING, YES.

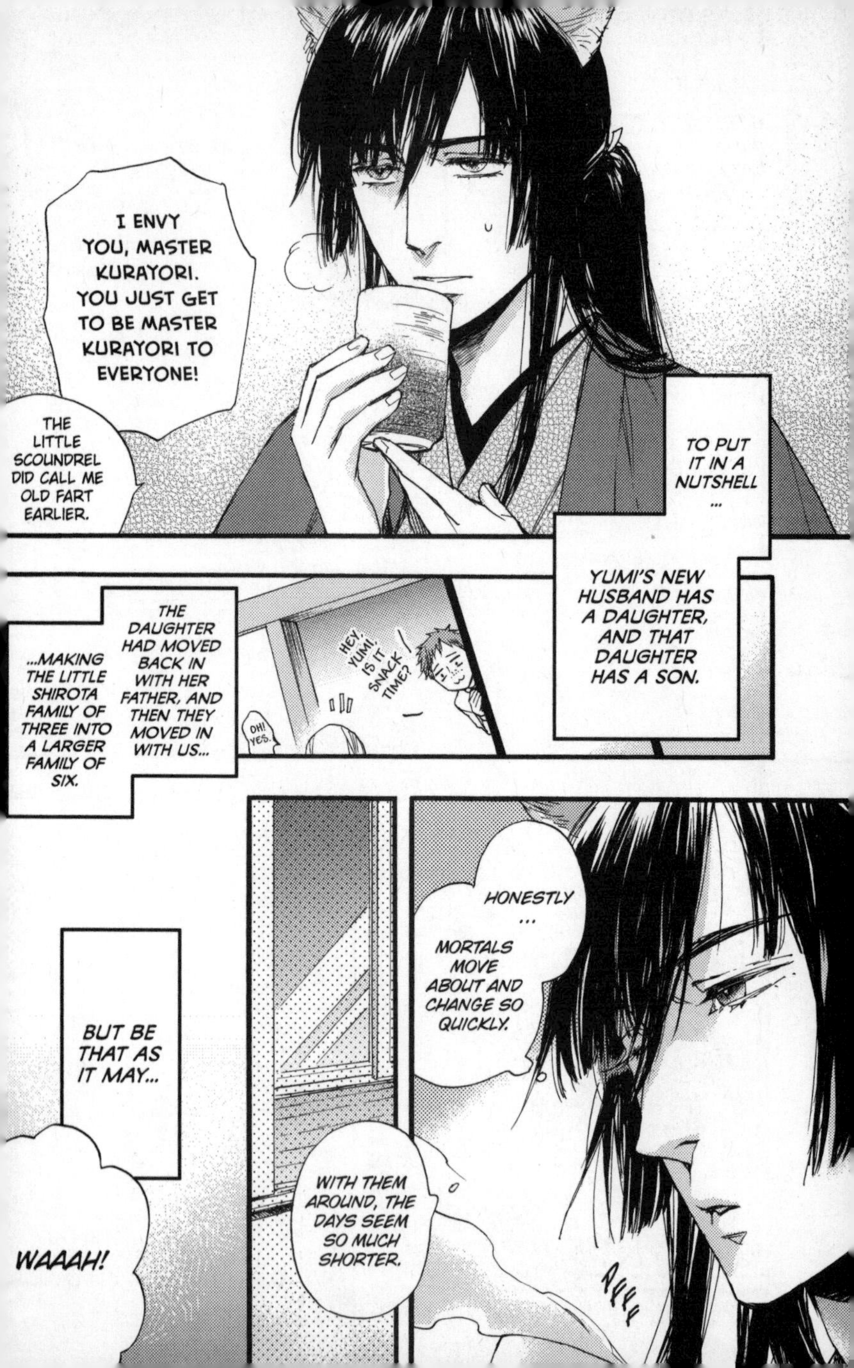
I ENVY YOU, MASTER KURAYORI. YOU JUST GET TO BE MASTER KURAYORI TO EVERYONE!
THE LITTLE SCOUNDREL DID CALL ME OLD FART EARLIER.
TO PUT IT IN A NUTSHELL ...
YUMI'S NEW HUSBAND HAS A DAUGHTER, AND THAT DAUGHTER HAS A SON.
HEY, YUMI, IS IT SNACK TIME?
OH! YES.
THE DAUGHTER HAD MOVED BACK IN WITH HER FATHER, AND THEN THEY MOVED IN WITH US...
...MAKING THE LITTLE SHIROTA FAMILY OF THREE INTO A LARGER FAMILY OF SIX.
HONESTLY ...
MORTALS MOVE ABOUT AND CHANGE SO QUICKLY.
WITH THEM AROUND, THE DAYS SEEM SO MUCH SHORTER.
BUT BE THAT AS IT MAY...
WAAAH!

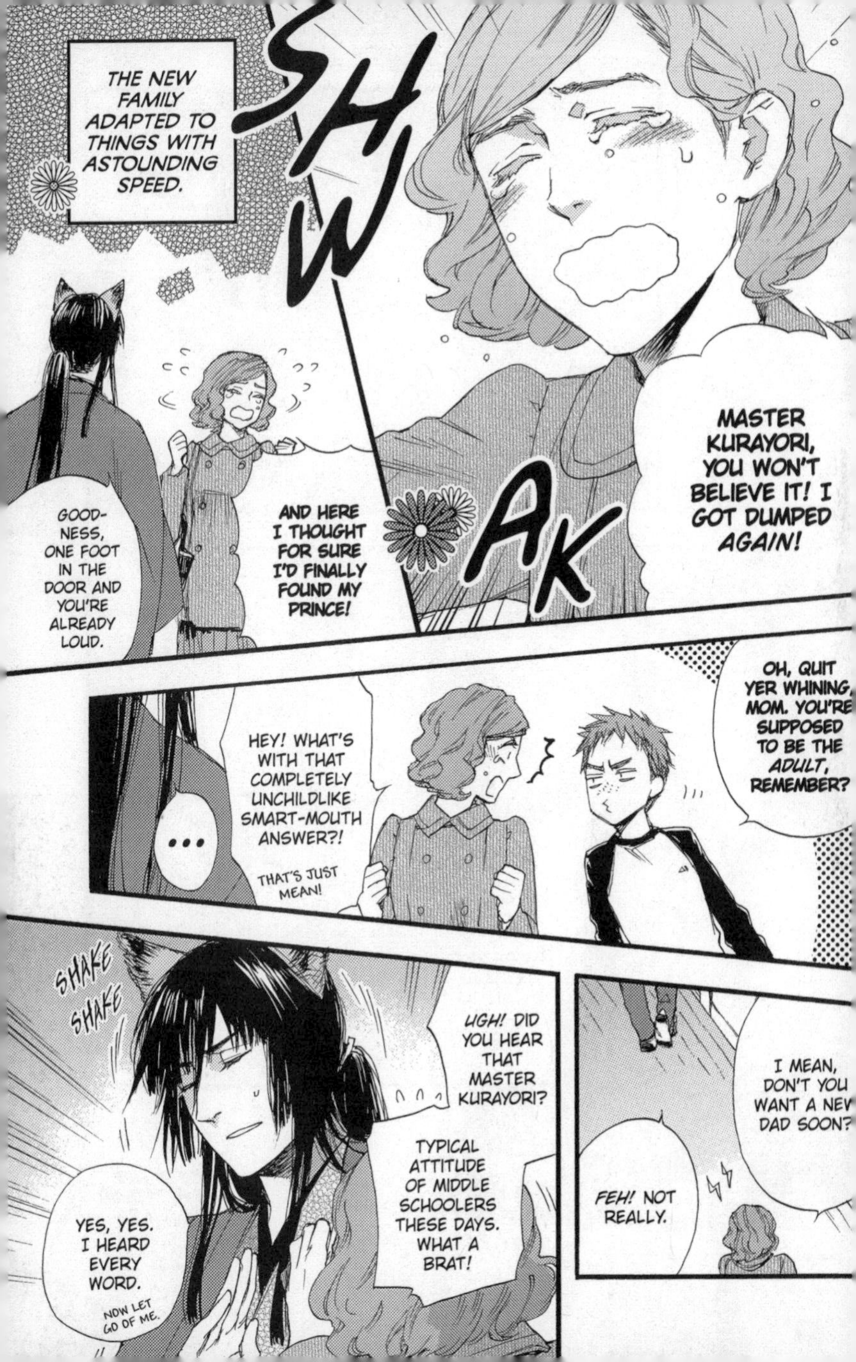
SHWAK
MASTER KURAYORI, YOU WON'T BELIEVE IT! I GOT DUMPED *AGAIN!*
THE NEW FAMILY ADAPTED TO THINGS WITH ASTOUNDING SPEED.
AND HERE I THOUGHT FOR SURE I'D FINALLY FOUND MY PRINCE!
GOODNESS, ONE FOOT IN THE DOOR AND YOU'RE ALREADY LOUD.
OH, QUIT YER WHINING, MOM. YOU'RE SUPPOSED TO BE THE *ADULT*, REMEMBER?
HEY! WHAT'S WITH THAT COMPLETELY UNCHILDLIKE SMART-MOUTH ANSWER?!
THAT'S JUST MEAN!
...
I MEAN, DON'T YOU WANT A NEW DAD SOON?
FEH! NOT REALLY.
UGH! DID YOU HEAR THAT MASTER KURAYORI?
TYPICAL ATTITUDE OF MIDDLE SCHOOLERS THESE DAYS. WHAT A BRAT!
SHAKE SHAKE
YES, YES. I HEARD EVERY WORD.
NOW LET GO OF ME.

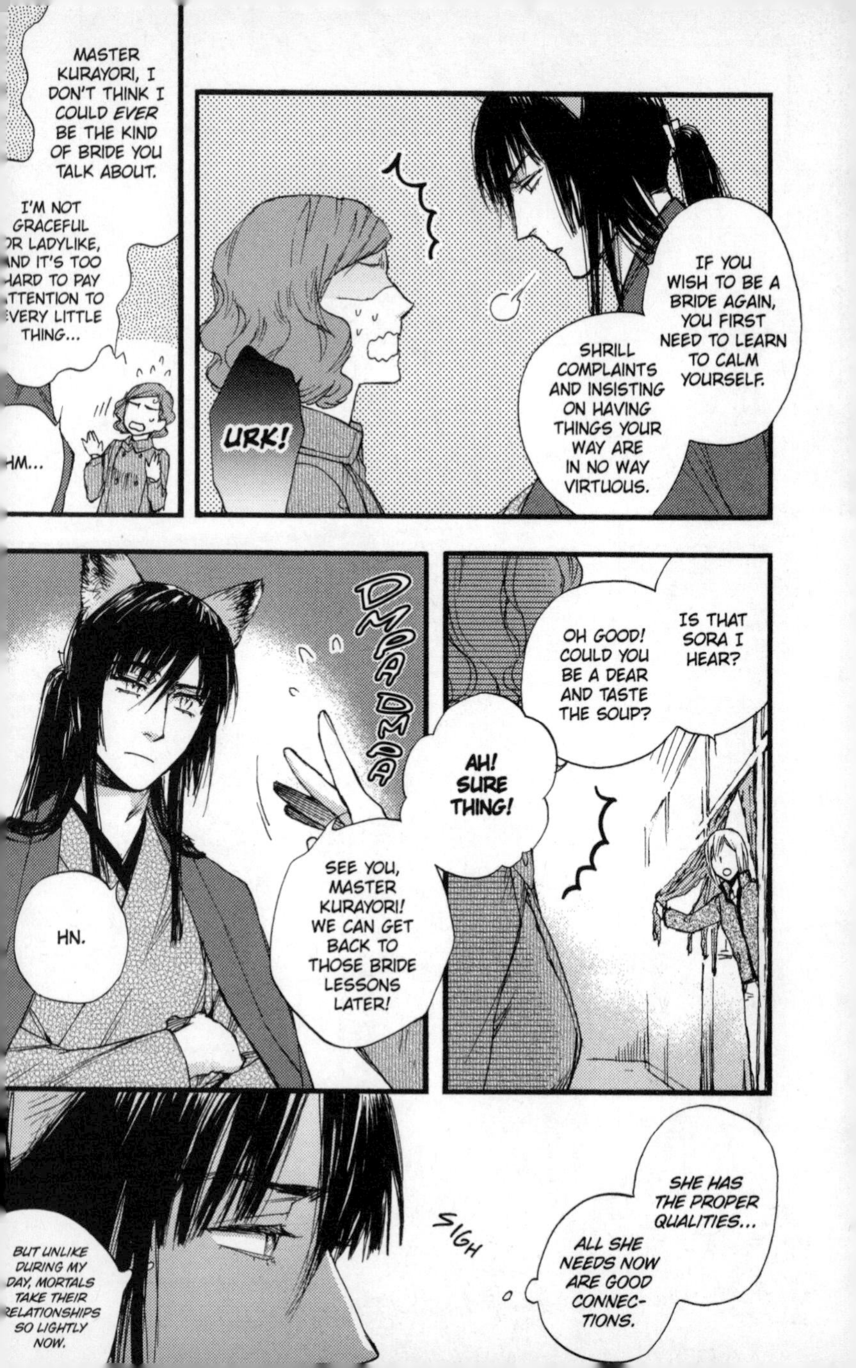
IF YOU WISH TO BE A BRIDE AGAIN, YOU FIRST NEED TO LEARN TO CALM YOURSELF.
SHRILL COMPLAINTS AND INSISTING ON HAVING THINGS YOUR WAY ARE IN NO WAY VIRTUOUS.
URK!
MASTER KURAYORI, I DON'T THINK I COULD *EVER* BE THE KIND OF BRIDE YOU TALK ABOUT.
I'M NOT GRACEFUL OR LADYLIKE, ND IT'S TOO HARD TO PAY TTENTION TO VERY LITTLE THING...
HM...
IS THAT SORA I HEAR?
OH GOOD! COULD YOU BE A DEAR AND TASTE THE SOUP?
AH! SURE THING!
DMPA DMPA
SEE YOU, MASTER KURAYORI! WE CAN GET BACK TO THOSE BRIDE LESSONS LATER!
HN.
SHE HAS THE PROPER QUALITIES...
ALL SHE NEEDS NOW ARE GOOD CONNEC-TIONS.
SIGH
BUT UNLIKE DURING MY DAY, MORTALS TAKE THEIR ELATIONSHIPS SO LIGHTLY NOW.

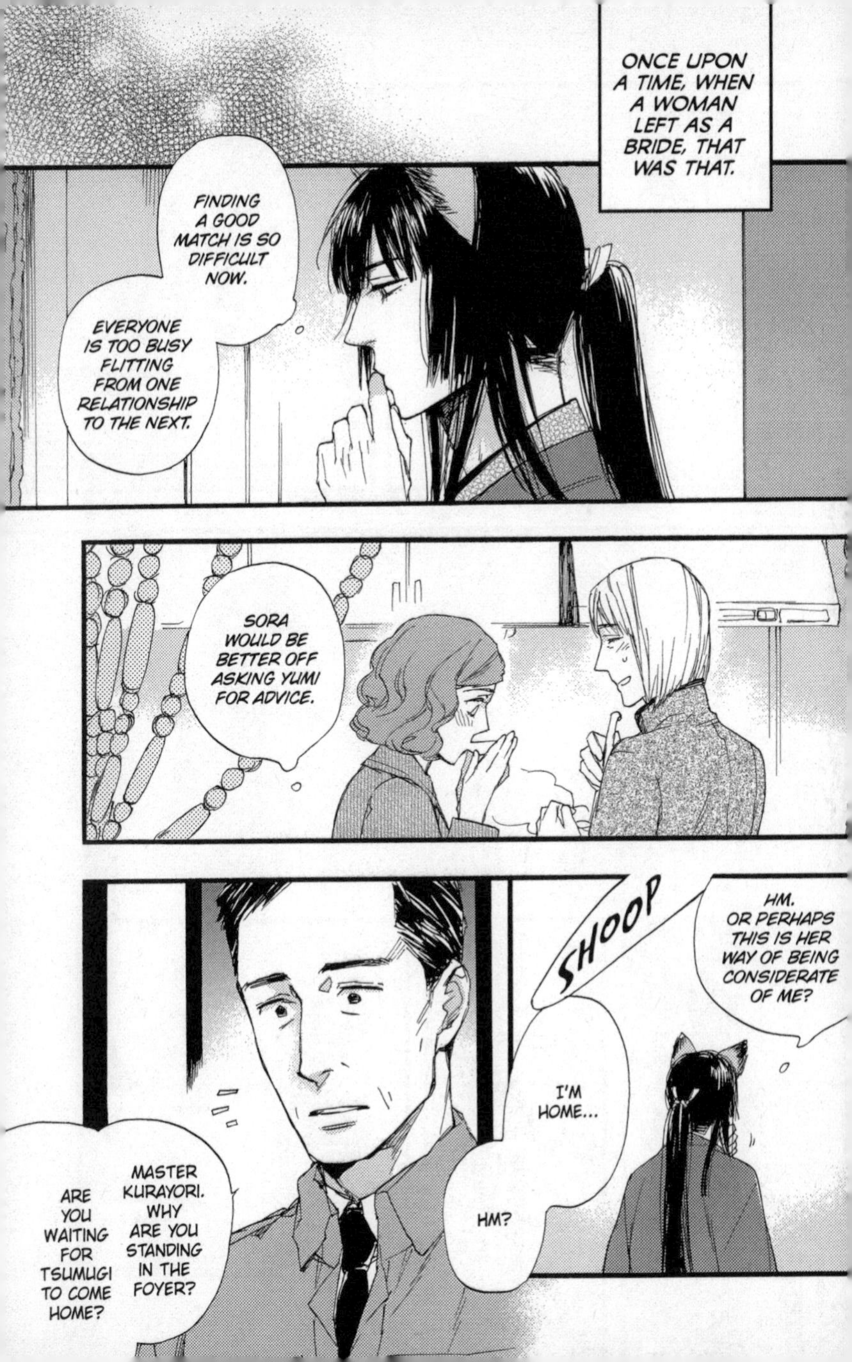
ONCE UPON A TIME, WHEN A WOMAN LEFT AS A BRIDE, THAT WAS THAT.
FINDING A GOOD MATCH IS SO DIFFICULT NOW.
EVERYONE IS TOO BUSY FLITTING FROM ONE RELATIONSHIP TO THE NEXT.
SORA WOULD BE BETTER OFF ASKING YUMI FOR ADVICE.
HM. OR PERHAPS THIS IS HER WAY OF BEING CONSIDERATE OF ME?
SHOOP
I'M HOME...
HM?
MASTER KURAYORI. WHY ARE YOU STANDING IN THE FOYER?
ARE YOU WAITING FOR TSUMUGI TO COME HOME?

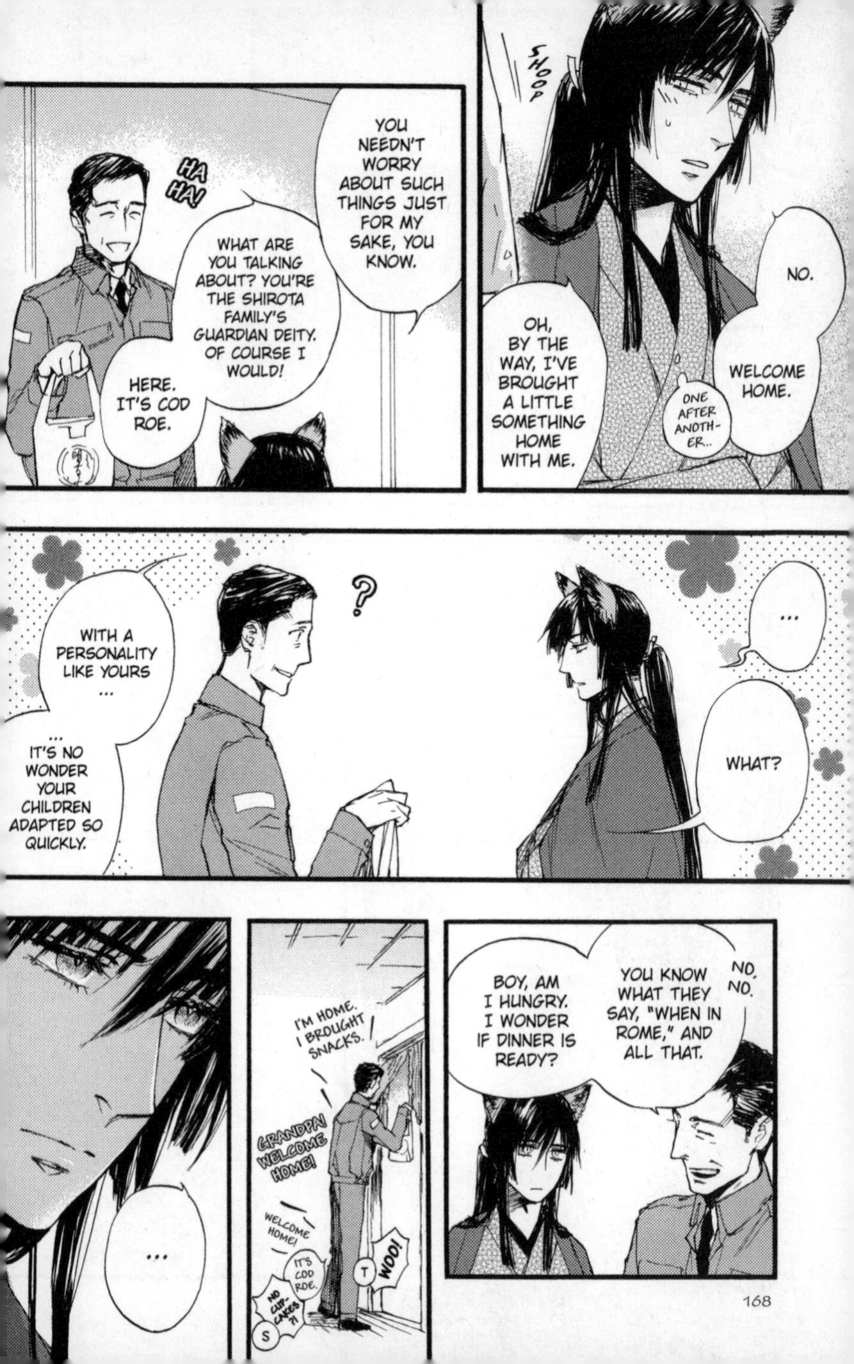
SHOOP
NO.
WELCOME HOME.
ONE AFTER ANOTHER...
OH, BY THE WAY, I'VE BROUGHT A LITTLE SOMETHING HOME WITH ME.
YOU NEEDN'T WORRY ABOUT SUCH THINGS JUST FOR MY SAKE, YOU KNOW.
HA HA!
WHAT ARE YOU TALKING ABOUT? YOU'RE THE SHIROTA FAMILY'S GUARDIAN DEITY. OF COURSE I WOULD!
HERE. IT'S COD ROE.
...
WHAT?
?
WITH A PERSONALITY LIKE YOURS ...
... IT'S NO WONDER YOUR CHILDREN ADAPTED SO QUICKLY.
NO, NO.
YOU KNOW WHAT THEY SAY, "WHEN IN ROME," AND ALL THAT.
BOY, AM I HUNGRY. I WONDER IF DINNER IS READY?
I'M HOME. I BROUGHT SNACKS.
GRANDPA! WELCOME HOME!
WOO!
T
WELCOME HOME!
IT'S COD ROE.
NO CUP-CAKES?!
S
...

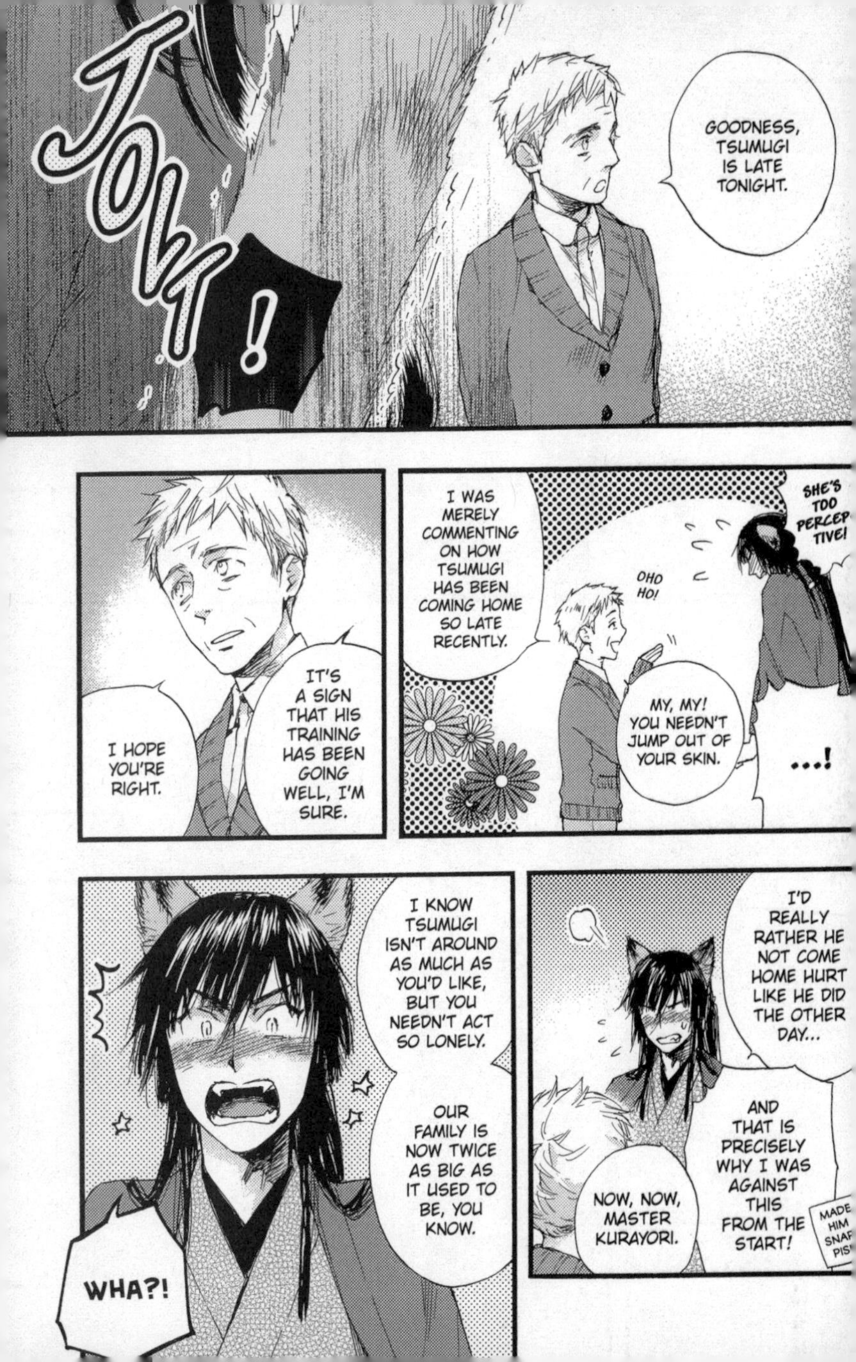
GOODNESS, TSUMUGI IS LATE TONIGHT.
JOLT!
SHE'S TOO PERCEPTIVE!
I WAS MERELY COMMENTING ON HOW TSUMUGI HAS BEEN COMING HOME SO LATE RECENTLY.
OHO HO!
MY, MY! YOU NEEDN'T JUMP OUT OF YOUR SKIN.
...!
IT'S A SIGN THAT HIS TRAINING HAS BEEN GOING WELL, I'M SURE.
I HOPE YOU'RE RIGHT.
I'D REALLY RATHER HE NOT COME HOME HURT LIKE HE DID THE OTHER DAY...
AND THAT IS PRECISELY WHY I WAS AGAINST THIS FROM THE START!
MADE HIM
NOW, NOW, MASTER KURAYORI.
I KNOW TSUMUGI ISN'T AROUND AS MUCH AS YOU'D LIKE, BUT YOU NEEDN'T ACT SO LONELY.
OUR FAMILY IS NOW TWICE AS BIG AS IT USED TO BE, YOU KNOW.
WHA?!

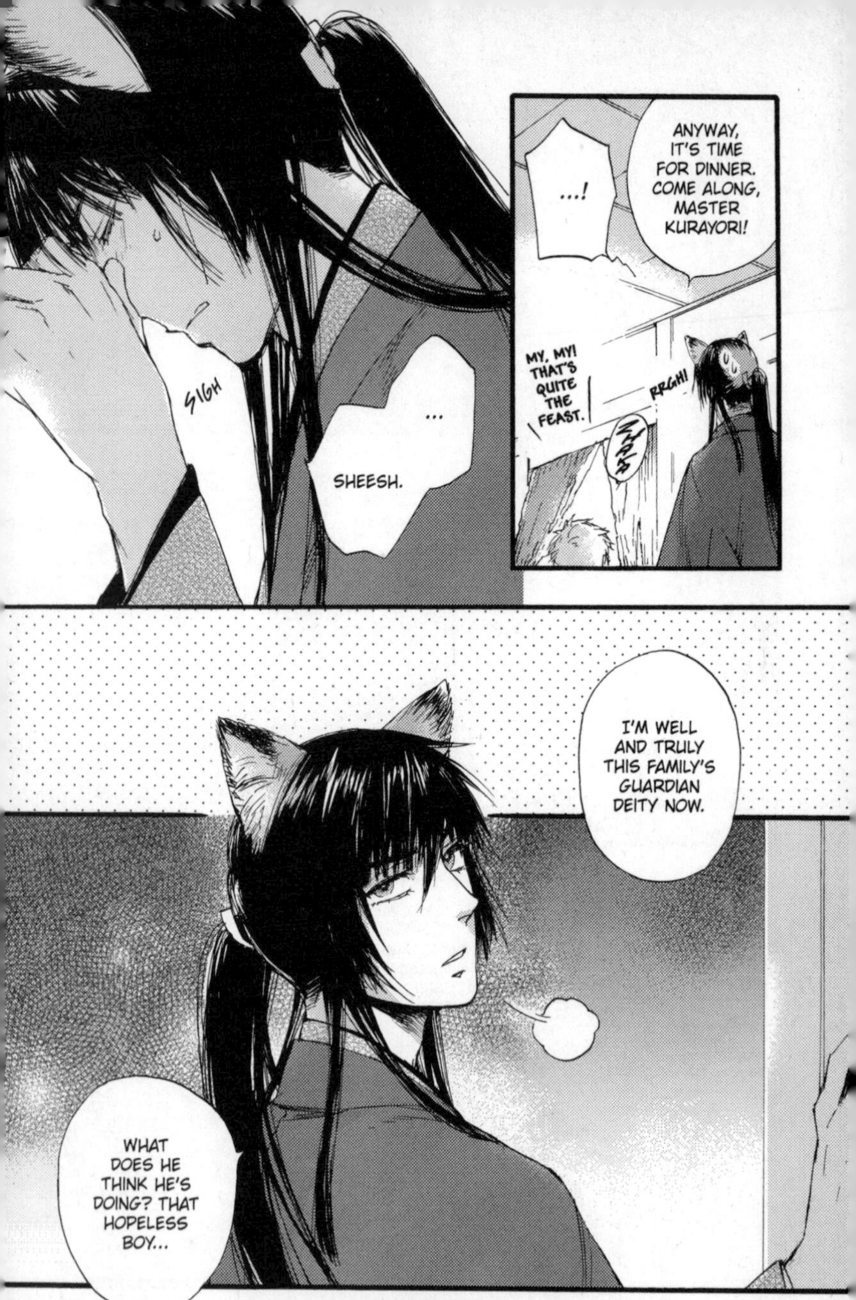
ANYWAY, IT'S TIME FOR DINNER. COME ALONG, MASTER KURAYORI!
...!
RRGH!
MY, MY! THAT'S QUITE THE FEAST.
SIGH
...
SHEESH.
I'M WELL AND TRULY THIS FAMILY'S GUARDIAN DEITY NOW.
WHAT DOES HE THINK HE'S DOING? THAT HOPELESS BOY...

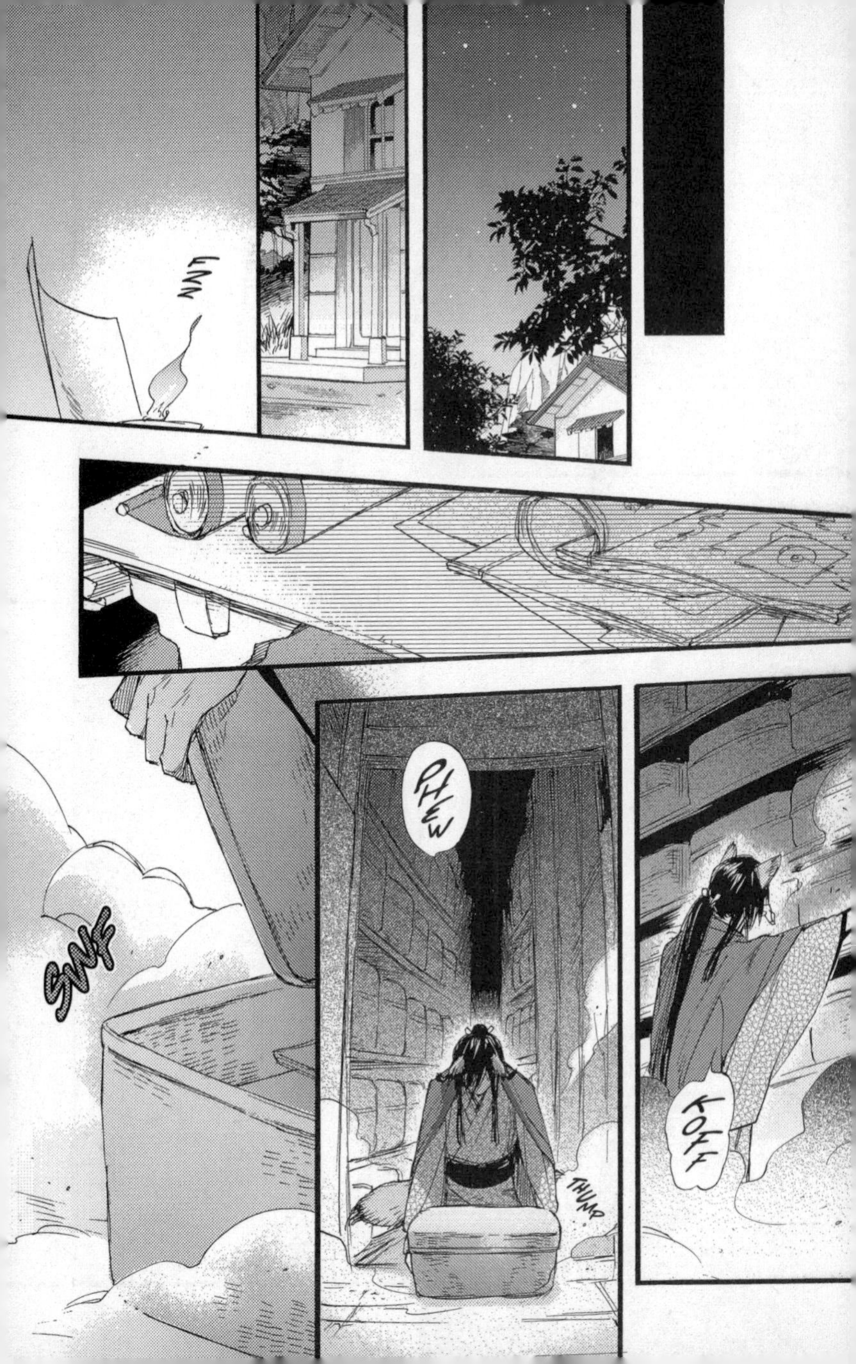
UNN
KOFF
PHEW
THUMP
SNIF

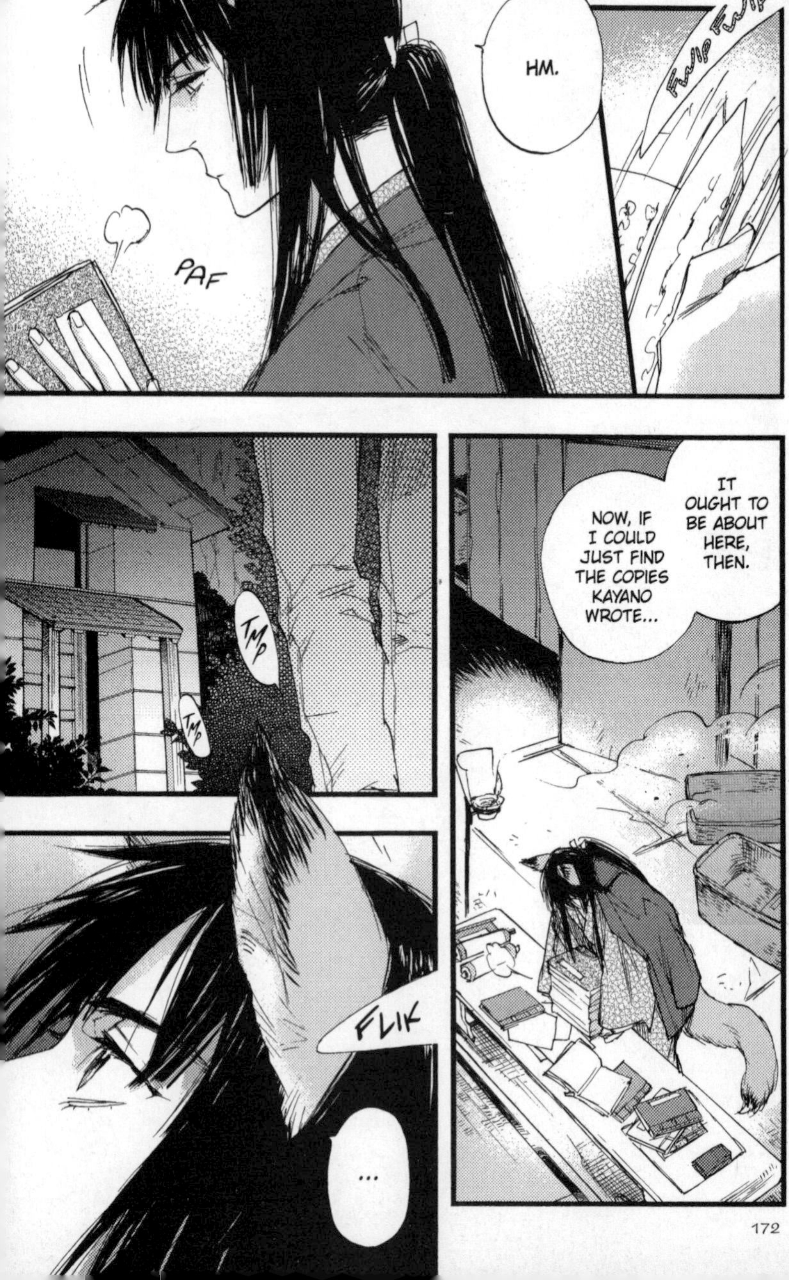
FWIP FWIP
HM.
PAF
IT OUGHT TO BE ABOUT HERE, THEN.
NOW, IF I COULD JUST FIND THE COPIES KAYANO WROTE...
TMP
TMP
FLIK
...

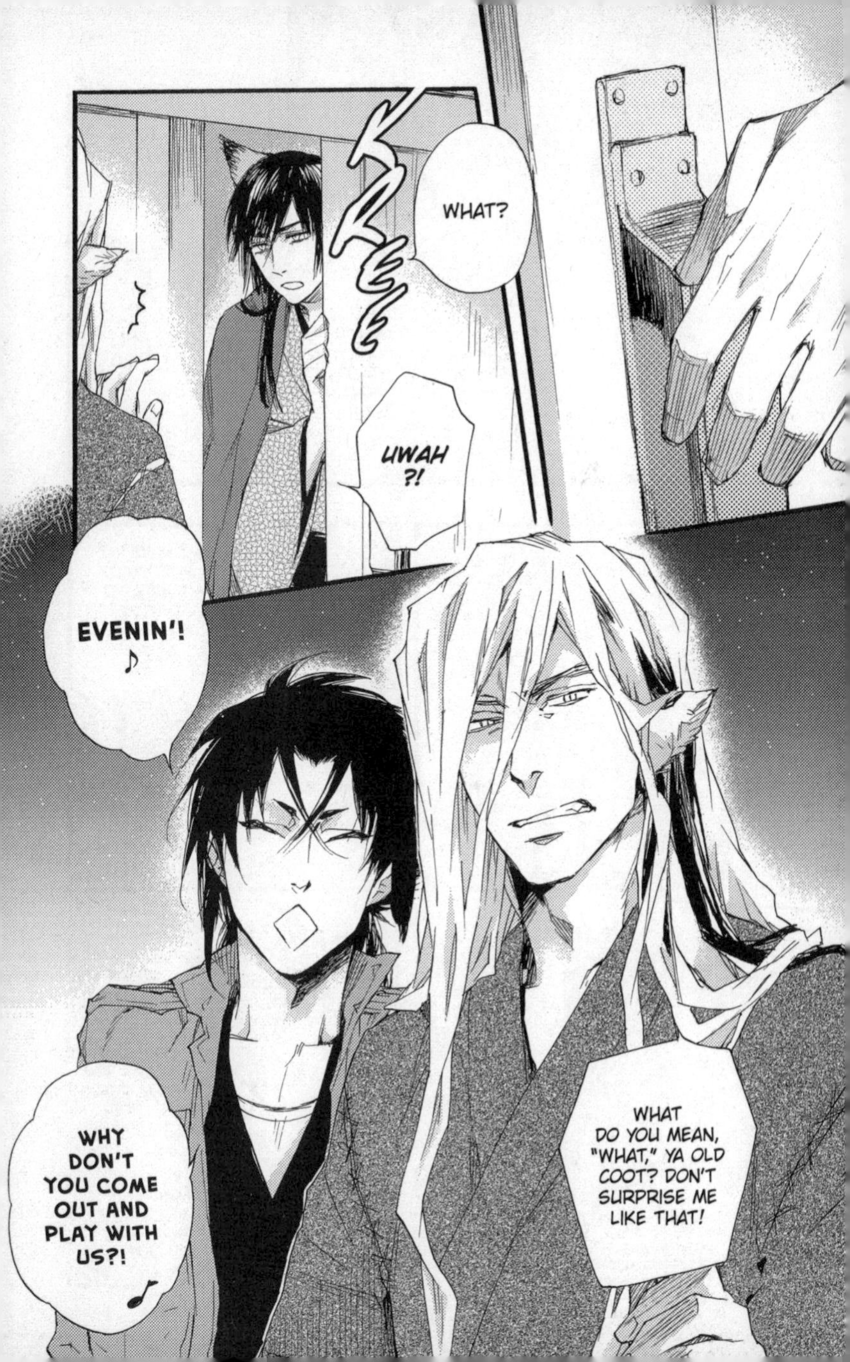
WHAT?
UWAH ?!
EVENIN'! ♪
WHAT DO YOU MEAN, "WHAT," YA OLD COOT? DON'T SURPRISE ME LIKE THAT!
WHY DON'T YOU COME OUT AND PLAY WITH US?! ♪

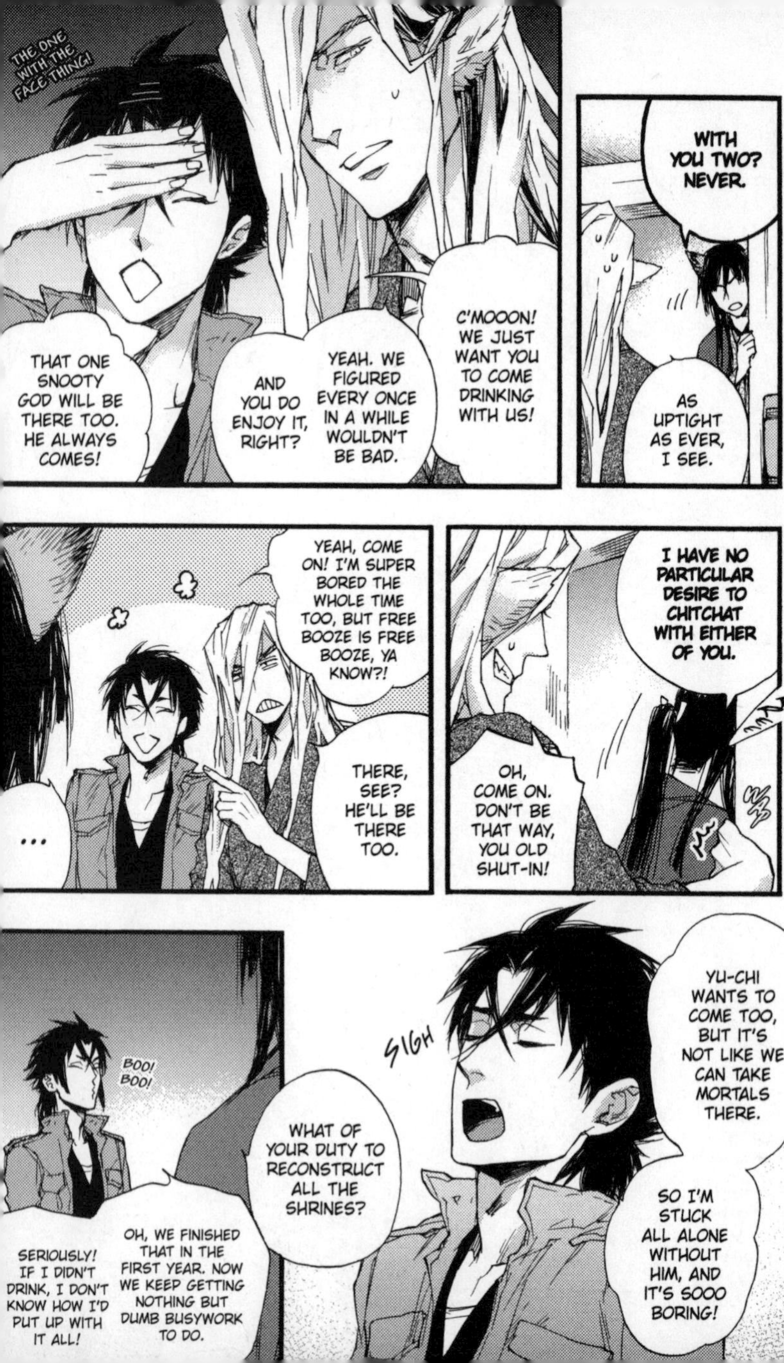
WITH YOU TWO? NEVER.
AS UPTIGHT AS EVER, I SEE.
C'MOOON! WE JUST WANT YOU TO COME DRINKING WITH US!
YEAH. WE FIGURED EVERY ONCE IN A WHILE WOULDN'T BE BAD.
AND YOU DO ENJOY IT, RIGHT?
THAT ONE SNOOTY GOD WILL BE THERE TOO. HE ALWAYS COMES!
THE ONE WITH THE FACE THING!
I HAVE NO PARTICULAR DESIRE TO CHITCHAT WITH EITHER OF YOU.
OH, COME ON. DON'T BE THAT WAY, YOU OLD SHUT-IN!
YEAH, COME ON! I'M SUPER BORED THE WHOLE TIME TOO, BUT FREE BOOZE IS FREE BOOZE, YA KNOW?!
THERE, SEE? HE'LL BE THERE TOO.
...
YU-CHI WANTS TO COME TOO, BUT IT'S NOT LIKE WE CAN TAKE MORTALS THERE.
SIGH
WHAT OF YOUR DUTY TO RECONSTRUCT ALL THE SHRINES?
SO I'M STUCK ALL ALONE WITHOUT HIM, AND IT'S SOOO BORING!
OH, WE FINISHED THAT IN THE FIRST YEAR. NOW WE KEEP GETTING NOTHING BUT DUMB BUSYWORK TO DO.
SERIOUSLY! IF I DIDN'T DRINK, I DON'T KNOW HOW I'D PUT UP WITH IT ALL!
BOO! BOO!

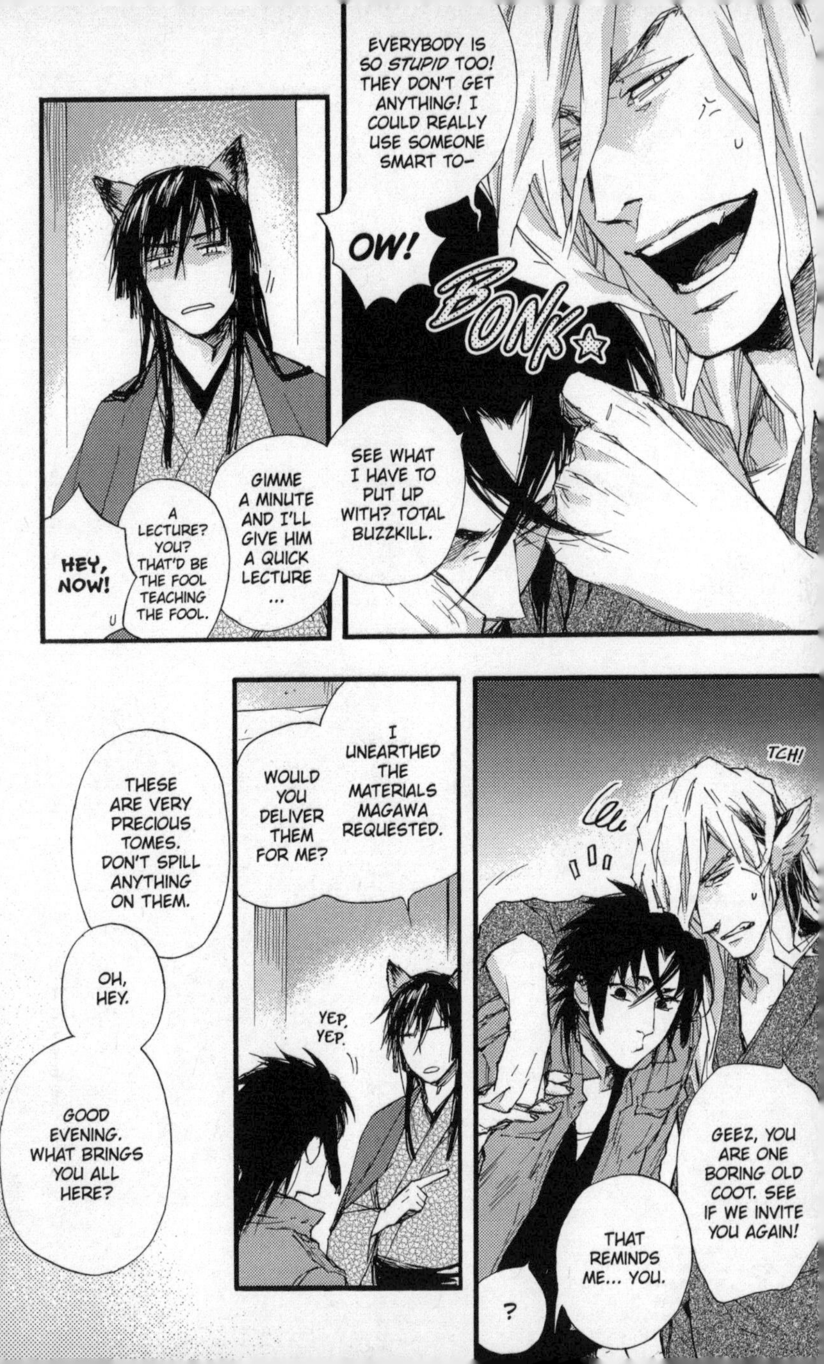
EVERYBODY IS SO *STUPID* TOO! THEY DON'T GET ANYTHING! I COULD REALLY USE SOMEONE SMART TO–
OW!
BONK
SEE WHAT I HAVE TO PUT UP WITH? TOTAL BUZZKILL.
GIMME A MINUTE AND I'LL GIVE HIM A QUICK LECTURE ...
A LECTURE? YOU? THAT'D BE THE FOOL TEACHING THE FOOL.
HEY, NOW!
TCH!
GEEZ, YOU ARE ONE BORING OLD COOT. SEE IF WE INVITE YOU AGAIN!
THAT REMINDS ME... YOU.
?
I UNEARTHED THE MATERIALS MAGAWA REQUESTED.
WOULD YOU DELIVER THEM FOR ME?
YEP, YEP.
THESE ARE VERY PRECIOUS TOMES. DON'T SPILL ANYTHING ON THEM.
OH, HEY.
GOOD EVENING. WHAT BRINGS YOU ALL HERE?

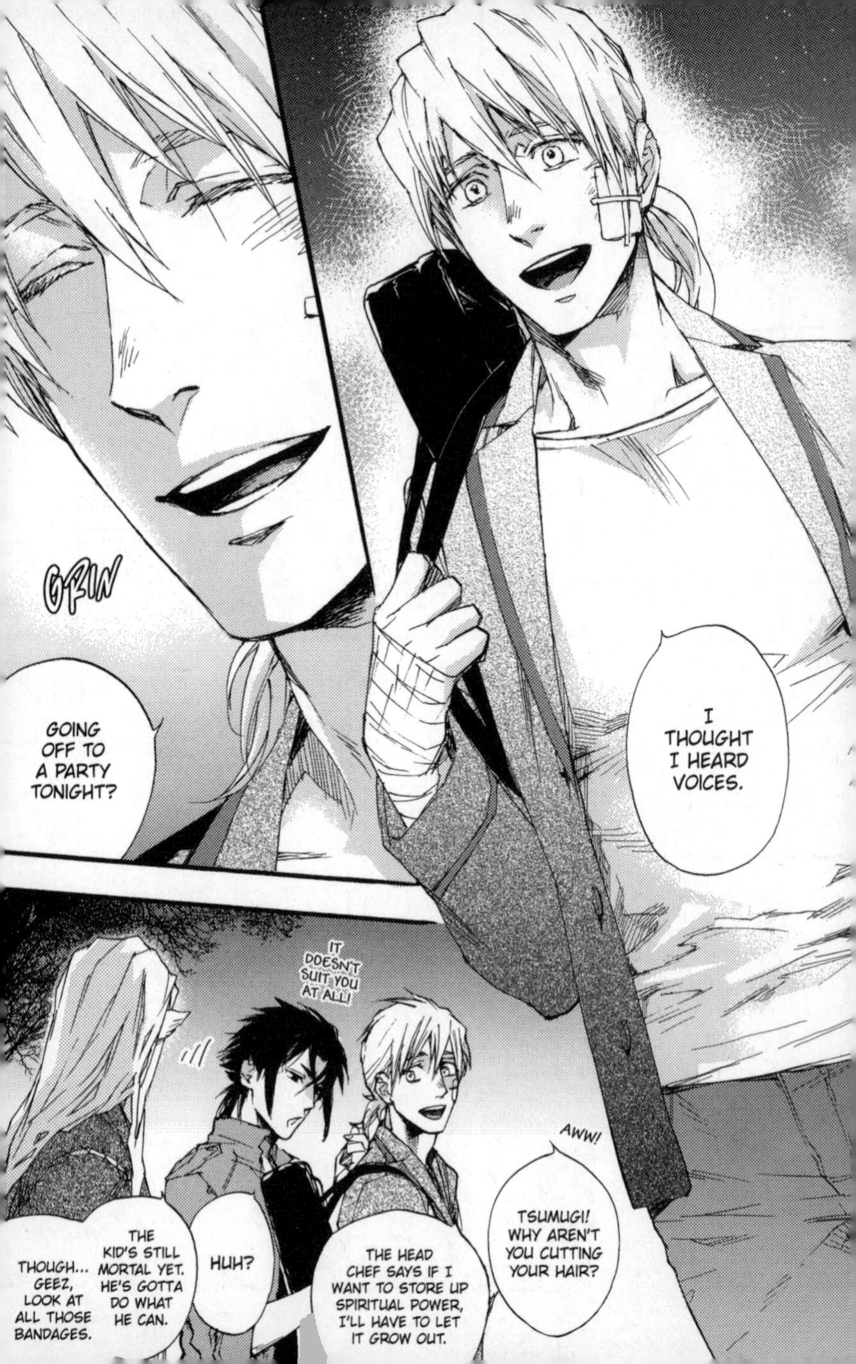
I THOUGHT I HEARD VOICES.
GRIN
GOING OFF TO A PARTY TONIGHT?
AWW!
TSUMUGI! WHY AREN'T YOU CUTTING YOUR HAIR?
IT DOESN'T SUIT YOU AT ALL!
THE HEAD CHEF SAYS IF I WANT TO STORE UP SPIRITUAL POWER, I'LL HAVE TO LET IT GROW OUT.
HUH?
THE KID'S STILL MORTAL YET. HE'S GOTTA DO WHAT HE CAN.
THOUGH... GEEZ, LOOK AT ALL THOSE BANDAGES.

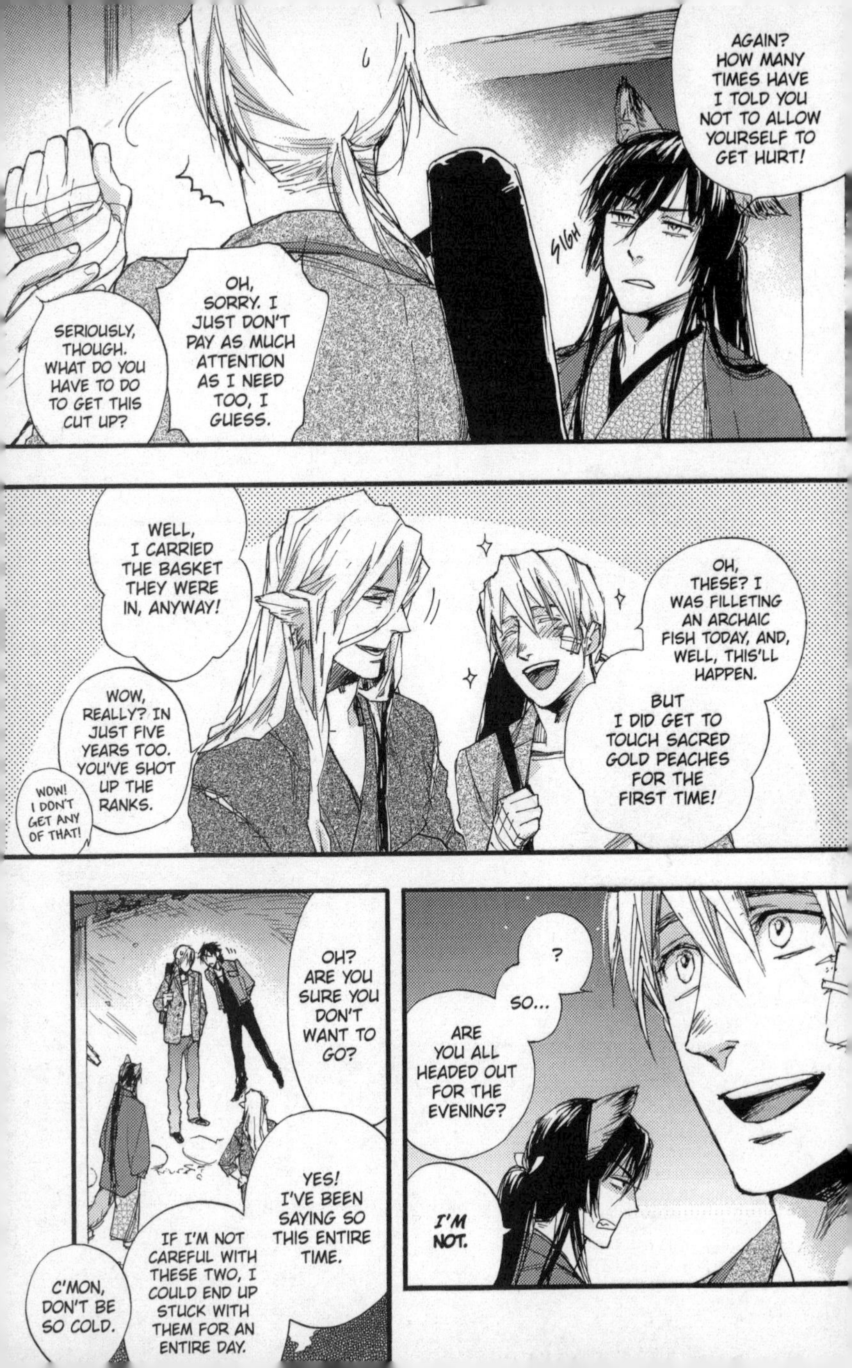
AGAIN? HOW MANY TIMES HAVE I TOLD YOU NOT TO ALLOW YOURSELF TO GET HURT!
SIGH
OH, SORRY. I JUST DON'T PAY AS MUCH ATTENTION AS I NEED TOO, I GUESS.
SERIOUSLY, THOUGH. WHAT DO YOU HAVE TO DO TO GET THIS CUT UP?
OH, THESE? I WAS FILLETING AN ARCHAIC FISH TODAY, AND, WELL, THIS'LL HAPPEN.
BUT I DID GET TO TOUCH SACRED GOLD PEACHES FOR THE FIRST TIME!
WELL, I CARRIED THE BASKET THEY WERE IN, ANYWAY!
WOW, REALLY? IN JUST FIVE YEARS TOO. YOU'VE SHOT UP THE RANKS.
WOW! I DON'T GET ANY OF THAT!
?
SO...
ARE YOU ALL HEADED OUT FOR THE EVENING?
I'M NOT.
OH? ARE YOU SURE YOU DON'T WANT TO GO?
YES! I'VE BEEN SAYING SO THIS ENTIRE TIME.
IF I'M NOT CAREFUL WITH THESE TWO, I COULD END UP STUCK WITH THEM FOR AN ENTIRE DAY.
C'MON, DON'T BE SO COLD.

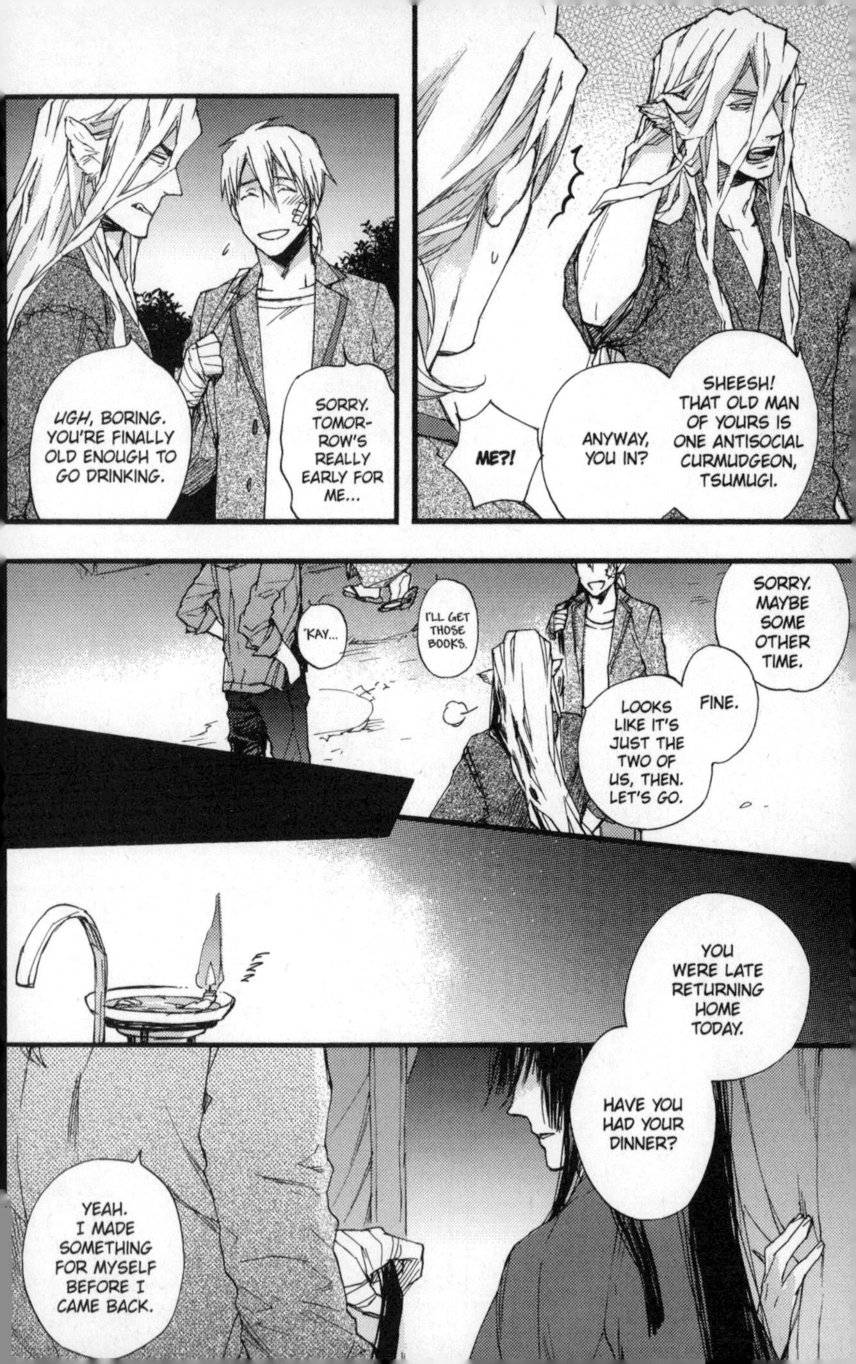
SHEESH! THAT OLD MAN OF YOURS IS ONE ANTISOCIAL CURMUDGEON, TSUMUGI.
ANYWAY, YOU IN?
ME?!
SORRY. TOMORROW'S REALLY EARLY FOR ME...
UGH, BORING. YOU'RE FINALLY OLD ENOUGH TO GO DRINKING.
SORRY. MAYBE SOME OTHER TIME.
FINE.
LOOKS LIKE IT'S JUST THE TWO OF US, THEN. LET'S GO.
I'LL GET THOSE BOOKS.
'KAY...
YOU WERE LATE RETURNING HOME TODAY.
HAVE YOU HAD YOUR DINNER?
YEAH. I MADE SOMETHING FOR MYSELF BEFORE I CAME BACK.

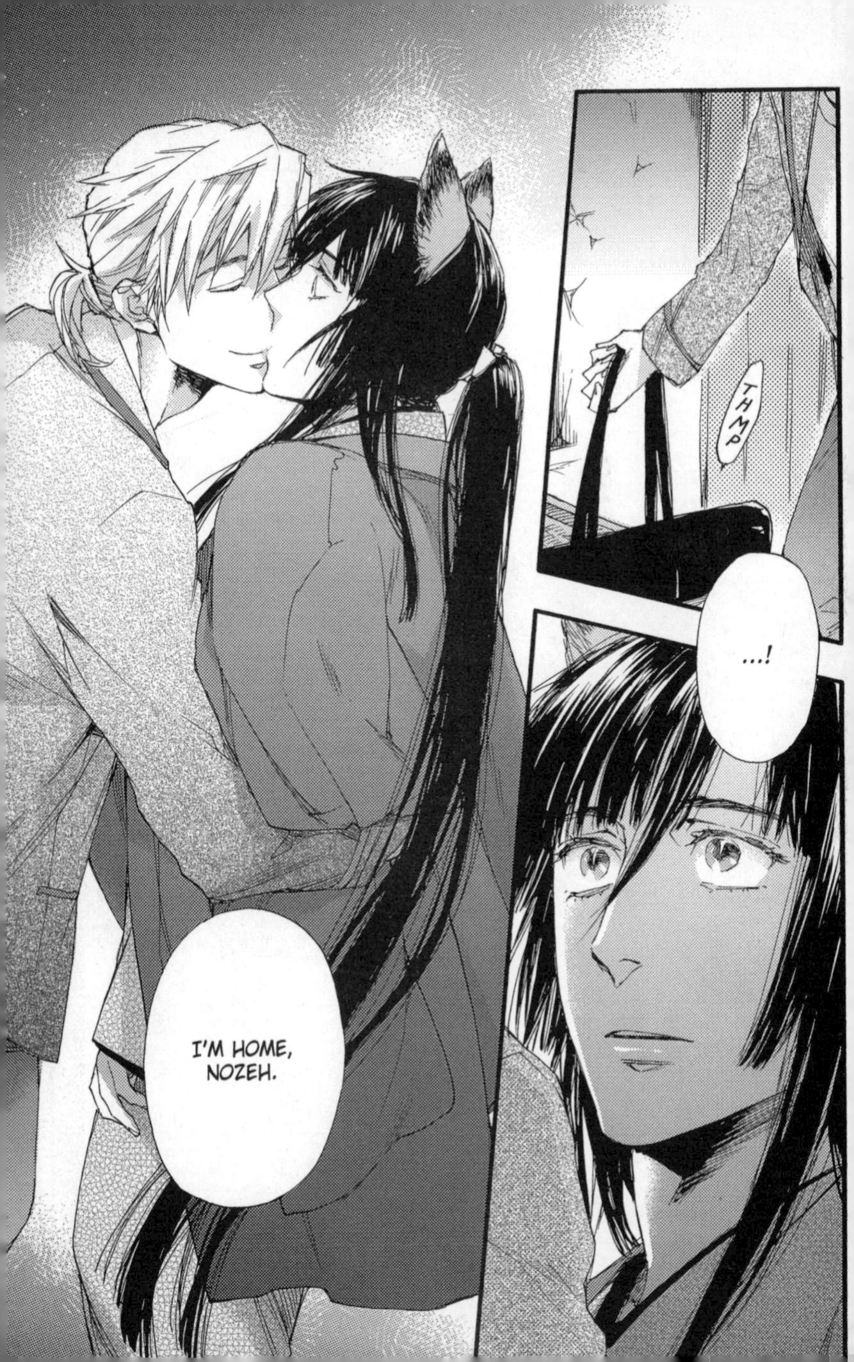
THMP
...!
I'M HOME, NOZEH.

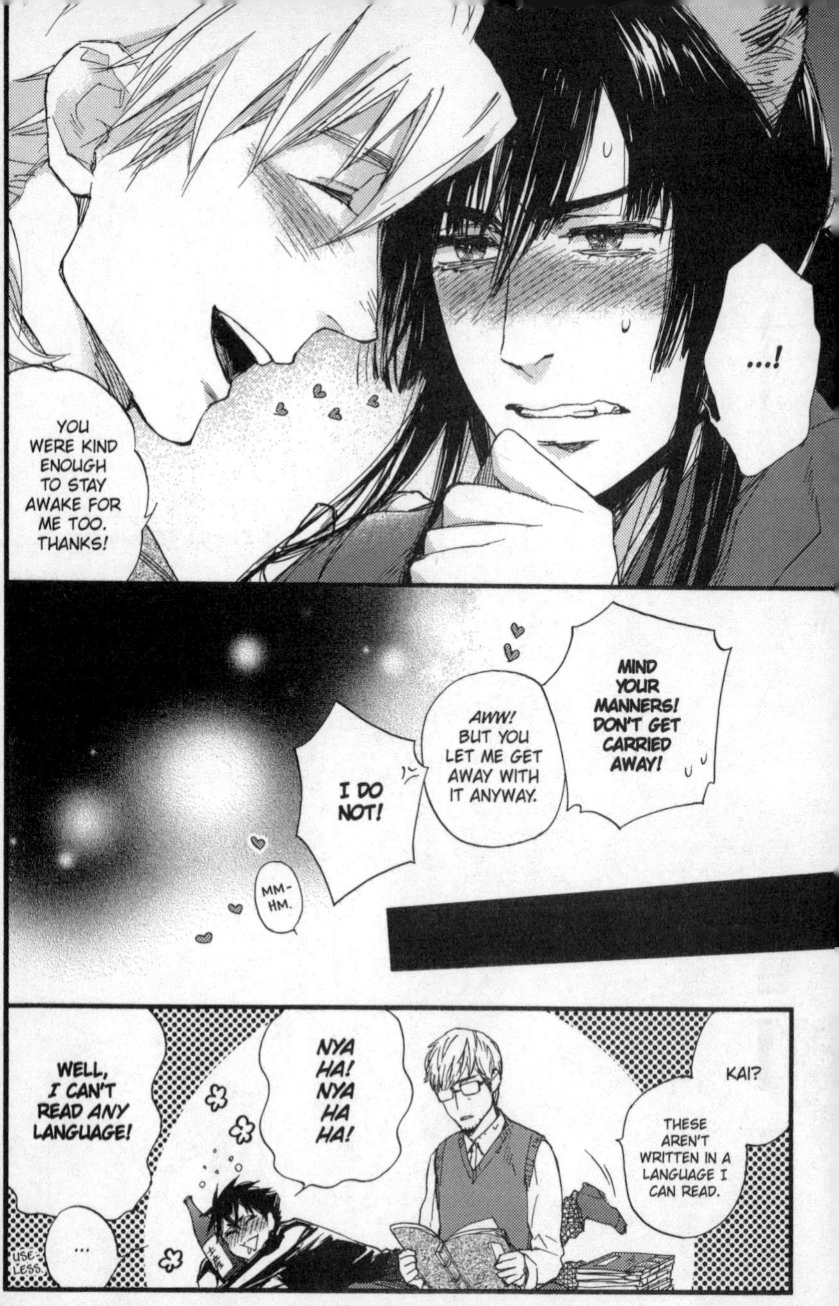
...!
YOU WERE KIND ENOUGH TO STAY AWAKE FOR ME TOO. THANKS!
MIND YOUR MANNERS! DON'T GET CARRIED AWAY!
AWW! BUT YOU LET ME GET AWAY WITH IT ANYWAY.
I DO NOT!
MM-HM.
KAI?
THESE AREN'T WRITTEN IN A LANGUAGE I CAN READ.
NYA HA! NYA HA HA!
WELL, I CAN'T READ ANY LANGUAGE!
...
USE-LESS.

A Strange & Mystifying Story Side Story / END

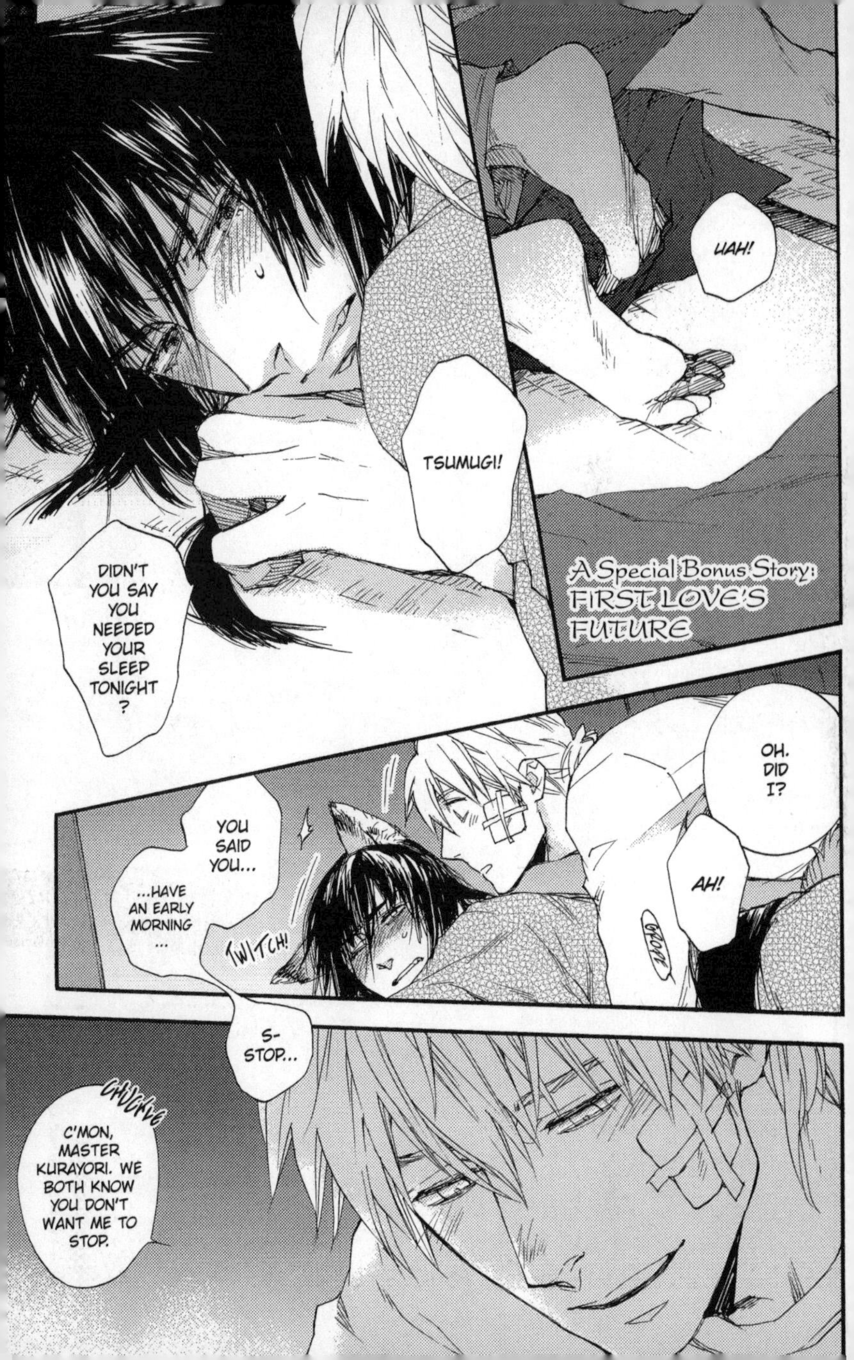
UAH!
A Special Bonus Story: FIRST LOVE'S FUTURE
TSUMUGI!
DIDN'T YOU SAY YOU NEEDED YOUR SLEEP TONIGHT?
OH. DID I?
AH!
TWITCH!
YOU SAID YOU...
...HAVE AN EARLY MORNING...
S-STOP...
C'MON, MASTER KURAYORI. WE BOTH KNOW YOU DON'T WANT ME TO STOP.

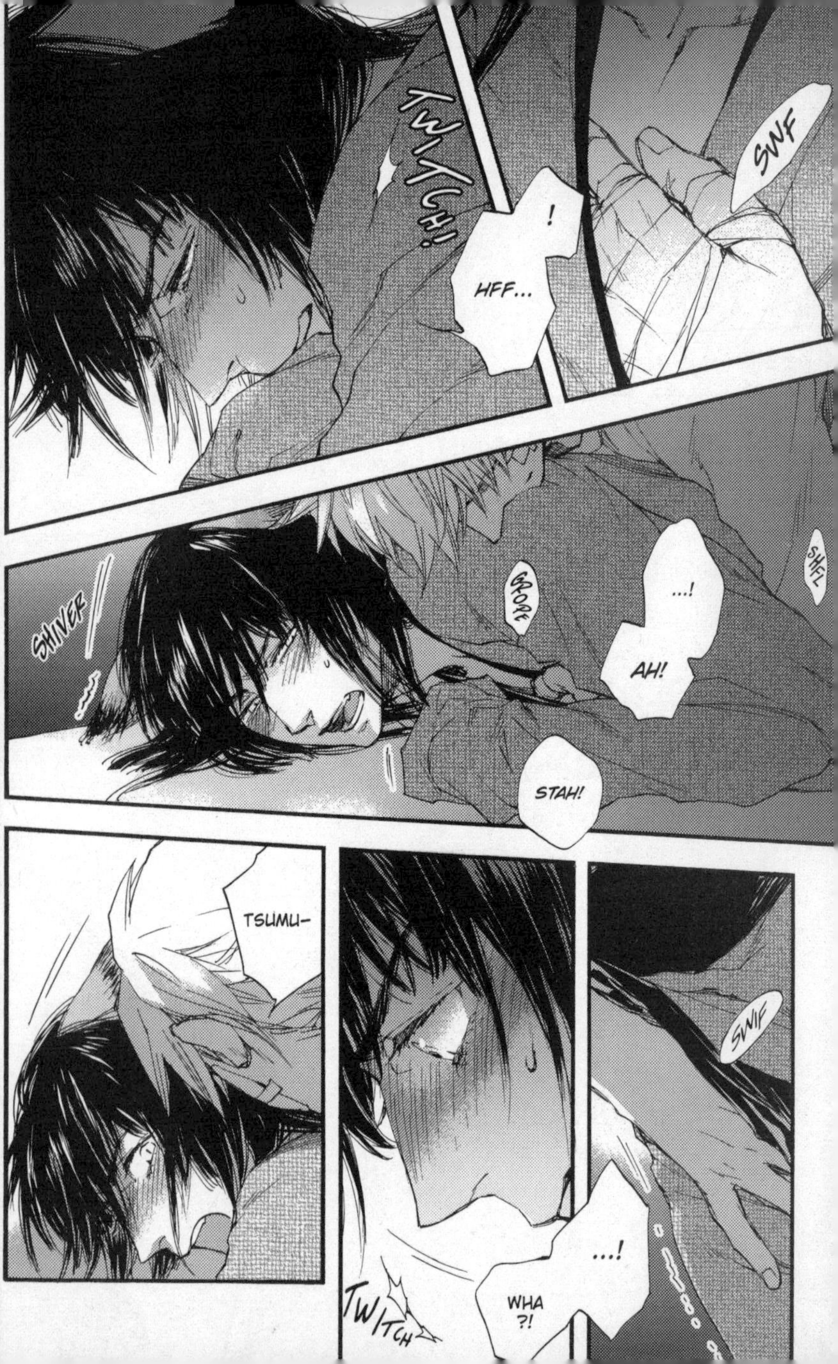
SWF
!
HFF...
TWITCH!
SHFL
...!
AH!
STAH!
GROPE
SHIVER
SWIF
...!
WHA ?!
TWITCH
TSUMU-

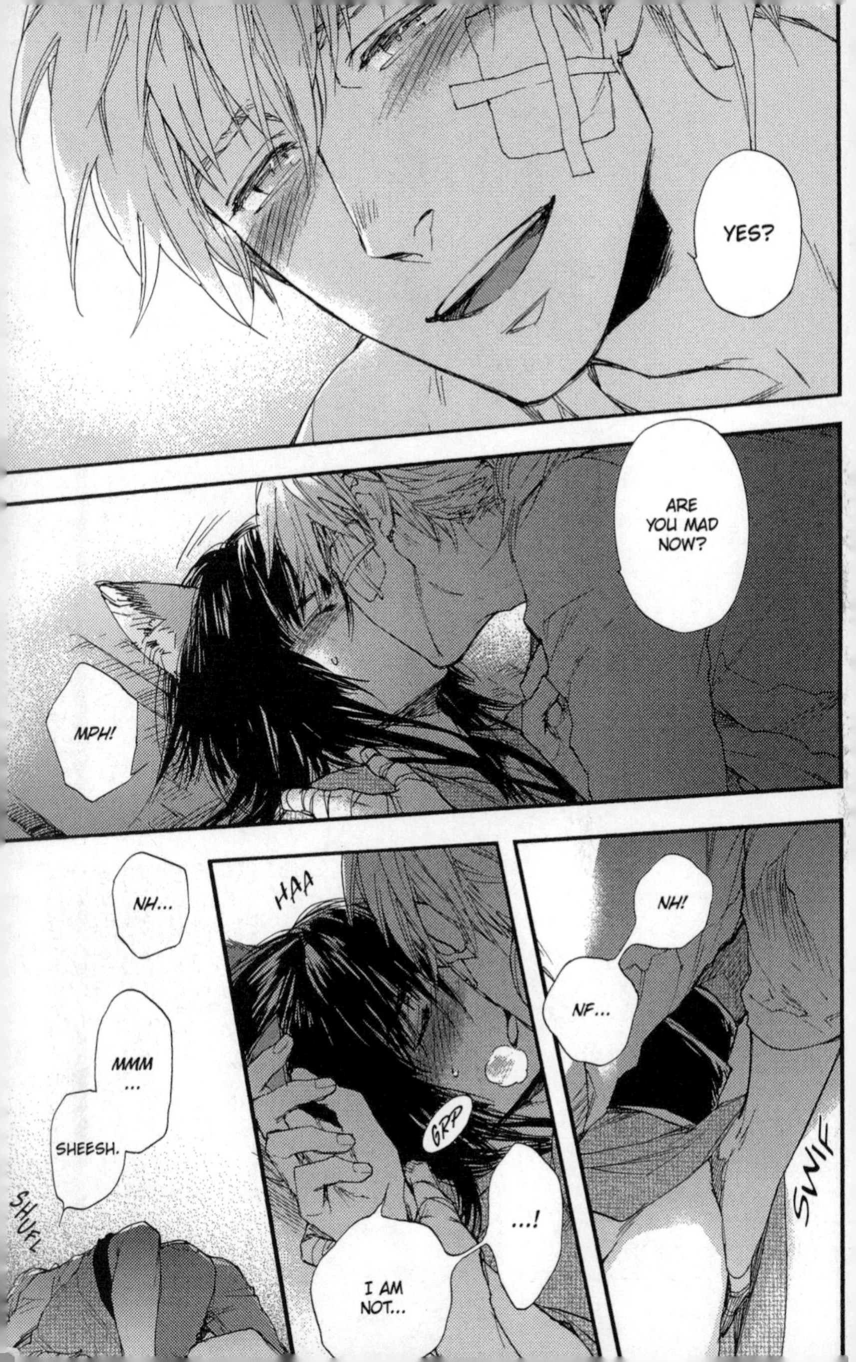
YES?
ARE YOU MAD NOW?
MPH!
NH!
NF...
SWIF
HAA
GRP
...!
I AM NOT...
NH...
MMM ...
SHEESH.
SHUFL

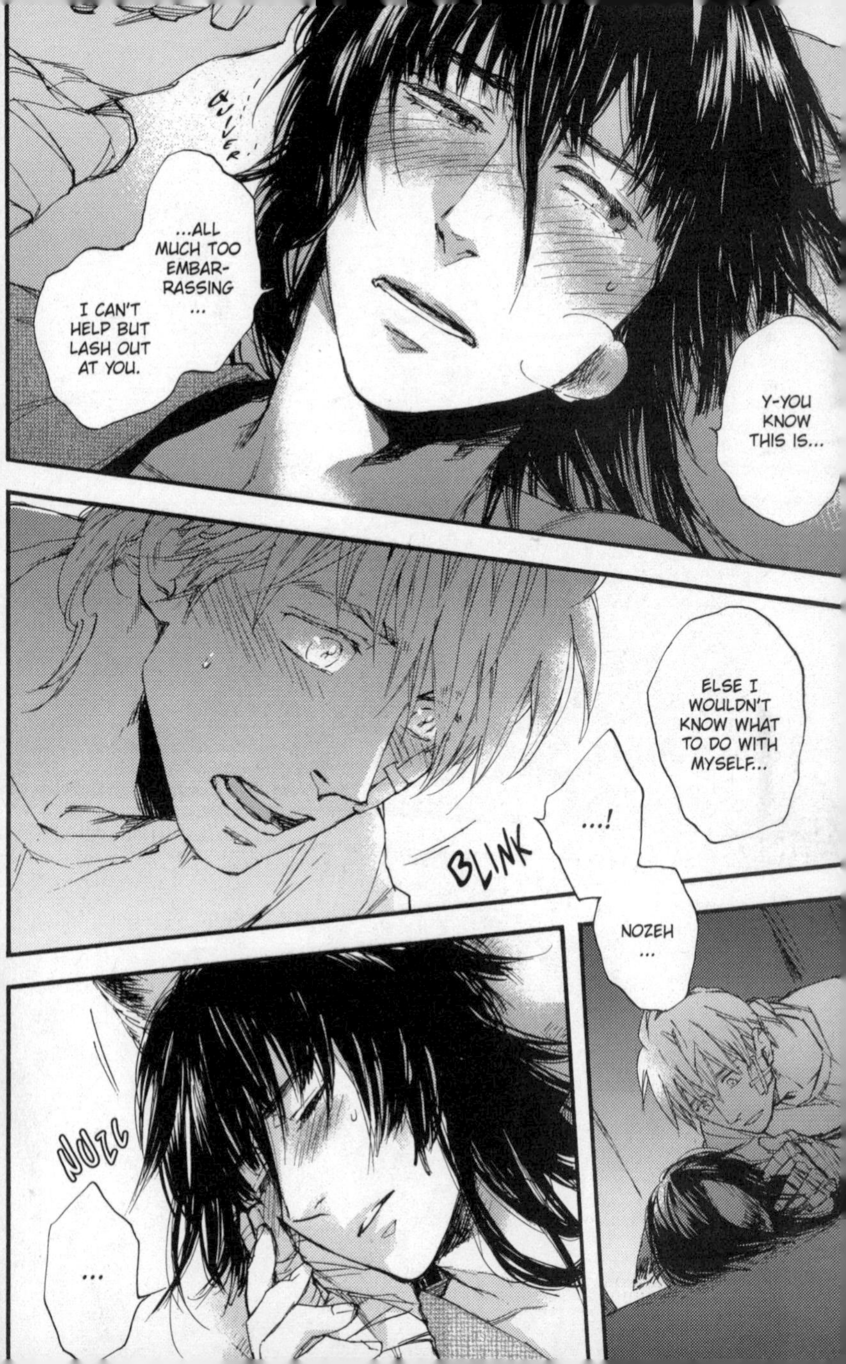
Y-YOU KNOW THIS IS...
QUIVER
...ALL MUCH TOO EMBARRASSING ...
I CAN'T HELP BUT LASH OUT AT YOU.
ELSE I WOULDN'T KNOW WHAT TO DO WITH MYSELF...
...!
BLINK
NOZEH ...
NUZZ
...

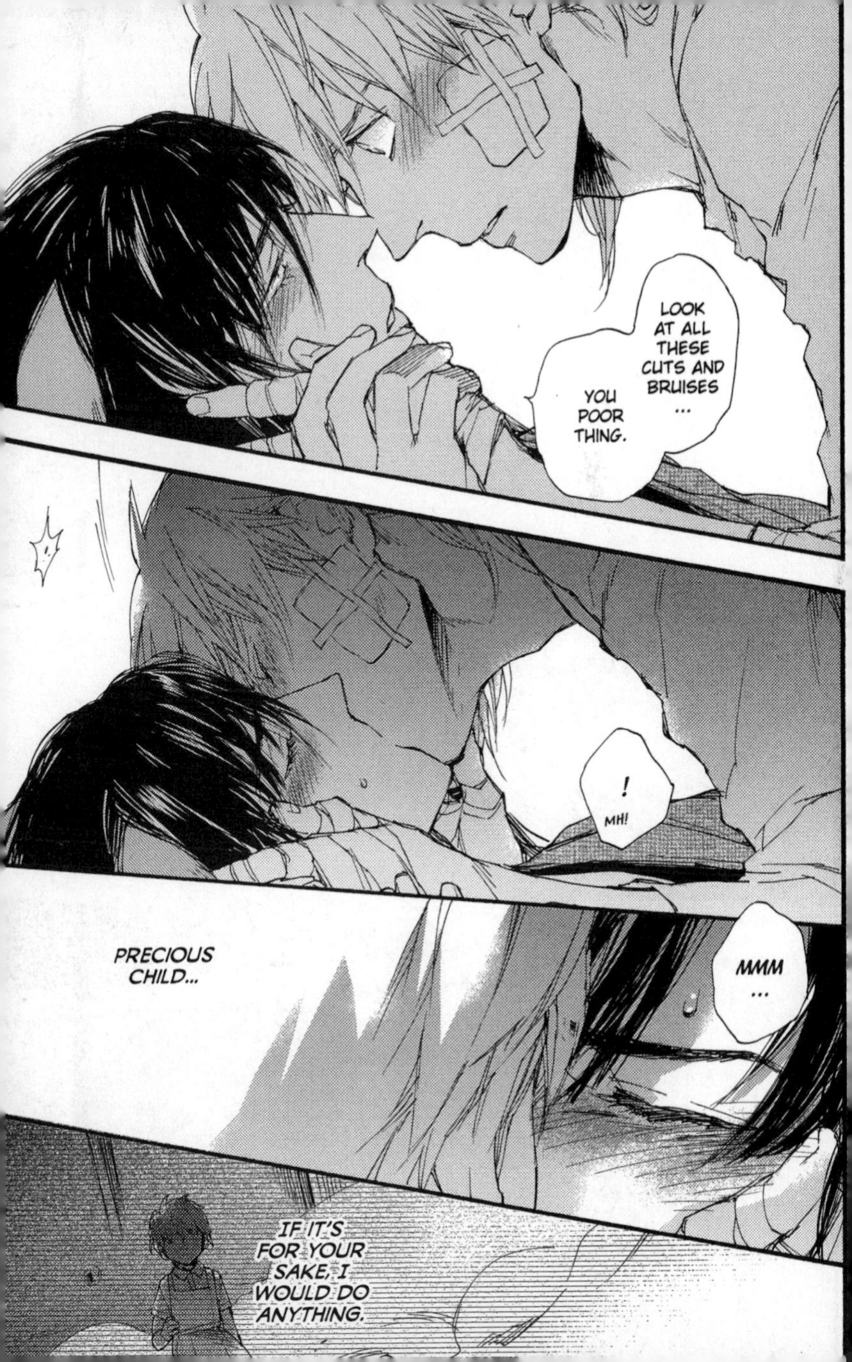
LOOK AT ALL THESE CUTS AND BRUISES...
YOU POOR THING.
! MH!
!
MMM...
PRECIOUS CHILD...
IF IT'S FOR YOUR SAKE, I WOULD DO ANYTHING.

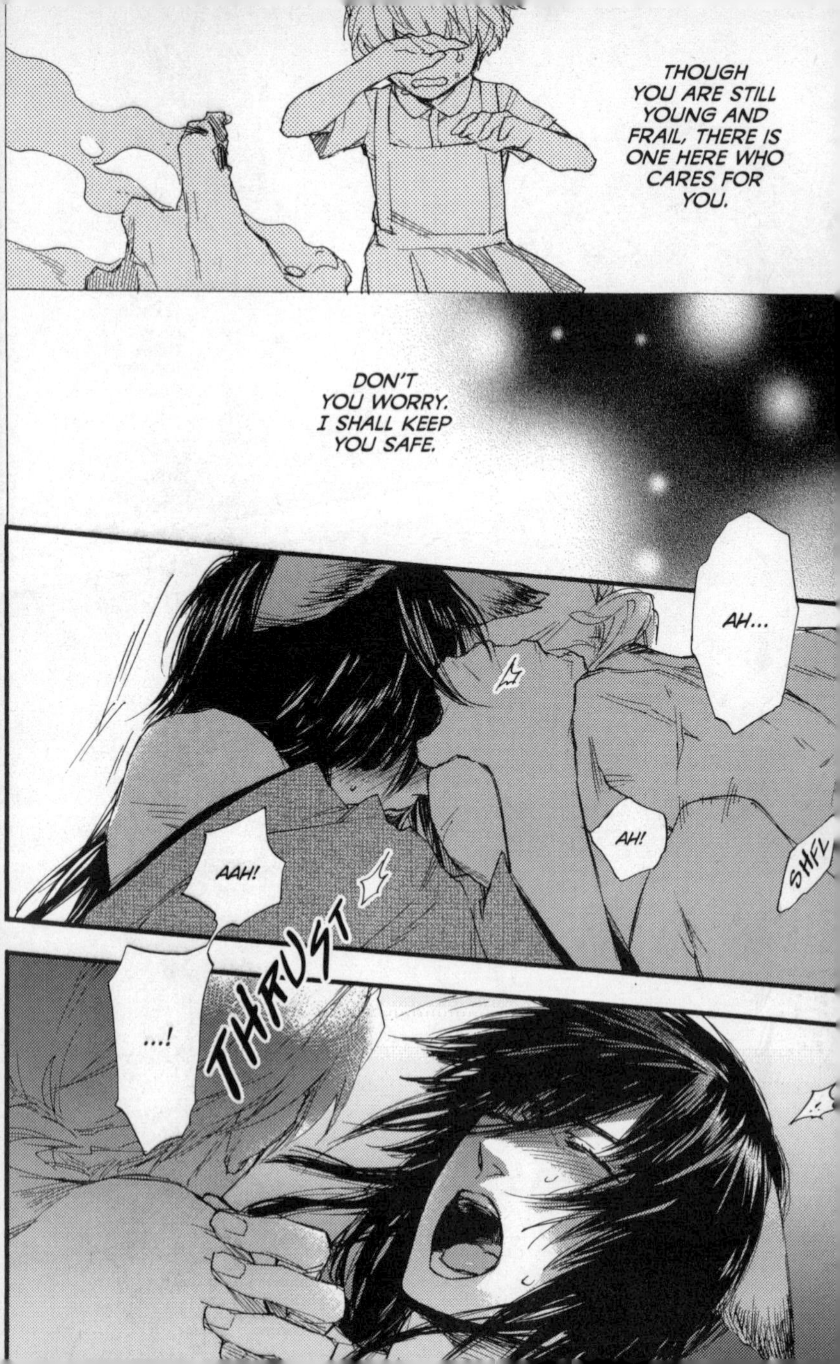
THOUGH YOU ARE STILL YOUNG AND FRAIL, THERE IS ONE HERE WHO CARES FOR YOU.
DON'T YOU WORRY. I SHALL KEEP YOU SAFE.
AH...
AH!
SHFL
AAH!
THRUST
...!

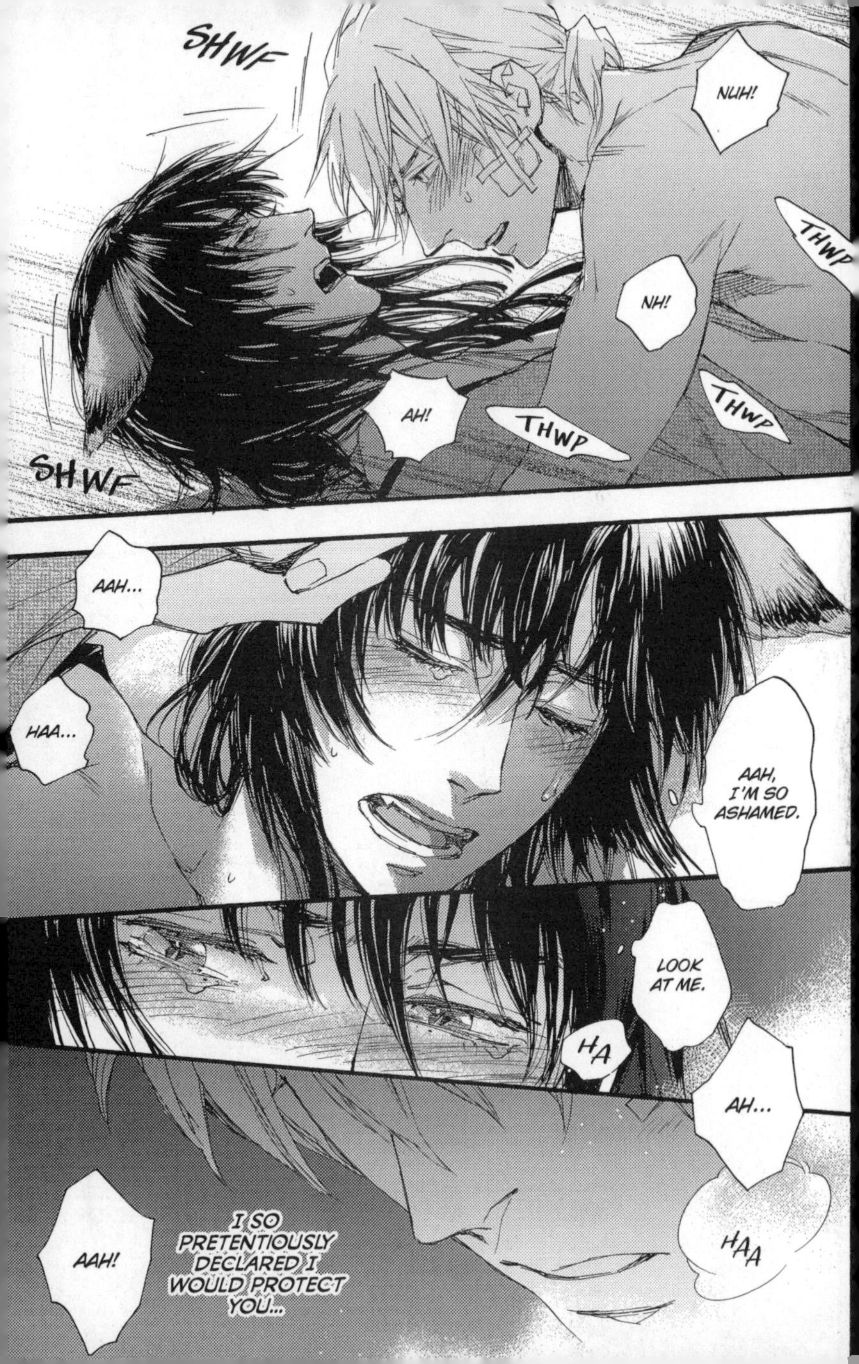
NUH!
THWP
NH!
THWP
THWP
AH!
SHWF
SHWF
AAH, I'M SO ASHAMED.
AAH...
HAA...
LOOK AT ME.
HA
AH...
HAA
I SO PRETENTIOUSLY DECLARED I WOULD PROTECT YOU...
AAH!

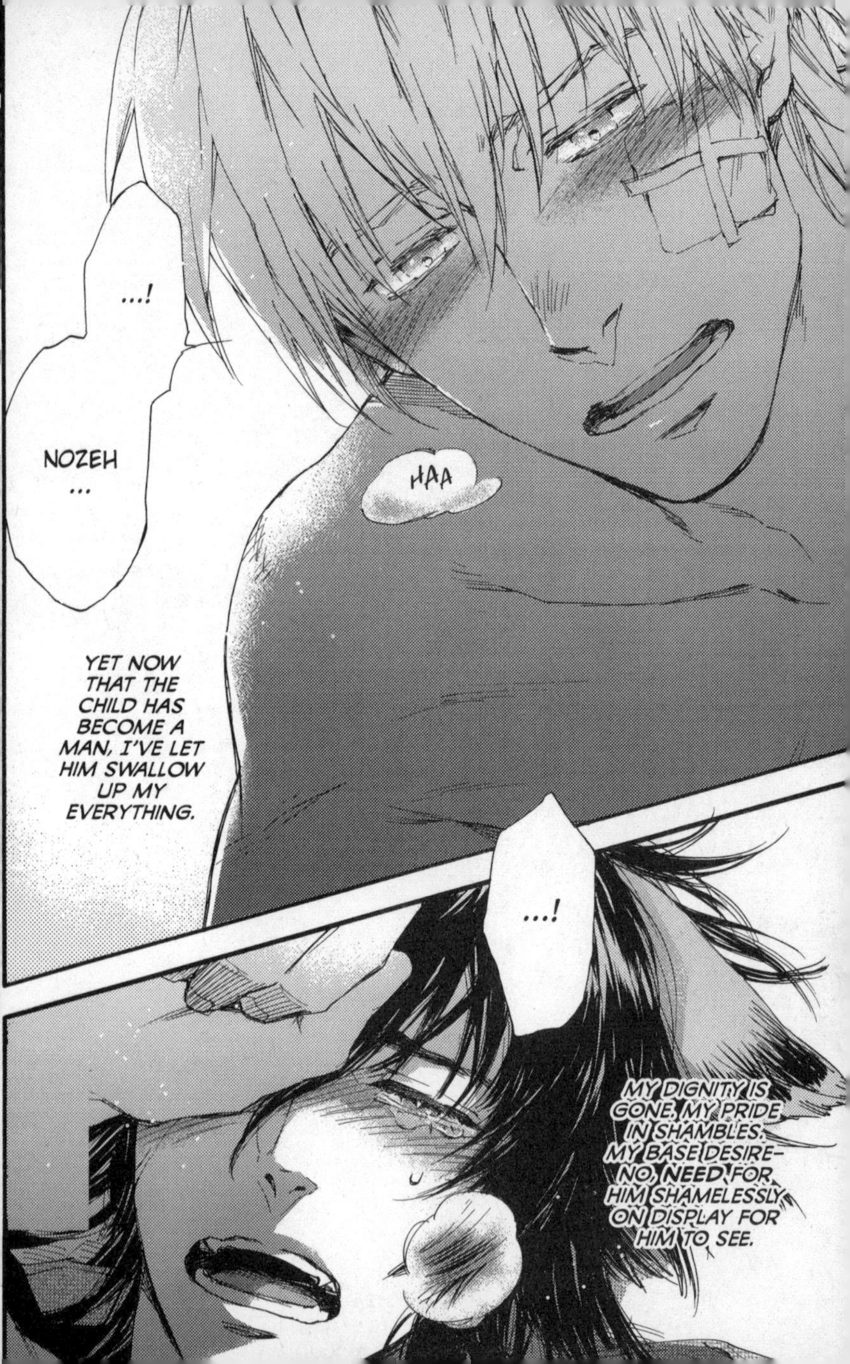
...!
NOZEH ...
HAA
YET NOW THAT THE CHILD HAS BECOME A MAN, I'VE LET HIM SWALLOW UP MY EVERYTHING.
...!
MY DIGNITY IS GONE. MY PRIDE IN SHAMBLES. MY BASE DESIRE—NO, NEED FOR HIM SHAMELESSLY ON DISPLAY FOR HIM TO SEE.

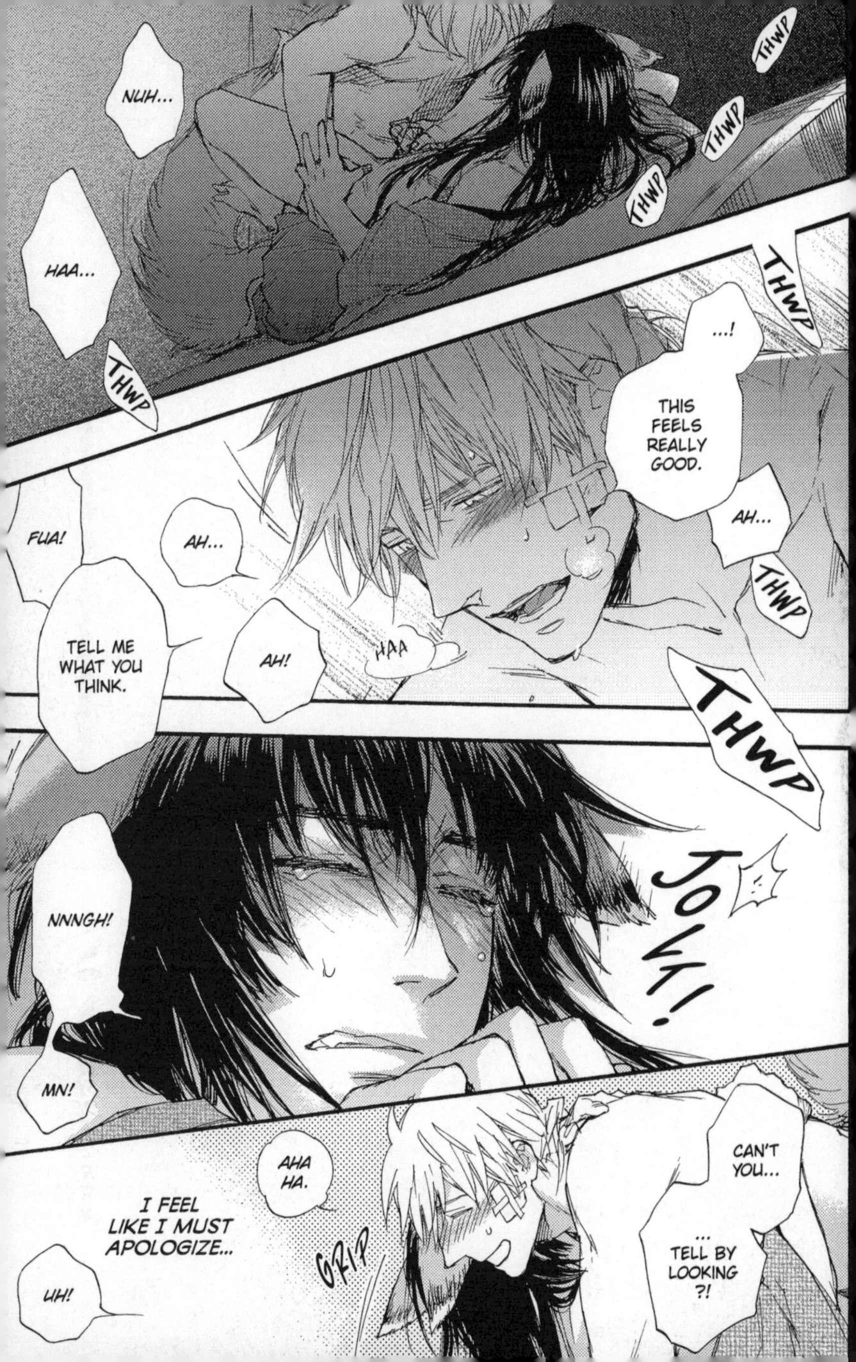
THWP
THWP
THWP
NUH...
HAA...
THWP
THWP
...!
THIS FEELS REALLY GOOD.
AH...
THWP
HAA
AH...
AH!
FUA!
TELL ME WHAT YOU THINK.
THWP
JOLT!
NNNGH!
MN!
CAN'T YOU...
...TELL BY LOOKING?!
AHA HA.
GRIP
I FEEL LIKE I MUST APOLOGIZE...
UH!

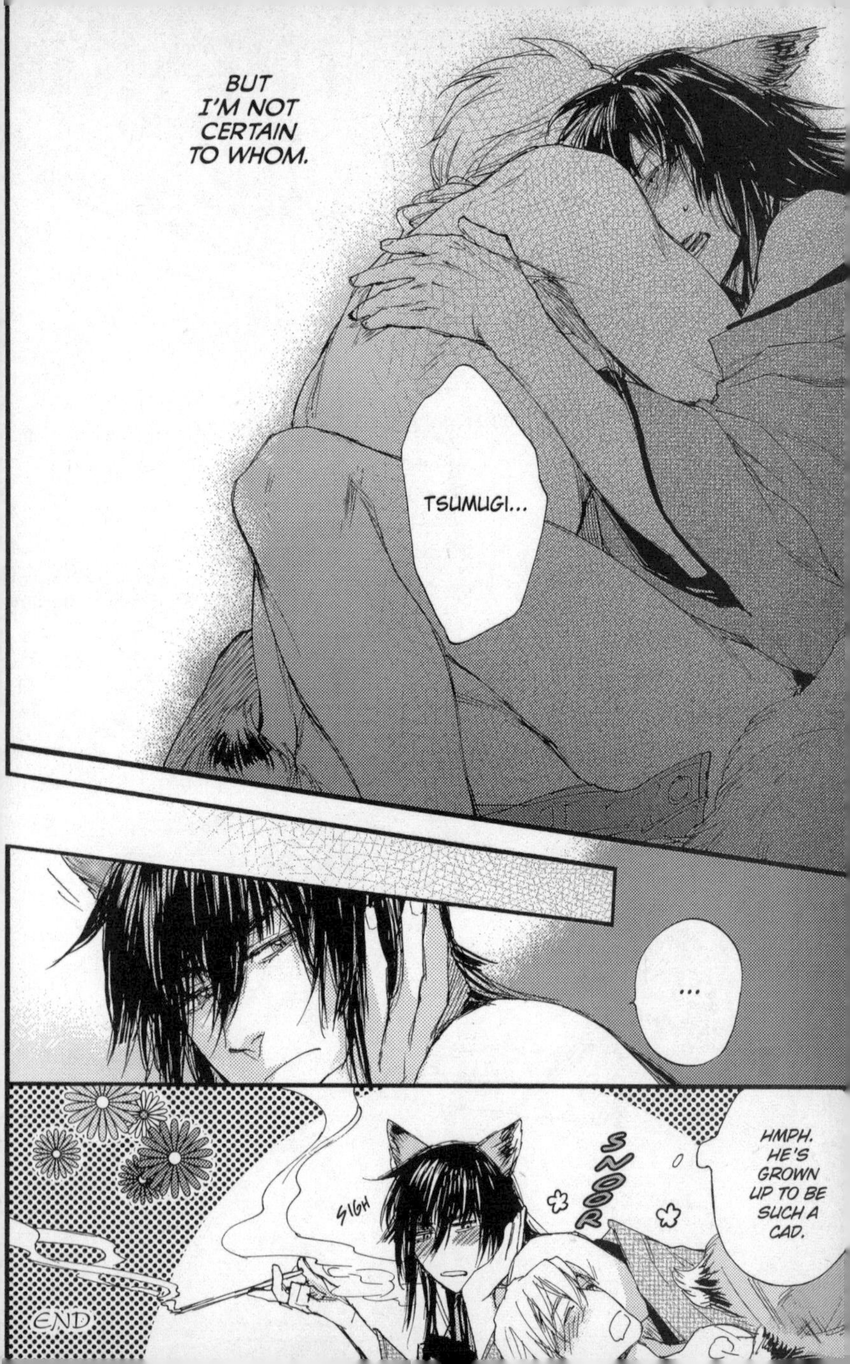
BUT I'M NOT CERTAIN TO WHOM.
TSUMUGI...
...
HMPH. HE'S GROWN UP TO BE SUCH A CAD.
SNOOR
SIGH
END

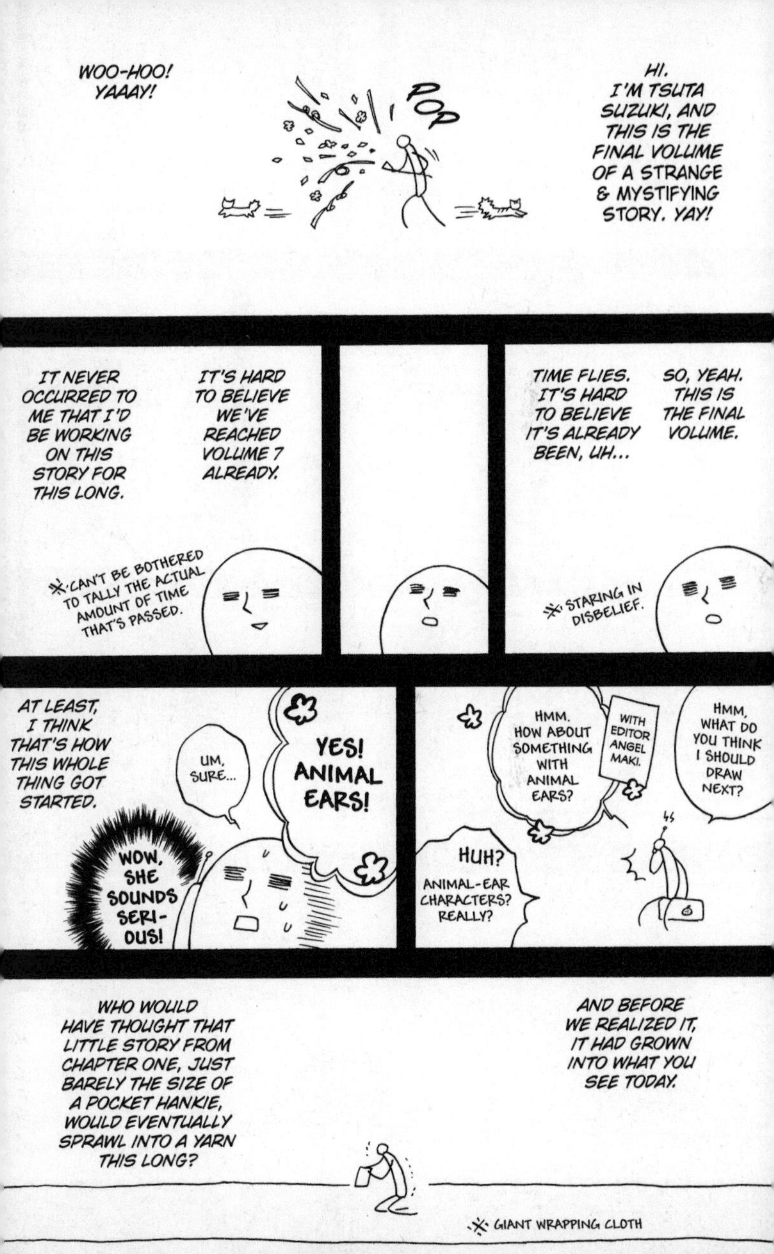
HI. I'M TSUTA SUZUKI, AND THIS IS THE FINAL VOLUME OF A STRANGE & MYSTIFYING STORY. YAY!
POP
WOO-HOO! YAAAY!
SO, YEAH. THIS IS THE FINAL VOLUME.
TIME FLIES. IT'S HARD TO BELIEVE IT'S ALREADY BEEN, UH...
※STARING IN DISBELIEF.
IT'S HARD TO BELIEVE WE'VE REACHED VOLUME 7 ALREADY.
IT NEVER OCCURRED TO ME THAT I'D BE WORKING ON THIS STORY FOR THIS LONG.
※CAN'T BE BOTHERED TO TALLY THE ACTUAL AMOUNT OF TIME THAT'S PASSED.
HMM, WHAT DO YOU THINK I SHOULD DRAW NEXT?
WITH EDITOR ANGEL MAKI.
HMM. HOW ABOUT SOMETHING WITH ANIMAL EARS?
HUH? ANIMAL-EAR CHARACTERS? REALLY?
YES! ANIMAL EARS!
UM, SURE...
AT LEAST, I THINK THAT'S HOW THIS WHOLE THING GOT STARTED.
WOW, SHE SOUNDS SERI-OUS!
AND BEFORE WE REALIZED IT, IT HAD GROWN INTO WHAT YOU SEE TODAY.
WHO WOULD HAVE THOUGHT THAT LITTLE STORY FROM CHAPTER ONE, JUST BARELY THE SIZE OF A POCKET HANKIE, WOULD EVENTUALLY SPRAWL INTO A YARN THIS LONG?
※GIANT WRAPPING CLOTH

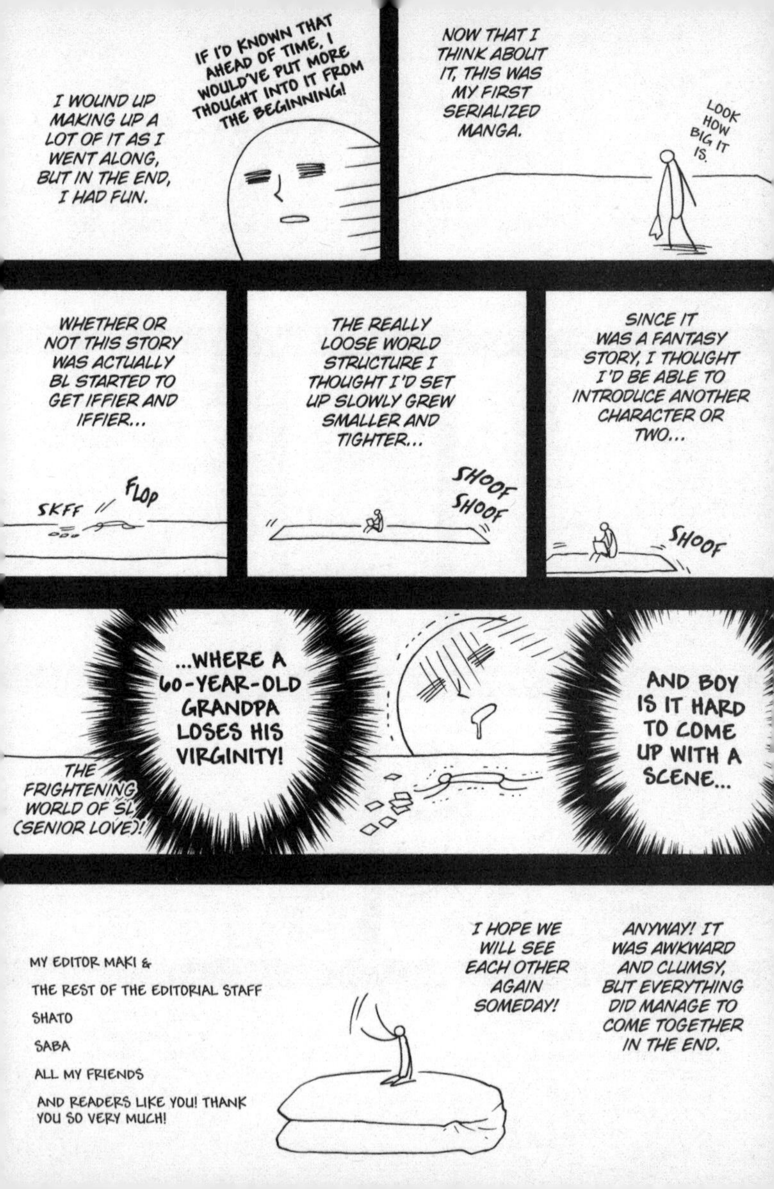
NOW THAT I THINK ABOUT IT, THIS WAS MY FIRST SERIALIZED MANGA.
LOOK HOW BIG IT IS.
IF I'D KNOWN THAT AHEAD OF TIME, I WOULD'VE PUT MORE THOUGHT INTO IT FROM THE BEGINNING!
I WOUND UP MAKING UP A LOT OF IT AS I WENT ALONG, BUT IN THE END, I HAD FUN.
SINCE IT WAS A FANTASY STORY, I THOUGHT I'D BE ABLE TO INTRODUCE ANOTHER CHARACTER OR TWO...
SHOOF
THE REALLY LOOSE WORLD STRUCTURE I THOUGHT I'D SET UP SLOWLY GREW SMALLER AND TIGHTER...
SHOOF SHOOF
WHETHER OR NOT THIS STORY WAS ACTUALLY BL STARTED TO GET IFFIER AND IFFIER...
FLOP
SKFF
AND BOY IS IT HARD TO COME UP WITH A SCENE...
...WHERE A 60-YEAR-OLD GRANDPA LOSES HIS VIRGINITY!
THE FRIGHTENING WORLD OF SL (SENIOR LOVE)!
ANYWAY! IT WAS AWKWARD AND CLUMSY, BUT EVERYTHING DID MANAGE TO COME TOGETHER IN THE END.
I HOPE WE WILL SEE EACH OTHER AGAIN SOMEDAY!
MY EDITOR MAKI &
THE REST OF THE EDITORIAL STAFF
SHATO
SABA
ALL MY FRIENDS
AND READERS LIKE YOU! THANK YOU SO VERY MUCH!

The chain of hate birthed by a serialization...

I had a lot of fun drawing all kinds of interesting characters. Thank you very much.

About the Author

This is **Tsuta Suzuki's** second English-language release, with her first being *Your Story I've Known*. Formerly working under the name "Yogore," she has also published *doujinshi* (independent comics) under the circle name "Muddy Pool." Born a Sagittarius in Shikoku, Japan on December 3rd, she has an A blood type and currently resides in Kyoto.

A Strange & Mystifying Story
Volume 7
SuBLime Manga Edition

Story and Art by **Tsuta Suzuki**

Translation—**Adrienne Beck**
Touch-Up Art and Lettering—**Bianca Pistillo**
Cover and Graphic Design—**Julian [JR] Robinson**
Editor—**Jennifer LeBlanc**

libre

Printed in the U.S.A.

Published by SuBLime Manga
P.O. Box 77010
San Francisco, CA 94107

10 9 8 7 6 5 4 3 2 1
First printing, May 2019

M
MATURE
PARENTAL ADVISORY
A STRANGE & MYSTIFYING STORY is rated M for Mature and is recommended for mature readers. This volume contains graphic imagery and mature themes.

SUBLIME
www.SuBLimeManga.com

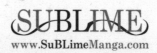